THE
SHOEMAKER

The Anatomy of a Psychotic

by Flora Rheta Schreiber

ALLEN LANE

ALLEN LANE
Penguin Books Ltd
536 King's Road
London SW10 0UH

First published in the U.S.A. by
Simon and Schuster 1983
First published in Great Britain by
Allen Lane 1983
Copyright © Flora Rheta Schreiber, 1983

Reproduced, printed and bound in Great Britain by
Hazell Watson & Viney Ltd, Aylesbury, Bucks

British Library Cataloguing in Publication Data

Schreiber, Flora Rheta
   The shoemaker.
   I. Title
   813'.54 [F]   PS3569.C/

ISBN 0 7139 1636 2

Acknowledgments

Thanks are in order to the persons who made it possible for me to work with Joseph Kallinger. Samuel S. Klein, Esquire, introduced me to Malcolm W. Berkowitz, Kallinger's lawyer in Philadelphia, who, with Arthur F. Abelman, acting for me, drew up my contract with Joseph and Elizabeth Kallinger. Berkowitz also introduced me to Paul J. Giblin, the attorney of record in the Kallinger 1976 Bergen County, New Jersey, murder trial.

Giblin secured my access to Joseph Kallinger by obtaining an order from the Appellate Division of the Superior Court of New Jersey and the sustaining of that order by New Jersey's Supreme Court. Because of the prosecution's request that the Appellate Division cite me for criminal contempt, access became possible, however, only after a panel of judges, headed by Robert A. Matthews, refused to make the citation.

In Bergen County I also want to thank Judge Thomas A. Dalton; members of the Leonia Police Department, especially Chief Manfred Ayers, Lieutenant Paul Ditmar, Detective Mashinski, Sergeant Robert MacDougall, Sergeant Chase (retired); Alden Todd and Professor Joseph Muzio, Chairman, Committee of Police, Town Council, Leonia; Katina Colombotos and other friends of Maria Fasching; and Professors Donal E. J. MacNamara and Raymond Pitt of John Jay College of Criminal Justice, and Dorothy Guyot (formerly of John Jay), who live in Leonia.

7

In Camden, New Jersey, I want to thank Judge I. V. Di Martino for signing the order that made possible my interviews with Joseph Kallinger; the late Bruce Robboy, Kallinger's lawyer; the Camden County Probation Department's Doris C. Guetherman; and, for his many daily kindnesses, Deputy Warden Eugene Salerno.

In Dauphin County, Pennsylvania, my thanks for many hours of intensive interviews with me go to Judge John C. Dowling, Judge William W. Lipsitt, District Attorney Le Roy Zimmerman, and Deputy District Attorney Richard Guida.

At the State Correctional Institution, Huntingdon, Pennsylvania, I want to thank Superintendent Lowell D. Hewitt; Director of Treatment Dennis Erhard; Dr. Frederick Wawrose, psychiatrist; Officer Dell; and Director of Education Stephen Polte.

Farview State Hospital in Waymart, Pennsylvania, has given me wonderful cooperation for over four years, and I want to express my gratitude to Superintendents Robert J. Hammel, Joel H. Hersh, Dale E. Newhart, and David W. Jay; to Director of Psychiatric Security Aides John Baldino; to superintendent-secretaries Sandra Thorpe and Barbara Kellogg; to therapists Dr. Ralph Davis, Dr. Marcella Shields, Dr. Ronald Refice, and Thomas Brennan; to Dr. Norman Wenger, Anthony Falvo, Gerald Stanvich, Thomas Williamson, John and Joan Gorel and Jerry Lewis, Assistant Superintendent; and to a host of supervisors and psychiatric security aides.

Crucial to this book are the findings of psychiatrists: the late Dr. Silvano Arieti and Dr. Lewis Robbins, mentioned in these pages, and also Dr. Dominick Barbara, who analyzed some of Joe Kallinger's dreams. Also crucial were the examinations by neurologist Dr. Howard Hurtig and Huntington's chorea specialist Dr. Edward Bird.

A special debt of gratitude is given to Arthur L. Gutkin, Esquire, for his herculean sleuthing in finding Joe's mother and half sister and in uncovering facts related to Joe's birth and adoption hearing.

This book is the more meaningful because of the observations of neighbors who knew Joe as a child and during his first and second marriages. Important contributions were also made by Carol Dwyer, teacher of Joseph, Jr.; Richard Kimmel, employer of Joseph Kallinger; Edward P. Aleszczyk for records of fires (the trailer fire as well as the fires Kallinger set); Michael's foster parents; Judith Renner, Joe's mother; and Muriel Gotshalk, his half sister.

For intensive interviews with me I want to thank Joan and Harry Carty, Helen and Henry Bogin, Ethel Fisher Cohen, and Annapearl Frankston, whose experiences are recounted in these pages.

My thanks go to the Reverend Eric Hayden for his work on the Kristorah chant; to Frank Reichl, Anna Kallinger's brother (and his son) who lives in Canada; to the late Stuart Long; to Emma Long; to Professor Ben Termine; to Lucy Freeman; to Bernice and Irving Statman; to Helen and John Vogel; to the late John Schreiber; to various lawyers: Deborah Glass, an assistant district attorney in the Kallinger child abuse trial; Assistant Federal Defender David Ruhnke; Charles Swigart; Phillip Kahn; and Steven Maury Greenberg of the Morrill Cole office in Rochelle Park, New Jersey; to Judge Glancey of Municipal Court, Philadelphia; and to newspaper men Thomas Gibbons (then of the *Philadelphia Bulletin*, now of the *Philadelphia Inquirer*), Ken Shuttleworth (of the *Camden Courier-Post*), Ron Avery (formerly of the *Camden Courier-Post*, now freelance), and Steve Jackson (formerly of the *Huntingdon Daily News*).

Credit for launching this book goes to my agent, Patricia S. Myrer of McIntosh and Otis, and for keeping it afloat to Michael Korda and John Herman of Simon and Schuster, and to Catherine Shaw, formerly of Simon and Schuster.

Laurels are due my own staff. John Shapiro not only typed the manuscript but as a reader was an incisive and imaginative critic and an indispensable literary aide-de-camp. James McLain made the first contact with Hilda Bishop Kallinger, Joe's first wife, and did the newspaper research on José Collazo. Curtiss Sayblack represented me in an important consultation with Judge Dalton. The late Brian Kiernan supplemented my work with Michael's foster parents. Paul Guzman regularly accompanied me to Camden and Farview and was present at an important interview with the neighbor who described the zoo incident and other brutalities inflicted on Joe as a child. Linda Frenchessetti not only was present at that interview, but arranged for it. Flossie Simmons was office manager and an aide to Joe Kallinger.

The Kallinger family—Elizabeth, Mary Jo, Stephen, Bonnie, and

James—have been indispensable aides. By reporting conversations he had with a neighbor, James gave me the first clue to the fact that his father had been an abused child. Especially I want to thank Joe himself not only for factual help in locating people and for his efforts in securing my access to him in Camden, but even more for many thousands of hours of soul-searching and painful revelation.

To John Shapiro, my alter ego
on this dark odyssey

CHANGE OF NAMES

I have used in these pages actual names when those names have appeared in the media—newspapers, magazines, radio, television—or during a trial and subsequently in the notes of testimony. Accordingly, the following names are different from what they are in fact: Judith Renner Scurti, James Scurti, Muriel Gotshalk, Dave Gotshalk, Tony Patelli, Lillian Rogers, Hilda Bishop Kallinger, Hilda Bishop, Sr., Hans Ibler, Freddy Prince, Thomas Black, Bobby Vane, and Johnny, Willie, and Susan Strong, Martin Slocum, David, Irving and Sarah Renner, and Willie (the boy at the creek). For purposes of further concealment I have also changed the names of places; Masher Street was not the actual street where Joe Kallinger and his first wife lived, nor was Palethorpe Street where Hilda lived before her marriage to Joe.

Contents

Prologue   17

Book One—Childhood

1—The Demon in the Bird   23
2—The Discarded Child   31
3—Two Against One   42
4—The Angry Child   50

Book Two—The Family Dream

5—The Secret World   69
6—Love, My Season   98
7—No Exit   115

Book Three—Descent into Hell

8—The Shoemaker's Castle   131
9—Mutiny in the Castle   146
10—The Naked King   170
11—The Total Gods   189
12—The Test of Strength   208
13—The Last Song   218
14—Case Number 4003-74   246
15—Dead End   254
16—Retaliation   264

Book Four—The Massacre of Mankind

17—A Gift for Bonnie   275
18—House Parties   294
19—The Hunting Knife   309

Book Five—Out of the World Forever

20—"You are an evil man"   333
21—Not Free to Die   346
22—Counselor in Handcuffs   358
23—Prisoner K-2719   370
24—The Endless Hills   386

Appendix 1—Poems by Joseph Kallinger   406

Appendix 2—Notes from the Author   417

General Index   425

Psychological Index   429

Prologue

In writing *Sybil* I took an astonishing journey with a woman possessed by sixteen separate personalities. At three and a half she ceased to be one person; at forty-two she again became one. This happened only after eleven years of psychoanalysis. "Never will you know," the integrated Sybil told me, "what it means to wake up in the morning and know you have a *whole* day as yourself!"

With Joseph Kallinger, the subject of this book, I have taken another psychological journey—a six-year journey into his life, his mind, and his crimes. Although not a multiple personality, he, too, was possessed.

When Kallinger, a thirty-eight-year-old Philadelphia shoemaker, and his son Michael, then thirteen, were arrested on January 17, 1975, there was shock and dismay at the father-son partnership. There was also terror that in seven weeks, beginning November 22, 1974, the duo had broken into five suburban homes in Pennsylvania, New Jersey, and Maryland; also there was horror at what had happened during the last break-in.

During that final break-in, in a small New Jersey town, father and son held eight people hostage, and Kallinger murdered a woman. The murder was grisly, brutal, and bloody. But it was not committed, as was generally believed, because the victim had refused to have sex with Kallinger. What actually happened will be told in these pages.

Headlines during the murder trial read: KALLINGER DESCRIBED AS

17

WEIRD; KALLINGER LEGALLY SANE, 2 PSYCHIATRISTS TESTIFY; 2 PSY-
CHIATRISTS TELL MURDER JURY KALLINGER IS INSANE; PROSECUTOR
TERMS KALLINGER A MURDERER FAKING INSANITY; KALLINGER WAS
OBSESSED ABOUT SEX—PSYCHIATRIST; KALLINGER ATTEMPTS SUICIDE;
KALLINGER FOUND GUILTY OF MURDER; KALLINGER IN JAIL TO 2,021.

I met Kallinger for the first time on July 19, 1976. He was in the
Bergen County Jail awaiting his murder trial. There, during eighty-
four hours of contact visits, I heard the ripple of unseen ghosts and
had my first clues as to the nature of his possession. On October 14,
1976, he received a mandatory life sentence for the murder, and was
then transferred to the Camden County Jail to await trial for the
first of the known break-ins. In a letter he wrote me from Camden on
April 17, 1977, he drew my attention once again to a terror he had
already expressed to me at Bergen. He was terrified because he
drifted in and out of contact with reality; after the period of unreality,
he became aware that something frightening had happened to him.
His letter, addressed to me at New York City's John Jay College of
Criminal Justice,* read:

"Please come to help me here at Camden County Jail. I need help
to find my self and I only feel comfortable when talking to you face
to face as we did for so long in Bergen County Jail. I trust you, and
I always felt better after our talks.

"If we can clear my thoughts that I can tell between visions and
life lived, then it's important for not only me but very important for
me to tell the court here.

"The trust is important to me. And I must know the truth or life
is not worth living and I only trust you.

"I know you're not a doctor, but you have experience from a
lifetime of working with life and doing research in many fields of
psychiatric writing.

"So if you can come every week for several hours at a time face
to face I just know I will be able to remember more clearly and
feel this Camden County trial will be fair and correct."

At Camden, where two months after receiving the letter I began
long daily conversations with Kallinger, the ripples flowed into a

---

* At John Jay, in addition to being a professor, I am the Director of Public
Relations and Assistant to the President.

18

stream of remembrance. Here our relationship grew and his trust deepened. He began to remember what until then had been buried in his subconscious; and remembering, he made dire revelations to me. These revelations are to be found in this book.

He fascinated me. He was verbal and analytical, charming, intelligent, and poetic. Extraordinarily sensitive, he was also a murderer who couldn't tell the difference between his visions and reality, between the phantoms that haunted him and the people who he thought were trying to destroy him. He was full of paradoxes.

As I probed into Joe's mind I realized that I was traveling some of the same terrain I had covered with Sybil. With Joe, as with Sybil, I was exploring abnormal psychology and an extraordinary developmental pattern. Both were victims of child abuse and of destructive parental attitudes toward them. Both were denied a child's right to self-realization. Sybil defended herself against these problems by becoming a multiple personality, with each of her selves protecting her against a particular trauma. One of the selves, Peggy Lou, dealt with Sybil's anger. Joe had no such defense mechanism. His rage festered, then exploded. He became insane, and rage was one of the elements from which the insanity sprang.

This book deals with crime, but essentially it is an exploration of madness. It is the first inside—that is, internal—look at a psychotic killer: a man whose psychosis drives him to kill.

A psychotic killer is very different from a psychopathic killer. The latter kills for money or the pleasure of killing, the former because of his psychosis. Joseph Kallinger would never have become a killer without his psychosis. With it he had no other course. This is not to say that all psychotics are killers, but that murder was the inevitable outcome of Kallinger's psychosis.

I have traced with Kallinger through many thousands of hours of conversation over a six-year period the origin and the development of both his psychosis and his crimes. This tracing, this reconstruction, was further interpreted by a world-renowned psychiatrist who examined Kallinger as a private patient. In addition there were also, of course, many other avenues of research.

The following pages tell a story and they explore madness. But they also provide a documented explanation for one man's criminal behavior. Already the case of Joseph Kallinger has become a landmark in psychiatry. For this reason the American Academy of Psychoanalysis in its May 1982 conference in Toronto invited me to present a paper on Kallinger.

The paper was startling and of exceptional scientific interest because in it I traced the genesis of murder from child abuse: from a specific childhood incident that became the origin of both a psychosis and of the crimes that were inseparable from the psychosis. The crimes were as clearly symptomatic of the psychosis as a particular rash is a symptom of measles or a special kind of cough of whooping cough. Because the crimes grew out of the psychosis, *three people would be alive if there had been psychiatric intervention at the proper time.*

Joe himself challenged me to search for what had turned him into a murderer. He did so on a scorchingly hot night in August 1977. We were sitting across a small wooden table in the empty infirmary of the Camden County Jail. We were perspiring heavily. He looked at me intently and said:

"Flora, what makes up a man? That's the question to ask. Well, apparently something within me had asked and I wonder, how sane am I? Yes. Yes. I talk sane at times, but without warning, something else emerges like the shadow but more concealed and deadly. What is the trigger? Yes, that's the question, Flora; find that answer and you got the man and you can start him moving on paper from the friendly neighborhood shoemaker to the living time bomb so deadly concealed that not even the most sophisticated detection device can spot."

As in the case of Sybil I found the trigger in childhood. It was a childhood of extreme emotional deprivation; and from the very beginning there was destruction.

—Flora Rheta Schreiber
New York City
July 4, 1982

BOOK ONE

Childhood

1 The Demon in the Bird

September 1, 1943. Nuns in black, nursing sisters, walked along the hospital corridor. They had pale faces and gentle smiles. Watching them, Joe, whose age was six years and nine months, stood in the open doorway of his hospital room and in his memory he heard the voices of his adoptive parents:

"Dummkopf! We'll send you back!" said his adoptive mother, Anna Kallinger. His adoptive father, Stephen Kallinger, a shoemaker, looked up from his work. Holding in a hand the knife with the green handle, he nodded his head and muttered, "Ja, Joseph!"

Like his bedroom and his clothes and the odors from his adoptive mother's cooking, the threat to send him back to the orphanage was a regular part of Joe's life with the Kallingers. Anna and Stephen had brought him to their home, had adopted—yes! had *rescued* him, they often said; but just as often they threatened to send him back.

Standing in the doorway of the hospital room, Joe thought of the orphanage. Over the sides of his crib eyes had peered at him through the black hoods of the nuns or from under funny hats with flowers and ribbons. As in a vague dream Joe remembered the steep high steps that led to swinging doors and behind them the long, dim halls where the nuns, like dark, gliding birds, went silently to and fro. One day Stephen Kallinger and his wife, Anna, had stood over the crib and had chosen him for their own.

The white hospital garment hung from Joe's shoulders to his ankles. He thought it looked like a Halloween costume. On December 11, Joe would be seven, but he had never dressed up for Halloween. His adoptive parents had never allowed him to join other children. Looking with wonder and yearning, through the windows of the Kallingers' shoe repair store, Joe had seen sheets and masks on the kids who ran along the Kensington streets and shouted "Trick or treat!" at front doors.

Joe's adoptive mother, Anna, had told him that he was going to have a hernia operation at St. Mary's Hospital, only a few blocks from his home. Joe didn't know what a hernia was—he thought it sounded like a girl's name—but he knew he was in the hospital and not back in the orphanage.

A nursing sister led him back to his bed. She took his temperature and said, "Goodnight, Joe. Sleep tight." The quiet of the hospital was as thick and fearsome as nighttime at the orphanage. Joe remembered that his adoptive father, Stephen, had said that during Joe's operation Dr. Daly would use a knife to "fix" the hernia. This made Joe think of the knife with the green handle that his adoptive father used for cutting the soles of shoes. Joe wondered whether Dr. Daly's knife had a green handle and whether the knife would kill him. Women gossiping in the Kallinger store often talked of people who had died in hospitals. If he did die tomorrow, then his soul would go to live with the butterflies. He had first seen butterflies at the Kallingers' Sunday and vacation cottage in the country. There Joe decided that butterflies were the most beautiful things in life and that he belonged to them.

Joe came out of the anesthesia. He was surprised to be alive and back in the hospital room. Dr. Daly's knife hadn't killed him. Later that day Dr. Daly came to see Joe. He wanted to ask why he wasn't dead, but he didn't dare. The doctor said that Joe had a six-inch incision low down on his left side. What's an incision? Joe asked. A six-inch-long cut, the doctor replied, his great eyes glittering. The knife that did that had magical power, Joe thought as he watched Dr. Daly put his instruments back into his black bag.

Joe was in St. Mary's Hospital for sixteen days. On the last morning a nurse dressed in white helped Joe put on his clothes. He felt a little weak, so the nurse held him with one hand while she helped him dress with the other. First went on his socks, underwear, his shirt and brown woolen sweater, then his tan double-breasted suit with a Fauntleroy collar. He sat down on a chair while the nurse put on his orthopedic shoes, for Joe was pigeon-toed.

An orderly wheeled him down the corridor and into the elevator. Near the street exit stood Joe's adoptive mother, Anna Kallinger. She wore her pancake straw hat, print dress, thin brown coat, and black, low-heeled shoes. Erect and unsmiling, she waited until the orderly had wheeled Joe down to her; then she turned sharply and walked out of the hospital, the orderly following her with Joe in the wheelchair.

Anna didn't speak a word during the short ride in the taxi to 2723 North Front Street, the Kallinger home. In a corner of the seat sat Joe. He clung to an assist strap and looked at Anna. The brim of her pancake straw hat rose and fell with the movement of the taxi, casting shadows on her tough, square face. Her eyes peered ahead intently through gold-rimmed glasses. The lenses were immaculate: Joe thought they looked like two small pools of water reflecting light and anger. She turned her lips down slightly at the corners and gave Joe a disapproving look.

The Kallinger house had been quiet during the sixteen days that Joe had been away. At the prospect of having him home again, Anna became anxious and vexed, but one would not have known that from looking at her stolid expression. Joe sensed that she was not glad to have him back.

Stephen Kallinger was working at his bench, one foot perched on a rung of the stool he sat on. He knew this was the day of Joe's discharge from the hospital, and he waited nervously for his wife to return with their adopted son.

As Anna and Joe walked into the shop, Stephen turned and looked at them over the tops of the small, rectangular lenses of his eyeglasses, which hung from behind his ears on earpieces attached to thin gold wire frames. He hopped off the stool with a shoe and a lip knife in his stained, muscular hands. This was the knife with the green handle that had figured in Joe's recollections in the hospital.

The handle and the blade were each four inches long. The blade, which was used for cutting heels and soles, had a curve at the end that was shaped like a human lip.

Though he was only five feet two inches tall and stocky (Anna was an inch taller), his movements were nimble and vigorous. Under his black hair, his eyes were gray, his wide lips thin and dry.

Anna grimaced at Joe, winked to her husband.

"So now we'll do it," Stephen said. He waved the knife at them in a nervous gesture and said, "I'll be in in a minute."

Stephen watched Joe as Anna, gripping Joe's upper arm with one hand, holding his little suitcase with the other, led him toward the living-room door. Stephen's face became stony, unyielding. It had to be done today—now!

Joe scowled, shaking himself loose from Anna, who opened the net-curtained French door. She went on without Joe directly into the living room and the Kallingers' living quarters, which Anna and Stephen called "in back."

Stephen was cutting the soles of shoes with the knife with the green handle. Joe stared at the blade as Stephen moved it swiftly through the leather. "You want to cut soles like your dad is doing, Joseph?" Stephen asked. "Very soon I will begin to teach you. If you will be a good boy and later a good man, you will learn. If not, then . . ." He looked hard at Joe over the rims of his eyeglasses, and turned back to his workbench, laughing softly to himself. Joe watched the fragments of leather drop from the slicing blade onto the floor. He wondered whether his skin had fallen like that when Dr. Daly made the long cut in his body. In the store, his adoptive father's knife was as menacing in reality as in the hospital it had been in fantasy. Grown-ups used knives, Joe realized for the first time, not only for cutting leather, but also for cutting a boy's flesh.

"Come inside, Joseph! *Schnell!*"

Joe slouched into the living room. Anna hastily removed his jacket and sweater. Then Joe ran to the staircase, but was stopped by Anna. "Stay downstairs," she ordered. "Your father and me have something we want to tell you." She added, "You mustn't run. You'll bust open your operation, then you'll have to go to the hospital again. *Ach! Was ein Kind!*"

At the foot of the stairs, Joe stood beside reproductions of paintings of Jesus and the Virgin Mary, which hung side by side on the wall. Anna brushed past him. He watched her strong, square body in the ankle-length print dress as she went up to his room with his sweater, jacket, and suitcase. Her thick legs moved with energy, her feet in the black, low-heeled shoes loudly thumping the stairs.

Hearing other footsteps behind him, staccato ones, Joe turned and saw his adoptive father coming toward him. Stephen had left an employee, Caesar, to manage the store. Chewing on a Philly cigar, Stephen carried a kiddy chair made of maple. What is he doing with *my* chair? Joe wondered. Stephen called up the stairs, "Ahnie! I am here. You coming down?"

"*Ja.* Right away." She appeared at the head of the stairs. Descending briskly, she gave a short, harsh laugh that scared Joe.

Stephen Kallinger pressed a light switch and the chandelier went on. Directly under it, he placed Joe's kiddy chair. "Sit down, Joseph," Stephen said.

Joe sat in his kiddy chair and looked up with fear at his adoptive parents. Anna and Stephen stood over him, looked at him intently through the immaculate lenses of their eyeglasses.

"Joseph, you must listen," Stephen said. "We have something important we want to tell you."

Anna said, "Dr. Daly did something to you in the hospital, he—"

"He fixed your hernia," Stephen interrupted, "but he also fixed . . ." He paused a moment. Bending down, he said in a low voice, his mouth close to Joe's ear, ". . . your little bird."

In the Kallinger home, "bird" was the euphemism for penis.

"What's wrong with my little bird?" Joe asked.

"A demon lived in your little bird before Dr. Daly fixed it," Anna replied.

"What's a demon?"

"An evil spirit," Stephen said.

"It works for the Devil, not for Jesus," Anna said darkly.

"It was in my little bird? What was it doing in there?"

Joe put his hand on his crotch, but Anna slapped it away.

"The demon makes your bird get hard," Stephen explained. "It makes it get hard and stick out so you got to do bad things with it. Then your soul goes to the Devil when you die."

"Dr. Daly drove out the demon, Joseph," Anna said. "He fixed your bird so it will *never* grow big. Demons can't live in birds that don't grow big, so your bird ain't going to get hard, understand?"

"But—but what did Dr. Daly *do* to my little bird?"

"That's a secret, Joseph," Stephen replied, smiling. He took a few strands of Joe's hair in his hand and pulled at them.

"Ja!" exclaimed Anna. "A secret. But you won't have no demon in *your* bird because your bird will always be small, small, small, small, small!"

To quiet her, Stephen put his hand lightly on her shoulder. She breathed heavily and her eyes were glassy. Joe thought she was sick, maybe she was going to die. He wondered whether her soul would go to the Devil.

"Didn't *your* birds grow?" Joe asked.

Stephen became angry. "Questions! Always with the questions!" He continued in a low, harsh voice, "Now listen! In the old country, the priest freed your mother and me from the demon. But in *this* country—*ja*, in *this* country," he repeated scornfully, "we had to get Dr. Daly to do it to you. Dr. Daly delivered you from evil."

"Mom, does your bird look like Dad's?"

Looking up, Joe again saw in the immaculate lenses of Anna's eyeglasses two small pools of water glittering with light and anger, her pupils disks of ice locking him into fear.

"Girls' birds are different than boys' birds," she snarled. She squatted on her haunches and put her face close to Joe's. "Pay attention!" she said. "Your bird won't get hard because the demon is gone. Always you will be soft there. So you're gonna be a good boy, a good man. Never get in no trouble. Never get a girl in no trouble. Not now. Not when you're a man." Anna sat down on the couch and leaned back. She was sweating.

Stephen turned to his wife and said, "We won't have no trouble with him now. Not like what other people have with *their* kids. That is so, yes, Joseph?" Stephen added, turning sharply back to Joe.

"Can I go now?" Joe asked.

"Yes, you can go," Anna replied. Dabbing her face lightly with a small handkerchief, she got off the couch and walked slowly toward the kitchen.

"Go to your room, Joseph," Stephen said. "You're sick. You gotta be careful now for a while. Your mother will call you when supper's ready."

On his way upstairs, Joe stopped in front of the rectangular mirror that hung on the wall above the staircase. As he always did, he moved his fingertips along the cool glass and wondered how the hand in the mirror could follow his hand, move when he moved, stop when he stopped. It was the other world, silent and clear, and he thought: I can go into the mirror and they'll never find me. Frightened, he wanted to run, but in awe he drew back against the banister. He saw, floating in the middle of the living room reflected in the mirror, a huge lip knife, the blade and handle vertical, and from the overlap on the tip of the blade hung his penis. In terror he brought his hand to his crotch and the image in the mirror vanished. A twinge of pain in the area of the incision brought him back from fantasy to present reality.

In his room he sat motionless on his bed. He wished he were a butterfly and could fly away to his butterfly family in the country. Although it was early, he kneeled down beside his bed and tried to say his prayers in German, as he had been taught to do by Anna and Stephen. But the prayers were gone. He couldn't remember a word. It was as if he had rejected his adoptive parents' native language for their unloving words spoken in English just now in the living room. Seeing him in their home again had made them angry; they told him strange things about his "bird" and sent him to his room. He looked out of the window and thought again of the butterflies.

In the years that followed, Joe remembered only five words from the vocabulary he had been taught by Stephen and Anna Kallinger. Two were the neutral *Danke schoen*. The third was *Coloffel*, Anna's private word for a big wooden spoon, one of the instruments of punishment. The fourth word was *Quatsch*, which meant rubbish, nonsense, bosh. The fifth was *Wanderlust*, which expressed Joe's desire to fly away.

Stephen and Anna knew, of course, that Dr. Daly had done nothing to Joe's penis. But, having overreacted to the normal sexual

29

curiosity he had shown at five and another episode two weeks before the operation, which they misinterpreted as sexual, they wanted him to grow up impotent. To achieve these ends, they had fabricated their grotesque story. The consequences of the scene they staged would be dark, hideous and tragic.

2 The Discarded Child

On the day Joe returned from St. Mary's Hospital, his adoptive parents by symbolic castration destroyed his capacity to grow up normally. Often talking to Joe during his puberty and adolescence about the demon and about soft, small penises and goodness, the senior Kallingers continued to warp his sexual instinct, though they did not uproot it as they had hoped. The "bird" scene in the living room and their never-ending assault on his sexuality were the origins of his later madness.

It is rare to be able to pinpoint a single episode from which a psychosis springs. But in the case of Joe Kallinger that episode is clearly his symbolic castration in the living room, strengthened by the process of destruction that had preceded it and followed it. The process that made Joe the more vulnerable to what the Kallingers did to him began while he was still in the womb.

Joe's natural mother, Judith Renner, was born in Montreal, Canada. Her parents were middle-class Jews of Austrian and English extraction. In 1918, when she was three years old, she was brought to the United States.

During the polio epidemic of 1916, Judith came down with anterior poliomyelitis. The handicap of a distinct drop in her left foot was not serious enough for her to use crutches, but she walked with a slight limp. When she was still a small child, her parents were divorced, and she and her brothers were placed in a foster home. When she was twelve years old she ran away from the foster home to a hospital to have her left foot corrected. Underage, she could not sign herself in, so she called her mother, who came and signed for her. After the operation, having refused to return to the foster home, she lived with her mother. But her memory of her childhood flight did not prevent her from looking for a foster home for the child in her womb.

Auburn-haired, five foot three, attractive even though plumpish, Judith Renner Scurti was ashamed because her child, though a love child, was illegitimate. The attitudes of the time—it was 1936—toward illegitimate children and toward the mothers who gave birth to them were priggish and censorious. She was also afraid because she was married, but not to her unborn child's father, whose name was Tony Patelli.

Judith had been not quite nineteen when in August of 1934 she married James Scurti. Because he was a Roman Catholic and she a Jew, they were married by a justice of the peace. He worked little, and Judith, a member of the International Ladies' Garment Workers Union, had a job as a sewing machine operator in a factory. The Scurtis' daughter, Muriel, was born in September 1935. Three months later, after having lived with Scurti for only sixteen months, Judith left him.

Judith and Muriel were living with Judith's mother, Sarah Renner, and Judith's brothers, David and Irving, when Judith met Tony Patelli. Like James Scurti, Tony was a Roman Catholic born in the United States of Italian parents. Unlike Scurti, Tony was someone with whom Judith could have a good time. He was an interior decorator and artistic. They both loved the theater, and they loved each other. Judith hoped to get a divorce from Scurti and marry Tony, but Tony stopped seeing her when she told him she was pregnant. Judith was then afraid that if she kept and acknowledged their unborn child, Scurti would secure custody of Muriel. Wanting to get rid of the intruder who threatened the safety of her legitimate child, Judith, although Jewish, paid a visit to the Catholic Children's Bureau one month before the new baby was expected and asked the agency to place the unborn child. She was told to come back after the birth.

* * *

32

On December 11, 1936, in Philadelphia's Northern Liberties Hospital, Judith, who would be twenty-one in five days, gave birth to a healthy nine-pound boy. She had had a difficult labor with Muriel, but an easy time with this second child, whom she named Joseph. In the hospital he was known as Baby Boy Renner, but his birth certificate stated that he was Joseph Scurti, the son of James Scurti and Judith Renner Scurti.

When Joseph was six days old, Judith sent Lillian Rogers, the only one of her friends who knew of his existence, to inform the Catholic agency of his birth. Two days later, however, when an agency representative came to the hospital to make arrangements for Joseph's placement, Judith refused to give him up. "He's a grand baby," she said. "I hate to part with him."

Leaving the hospital the next day, Judith took her son to the home of Lillian Rogers. For three weeks at the Rogers home Judith breast-fed Joseph, cooed to him, sang to him, touched him lovingly. Doing everything a loving mother should, she gave him the bliss of infancy. She did this because she knew he wouldn't have it very long.

At the end of the three weeks, Judith went back to work. She placed Joseph in a private boarding home and saw him once a week when she paid his $5 weekly board. The bliss of infancy turned into separation anxiety, which was the greater because of the three weeks of extreme closeness and the permanence of the separation. From this anxiety would spring rage, intense and cumulative.

Judith's work became irregular. She was unable to keep up with the payments to the boarding home. She thought briefly of taking Joseph to her mother's house, then changed her mind. She was still afraid of losing Muriel if she acknowledged Joseph. She told herself that she couldn't take Joseph home because her mother was already taking care of Muriel. Boys were harder to raise than girls, and her mother had a heart condition; it wasn't fair to Mom. Joseph, the intruder, was still last in his mother's considerations.

Judith turned to a priest. She promised to have Joseph baptized if the priest would find a place for him at St. Vincent's Hospital, a Catholic orphanage. Joe had already had a *brith*, the traditional Jewish initiation ritual for a male child. The conversion from Judaism to Catholicism was part of the confusion and instability that surrounded Joe's babyhood.

At three months and nine days old, Joseph left the boarding home for the place with the swinging doors and high steps that he remembered vividly during his stay at St. Mary's Hospital for his hernia operation. A nun in black, seeing him that first day at St. Vincent's, observed that he was "a bright, healthy-looking child, rather Jewish-looking, seems to have a nice disposition."

At first, Judith refused to have the Catholic Children's Bureau put Joseph on its Possible Adoption List. She wanted to divorce Scurti, find a new husband, and give her son a home. She had resumed her affair with Tony, Joseph's father, while Joseph was in the boarding home, and she hoped that Tony would be the new husband. But when she pressed for marriage, Tony told her what she had never known: He was married and had a family.

By December 1937, Judith saw no prospect of an immediate marriage and lost hope of making a home for her son. She asked the Catholic Children's Bureau to put Joseph, who was then one year old, on its Possible Adoption List. St. Vincent's advised the bureau that he was "a very attractive child, round, chubby face, dark hair and eyes; he's in good condition and seems suitable for adoption."

Judith was often delinquent in paying Joseph's $3.50 weekly board. When he was fourteen months old, she finally served notice that she couldn't pay and would file a petition to that effect. For the petition to be valid, she had to give the name and address of Joseph's father. When she refused to do this she was told to take Joseph home. She agreed, but changed her mind a few days later. The old fears about bringing Joseph into the open had reasserted themselves. In addition, her mother felt that since the boy was now a Catholic, the Catholics should take care of him. Judith began paying a small amount toward Joseph's board, and he remained at St. Vincent's for just under ten months after his name had appeared on the Possible Adoption List.

On October 15, 1938, Judith was greatly relieved to be told that "a very nice family" had selected Joseph and the problem of board had been solved.

Stephen and Anna Kallinger—the "very nice family"—had chosen Joseph the very first time they peered over his crib at St. Vincent's. His jet-black hair couldn't have been more like Stephen's hair if they were father and son; Stephen wanted him out of vanity. The child also met Anna's specifications: He was toilet-trained, he walked and talked, and according to St. Vincent's, he was in good health.

Originally, Anna had wanted to adopt a girl, and she would later tell Joseph that because he was not a girl, he had been a disappointment to her from the beginning. But though usually more dominating than her husband, she had acceded to his wish for a son. She saw the wisdom of Stephen's wanting to adopt a male child to whom he could teach the craft of shoe repairing and who would eventually inherit the business Stephen—and Anna as well—had worked so hard to build.

The Kallingers met in Philadelphia, but were emigrants from the Austro-Hungarian Empire. Anna came from the town of Bocksdorf in the province of Burgenland in the lowlands of Austria; Stephen came from Unter-Petersdorf Bezirk, Oedenburg, Hungary. He arrived in the United States in 1921 at the age of twenty-three, and Anna in 1925 when she was twenty-eight. They became naturalized Americans, Stephen on August 17, 1928, and Anna on December 2, 1930.

They came for different reasons. Anna emigrated because of family hardships and misfortune. Her father, Michael Reichl, worked in the building trade, and in the course of his work fell off a construction site. He died of head injuries resulting from the accident. After his death, Anna's mother went to work on a farm, placing her two-year-old son in foster care. Her twelve-year-old daughter—the future Anna Kallinger—went to work in a factory.

For Anna, who could scarcely read or write, life in Austria was tough and hopeless. She thought of the United States as the land of milk and honey. Until her marriage a year and a half after her arrival, she worked in Philadelphia in the kitchen of a restaurant and as a waitress.

Stephen came to the United States because his cousin, Henry Kallinger, had offered him a home and a job. In his notarized deposition of June 10, 1921, Henry Kallinger stated that he was often incapacitated because of asthma and wanted Stephen, who was "an experienced shoemaker, fully dependable and trustworthy," to help him in his business.

The Kallingers, who were married on October 2, 1926, in St. Peter's Roman Catholic Church, Philadelphia, had observed their twelfth wedding anniversary twenty-three days before bringing Joseph to their home.

That Stephen was sterile was a fact known only to the Kallingers and their family physician, Dr. Joseph Daly. The doctor (it was the same one who would perform Joe's hernia operation) had urged them to adopt a child. But, busy building the shoe repair business that was the pivot of their existence, they had procrastinated. Stephen's fear of growing old without an heir and Anna's fear of not having a younger person to lean on in her old age eventually brought them to St. Vincent's. Now, when Anna was forty and a half and Stephen was two months away from his fortieth birthday, they finally became parents.

Joseph's new home was a two-story red brick row house on the northeast corner of North Front and East Sterner streets in the Kensington section of Philadelphia. In 1938, Kensington, which was older than Philadelphia itself, having been on the map since 1655, was a combined residential and industrial area. It had a few apartment houses, but mostly small buildings, including many that, like the Kallingers', were combined stores and homes. Realty values and rentals had been hard hit during the Great Depression, but were on the upgrade in 1938. Both the Frankford elevated, which opened in 1921, and the coming of the automobile had contributed to solid growth.

The neighborhood was clean and well kept. There was almost no poverty, almost no street violence or other crime. Although there were some Protestants and a very few Jews, Catholicism was the dominant religion. The residents, chiefly German, Italian, and Irish immigrants or first-generation Americans, either had their own small businesses or worked in the area's factories and mills. At one time Kensington had been one of the richest areas in the world and Philadelphia's industrial center. Most residents were proud of being from Kensington.

The Kallingers, who were German-speaking immigrants and Catholic, felt at home. Highly respected shopkeepers, they were more prosperous than those of their neighbors who were blue-collar workers. Stephen and Anna could have afforded to move to a more fashionable area of Philadelphia, or to the suburbs. Kensington,

36

however, was where Stephen, a first-rate shoemaker who had won awards for his work, had built his business and where he chose to remain.

The red brick row house which the Kallingers owned and where they had their shoe repair store, was a lonely and austere place. No child had lived there before Joseph; after his arrival, no child was ever allowed in to play with him. From early Monday morning until Saturday evening, there were many people going in and out of the store to leave shoes or to pick them up, but nobody ever went into the living quarters, not even on Sundays. Anna, Stephen, and little Joe lived withdrawn from the world, the window shades always down and the door to the living quarters always closed.

Since his birth at Northern Liberties Hospital, Joe had spent three weeks with his natural mother, Judith Renner Scurti, at her friend's home; two months and nine days at a private boarding home, and nineteen months at St. Vincent's. He had been taken from the orphanage by the Kallingers when he was twenty-two months and fourteen days old. Now, through the rooms of his fourth home since leaving the hospital where he was born, Joe wandered day after day, exploring his bedroom and, downstairs, the living room and the kitchen.

On the wall beside the staircase was a three-panel rectangular mirror. Joe often amused himself by looking into it. He thought that the boy whom he saw in the mirror had come to play, for Joe didn't know until he was older that what he saw was his own reflection. He often pretended to change places with his reflective playmate, and believed that *he* was in the mirror and that his playmate was standing in front of it. It was the same mirror in which Joe at six years and nine months, after being told that Dr. Daly had "fixed" his "little bird," had his first hallucinatory experience, when he saw his penis floating toward him on a lip knife. When Joe first came to the Kallingers, however, the mirror was simply part of his richly evolving fantasy life. The need for fantasy was the stronger because lack of companionship and the stress and uncertainties of Joe's first twenty-two months had already made him retreat within himself.

Joe continued, however, to give the impression, as he had at St. Vincent's, that all was right with his little world. A social worker was sent to the Kallinger home by the Catholic Children's Bureau. "Joseph," the social worker wrote in a report of January 20, 1939, "is a pretty, dark, curly-haired boy with bright brown eyes. He has gained in weight and seems very happy and contented in this home. Mr. and Mrs. Kallinger are both very fond of Joseph. They gave him many pretty toys and also had a lovely Christmas tree for him. They were well repaid when Joseph came down on Christmas morning . . . the beautiful look of happiness on his little face. It made them so happy." The social worker also reported that Joe had his own room and that he was insured for $1,000.

Having emerged with good marks from the probationary period, the Kallingers definitely wanted to adopt Joseph. The adoption hearing was set for December 19, 1939, in Municipal Court, but did not take place that day.

The day before, Stephen and Anna had been working in the store. Three-year-old Joe, sitting on his maple kiddy chair, was playing with a Philly cigar box. The telephone rang, and Gerald A. Gleeson, the Kallingers' lawyer, told Stephen that Judith Renner, Joseph's natural mother, was on her way to the Kallinger store. The lawyer said that Judith Renner was ready to agree to the adoption, but first she wanted to see the home where her child would be placed. Gleeson had given Judith Renner the Kallingers' address and telephone number.

Furious, Stephen hung up. In an effort to prevent Judith Renner's visit, he called the Catholic Children's Bureau. He was told that since his own lawyer had given her the address, nothing could be done.

Judith arrived and introduced herself to Anna, who was in the store at the counter. Stephen didn't look up from his workbench. The two women, one in her twenties, the other in her forties, were a study in contrasts. Judith was vibrant, sexy, and, in spite of her hardships, cheerful. Anna had a dumpy figure and plain features. She was joyless and rigidly devoted to hard work and self-denial. Judith was unstable and full of *joie de vivre*. Anna was disciplined and morose.

Joseph was not in the store. When she learned that Judith was coming, Anna had taken him "in back." But Anna talked to Judith about him. He had to wear orthopedic shoes, Anna said. She also said, "He's mischievous!" A three-year-old's normal mischief had led Anna to this conclusion.

Judith asked to see Joseph. Anna brought him back into the store. He did not know the lady with the auburn hair, nor, of course, did he connect her with the breast, the cooing, the touching of which Judith had deprived him when he was three weeks old.

When she kissed him and stroked his hair, Stephen called, "Ahnie, that's enough."

After Stephen had introduced himself he asked abruptly, "What are you here for, Mrs. . . . or is it *Miss* Renner?"

Judith flushed, but didn't answer. Then she said, "I want to see the home where my child will live."

"You have no right to be here," Anna said. "But since you are, I'll show it to you. It's better than you can give him."

They took a tour of the house. Joseph went with them, and Anna held his hand tightly. When they came back to the store, Judith said, "It's a nice place. I'm going to let you have Joseph if you give me five hundred dollars."

"Blackmail!" Stephen screamed. "Get out of my store!"

Ignoring this, Judith asked, "Do you mind if I use your phone?" Stephen didn't reply. Judith called the Catholic Children's Bureau. She told a bureau official: "I want to take Joseph myself."

When she got off the phone, Stephen telephoned Gerald Gleeson, his lawyer. Stephen said, "We don't want to go ahead with the adoption." Then, turning to Judith, he again told her to leave.

"I want to take Joseph today," Judith insisted. "Will you please pack his belongings?"

The phone rang. It was a Children's Bureau representative. She said that Gerald Gleeson had just told her that because of what had happened, he would have the adoption hearing postponed to a later date by the court.

"We're not going ahead with the adoption," Stephen replied. "Judith Renner is still here. She wants to take Joseph today."

Stephen was told that under no circumstances should he let Judith have Joseph. The child was under the care of the Children's Bureau, and if Judith wanted him, she could have him only through the bureau.

"We'll keep Joseph," Stephen agreed, "until after the Christmas holidays. But then we'll return him to you. Even if Judith Renner changes her mind and consents to the adoption, now that she knows where we are, she can always come back and bother us. She might take Joseph in the end. My wife and I feel it's better all around for us to give Joseph up."

Stephen explained to Judith why he couldn't let her have Joseph that day, and she left. Ten days later, the Christmas holidays being over, the Kallingers—as they had said they would—took Joseph to the Children's Bureau offices. But not to return him. They were there to say they still wanted to adopt him.

Judith had promised the Kallingers that if they adopted Joseph, she would remove herself from his life and theirs. "I will never bother you again," she said very solemnly in a telephone conversation after her visit. It was a repeat performance of her on-again, off-again behavior while Joseph was at St. Vincent's and even when he was an infant at Northern Liberties Hospital.

The Kallingers disliked Judith. They would tell Joseph, when he was a few years older, that she had tried to blackmail them into paying five hundred dollars for him. They pointed out that at the time Joseph had not even been legally hers "to sell." Yet the Kallingers, wanting to keep their future shoemaker, believed Judith when she said she would leave them alone. She did!

The adoption hearing took place in the Municipal Court of Philadelphia County on January 9, 1940. The Kallingers, having been instructed to bring "the said minor, Joseph Renner Scurti," had him with them. Now three years and one month old, he entered a courtroom for the first time.

Judith was not present, but she had signed a surrender form, stating that she did not want Joseph as her child and was giving him up to adoption. She had signed the document as Mrs. Judith Renner. Then she had struck out the *Mrs.* three times.

Judge Joseph G. Tumolillo pointed out that the child, according to his birth certificate, was Joseph Scurti, but that other documents, including the surrender form, stated that he was Joseph Renner. The adoption petition was therefore amended to read: "Adoption of Joseph Scurti, a.k.a. Joseph Renner."

The judge, in his "findings of fact," declared that "the child,

Joseph Scurti, also known as Joseph Renner, is an illegitimate child born out of wedlock to Judith Renner Scurti and an unknown putative father." His honor continued, "The putative father's name is unknown and his whereabouts are unknown, and likewise it is unknown whether he has acknowledged the child."

It was a closed hearing. In the hallway outside, a man of medium height, swarthy, with charming manners and trim and neat in dress, waited. He had tried to get into the hearing, but couldn't. Inside the courtroom it was said that the whereabouts of Joseph's putative father were unknown. But the man waiting outside was Tony Patelli, that father. He wanted to get a glimpse of the boy he had sired.

The moment came when the hearing was over. Joseph, now Joseph Michael Kallinger, walked between Stephen and Anna Kallinger. They had kept the name of Joseph, but had given him a middle name in memory of Anna's father, Michael Reichl.

Tony Patelli kept his eyes on Joseph until the boy was out of sight. "A wonderful little boy," he later told Judith. Then Tony walked toward the street and got there just in time to see Joseph and his adoptive parents drive away. They were driving toward the red brick row house which was Joseph's prison in childhood, which in adulthood he would turn into a prison for his family, and from which, on January 17, 1975, he would be taken to prison, never to return.

3 Two Against One

The Kallingers had a two-room country cottage in Neshaminy, Bucks County, Pennsylvania, that they used for weekends. It was made of white clapboard and sat on cinder blocks. There was no plumbing, just an outhouse.

The cottage was two miles from the naval air station at Willowgrove. One hundred and fifty feet from the cottage there was a springhouse, covered by brush and weeds, that could have been passed unnoticed unless the passerby knew it was there.

Little Joe did know. The springhouse in the country, like the mirror in the city, was part of his secret world. Lying in the grass beside the springhouse, Joe, at three, four, five, and even six years, would play with the brush and weeds. He would spin fancies about the spirits he had created for himself and whose home, he imagined, was in the well; and also about the butterflies that fascinated and delighted him as they fluttered around him and through the tall grass.

Alone with his fancies, Joe seldom looked toward the front of the cottage, where his adoptive parents dozed in their wooden beach chairs. A double generation gap (they could almost have been his grandparents) separated them. There was also the powerful separation of temperament.

Joe was imaginative and volatile. His adoptive parents were icy, leaden, and emotional only when angry. Temperamental differences showed in the faces of Stephen and Joe. Both had black hair, which was one of the reasons for Stephen's wanting to adopt Joe. The hair, however, was the only similarity. Stephen's face was square, hard-boned, and disciplined; Joe's was full of feeling, the bone structure delicate.

Joe wanted to forget that the people in the beach chairs were there. He called them Mom and Dad, but he didn't feel like their son. Didn't they tell him and everybody else that he was adopted, that they had rescued him from an orphanage and had given him a home? Didn't they say he was their good deed, and didn't they keep reminding him of what they were doing for him and that he had to pay them back?

The Kallingers seemed to Joe as inseparable as if they had been glued together. They were a team, he thought, and he an outsider. "I had a lack of feeling," he would tell me, "that I was a part of anybody—or that anybody was a part of me!"

To the Kallingers, however, Joe was an insider. For the fulfillment of their own needs and purposes they were binding this child to themselves. The binding had nothing to do with *his* needs (and later his potentialities). It had nothing to do with affection or emotional closeness. The Kallingers didn't kiss Joe, stroke him, pet him, or play with him. They touched him only to hit him or to take his hand on the way to kindergarten. (Until he was thirteen Anna would take him to and from school.) Even when he was a tot, they kept him in the store most of the time. Sitting on his maple kiddy chair, he would often collect money for war bonds. He put the money into one of Stephen's Philly cigar boxes. Each time there was $18.50 in the box, the Kallingers bought a war bond in Joe's name. They were teaching Joe the value of saving and also telling him how much they were doing for him.

Some neighbors called him Joey, but to the Kallingers he was always Joseph. They wouldn't call him Joe until he was an adult. When he annoyed them, they called him *Dummkopf*. He couldn't help thinking that *Dummkopf* was the only pet name for him.

"We will be strict with him," Anna told people when he first came. "Like the old country. He will be a good boy. He will respect my clean house, no throwing his stuff around."

"*Ja*, he'll be a gentleman!" Stephen told neighbors. "He is going to learn the business early. No fooling around. No playing with other kids and get in trouble. I am going to make him an expert shoe-maker, like me, his dad."

As Joe put it to me many years later, "You couldn't communicate with my mother. She just didn't understand feelings. Stephen didn't, either. Except when they got angry, they were like two pieces of ice."

Joe didn't feel close to the Kallingers even when he helped them rake together the fallen leaves in autumn. Yet he was excited by what was happening. He would watch Stephen kneel in front of the large, loose mound of leaves and carefully ignite it around the base with a match. Entranced, Joe would watch the flames grow and spread, curling the edges of the leaves, twisting them into burned and fragile shapes, with hot, red sparks rising in the smoke. The crackling sound of the yellow flames, flashing and capering in the wind, thrilled him. Fire became part of his secret world in which he lived with sights, sounds, and objects, all of which took the place of people.

At the springhouse and in the surrounding woods, Joe found worms in the earth. In back of the cottage, on the bank of a creek where his adoptive father took him fishing, Joe watched as Stephen put a hook through a worm's squirming body. Joe refused to bait his hook with a worm, for he believed that worms were the spirits of dead people. He imagined that if he made a worm suffer, a dead person, holding in a bony hand Stephen's lip knife with the green handle, would come out of its grave to kill him.

A boy of four or five or six, Joe didn't want to be destroyed. The life force was strong in him, and he didn't know that dark forces of destruction were at work around him; that on September 16, 1943, the day of his discharge from St. Mary's Hospital, they would move even more relentlessly to overpower him.

Afraid of being destroyed by the worms, Joe fished only for minnows, which he would catch with a net and sometimes with his hands; or he would put on the hook a small ball of oatmeal mixed with dough, and he would sit by the creek, line in hand, usually by day, but sometimes by night, while the fish nibbled at the crude bait or swimming by, ignored it.

As an adult Joe made idyllic his recollections of the creek, giving voice to the poetic sensibility he already had as a child:

the waiting darkness holds things:
the occasional tinkering of a cow bell,
little yellow windows that are like eyes
peering into the depths of a darkness;
insect sounds all around,
and from the distance the mournful sounds
of baying hounds; the sound of running
water, and memories flashing back
to childhood days in the country,
with the shallow crick in the back
of the old bungalow, the eager thrill
of fishing in the night by the glow
of a lantern as I sat quiet in the darkness
waiting for a bite and my first fish by night.

Joe thought of the spirits in the springhouse well as good spirits that would protect him in the way his guardian angel, a female figure with small breasts and two wings, watched over him. And communing with them, he knew peace. The worms frightened him because they were the spirits of the dead. But he was happy living in fantasy with the butterflies. They looked like angels, he thought, for, like angels, they had two wings. Lolling at the springhouse or pushing through the high grass or fishing in the creek, he decided that the most beautiful things in life were the butterflies, and, sensing that *to be* is to belong to someone, he saw himself as belonging to them.

"Everyone has people, right?" Joe reminisced to me. "I used to think, when I was a kid, that the butterflies were *my* people. I didn't know where they lived, but I thought I was a spirit who lived with them, that I could penetrate them maybe like other kids think they can fly to the moon on broomsticks. I thought I had lived on earth before and had died; that while I waited for a body in which to return I had been a spirit freely going into one butterfly or another.

"But I thought," he added, "I had no home until Anna and Stephen came along and wanted this baby boy. And I thought that I was born through another mother and my spirit that had gone in and out of the butterflies went into the body of this baby and then Anna and Stephen were sent to pick me up."

Feeling rootless, little Joe found comfort in this fantasy. In fantasy his mother, who was merely incidental in the divine scheme of things, had not abandoned him. She had given birth to him for the express purpose—the divine purpose—that the Kallingers would make him theirs.

The fantasy grew each time the Kallingers said they were proud of Joe. And in these early years they were proud when the nuns at the St. Boniface kindergarten marveled that Joseph could recite his prayers in German; that he had "an excellent memory" and that he was "smart." Joe knew that the Kallingers were especially pleased because St. Boniface was a German parish where they did most of the advertising for their store.

But the fantasy faltered whenever the Kallingers threatened: "We'll send you back where we found you." This was the Kallingers' bogey man, their means of frightening the child with his own insecurity. He never knew when the threat was coming. It came when he didn't eat his spinach or forgot to take off his rubbers before coming into the house. When he cried because Anna hit him on the head with a wooden spoon for not taking off his rubbers, she repeated the threat and hit him again. And Stephen! Joe would always remember how Stephen waved the knife with the green handle at him and ordered, "You do as I say or we'll send you back."

From the time Joe was five until just before the hernia operation when he was six years and nine months, three incidents took place that widened the distance that separated him from the Kallingers. These incidents also threatened finally to put to rest his fantasy that he was especially meant for the Kallingers.

The first incident occurred on an autumn afternoon in 1941. Anna brought five-year-old Joe home from kindergarten. She allowed him to ride his tricycle on East Sterner Street. He overheard some older boys say "fuck"—a word that was new to him. When he pedaled his tricycle back to the Kallinger store, he saw Stephen through an open window.

"Dad," Joe called, "what's 'fuck' mean?"

Stephen rushed outside, yanked Joe off the tricycle, and dragged him into the store, then "in back," where he flogged him with leather. Then Anna hit him with the wooden spoon. The child was "left in" for a week. During the week the Kallingers repeated their punishments, told him that he was "bad, bad," that they had room in their house only for a good boy, and if he continued to be bad, they would have to send him back. But they never told him in what way he had been bad nor what "fuck" meant.

Three weeks later, the second crisis occurred. Anna brought Joe home from kindergarten and served him a glass of milk. After finishing the milk he headed for the street door. Grabbing him by the shoulders, she scolded, "You ain't going out, Joseph. Not after what you did in the alley yesterday."

"What did I do?" Joe asked.

"You know perfectly well," Anna replied. "You tried to pull a little girl's panties down. She didn't let you and you ran away. The lady next door told me." Anna picked up her wooden spoon. Joe threw up his arms to shield himself against the blow. But it came. He cried, and Anna raged, "Stop the tears. You cry and I'll give you something to cry about. This time we're really going to send you back."

Anna grabbed her broom and went outside, slamming the door behind her. Through the window Joe watched her wave the broom at two teenage boys and heard her yell, "You messed up my clean sidewalk! Do it again and I'm going to call the cops." She chased the boys with the broom, and when they were out of sight, swept away with large, furious strokes the two small Dixie cups the boys had thrown on her clean sidewalk.

Watching, Joe wished that she would sweep *him* away. He was terrified that she would send him back, but just as terrified that he would not be able to break free of her. For he could not escape from the central fact of his existence: that not having been born to the Kallingers, he lived with them on sufferance, as if he had come into their lives as an ugly changeling and had to endure a changeling's pain and hardship.

It was not until two weeks before Joe's hernia operation, however, that the fantasy that he was especially meant for the Kallingers actually died. Joe opened the door to the Kallinger store partway, then stood still, frozen by fear.

"Shut that door," Anna scolded from inside.

Joe closed the door and found himself standing close to Anna, who had left the counter to meet him.

"What happened to you?" she asked angrily. "You got mud all over you. You look pale. You smell awful."

"I was climbing a fence," Joe explained. "A redheaded girl kicked me. I got sick and vomited."

"Kicked you?" Anna asked. "What did you do to her?"

"Nothing," Joe said.

"You're a liar! She kicked you because you did something *bad* to her, like the little girl in the alley. You were five then. Now you're more than six. What you did now had to be worse. I just know it."

"I didn't even see her before she kicked me," Joe protested. "Honest I didn't."

"Go to your room," Anna ordered. "You ain't getting supper to-night. In the morning we'll send you back."

That night, lying alone and miserable in the dark of his room, Joe stifled his tears as pain shot through his left groin. He murmured to himself: "I hate girls. I hate the Kallingers. I hate everybody. Except Tommy."

Tommy, Joe's imaginary companion, stayed with Joe all night.

Tommy lived in Joe's stomach, came out through Joe's throat and mouth, took Joe by the wrist and held Joe's left index finger in the mirror. Joe sometimes wondered why he could see his own finger in the mirror, but not Tommy's hand on the wrist. It didn't matter. Joe knew that Tommy was there. Joe didn't actually hear Tommy's voice, but knew when Tommy was talking to him. When Joe was lonely, as he was most of the time, Tommy was his friend. Feeling Tommy's presence, Joe would stand at the mirror for hours sometimes, anyway until Anna dragged him away. Anna was cross because Joe kept looking into the mirror. But not this night. This time Tommy, without leaving Joe's stomach and without making any sound, just kept saying: "You're going to be all right, Joe, all right."

The next morning Joe wasn't all right, and the Kallingers, instead of "sending him back," took him to Dr. Daly. Even though the diagnosis was "left indirect hernia (congenital)," Anna was certain that the kick the redheaded girl had given Joe had caused the hernia.

During the sixteen days Joe was at St. Mary's, the Kallingers were probably getting ready to stage their symbolic castration scene in the living room. In all likelihood they were going to do so because they had misread the meaning of the incidents when Joe was five: his asking the meaning of the word "fuck"; his having tried to pull down a little girl's panties; and the recent episode with the redheaded girl, who was several years older than Joe.

The Kallingers did not realize that only the pulling down of the little girl's panties had any sexual meaning. Joe had asked what "fuck" meant out of sheer curiosity about a word that was new to him. With the redheaded girl he was the passive victim of her aggression, an aggression that had nothing to do with sex. Even the one incident that did involve sex reflected the perfectly normal curiosity of a little boy. If the Kallingers had known anything about how to bring up a child, they would have recognized normal curiosity, even normal sexual curiosity, when they saw it. In their unenlightened way they saw sex where it did not exist. On a conscious level, they may have staged the "bird" scene to save little Joe from the sexual damnation toward which, because of the three unrelated episodes, they thought he was heading. On the unconscious level, they may have wanted to destroy him for representing their own failure to have a child. "Behave yourself," they screamed at him again and again. Now they had put their verbal commands into grotesque action.

After Joe had returned from the hospital, the Kallingers tightened the security of his prison house. No longer was he allowed to play outside. The punishments inflicted upon him became more cruel and more numerous. Having given up his fantasy that the Kallingers had been sent to pick him up, Joe himself became less docile and more rebellious. For the most part he would still be the Kallingers' obedient robot. But there would also be lapses.

So it was that Joe's childhood with the Kallingers fell into two parts: *before* and *after* the hernia operation.

Before had been a time of compensating through fantasy for the feeling of not being "a part of anybody." *After* would be a time of expressing through unhealthy anger directed chiefly against himself his reactions to the emotional deprivation and the traumas the Kallingers had inflicted and would continue to inflict.

4 The Angry Child

Joe stood beside a small table at the back of his first-year classroom at St. Boniface. On the table, next to an unlighted candle, was a missal, a tiny book of daily prayers and devotions. Bound with black paper, the missal had gilt-edged white pages and, on the front cover, gilt lettering. Joe thought of it as a "beautiful black-and-gold Bible."

He lifted the "Bible," closed his fingers over it, and held it tightly. He put it back on the table and walked with the rest of his class into the hallway for morning recess.

He kept thinking about the missal, which he not only wanted as his own, but also felt strongly compelled to have. He had fallen behind in his schoolwork because of the hernia operation and the long convalescence that followed. Back at school for three weeks now, he felt that the nuns who taught him no longer regarded him as "smart." He felt stupid, humiliated, worthless.

The missal began to assume magical powers, and Joe thought that by praying with it, he could become "smart" again.

As they were coming back to the classroom, he asked the teacher where he could buy the missal. When she said the stores didn't carry miniature prayer books, he was crushed. But knowing that he *had* to have the missal, he tried to make Anna, on the way home for lunch, stop at the Holy Shop, a Front Street store that sold religious items.

"What you want to go there for?" Anna asked, tightening her grip on his hand.

"I want to see if they have a little Bible I want," Joe explained. In spite of what the teacher had said, he was going to *try* to buy it.

"You want to see?" Anna snapped. "You know I have to get you home and back to school. Look at you. You have dirt on your shirt. I have to change you."

"Just a minute," Joe pleaded as he pulled closer to the Holy Shop. "Let me see if they have it."

"Shop? Stop? I'll give you shop and stop," Anna ranted as she pinched Joe on the flesh just below his elbow and made him walk on.

During the next morning's recess, Joe took the tiny missal from the small table and held it in his hands. He opened it, turned the gilt-edged pages, and closed it. He slipped it into his pants pocket and followed the other children out of the classroom.

Once Joe had taken the missal, he thought of it as *his*. He felt it belonged to him in the way that the good food, the good clothes, even the good toys the Kallingers gave him never did. Didn't the Kallingers always say, "Look what we do for you—when you're big, you will have to pay us back"?

Joe had acted not only out of intense desire to possess the little book, but also out of rage, both immediate and cumulative. To the immediate anger at feeling worthless because he couldn't keep up with his lessons had been added the rage that began with separation anxiety in infancy and had been reawakened and intensified by the symbolic castration in the living room on the day of his discharge from the hospital on September 16, 1943. Any child, driven as Joe was driven, could have done the same thing. But nobody bothered to find out why Joe had done it.

The next day, when the teacher noticed the missal was missing, she accused Joe of having taken it. For he had talked to her about it.

"You're a thief," the teacher said.

"A thief," said Anna, who was called to school.

"A thief," Stephen echoed when Anna brought Joe home.

That evening Joe overheard Stephen saying to Anna: "Keep the money locked up. We have a thief in the house."

For an hour each night during the next week the Kallingers made Joe kneel with bare knees on a strip of coarse sandpaper used for sanding leather and rubber. When the hour was over, Joe would take refuge in the bathroom. After putting Vaseline on his stinging knees, he would retreat to his own room. Almost always he reached for his "Bible." He would stand on a chair and pull the tiny book down from the top shelf of the closet, where it had remained undiscovered when the Kallingers searched his room for it. Sometimes he sat with the missal open on his lap, not really reading but pretending to do so. At other times he paced with the "Bible" clutched tightly in his hand. And there were times when he used the missal to pray, as he had originally intended to do, that he would catch up with his schoolwork. But he never kneeled. The stinging sensation in his knees made kneeling painful, and he knew that the next night he would have to kneel on sandpaper again.

Like the butterflies in the country and Tommy, the imaginary companion, the missal was Joe's friend. Yet Joe knew that the missal was a dangerous friend. Before he had taken the missal his teachers considered him a good boy, but now they said he was a bad boy: a thief.

For weeks Joe struggled between the desires to keep and to throw away the missal. Finally he threw it down the sewer on the way to school. But throwing away the missal changed nothing.

Joe was now trapped in an unending capture-control-imprisonment syndrome, with one escape door from cruelty after another closed. He was treated not as a child, but as a shoemaker's robot that, duly programmed, would become a shoemaker. While other children played, Joe, from the time he was seven, did shoe repair work after school and part-time or full-time on Saturdays. He pulled heels off shoes and filled bushel baskets with heel pads. He also had to run errands and do other chores for the Kallinger store. After supper he was given an hour off to do homework, and usually his work day didn't end until nine in the evening.

Joe wasn't allowed to go to block parties, to stand under a hose with other kids in hot weather, or to throw snowballs with them in cold weather. He wasn't allowed to skate or ride a bike or wear a Halloween costume. He wasn't allowed to go into other children's houses or bring anyone into the Kallinger house. However, when Joe's class at St. Boniface was going to the zoo during the afternoon school hours, Joe, then eight years old, thought that this one time the Kallingers would allow him, as he wrote in a poem, to "walk to the beat of the drums."

Joe did not mention the zoo to Anna while they were walking home from school. But when they got into the store, Joe told Stephen and asked for a quarter for the outing. Stephen called to Anna, who was behind the counter, to give Joe twenty-five cents from the cash register. But Anna rushed up to her husband, shook her head angrily, and said, "Steef, *bist du wohl verrückt?* When will he do his work?"

"It's during school hours," Stephen said.

"No," Anna insisted. "The zoo will take longer than school. He's gotta work *now*."

Anna then ordered Joe to go "in back" and eat his lunch. "Your class will go to the zoo," she told him, "but *you* will work! You're not here to play. You're here to repair shoes. No fooling around. No waste time. Someday you will own the business. You got to learn."

"Dad said I could go to the zoo, and I'm going!" Joe replied.

Infuriated by Joe's first act of defiance, of open rebellion, Anna grabbed Joe by the arm and with her free hand reached for a hammer. It was a short but heavy instrument used for driving nails through layers of leather. "Zoo?" Anna screamed in the presence of a customer and neighbor who would remember the incident for the rest of her life. And she hit Joe on the head four times with the heavy steel instrument. "You want zoo? I'll give you zoo!"

After the fourth short, sharp blow, Joe finally managed to pull away. Screaming and rubbing his head to ease the pain, he ran "in back." He sat at the kitchen table, rubbing his head and staring at the drops of blood on his fingers. Everything seemed to be spinning around him. The ceiling looked as if it were going to fall. Then, turning his rage against himself, he leaped blindly from the chair and ran from one room to the other, banging his head first against the kitchen table and then on the kitchen and living-room walls. Anna, who had left the store to see what Joe was doing, ran after him with a broom.

"You can never get away from me," Anna shrieked after Joe.

He ran up the stairs. She ran after him. Catching up to him, she saw the blood on his fingers for the first time.

She pulled him into the bathroom, took iodine out of the medicine closet, and applied it to the cut on his scalp. Joe kicked and screamed.

"Ach! Always with the tantrums," Anna complained. As soon as the bleeding had stopped, she walked out of the bathroom.

Joe sat down on the edge of the bathtub, fighting tears as he thought not only of the hammer blows, but also of other punishments. Vivid were the frequent floggings Stephen gave him with a homemade cat-o'-nine-tails he had fashioned out of leather and rawhide laces.

Holding in his hand two thick, hard soles placed together, Stephen would chase Joe, who would run to his room and hide under his bed. Stephen, right behind him, would pull up the mattress and the spring and reach for him as he cowered on the floor in the corner of the bed frame nearest the wall. Stephen would crack him on the back, the arms, the head, all over.

That night in bed, his head still aching, Joe wanted to go into Stephen and Anna's bedroom to be with them, to try to talk to them. He wanted to tell them his head still hurt. Maybe if he was a good boy and worked very hard in the store, they'd let him go to the zoo the next time his class went. But he knew it was no use. As far back as he could remember, he had never been allowed to go into their bedroom at night. By day they didn't mind if he stuck his head through the bedroom's open doorway or went in and looked around—provided he didn't mess anything up. At night he was forbidden to enter. Once or twice he had tried to go in after he had been told their bedroom was *verboten*. They had chased him out, back to his own room, back to darkness. They kept him out of their bedroom in the same way they made him sit in the back of the Plymouth by himself on trips to and from their Neshaminy cottage when he wanted to sit up front with them. Lying in his bed, he wondered what they did in there, what magical things happened during the night that they didn't want him to see.

Then Joe fell asleep. He dreamed he had entered the Kallingers' bedroom. They lay on their beds, their faces turned away from him, their eyeglasses on. They would punish him if they found him there.

Through the immaculate lenses of their glasses would come the hot light of anger to burn him.

Joe's feet were bare. Noiselessly walking out of the bedroom, he went down the long hallway to the door that opened into what the Kallingers called "the empty room," for nobody slept in it. It was filled, however, with Stephen's shoe repair display materials and Anna's jars of preserved fruits and vegetables. Joe released the slip-bolt lock and the door opened. "The empty room" having always been off limits to him, Joe entered it as a triumphant intruder.

He opened the closet door. Where the wall had been was a window with bars shaped like half-moons. He turned to face the closet door, which closed after he had entered the closet. He pushed himself against the door. It opened, but "the empty room" had vanished. In its place was a roof bathed in sunlight. The roof merged with the neighboring roofs, forming one big roof.

On the big roof were people in swimming pools and in groups talking and laughing in the sunlight. For the first time in eight years, Joe made friends, but he knew he could never bring them into the house of his adoptive parents.

Suddenly the sunlight was gone. The merged roofs began buckling and swaying, cracks appearing in the surface. Trying to come through a window of the Kallingers' house was a big, hairy man.

"Don't jump!" Joe cried. "Don't jump!"

But the big, hairy man leaped through the open window and tumbled over and over in the air, becoming smaller and smaller until he vanished.

Then the people, Joe's new friends, vanished. Joe was desolate. The merged roofs were violently shaking and splitting. He tried to get back into the house to warn his adoptive parents that the world was going to pieces. At that moment, Joe awoke.

For many years Joe remembered the dream; he told me about it thirty-five years later. It was a painful memory, for the dream was a representation of psychic pain. The dream expressed his awareness of his exclusion from the intimacy of the Kallingers in their own house, which, because he had no other, he called home. The shaking and splitting of the merged roofs expressed the child's uncertainty about his identity. Quite literally he didn't know who he was, for his natural parents' nationalities, religions, and ethnic origins were unknown to him. This bothered him, because he and everyone else knew that he was adopted.

"The empty room" in the dream represented his eagerness to have what had been denied him in his waking life. The disappearing wall in the closet represented his desire to break through the imprisoning walls of the Kallinger house. The half-moon bars on the window where the wall had been had to do with Joe's natural mother and the Kallingers. The shape, representing a woman's breasts in profile, expressed the child's separation from his real mother. The bars themselves were symbols of his imprisonment in the Kallinger household. The merged roofs and the people on them expressed his wish for freedom and inclusion, his wish to have friends and to be like everybody else.

The big, hairy man was, perhaps, a dream transformation of his adoptive parents into a figure representing Joe's ambivalent feelings for them. Even though he had begged the hairy man not to jump, Joe's fear and hatred of the Kallingers also made the hairy man vanish. However, the house into which Joe was trying to return belonged to his adoptive parents and was the only home he had. Therefore, he had to warn the Kallingers of the danger, even though he had symbolically destroyed them in the vanishing of the hairy man, their transformation.

Two weeks later, eight-year-old Joe was on an errand for the Kallingers. Before going back to the store, he stopped at a lot on the corner of B and Cambria streets, four blocks from the Kallinger house. On the lot were three big, round abandoned oil tanks that were Joe's city equivalent of the springhouse in the country. He often came to the tanks, which he called holes, when he was sent out on an errand. For him the "holes" represented escape and safety.

He would climb up a twenty-foot vertical ladder and go over the top of the tank onto another ladder and climb down to the bottom. Sitting on the floor of the tank, he would look at the sky and watch the drift of clouds, or he would follow a bird bobbing up and down in the air currents as it flew to the limit of Joe's vision, which was marked by the top of the tank. He would talk to the spirits he thought inhabited the tank and feel at peace.

56

This summer afternoon in 1944, while the world was at war, the peace of the tank sanctuary also came to an end. As eight-year-old Joe stepped from the ladder onto the floor of the tank, he discovered that he was not alone. He had come upon three boys whom he knew by sight, but not by name. They were much older than he, which made him feel weak and little. Joe wanted the boys to go away, because he felt that his privacy had been violated and that the spirits would resent the intrusion of the strangers.

They were making strange movements with their bodies, movements that he had never seen anybody make before. Never having had any sex and knowing nothing about it, he didn't know that one of the boys was committing fellatio, and that the third boy, who was watching them, was masturbating. Joe noticed that the boy whose hand was going rapidly back and forth in front of his open pants was smiling strangely; that the boy who stood in front of his kneeling companion was moving the lower part of his body in slow, thrusting motions. His sports shirt was rolled above the top of his pants.

The one who was masturbating turned his head in Joe's direction and suddenly stopped. "Hey," he said, "there's that shoemaker's kid, standing over there." The kneeling boy pulled back his head, wiped his mouth with the back of his hand, and swung around, crouching, to look at the little kid standing by the ladder on the other side of the tank. Then he got to his feet, ran over to Joe, and grabbed him by the shirt. He dragged Joe across the tank to his two friends.

The boy who had been masturbating took a thin knife from his pocket. He clutched Joe's hair with his other hand, and placed the flat of the knife blade against Joe's throat. He said, "Don't scream or you'll get cut, understand?" Pressing the flat of the blade harder against Joe's flesh, he continued, "We're going to take your pants off and this other guy here is going to give you a blow job. If you make any noise, you're dead, get it?" They pulled down Joe's pants and pushed him to the floor of the tank so that he was lying on his back. Then the boy who had dragged Joe across the tank kneeled beside him and covered Joe's penis with his mouth. His two friends stood with knives in one hand and masturbated with the other while they watched.

* * *

57

From the tank Joe went to the shoe repair store. As he pulled heels off shoes and filled bushel baskets with heel pads, he felt dirty and sick because of what had been done to him in the tank. But he also kept thinking of what he had seen the boys in the tank doing to each other. He wondered whether what mothers and fathers did to each other was like that.

He had never been given any sex instruction beyond being told that sex was nasty, dirty, sinful! Sex, he had been told, was connected with a demon, and when the demon is made to go away, one never gets into trouble. He was very confused.

Sex is trouble, he pondered. I got into trouble in the tank. But Dr. Daly drove the demon out of my little bird. With the demon gone, I can't get into trouble. But I did. It's all very mysterious. Mothers and fathers do something to each other. Is that trouble?

In the tank Joe was a silent witness for the first time to the sexual experience of others, and it was in the tank that, with a knife held at his throat, he was himself initiated into sex.

That night, without knowing what to expect, he stood on a chair and peered through the transom into his adoptive parents' bedroom. He heard nothing, but he could see the Kallingers, each alone in a twin bed. They were lying silently, and he couldn't tell whether they were asleep.

When he looked through the transom a few days later, he again saw the Kallingers in their own beds. But this time they were talking to each other about the business of the day that was over and of the one that had not yet begun. Then they began talking about all the money they were spending on him and how they hoped the money wouldn't be wasted. He didn't like being thought of as a waste of money. He went back to his bedroom and to bed.

Any child—or any adult—would be terrified at having a knife at his throat. For Joe the normal terror was complicated by the knives in his past: the knife with the green handle in the Kallinger store that cut leather; the knife Dr. Daly had used to cut a little boy's flesh and allegedly to drive out the demon from the "bird"; the knife with Joe's penis in the mirror after the symbolic castration in the living room. But while these knives were part of Joe's fantasy life, the knife held at his throat in the tank was a hideous reality. It was a reality that he would make part of his fantasy life, and later realities would be influenced by the fantasy.

Like the symbolic castration in the living room, the scene in the tank was fundamental to Joe's development. The boys in the tank, like Dr. Daly, were to Joe giants who controlled him. He therefore linked sex with violence, especially with knives, and both sex and violence with power.

Other children have had similar experiences without suffering serious psychological damage. In Joe's case this oral rape in the tank was complicated by past experiences. At the time, he already had the underlying violent trauma that grew out of his symbolic castration and that became the matrix of his adult psychosis.

To both the tank episode and the violent trauma Joe brought his preoccupation with the knives he had seen in the Kallinger shoe repair store, his enforced alienation from people, and his shaky sense of his own identity as revealed by the dream in which the roof shook. He also brought the emotional and cultural barrenness of his childhood in the Kallinger home, and the sense of shame connected with sex that, apart from the repeated exorcisms of the demon from the "bird," the Kallingers had instilled.

Tuesday, December 11, 1945, was Joe's ninth birthday. Tall for his age and lean, he was a handsome boy. He no longer had a round, chubby face, but a long, narrow one. The eyes were sad, the face sometimes petulant or scowling.

That morning, walking with Anna to St. Boniface Church and School, Joe sang softly, "Happy birthday to me; happy birthday, dear Joe."

"What is this nonsense you're mumbling?" Anna asked as they turned from Lehigh Avenue into Mascher Street.

"It's my birthday," Joe replied quietly. He stopped walking.

Anna jerked his hand roughly and said, "Stop that nonsense! Listen. I have something to tell you. You don't obey your mother. I *told* you not to hang that dirty thing in my window."

"It isn't dirty. It's a lovely Christmas tree. I made it all by myself. It's papier-mâché, the sister said."

"Well, it isn't in the window now. I took it down," Anna replied.

"Where is it?" Joe asked tensely, moving from side to side and shaking Anna's hand up and down. "Other kids have things in *their* windows."

"Hurry up!"

Again Joe stopped walking. Anna pulled his hand, but he wouldn't move. "Where is it?" he asked again, this time in a high-pitched, screechy voice.

"I put it away, but you carry on like this and I'm going to burn it. Come *on*! Behave yourself!"

"You can't," Joe pleaded, still refusing to walk. "It's mine! It's mine!"

"I do what I want, you understand that, *Dummkopf*? And *you're* going to do what I want. Walk, Joseph, or I'll burn you up, too!"

"I'm going to go home and save my tree," Joe screamed as he tried to break free of Anna's grip.

"Don't you have a fit here," Anna panted. "A truant, a thief. That's what you are! And a crazy boy. I wish I never took you to my house."

"I wish you didn't, too!" Joe replied in a tight voice.

Through the immaculate lenses of Anna's eyeglasses, Joe saw her eyes go steely with anger. *"Ach so!"* she said. "We will send you back and good riddance."

"It's my birthday," he went on, "and you didn't give me a present. You *never* did!"

"Every day is your birthday. Your father and me, we give you presents all the time: a good room to sleep in, better clothes than the other kids—the sisters asked us to give them your hand-me-downs for the poor kids. In summer, and Sunday in the country, you ride like a prince in the Plymouth. And when you were little, we gave you plenty toys, believe me! So, these things are not real for you? *A present*? You are a bad boy, a *greedy* boy. I tell you now, first and last time, birthday or no birthday, no present! Understand? Come! Walk!"

After the morning Mass was over, the children, led by the sisters, filed out of the church by a side door, walked across the courtyard into the school, and then fanned out, section by section, to their classrooms.

In the church Joe had prayed to God, but he had kept his eyes

60

on the face of a statue of the Virgin Mary. He was sure that *She* would never have removed his papier-mâché Christmas tree from the window where he had hung it the day before, after he had gotten back from school. But Her stone face had told him nothing, and Her stone garments—the long cloak and under it the dress that reached, like Anna's, down to Her ankles—were rigid; Joe had almost expected that She would step down from Her niche and tell him that Anna would put back his Christmas tree in the window and that he would not be taken back to St. Vincent's.

He went directly to his seat, which was in the rear of the classroom. He sat with his eyes lowered and his hands in his pockets. With his right hand he squeezed the penknife that he had found in a trash can. He would have as usual no birthday present; his Christmas tree would be burned; and he would be sent back to St. Vincent's. Furious, he couldn't understand anything that the sister was explaining to the class, and he thought that this morning would be his last at St. Boniface. He was shaking with anger and didn't want anyone to ask him what was the matter. What could he say? He couldn't talk against his mother. No good little boy did that! How many times had the sisters drummed *that* into his head? He had tried to honor the Kallingers, had wanted to be loyal to them, but what was the use? His fingers tightly squeezed the penknife in his pocket as anger ate at him, gnawed at his insides, and made him feel that he was being torn apart. And the kids here at St. Boniface: He looked around the classroom and hated everyone he saw. They laughed at him because, they said, he was a sheltered mama's boy: too clean, too neat, dressed up like a little Lord Fauntleroy, but still wearing short pants when the other kids his age were in long pants.

These thoughts were racing in Joe's mind at great speed when he heard his name called. That meant it was his turn to take the composition he had written at home to the sister's desk. He was glad that the shaking had stopped, but he still felt the gnawing at his insides.

While the sister read and corrected his paper, he stood at her desk staring at the children's wardrobe key in the corner of the desk blotter. Knowing that the sister was paying attention to his paper and not to him, he reached for the wardrobe key and put it into his pocket.

After the English lesson, the sister told the children that they were going to spend the next period decorating the school library for Christmas. As the children left their classroom, Joe made sure that he was last in line.

He began walking with the others toward the staircase, then he peeled off from the line and returned to the empty classroom. He removed the wardrobe key from his pocket, opened the wardrobe door, and went inside.

He stared with hatred at the coats on the hooks. The coats belonged to children who were allowed to hang what *they* made in *their* windows, who got birthday presents and didn't have to sing "Happy Birthday" to themselves. They could also go to the zoo with their class. They weren't cooped in behind walls all the time— walls that sprang up in dreams.

The coats, like the children who owned them, were part of loving families and were not discarded like the objects found in trash cans. He felt close to the things in trash cans because they and he were discarded. When he picked them up, he was looking for identity and saw himself playing the role of adoptive parent to found treasures. He would never harm these treasures. Never!

But the coats! He pulled the penknife out of his pocket, then slashed the pockets of two coats and cut off the buttons of three others. He locked the wardrobe, put the key back on the teacher's desk, and raced out of the classroom. He was last in line, back in his place, as his class filed into the library. Having vented his rage in his first destructive act, he felt calm.

With the cutting of the coats and the stealing of the missal earlier, Joe had become conscious of what he later described to me as "an awareness to do something wrong." Both times he had acted out of rage. In the case of the missal it was rage at feeling worthless. The coat-cutting was the rage of an outsider against insiders; of a child denied love against children who had it. The rage in both instances had been both immediate and cumulative: To the immediate compulsion to do something wrong had been added the rage that began with separation anxiety in infancy and was awakened and intensified by the symbolic castration after the hernia operation.

Joe did not have this "awareness to do something wrong" again until he was eleven. By then he had been graduated from small jobs in the Kallinger store to more complicated ones. He would sit on a chair with a bushel basket beside him and a wooden block in front of him on which he would place a large sheet of leather hide. He would put a steel die on the hide and would hit the die with a wooden mallet, thus cutting out heel pads for men's shoes. Then he had to fill the bushel basket with the heel pads. The only payment for his work was the movie money he got by filling the basket.

For on Saturday afternoons Joe, who still could usually go out alone only on an errand for the Kallingers, was allowed to go to the movies by himself. Not having an allowance, he could go *provided* that he earned the movie money by working with the heel pads in the Kallinger store on Saturday mornings. He would sit on the chair and work furiously to meet the movie deadline.

Sometimes when the morning was almost gone and the basket was not yet full, he would stuff newspapers into the bottom of the basket and then put the heel pads on top of the newspapers. Knowing that Stephen was too busy to notice, Joe would go to the movies unperturbed. During the week he would take the basket to the cellar and empty the heel pads into the bin where pads were kept. The ruse was never discovered, but in time Joe became unhappy about going to the movies alone while other kids went in groups. Only by paying the other boys' way could Joe, who had not been allowed to have friends, persuade them to go to the movies with him. But the heel job paid only for a movie ticket for himself. Realizing this, Joe, for the third time, had an "awareness to do something wrong."

One Saturday morning while the Kallingers were in the store and before he himself went downstairs, Joe walked into their bedroom and opened the closet where they kept rolls of nickels, dimes, and quarters. Taking a roll of quarters, he returned the other rolls to the shelf. By paying for one of the boys in the neighborhood to go to the movies, Joe was a big shot that day. Having succeeded once, he continued to "bribe" kids to go to the movies with him. He began taking more money from the closet than he needed for the day's outing, putting the "balance" underneath a loose brick in the pavement, surrounded by high grass, near a fence on the other side of East Sterner Street. He would place the brick over the coins in the ground and feel secure about the money in his improvised "bank."

Whatever the Kallingers did when they discovered that the coins were missing, he felt it would be worth the price of not being lonely on Saturday afternoons.

One Wednesday morning early in January 1947, Joe knew the moment he walked into the kitchen for breakfast that he had been caught. Anna was frying bacon, and Stephen, having improved his English, was reading the *Philadelphia Inquirer*. When the Kallingers saw Joe, Stephen scowled, and Anna, holding the pan over the flames, snarled, "Thief!"

"You bring us shame again, Joseph," Stephen said, putting down his paper.

Standing awkwardly between Anna at the stove and Stephen at the table, Joe said nothing.

"We give you everything," said Anna. "But you steal from our closet. Our hard-earned money you take."

"I'm counting the money in the closet before I come down for breakfast," Stephen explained. "I see some rolls are missing. How do I feel? Ashamed! And why? Because I have a thief in my house. I feel like it isn't safe to have anything valuable around. When you stole the missal from St. Boniface, I told your mother to lock everything up. She didn't listen to me and now this is what we got."

"Four years ago, Joseph," Anna said, "we brought you home from the hospital. We told you that you were going to be a good boy. . . ."

"We were afraid you would do wicked things with your little bird when you got older," Stephen said. "We got Dr. Daly to drive the demon out of it. He did, but . . ."

"*But*," said Anna, "we didn't think to get the doctor to drive out *this* badness, so now . . ."

"We were wrong, Joseph," said Stephen. "We should have done that also. But how could we dream that you would do this, rob us of our money? First the missal and now *this*! *Mein Gott!* What are you going to do next? Dr. Daly drove the demon out of your little bird. But you still have a demon in you. A demon that makes you a *thief*! What do you have to say for yourself, you model little boy, you?"

Standing stiffly, Joe still said nothing.

Anna walked away from the stove and stood close to Stephen. "Steef," she whispered in his ear, "we must drive the demon out of the fingers."

"*Ja*, Ahnie, that is what we must do," Stephen replied.

Having heard what Anna had whispered to Stephen and sensing danger, Joe started toward the door. Before he could get there, Stephen had grabbed him by the shoulders, turned him around, and, tightly holding his arm and pulling, walked Joe to the stove.

Anna, who was waiting, had removed the pan of frying bacon, but she had not turned off the flame. Instead she turned it all the way up.

"It's ready," Anna told Stephen as if she were a nurse handing a doctor a surgical instrument.

"*Ja*, very good, Ahnie," Stephen replied.

With his left hand Stephen gripped Joe's left wrist; with his right hand he gripped Joe's right wrist. Standing directly behind Joe, his grip around Joe's wrists squeezing the bones, Stephen slowly brought the fingertips of Joe's right hand over the burner and then pushed them into the flame. Joe screamed while Stephen intoned: "This will burn the demon thief out of the fingers that steal."

Stephen shoved the fingertips of Joe's left hand into the flame and withdrew them. The pain was great. Then Stephen pushed the fingertips of Joe's right hand into the flames. Joe screamed again and thrashed. Again Stephen intoned: "This will burn the demon thief out of the fingers that steal."

When Stephen had finished punishing Joe, Anna turned the burner off with a swift movement of satisfaction. "You did it well, Steef," she said, her face bright with admiration.

Stephen released his grip on Joe. His fingertips throbbing and smarting, Joe ran to the door that led into the living room.

"Where do you think you're going?" Anna asked.

"No place," Joe replied, gasping and sobbing. He clenched his teeth against the pain and held his hands away from his body, the palms up, the fingers curled. He couldn't stop shaking. He stood and looked at Anna, and waited for directions.

"Have you learned your lesson?" Anna asked.

"My fingers hurt terrible," Joe said softly.

"Of course. You must suffer for your great sin," Anna said.

Joe walked to the sink. He turned on the cold water, but Anna pushed him away and closed the faucet.

"You can have no water and no ointment. You must feel the pain with your body and soul. Then maybe God will forgive you. You must ask the blessed Virgin to intercede for you," Anna said.

But even more powerful than the pain from the exorcism of the "demon thief" was Joe's intense yearning not to be alone on Saturday afternoons. Whenever the supply of coins in his improvised bank was depleted, Joe returned to the Kallinger closet. He continued to steal the coins and to endure the pain of having his fingertips burned, so great was the loneliness the Kallingers had created for him.

The Kallingers burned Joe six times. Sometimes Anna placed Joe's fingertips in the flame, but more often it was Stephen who did. The burner was small and the fingertips were placed in the flame briefly. But on that burner, along with other punishments and indignities the Kallingers imposed, a human being with great potentiality was being destroyed.

By the time Joe was twelve, he had lost interest in bribing neighborhood children to go with him to the Howard Movie Theater on Saturdays with money he had stolen from the Kallingers.

In stealing the coins, Joe was trying through desperate means to assuage his loneliness. But he was also punishing the Kallingers by giving vent to the rage born of the indignities to which they had subjected him. They had created Joe's transgressions by denying him the right to find and to be himself, to play and enjoy being alive.

BOOK TWO

The Family Dream

5 The Secret World

Late one night, with only his desk light on, Joe, twelve years old, kneeled on his bed. He was in his pajamas. In his left hand he held the knife with the green handle. He pressed the point against the flowered wallpaper of his bedroom and quietly pivoted the knife from right to left, over and over again. His dark eyes watched bits of wallpaper and flecks of plaster fall onto the bed. From time to time he stopped and listened. All was quiet. Turning the blade farther into the wall, pressing on it, he felt a strange and wonderful power running through his body.

Joe wondered whether the power came from the knife with the green handle or from his left hand. The knife had scared him in the shoe repair store when Stephen used it to cut leather. But now at night, when the store was closed, the knife no longer frightened Joe. He had taken it from the shop to cut the hole in his bedroom wall and would return it in the morning, so there was nothing to fear on that score. As for the power, he decided that it came both from the knife with the green handle and from his left hand. He couldn't know that his left hand would become the stabbing hand, the hand of destruction.

The hole Joe cut in the wall, like the springhouse in Neshaminy and the tank in Kensington, was part of his secret world. Unlike them, however, the hole would not be used to communicate with the spirits or to spin fancies about the butterflies. Joe had created the hole for the pleasure of masturbation, and symbolically to conceal his penis, of which he was ashamed.

Joe removed the blade of the knife from the hole. To make sure the hole was the right size, he put his thumb into it. He turned off his desk lamp and lay down on the bed. Through the fly of his pajama bottoms, Joe placed the fingers of his left hand around his tumescent penis and masturbated. Becoming excited, he got on his knees and put his penis into the hole. Thrusting a few times with his hips, he came to orgasm.

For a while Joe lay on his bed, feeling calm and peaceful. But then he was overwhelmed by sadness, guilt, and shame. For, as his Catholic upbringing had taught him, he had "touched himself in an impure way."

He was bewildered and confused. Here he was lying beside the hole in which his erect penis had given him so much pleasure when a small penis free of the demon was supposed to have made him a good boy. He had enjoyed the hardness of the penis followed by the explosion of the orgasm. He knew that the demon that was supposed to have been driven out of his penis was still there.

The hole in the wall did not remain secret. Stephen discovered it, flogged Joe, and replastered the wall. Joe cut the hole again, was again beaten, and again Stephen covered up the hole with plaster. This happened repeatedly, but Stephen did not know that the hole was an indication that his plan to keep Joe's "bird" from ever getting hard had failed.

Joe half believed, half disbelieved what Stephen and Anna had told him about his "bird" six years ago and had frequently repeated since that time, particularly of late. He was convinced that the demon had not been driven out of his penis. But, according to prediction, his penis *had* remained small.

Actually, Joe's penis was not abnormally small. But it was small enough when compared to those of the older boys he had seen in school lavatories to feed the small-penis delusion Stephen and Anna had planted.

From time to time Joe gazed dreamily at the hole in his wall and spun fantasies. Many were about knives; the knife with the green handle, the unseen knife used to "fix" his "bird," the knife with the penis on it that appeared in the living-room mirror, and the knife in the tank, the sinister reality that marked his first sexual experience.

"When normal things should have taken place," Joe explained to me years later, "this *other thing* developed." This *other thing* was an adolescence in which the use of a knife was wedded to sexuality. For as Joe grew a little older, he was not content just to spin fantasies about knives. To heighten the pleasure of masturbation, he laid a real knife on his bed near the hole in the wall. He also brought to his room photographs of partially naked men and women that he found in pornographic magazines he picked up in trash cans.

In real life a buxom woman both sexually aroused and frightened Joe. Once when a large-breasted girl flirted with him at the movies, he literally ran away. Not feeling "macho," he didn't dare to compete for her favors with macho men. He thought that she, like everybody else, was laughing at him. But the nude, big-breasted women in the photographs excited him sexually without scaring him.

In time, however, the knife and the pictures ceased merely to enhance the pleasure of masturbation; they became essential. Joe was no longer able to achieve climax unless he had first cut a hole in a picture of a woman's breast or stomach. When he stabbed the breast or stomach, he felt very potent. The knife had returned to him the power that Dr. Daly's knife had allegedly removed.

In moments of anger, and not for sexual climax, Joe stabbed the penises in photographs of men. Again he was retaliating against the knife the surgeon had used.

What Joe was doing, he knew, could send a boy to Hell. He thought of Hell not as a place located on earth, but as a state of mind, although at that time he couldn't express the distinction. But even though he didn't think Hell was a place, with his rich imagination he had many pictorial images for it.

Hell was a great hole (a hole had again become important in Joe's imaginative life) in the earth into which all sinners were thrown after they had died and where spirits (the spirits did not have the shape of human beings) would torture the sinners. The lesser sinners, Joe thought, stayed near the top of the hole and the greater sinners near the bottom. There were fires in Hell, and these fires, giving off light like fires on earth, burned the sinners but did not consume them.

Hell was also a mountain, so high that it could be seen over the horizon. The mountain was made of men and women, their limbs, heads, and torsos intertwined and twisted into shapes expressing agony of mind and body. They had died while having sex or while masturbating; after death, they had had their penises or their breasts cut off with flaming knives by invisible demons that flew over and around the mountain in eternal patrol, only their flaming knives visible, and swooped down from time to time to cut off the penises or breasts of a newcomer, the mountain growing larger by the addition of each new sinner. Women had gaping, bloody holes in their stomachs. And this huge mountain, made up of those who in life had sinned through sex, gave off groans, lamentations, and wailings, all of which would continue forever.

Hell, too, was a place where short, squat devils, both male and female, who spoke a strange language that sounded like that of his adoptive parents, were chasing little boys and girls who had been caught having sex with one another or masturbating alone in their beds. In this Hell were five-year-old boys who had pulled down little girls' panties and twelve-year-old boys who had masturbated while ripping holes in pictures of women's bodies. Believing that both the people in the illustrations and he himself belonged in Hell, he imagined that the short, squat devils, speaking their guttural, incomprehensible language, were going to punish Joe Kallinger not only for his sinful actions, but also for his sinful thoughts.

Burdened by guilt, Joe felt more than ever that he was not "a part of anybody." But, seeking compensation, he told himself that he was "God's child," that he was "better than anyone else," and that he was "ahead of his time." The defense mechanism was clear: He thought himself ahead of his time because he was not *of* his time, and to be ahead explained his alienation and loneliness. He often thought of the guardian angel of his childhood, a female figure with small breasts who he hoped would still protect him. He prayed to her to save him from damnation. He also prayed that she would help him find the parents he had never known.

Joe had seen his mother in the Kallinger shoe repair store before the adoption, but didn't know that he had. Nor did he know that she lived—and always had—within a short trolley or bus trip from the Kallinger home. But fantasizing for no reason at all that she lived on the corner of Girard and Montgomery avenues, he went there one Saturday afternoon when the Kallingers thought he was at the movies.

Standing at that corner, he thought at first not of his mother, but of the Kallingers. He remembered how he had tried to get close to them by doing little things to please them. He had spent many hours in the cellar, where he constructed out of old boxes a chest of drawers in which Stephen could keep small objects. The past Mother's Day Joe had given Anna a flowering plant in a small pot. He had saved his movie money for it. But she remarked irritably, "Now, why did you go spend money on that? It's just going to die anyway."

The distance Joe had felt from the Kallingers when he spun fancies at the springhouse and they dozed in their beach chairs had never been bridged. He had always sought companionship elsewhere. He found it with the butterflies. He also found it with trolley transfers and discarded motors from electric clocks, vacuum cleaners, dishwashers, and other appliances. He consciously thought of himself as having been discarded by his natural parents. The transfers and motors had also been discarded. He felt that they and he were alike. Whenever Anna caught him with transfers, she tore them up.

He had plucked transfers from wooden telephone poles, out of gutters and assorted crevices, for he wanted to have as many transfers as a motorman. He even wanted to be a motorman so that people would have to go where he took them and he could *run* things.

He thought of his real parents as *his*, even though they had sentenced him to abandonment for the crime of having been born. He couldn't forgive them, yet mourned the loss of them and felt he belonged to them. He wanted them to call him son and love him.

In poems Joe wrote as an adult, he explained his feeling about his unattainable parents. He lamented that "there was no one to show me how to see and hear"; he likened himself to "the snow, beautiful to look at but unwanted and shoveled from side to side." He expressed his wish for a sister and brother, and underlying this desire was the more sweeping longing "to feel alive, to feel needed, to feel wanted, to belong to a loving family."

That summer Joe felt the old urge to escape from the unloving Kallingers, if only for a little while. He had never run away from home and was not doing so now, but he had persuaded his adoptive parents to send him to camp for a few weeks. So on the morning of a hot, sunny day early in July 1949, Joe, carrying a duffel bag, walked to the Lighthouse, a neighborhood recreation center that operated Downington Camp in the suburbs of Philadelphia.

For years Joe had begged his adoptive parents to move to the suburbs, and he was delighted that the camp was there. He was unhappy in Kensington and had a fixed idea that he would be happy in the suburbs. The suburbs, he was certain, would bring an end to his loneliness and to the occasional bullying by kids he didn't even know. He was indulging in a form of magical thinking, a form of thinking characterized by lack of any realistic relationship between cause and effect.

Walking to the Lighthouse, Joe again had this feeling about the suburbs as he recalled an incident of bullying in Diamond Square Park that had occurred when he was ten: School had been let out on a warm spring day and Joe, in his knickers (when other boys his age were wearing long pants) was waiting for Anna just inside the entrance to the park. Three teenagers taunted him about his knickers. They threw him down, called him "Mama's boy." One of the teenagers jumped on his stomach. Lying there terrified, Joe saw Anna coming.

As soon as Anna arrived, the three teenagers fled. Joe would not have fought them; he had never fought back when attacked. "Good little boys don't fight," Anna had always told him. Yet, in the past she had also called him "chicken and yellow" for not fighting back. He felt himself trapped. That was his life. With his parents he couldn't win!

The chartered bus was waiting when Joe reached the Lighthouse. He went to the rear and sat down. He was the last to get out when the bus arrived at Downington Camp.

While the counselors organized the campers in cabin groups, Joe stood at the edge of the crowd. From a distance he looked for familiar faces. There were some from Kensington. There was also one—the face of a counselor—that Joe couldn't place, but that made him uneasy. Then he recognized the counselor as the boy who four years earlier had given him the "blow job" in the tank. Ashamed

74

and revolted, Joe was relieved, however, to find out that *his* counselor was not the same boy.

In the early-morning hours when everyone else was asleep, Joe would leave his cabin and walk alone on the trails in the woods. He started collecting turtles from the bases of trees and under rocks. He wondered which was better: To fly away with the butterflies as he had thought he could do when he was younger, or to crawl into a shell like the turtle.

Joe's counselor urged him to take part in target practice on the rifle range, but Joe had never held a gun and kept refusing. However, on Monday morning of the second week of camp, he agreed. Having secured his rifle, he shot two rounds. Joe didn't fire a third round, but, while lying prone, the rifle cradled in his right arm, he removed the telescopic sight with his left hand, the hand whose power he had felt when he first carved a hole in his bedroom wall. He put the telescopic sight into his pocket and pulled his shirt over the pocket to hide the eyepiece. When the other kids left the range for their cabins, he did not go with them but went into the high weeds near the range.

Protected by the weeds, he took the telescopic sight out of his pocket. He held it tenderly in his hand the way long ago he had held the missal. Then he took the telescopic sight apart. Discarded motors were a passion of his life. Now as he studied and examined the scope's parts, he found this new mechanism even more fascinating. This was especially true of the magnifying glass. He kept the lens, but threw the other pieces into the weeds.

Joe focused the lens on his hand, and the magnification gave him a sense of power. Removing the lens, he again felt weak and defenseless. But when he put his hand under the lens, he again felt powerful. His left hand seemed particularly big. He wanted to stay forever, hidden by the weeds and looking at the magnification of his left hand. When the first gong rang for lunch, he put the lens into his pocket and walked quickly to the dining hall.

During the afternoon activities, Joe stayed, as usual, on the sidelines. The lens was in his left pants pocket. He caressed it with his thumb until the smooth, slightly humped surface became moist from the sweat of his hand. Power coursed through his body, as it had on the night he had first carved the hole into his bedroom wall. He felt superior to the other campers; the hatred and envy, and the loneliness, with which he always watched them at play were replaced by scorn. Near him two cabins were playing baseball; beyond them, near the trees, other campers played volleyball. They were wasting their time. *He* knew things, he assured himself, that his fellow campers—and the counselors, and, maybe, the entire world—didn't know. Holding the lens tightly now with his left thumb, forefinger, and middle finger—his masturbating fingers—he believed that he had found a source of magical power that could make him unconquerable: By placing the lens over his left hand, he could turn himself into a giant.

That evening at dinner an announcement was made that one of the telescopic sights was missing. The camp was searched, but the missing sight was not found.

The next morning Joe counted to one hundred as he walked along the dirt path from his cabin to the swimming pool. Never having been in a pool before coming to camp, he didn't know how to swim. He had refused to take swimming lessons at camp and stood in the shallow end of the pool by himself while the other campers splashed and swam. Hatless beneath the summer sun, he wanted to get dressed and go into the shade. At poolside he took off his wet trunks and hastily stepped into his white linen short pants. As he was getting out of his trunks, he heard the lens of the telescopic sight hit the ground, and then his counselor's voice sternly asking, "Where did you get it?"

"It's mine," Joe said softly. He looked down at the lens. It lay on the ground, wet, sunlight glistening in the drops that coated its surface. He had forgotten that he had transferred it from his shorts to his trunks. He kept protesting, "It's mine," as the counselor bombarded him with questions. In his delusion, Joe leaped beyond the borders of reality to make *his* any object that had special meaning for him. Like the missal in the school, the magnifying glass that he had taken from the rifle became *his*. Joe believed that the magnifying glass gave him powers that set him above the other campers, making him feel strong and secure.

With a vacant stare that, like the turtle's shell, was a form of protection, Joe walked meekly beside the counselor to the director's office. There Joe admitted having stolen the lens, saying that he wanted it because "it makes things big." Then he took his counselor and the director to the high weeds, where he pointed out the scattered parts of the dismantled telescopic sight.

The Kallingers had paid for two weeks at camp, but had told Joe that if he liked, he could stay another two weeks. Now there was no choice. The camp director said that Joe had to leave when his two weeks were up.

Joe had destroyed the telescopic sight, and destruction was now a compelling need of his. The torture he had endured in the tank when a *real* knife was held at his throat continued to haunt him and to call out for retaliation. He had already felt power in his left hand, and the magnification of it intensified the sense of power. Later the left hand, the hand of power, would become his stabbing hand. But the impulse to stab, to torture with a knife, derived from a single incident: his symbolic castration during the hernia operation. His fantasy life, the source of his murderous impulses, had begun with that incident. He had to restore to himself the power—sexual and otherwise—he believed the surgeon's knife had removed.

Ten days after coming home from Downington Camp, Joe, with a lip knife in his pants pocket, boarded a bus on a Saturday afternoon. He had heard what he thought was the "voice of the demon" ordering him to go out and cut somebody. The demon was no longer supposed to be in him, yet it seemed to be there. Joe was acting out with a knife the fantasy of restoring to himself the power which he believed Dr. Daly's knife had shorn from him.

Joe looked for a victim through the bus window. One mile from the Kallingers' Neshaminy cottage, he saw a boy about his own age walking along a dirt road parallel to the highway on which the bus was traveling. Joe got off the bus, leaned against an old oak tree, and waited for his prey.

He stopped the boy with a cheerful "Hi!" and chatted with him amiably, then lured him to the creek on the pretense of going fishing.

The two boys crossed the highway and reached a dirt embankment. They walked down the embankment, their shoes kicking aside twigs and scattering dead leaves.

"Where's your rod and reel?" Willie asked when they reached the creek. Joe had told him that his fishing tackle was by the stream. "Might as well start fishing." Receiving no answer, the boy rattled on, "C'mon, let's get your rod and stuff and start fishing." Joe still didn't answer. The only sound was that of the traffic from the highway. "It isn't here," Willie said. "I just know it isn't. What's going on?"

The two boys stared at each other, and Joe squeezed the knife in his pocket. Then Joe said coldly, as he slowly moved the lip knife toward the boy, "Drop your pants, Willie."

"Hey, Joe! You're kidding," Willie said in a tight voice, his eyes on the point of the knife. "We came here to fish."

"Fish? You want fish?" Joe ranted. "I'll give you fish." He was unconsciously mimicking Anna Kallinger's "Zoo! You want zoo? I'll give you zoo."

Joe raised the point of the knife higher, and Willie, terrified, dropped his pants. Underneath them, he was wearing jockey shorts.

"Take them off, too," Joe ordered as he moved the knife closer to Willie.

"Jesus, Joe, what are you *doing*?"

"Ach, always with the questions," Joe replied angrily. He sounded like Stephen Kallinger, who had always squelched Joe's questions.

Again Joe ordered Willie to take off his shorts.

Willie, who was shivering and too frightened to run, dropped his underpants. Joe felt powerful at having commanded obedience, and, as he looked at the boy's penis hanging limply, he was elated that he was going to do to his victim what Dr. Daly had done to him.

But instead of plunging the knife into Willie's groin, Joe put the knife back into his pocket and fled into the fields and then into the woods. For the penis of the other boy and Joe's penis had, in Joe's mind, become one: the object not of hatred and castration, but of self-love and preservation. The penis belonged to all mankind, and to destroy it was to destroy all men, including Joe Kallinger.

Joe did not stop running until he collapsed on the front lawn of the Kallingers' cottage, which was a mile away from the scene of terror.

What if I had killed that kid? Joe thought as he lay there. He did nothing to me. I'll never do this again. *Never!*

Then Joe thought: It controls me. I don't control it.

He didn't know what "it" was, and didn't know that for the first time his use of the knife was wedded to feelings of aggression. He felt like a "whopping puppet," for a force outside himself seemed to be controlling him the way a puppeteer manipulates the puppet's strings. It was the same feeling Joe would have as an adult caught in the grip of destructive delusions.

Now Joe was filled with a sense of doom. His future was beyond his control, beyond his own making. In that instant, Joe Kallinger, five months away from his thirteenth birthday, saw his life as destruction and disaster. His child's world of butterflies, minnows, and the shallow well in the springhouse had vanished. He got up, walked slowly to the springhouse, and dropped the lip knife into the well.

Joe had committed his first act of terror; in adolescence, "when normal things should take place," as he put it, "this other thing developed." He had wedded the use of a knife to feelings of aggression.

But Joe did not seek the usual outlets for adolescent aggression: the punching, hitting, fighting that the boys in Diamond Square Park had used on him. By terrorizing with a knife, he turned to a form of aggression that grew out of his childhood fear of knives and his conviction that through a knife he could achieve power. His use of the knife at the creek restored to Joe the power that Dr. Daly's knife had allegedly removed from him. Terrorizing with the knife also made it possible for Joe to avenge himself against the boys in the tank, who, by seducing him with a knife, had made him powerless. By terrorizing the boy at the creek Joe momentarily relieved himself of the anguish that knives had caused him. And, by making another boy suffer, Joe transformed himself from victim to victimizer, avenging himself against the world that had humiliated and tortured him.

In the next few months, Joe used retributive power on three more victims. Each time he still thought of himself as a puppet, but now he knew that the puppeteer was a demon, whom Joe had never seen, but whose voice he heard. Each time he held the weapon in his left hand, the stabbing hand. In all three encounters, Joe terrorized the victim, but, as with the boy at the creek, fled before inflicting bodily harm.

The second victim was a girl Joe pursued after a second bus trip to the suburbs. This time the weapon was not a knife, but a piece of glass shaped like and symbolizing a knife.

The other two victims were boys whom Joe terrorized with a lip knife under Silver Bridge, a short distance from the Kallingers' Kensington home. With one of these boys Joe repeated what he had done to the boy at the creek. But with the second of the Silver Bridge victims, Joe partially reenacted what as a victim he himself had experienced in the tank almost five years earlier.

Joe had linked his fantasies about knives to both aggression and sexuality. But it was not sex that interested him when, holding a knife, he put the boy's penis into his mouth as if to give him a "blow job." Hearing the "demon" say, "Chew it off," Joe bit the boy's penis. Then Joe panicked and ran home. The biting had been part of Joe's desire to castrate his victim but also the expression of Joe's fears about his own "castration." What he had done to the second boy under Silver Bridge was also the first glimmer of a cannibalistic complex which would play a large and tragic part in his later life.

Joe had performed four aggressive acts with criminal intent between his twelfth and thirteenth birthdays. But never again during the next twenty years did he return to crime. It was as if the criminal aspect of his incipient psychosis, spawned by his symbolic castration, had gone into hiding.

After the second confrontation under Silver Bridge, Joe desperately wanted to confide in someone. But there was no one—not even the living-room mirror, which Anna had taken down to punish Joe. "It's all alone that drives to madness," Joe scribbled on a pad.

At the time of his thirteenth birthday, on December 11, 1949, Joe had a reprieve from the aloneness that drives to madness. The director of the YWCA Christmas play, a woman who was one of the Kallingers' customers, had asked Stephen to let Joe try out for the play. Stephen agreed. "It will be good for business," he told Anna.

Joe had never been in a play and had not even seen one. But he tried out for Dickens's *A Christmas Carol* and got the role of

Scrooge, the lead. Never before had he been allowed out of the Kallingers' store alone except to run errands or to go to the movies on Saturday afternoons. But now he went to rehearsals at the YWCA almost every night.

On stage he was not Joe Kallinger but Ebenezer Scrooge. He enjoyed working to get just the right grating, growling tone for the role. Delighting in memorizing the Dickens lines and with an instinctive ability making them his own, he would silently say them over and over to himself, not only in his room, but also on his way in the morning to Visitation School and in the evening to the YWCA at Second and Allegheny.

On stage Joe reveled in having makeup on his face, a mask that gave him a sense of calm and a new persona, releasing emotions he was not otherwise able to express. His costumes, including an old greatcoat, took him back to the middle of the nineteenth century and made remote the painful present. Being someone else in a world of illusion put to rest the delusions and fears of Joe's daily life.

On the day of the performance, which was close to Christmas Day, Joe walked across the stage with an ease he had never known offstage. This was a transformation as real as the one that had taken place on the day he had terrorized the boy at the creek. But this transformation was on the side not of madness and crime, but of wholeness and aesthetic beauty.

Each step of the way onstage Joe knew that he held the audience in the palm of his hand. The audience was with him when, after the clanking of heavy chains and the booming sound of a cellar door flying open, he bellowed, "It's all humbug!" Joe, as Scrooge, thinking of himself as the solitary child, sobbed with the tears that since his early childhood he hadn't dared to shed. It was then that he heard a woman in the first row whispering to the man who was with her, "That kid's good!"

After the curtain fell, the audience of three hundred called "Scrooge" back for curtain call after curtain call. For the first time Joe knew the thrill of applause and approbation. He had been adopted to become a shoemaker, but now felt he had found his own métier.

The Kallingers had not seen the play. Stephen had written the director a note explaining that even though Anna and he wanted to come, they couldn't because on Saturday, as on every other day except Sunday, the store didn't close until well after curtain time.

At breakfast the next morning, a Sunday, a euphoric Joe told the Kallingers that the director of the play had encouraged him to study acting and to become an actor. "*That's* what I want to be," Joe said.

"Nonsense!" said Stephen. He banged the table with his coffee spoon.

"He's crazy!" Anna exclaimed.

She turned to Joe and said, "Actor? You want to be an *actor*? I'll give you . . . Stephen, why they didn't tell us at St. Vincent's that our little Joseph was an actor?"

Anna winked heavily at Stephen and then said commandingly to Joe, "Go, act! Here! Right now! Your dad and me will watch. Now, Joseph, *act!*"

Joe got up from his chair and picked up a wooden box, which he placed on the floor about six feet away from the table where his adoptive parents were sitting. He stood on the box and faced his audience. He didn't feel the ease and power that he had felt onstage Saturday night. The director of the play, as a reward for a fine performance, had given Joe a copy of *Hamlet*, and he had committed to memory one of Hamlet's soliloquies.

"O, what a rogue and peasant slave am I," Joe said, watching, as the words came, the faces of Anna and Stephen. He stopped.

Anna said, "My God, that's *all*? What are you stopping for?"

"What's all this *Quatsch*," Stephen asked, "about peasants, about slaves? You make this business up, Joseph?"

"No, it was . . ." Joe tried to explain.

"Steef, we must not interrupt. Go on, Joseph, the whole world is waiting to hear you."

Joe began again. "O, what a rogue and peasant slave am I. . . ."

"*Again* with the peasants," Stephen muttered.

"Ssh, Steef." Anna winked again at her husband.

"Is it not monstrous . . ." Joe went on.

"Ach, a professor from the university he is!" exclaimed Stephen. "Not an actor. Pfui! Always with the big words now. What means *monstroos*?" Stephen looked from Joe to Anna, his eyes wide with feigned admiration and amazement.

Anna giggled. "Maybe our Joseph is an actor with an education?

Ja, Joseph?" She put her finger into a glass filled with water and flicked a few drops at Joe.

Joe forgot the next line. He froze and stood helplessly on the box. He wished he were a turtle.

"An actor?" Anna sneered. "*You* ain't an actor."

"Better you come down from cloud-cuckoo-land. *That* is for actors," said Stephen.

"Get off the box!" Anna ordered. Joe stepped down.

"With God's help and your parents' help," Stephen said as he rose from his seat at the kitchen table, "you will be a—*shoemaker*!" He snapped his fingers at Joe and glowered at him. "But if you don't want to be a shoemaker, then you will be a bum, understand?"

"But I'm *good* at it," Joe replied. "The director of the play said I could be a *good* actor. I could be in the movies. I could make a lot of money."

A few weeks later the director came to see the Kallingers and asked them to let Joe be in the spring production. She also strongly advised sending Joe to drama school after his graduation from Visitation.

"Once is enough," Anna replied sharply.

"You're a wonderful woman and we appreciate your interest in our son," Stephen put in, "but our little Joe, he is busy with the school and the store. Maybe next year. But not now. You understand."

The director tried several times in the next year or two, but was always politely rebuffed.

Joe was brilliant and whole on the stage. But offstage he was a mess. He was haunted by the foreboding that his life would end in disaster. He lived with feelings of worthlessness that had come from the Kallingers' belittling of him, and also with gnawing doubts about his masculinity. Acting eventually faded into Joe's world of yearning, along with a variety of other abandoned aspirations, from trolley motorman to detective; from writer to lawyer to monk in a distant monastery.

Joe was now on the way to becoming a shoemaker. He had been the odd-job boy in the store since he was seven. Now, at thirteen, he became an apprentice shoemaker, starting to fulfill the purpose for which the Kallingers had adopted him.

The Howard Movie Theater on Saturday afternoons became part of Joe's secret world—the secret of his frustration about acting, which he shared with nobody. He stared at the actors on the screen and knew that what they had would never be his. His frustration was so intense that it had a tangible presence. He reached out to touch it, but, uncertain as to where it was, he drew back to look at the tormenting shadows on the screen. These actors, confident, triumphant, were an affront to his frustration. Never would he share their fulfillment in the world of illusion. Whatever lines they spoke, it seemed to Joe they were singing a dirge for the lost dream of Joe Kallinger.

On the screen, however, Joe also found the vengeful fulfillment he was afraid of having in the world outside. But love scenes made him nervous. He became even more nervous as he watched the boys and girls in the audience clasp hands and kiss. In his mind's eye he saw himself at the dances at the YWCA, where, after the play, he was a volunteer ticket-taker. He never went with a girl onto the dance floor, but sat alone near the wall on a hard chair and hated the dancers and the music. He was even frightened by the game called Spin the Bottle, in which the boy who spins the bottle kisses the girl at whom the spinning bottle, coming to rest, finally points. The theater, like playing Spin the Bottle and the YWCA dances, was a grim reminder that Joe was not "a part of anybody."

Before cutting the hole in his bedroom wall Joe, watching the intimacies of the couples in the theater, had explained to himself that the boys making love were different from him because nobody had driven a demon out of *their* "birds"; that their "birds" had not been made small like his. Now he no longer could account for the difference because he was certain that the demon was still in him. But his penis *was* small, he told himself, and he wondered whether the Kallingers were wrong about demons not liking small "birds." For as he watched the kissing of the couples in the theater, he would feel the warm swelling under his pants and the lump in his throat that always came when the "bird" got hard.

Often when Joe felt his penis swell he would wonder whether back in the store Stephen and Anna could see his hard "bird"; and he also wondered whether at that very moment they might be making plans to send him back to Dr. Daly, who *this* time would succeed in driving the demon out by making Joe's penis even smaller than it was. Joe would also wonder exactly *what* Dr. Daly was *supposed* to have done to him seven years ago and would do to him again.

Had the doctor known how to do it by himself? Or had the Kallingers helped him as they stood beside him while Joe was unconscious on the operating table? Although the Kallingers had remained in the store on the day of his operation, Joe could see them in masks and long white gowns, growling instructions to Dr. Daly as he pushed the knife into Joe's groin.

Joe could not understand that the Kallingers *couldn't* be in the store and at the same time see him at the movies. Nor could he understand that they could not be in an operating room, giving orders to a surgeon. For Joe was caught in the grip of a delusion that the Kallingers, who controlled him, were omnipresent, omniscient, and all-powerful.

In the spring of 1950, on a Saturday afternoon, Joe saw a thin girl, with a gaunt face, flat-chested and awkward, move sideways into the row ahead of him at the Howard Movie Theater. She sat down three seats to his right, and gently rocked a baby in her arms. Once she turned quickly in Joe's direction, and he saw by the light of the screen that the corners of her lips were drawn down as if some dissatisfaction were gnawing at her. Her thin shoulders under her flimsy print blouse and her hungry face called out to Joe for rescue.

He leaned forward in his seat and whispered, "Hello." She turned and whispered back, "Hello." He felt nervous. But her flat chest and fragile appearance gave him courage. He invited her out for a soda.

Ten minutes later Joe and the flat-chested girl left the theater together. The girl said her name was Hilda Bishop and that the baby, whom Joe was now carrying, was not her own. She had been baby-sitting, had gotten bored, and had brought the baby to the movies.

After they took the baby home, they looked for a restaurant. Walking with Hilda, Joe wondered whether the Kallingers were watching him from the shop. If they were, he would catch it when he got back home. But he no longer cared. Hilda had called out to him for rescue with her hungry look and gaunt cheeks. He felt strong and protective.

* * *

The Saturday-afternoon crowd, chiefly teenagers, was beginning to fill the tables and booths of the noisy restaurant as Joe and Hilda made their way to one of the booths. Joe had never taken a girl to a restaurant. It hadn't been difficult to say hello in the theater, but now everything was different. He felt light-headed and his fingers tingled; he was worried that Hilda might laugh at him if he was awkward or said the wrong thing. He smiled at her. She was watching him, her head tilted a little to one side.

Hilda had thin brown hair. Her skin was taut over the jawbone, and under her cheekbones there were dark impressions, as if a strong hand had closed around her face. Her lips were thin; she drew them over her pitted and discolored teeth whenever she smiled. Sitting near her at the table, Joe smelled an odor of decay mixed with breath sweetener. Her arms were long and thin, and as she bent to tighten the clasp on her sandal, Joe saw that her fingers were bony and her fingernails ragged and bitten.

"What'll you have, kids?" The waiter handed them menus.

Joe saw the outline of bones just above the low-cut collar of Hilda's blouse, so he told the waiter: "My friend'll have steak, well done, with mashed potatoes. Also some French-fried onions. Uh— I'll have a hamburger, well done. And please bring two large Cokes."

"I'm starving," Hilda said after the waiter had gone.

"Me, too. But I can't have much because I have to be home for supper. I'll get it if I get back late."

"Your folks sound awful strict," Hilda said.

"Most of the time it's worse than that! Besides going to the movies once a week by myself, they didn't let me do anything till I was twelve. And we don't talk much. It's awful quiet in my place— except when they're yelling at me."

"I don't have that trouble," Hilda replied. "I can go out or stay home with nobody interfering. Mom's usually in a bar drinking or she brings some guy home; and Grandma and Grampa—well, he works all day at the Motor Vehicle Bureau and she doesn't care *what* I do. But it ain't quiet where I live; somebody's always yapping about this or that and the radio's going *all* the time."

"Don't you have brothers or sisters?" Joe asked.

"Uh-uh. I'm an only child."

"Me, too," replied Joe.

Joe watched a fly crawling along the ring of sugar around the edge of an open sugar bowl. He thought of the tank and of what the big boys had done to him in there.

They ate quickly. Hilda, her legs crossed, waved her little finger in the air as she brought large forkfuls to her mouth. After they had finished and were waiting for ice cream and more Cokes, Joe asked, "Is your mom your *real* mom?"

"Sure! Isn't *your* mom your real mom?"

"No. I'm adopted. I've never seen my *real* folks. Don't know anything about them."

"That's a shame. My mom and dad were separated. A long time ago. I don't remember him. I was just a small kid and he got up one morning, left the house, and never came back."

"At least you have your mom," Joe said wistfully.

Hilda gently put her hand on top of Joe's. "I'm sorry for you, Joe, that you don't have your real folks."

"I guess it wouldn't be so bad if the folks I have just wouldn't blow up at me all the time, always hitting me, and they never listen to anything I say. One time, Hilda, I wanted to be an actor, but they wouldn't let me."

"An actor? Golly, really?" Hilda looked keenly at Joe. She took a big spoonful of ice cream and looked at Joe again, her eyes wide.

"I was in this Christmas play at the YWCA, and the director told me that I was real good, that I should study acting, get into the movies or something, make a lot of money, too. It was fun. But my folks—well, they kind of laughed at it and told me I had to be a shoemaker like my dad."

Joe never talked like this about his adoptive parents. He was still under the delusion that Anna and Stephen could remain in the store while spying on what he was doing somewhere else. He was sure that they had special ears that could hear him talking to this girl in the restaurant. Now he felt frightened; the courage he had felt in the street an hour ago had left him. He imagined Anna saying to him, "*Dummkopf!* In hell you will be punished!" And he saw the mountain of people who had been damned and sent, after their deaths, to feel the pain of the flaming knives that were carried by invisible devils.

"What school do you go to?" Joe asked.

Hilda hesitated, and then said, "Carroll. It's a kind of school where they teach you a trade, like being a mechanic or a seamstress. What school do you go to?"

"Visitation Elementary," Joe replied.

"Do good there?"

"Yeah, sometimes. Sometimes, no. The teachers say my work's uneven. You see, I'm moody."

"That ain't bad, being moody," Hilda said. "My mom's moody. Either she's giggling and having a good time or she's drunk and smashing things."

Joe thought of his bedroom and of the bad things he wanted to do to women when his "bird" got hard and he put it into the hole in the wall. He could see his penknife slashing, blood flowing. Slowly the image vanished, and he was aware again of Hilda.

On Palethorpe Street in front of the red brick row house in which Hilda lived, Joe and Hilda held hands and planned for their next meeting. He thought of kissing her, but, restrained by old fears, didn't. He told himself that because they had just met, she would think him crude. As he was about to leave her, she said, "You made me feel like somebody. Nobody did that before."

Joe and Hilda had been seeing each other for several months when a customer told the Kallingers that Joe was dating an Irish girl, Hilda Bishop. The Kallingers gathered information about Hilda. "She comes from a broken home," Anna told Joe. "Her family is poor. Her mother hangs around bars. We won't let you see this girl again."

Getting up from the table, Joe started walking toward the door. Stephen followed him. "Look, Joseph," Stephen said, "give up this girl. What you need a girl for, anyhow? Remember what we told you about your 'bird.' Many times we told you."

Joe didn't answer. He wanted to tell Stephen that Dr. Daly had made the bird small, but had done *nothing else*; that the "bird" got hard and that the demon was still in the "bird" and in Joe Kallinger! Not daring to tell Stephen this, Joe returned to the table, finished his breakfast, and went right on seeing Hilda.

On Saturdays they went to exhibitions at the Franklin Institute, went to the movies, and even went shopping together. Weeknights after work Joe managed to get out of the house by offering to walk

Sporty, the Kallingers' fox terrier. Hilda waited for Joe across Front Street on the steps of a three-foot walkway between the street and the door of an old mill. Sometimes they took a walk with Sporty cavorting beside them. But when they found even the presence of a fox terrier intrusive, they tied him by his leash to a pole and, after the walk, came back for him. They held hands, kissed on the cheek, or lightly on the lips, but for a little over a year did not have sex.

On a mild September night in 1951, however, Joe suggested that they walk to the mill on Lehigh Avenue. When they got there, he said with a smile, "Well, I guess we're far enough from home!" Then they stood three feet away from the street in the unlighted walkway leading to the door of the mill. Overhead there was nothing but sky. Joe took Hilda in his arms and held her tightly. She slipped out of her panties; he opened his fly. They fondled each other and the "bird" got hard. They had full intercourse, each of them having an orgasm, and Joe delighting in Hilda's tiny breasts.

There was no blood and Joe was glad. The sight of *real* blood would have made him feel guilty. In spite of his resolve to keep his thoughts clean, he knew that it was the fantasy of slashing and ripping the women in the photographs he used near the hole in his bedroom wall that made him potent with Hilda. She knew only that he had been a tender, ardent, and passionate lover. "It was worth waiting for," she told him.

Successful with Hilda, Joe was at this time also successful in the Kallinger store. An apt pupil when Stephen first started teaching him, Joe was now doing actual shoe repair work. He was a full-time student at Jones Junior High School, but had a part-time working permit and received wages for his work. The working permit made it legally necessary for the Kallingers to pay him. Being very practical, they were glad to do this. For they believed that to learn how to use money was an essential part of Joe's training. Besides, one of the ways he used his money was to pay the rent and board his adoptive parents required after they had begun paying him wages.

Joe had two nights off a week, which he spent with Hilda. Often they went to the walkway of the Lehigh Avenue mill. But after Joe had entered Northeast High School they made the schoolyard the scene of their rendezvous. They usually sat on a bench, just talking. Then they went to the rear of the yard where the cars, used during the day by students in the auto mechanics classes, were parked. Standing behind rows of cars and hidden from anyone who might come into the yard, Joe continued to be Hilda's tender and passionate lover. And his aphrodisiac continued to be the savage thoughts, so different from his behavior, on which his potency turned.

To restore to himself the potency that Dr. Daly's knife was supposed to have removed from him, Joe had to visualize himself cutting with a knife as the surgeon during the operation had allegedly cut him.

The "bad thoughts," as he called them, turned Joe on, but were not directed at Hilda. He didn't want to hurt her, and she didn't figure in the fantasies. But when he shut them off as he sometimes tried to do, his penis remained limp and lifeless. To be passionate and potent he had to turn the restitutional fantasies back on.

At fifteen—the time of Joe's success at the store and with Hilda—there were new terrors. He began associating *The Shadow*, his favorite radio program, with what was actually happening to him. The Shadow in the program disappeared and reappeared, and it seemed to Joe that the Joe Kallinger he knew was also disappearing. For he saw in the mirror that his looks and facial expressions were no longer the same.

Another important thing was happening. As an adult he would be plagued by the twisting and turning of his body with undulating movements. These movements now occurred for the first time. His head sometimes jerked from side to side, especially when he laughed. He also had another laugh completely different from the one he recognized as his.

This other laugh rolled, roared, and hissed. It gushed forth without outside provocation and it was accompanied by convulsiveness in the stomach. When this laughter took over, Joe could feel a large smile dominating his facial expression and spreading across his face. Sometimes when he looked in the mirror, he could see the smile changing into a grin. And the hiss in the laughter seemed to be erupting through the grin.

Joe tried to turn the laughter off, but the cavernous laughter from deep within himself just roared. He tried to shut the laughter off by holding his hand over his mouth, but the laughter continued. The laughter, he realized, had a will and a personality of its own. Just as he had thought himself the puppet of the "demon" on one of the bus trips and under Silver Bridge, so now he was the laughter's puppet. He wondered whether the laughter was a part of the "demon" and whether the "demon" was transforming him, Joe Kallinger, into someone else. If so, would the "I" he thought he knew, like the Shadow in the radio program, reappear?

What remained solid was Joe's shoe repair work. He was a perfectionist, and customers asked for him because the finishing touches he put on shoes really lasted. By fifteen he was also expert at orthopedic work.

One afternoon, while Joe was standing at his workbench, he looked up and saw a bright light. In the center of the light was a large figure that made him feel that he was in the presence of God. He heard a deep, resonant and commanding voice:

"Joe Kallinger, you are a special person, and you must undertake a special mission. Already, through your orthopedic work, you are easing pain in the feet. The feet are also the key to the brain. Your mission is to control the brain through the feet. This is what I, God of the Universe, command you to do. You will use this method to heal yourself and heal mankind. You must heal and save!"

The white light disappeared and with it the figure that was God, but the feeling of elation that had overtaken Joe in the presence of God persisted even after he went back to repairing shoes.

Joe was troubled by the command to heal himself. He was disturbed by his strange movements and strange laughter, but he didn't like to admit that there was something wrong with him that he had to correct. Yet the order to correct himself was a challenge. Maybe, he thought, he could make the movements and the laughter disappear. He didn't know that he was mentally ill.

Also compelling was the command to save mankind. He would begin with Americans, but eventually he would heal every man, woman, and child on Earth. "There's a destiny that shapes our ends," he remembered from *Hamlet*. Then he thought with irony, but not bitterness: I have never been a part of *anybody*. But now I'm going to save everybody.

Under the spell of these delusions and the hallucination of having seen God, Joe went immediately to work on the first of the more than 40,000 orthopedic experiments he would perform between

1951 and 1972, from the time he was fifteen until he was thirty-six.

For his first experiments Joe used a straight knife or a lip knife to fashion heel wedges out of leather or rubber. The wedges were from one-sixteenth to one-quarter of an inch high. Using himself as a guinea pig, he placed a wedge on the heel inside his shoe. High on the outer side of the heel, the wedge tapered off to nothing on the inner side. By raising the outer side, he was able to tilt his foot inward. Doing this, he had a feeling of relaxation through his leg and spine. From this he developed his theory that the wedge could change the position of the body; that the changes in the body produced chemical changes in the brain; that these chemical changes would lead to the mental and emotional healing God had instructed him to accomplish.

Joe worked on the experiments during his free time in the store and sometimes before the store opened and after it had closed. But he talked to nobody about them. He put them in his secret world to replace Tommy and the butterflies.

What took place in the secret world, however, did not silence the roar in Joe's belly laugh. Afraid of the laughter, Joe was also afraid of himself. The Kallingers had also noticed Joe's facial expressions, the twisting and turning of his body, and the jerk of his head. They had heard his belly laugh and had seen other new and disquieting signs in Joe. There was also a coldness about him that made him different from what he had been before.

One night, in the upstairs hallway of the Kallinger house, Joe discovered that the Kallingers had installed a standard-size Yale lock on their bedroom door. The lock could be controlled only from inside their room.

The Kallingers, Joe thought at first, had put in the lock to keep out burglars. He was less sure about the burglars when he noticed that the Kallingers used the lock only when they were in their room. When, through their open door, he saw that they now kept a baseball bat close to the door, he felt beads of sweat on his brow, for he knew that the lock and the baseball bat were there because his adoptive parents were afraid of *him*!

He didn't know why. He had never struck them, never so much as raised a hand to them even when they beat or burned him—not even when he went wild with rage. They knew nothing of the bus trips nor of what had happened under the bridge. They didn't even know about the rifle range at Downington Camp. All that was in the past anyway. Did they know about the thoughts of cutting he had during sex? They couldn't know. He couldn't understand why they were afraid of him.

When he asked the Kallingers why they had barricaded themselves against him, they told him only what he himself had observed.

"You have strange looks on your face," Stephen said. "You twist around and look like a snake."

"You smear lipstick on the walls, the windows, the mirror," Anna said. "You lock yourself in the bathroom or in your room and you talk to yourself or laugh so crazy loud that it's like the house will come down."

"You're not like anyone we know," said Stephen. "You're cold. It's like we don't know you now." And then, accounting for the lock and the baseball bat more directly, he added with a twisted smile of foreboding, "We can't tell *what* you'll do."

The Kallingers had barricaded themselves against Joe because they obviously thought him dangerous. Yet the behavior that frightened them was not a sign of dangerousness but of mental illness. This was the time to have sought psychiatric help for Joe. He was between his fifteenth and sixteenth birthdays, an age when this help could have proved effective.

A few days after the conversation with Anna and Stephen, Joe moved into a large furnished room on the second floor of a three-story row house on Sixth and Somerset Streets. The rent was $12 a week—exactly what, since he had been getting wages, he had been paying for his room at the Kallingers. The new room was only a few doors away from where Hilda and her family lived. The room was six blocks away from the Kallinger store, where Joe still worked.

Stephen knew that Joe was a superb shoemaker who had his own following, and he didn't want to lose him. So even though Anna complained to neighbors—"Joe left. He ran away. He's making money from us and paying it to strangers"—Joe went right on working in the store which he had been adopted to inherit.

When Joe wasn't in the store or at Northeast High School, he was with Hilda. He had never been allowed to ride a bike or to skate, but with Hilda he went roller-skating. They had sex in the home where she baby-sat, for he didn't want to take her to his room because of what the neighbors might think. He was a frequent visitor at the lively Bishop menage and now had friends for the first time. He learned to play pool and poker, to gamble and to drink. The liquor, at first, made him dull, sullen, and sick, but he was at last part of a crowd. Never before, except when he played Scrooge, had he felt that he was a part of anybody or anything.

Seven days after his sixteenth birthday, Joe dropped out of Northeast High School. He did so, according to the school records, because he "had obtained full employment." His employer was Stephen Kallinger, who did not know that Joe wanted to work full-time in order to marry Hilda. But Stephen and Anna did hear about Joe's new life with Hilda's family, and by April of 1953, they had learned through the Kensington grapevine that Joe was planning to get married.

Probably because they were afraid of him, the Kallingers had let Joe move out of their house without protest. But his latest act of defiance they could not tolerate. He had defied not only their order for him not to see this girl, Hilda Bishop, but, more fundamentally, their determination to make him "a good boy and a good man." Their myth about the "bird" had miscarried, and their adopted son was acting as if they had not gone to the trouble of inventing it. Because of Joe's odd behavior, which they saw not as mental illness but as wickedness, they had put the lock on their bedroom door. Now, because of his decision to marry, Anna Kallinger, on April 18, 1953, filed an incorrigibility petition against him. Joe was then sixteen years and four months old.

The complaint was that Joe was undisciplined and headstrong, that he had little sense of obligation to his parents or the community, and that he associated with questionable persons. Presumably he had little sense of obligation to his parents because he had defied them by planning to get married. The questionable persons were undoubtedly Hilda, her family, and her family's friends.

The petition, however, was dismissed because Anna Kallinger could point to no instance of violence or wrongdoing on Joseph's part. In 1972 William Iezzi, an investigator for Philadelphia's Court of Common Pleas, in reference to another matter, made an observation that leads us to speculate why the petition might also have been rejected:

"Family Court records," the investigator stated, "reveal that the subject's [Joseph Kallinger's] parents were incapable of providing him with the constructive, judicious supervision, guidance and discipline that he required."

The Kallingers, like most people, confused mental illness, or at any rate its symptoms, with dangerousness. They were treating a sick boy as a bad boy. It was a failure of perception and comprehension that would be repeated by other of Joe's authority figures and would plague him all his life.

Joe had come to the Kallinger home as a healthy baby of twenty-two months. The seeds of his adult schizophrenia were sown there. When he left at fifteen years, the seeds were already sprouting and he was on his way to the severe paranoid schizophrenia he has had as an adult. He had been the more vulnerable to the abuses of his adoptive parents because of the insecurity and rage, born of abandonment, which he brought to their house. But it was not the first twenty-two months of Joe's life nor a genetic defect that created his psychosis. Even if the insecurity and rage of those twenty-two months or a genetic defect had veered him toward psychosis, it would have been "a mild schizophrenia," in the opinion of Dr. Silvano Arieti, unsurpassed as psychoanalyst, creative thinker, and writer in the field of schizophrenia, who examined Joe Kallinger in 1980 and in 1981. What determined the severity of the illness and the particular shape and form that it took was *what was done to Joe by his adoptive parents*. As Dr. Arieti, who, in addition to his examinations of Joe, studied this book and Joe's medical records, put it:

"The case of Joseph Kallinger is unusual because the schizophrenic symptoms led directly to horrible sadistic crimes and because a specific childhood incident became the origin both of the low self-esteem that is conducive to schizophrenia and the nature of the sadistic acts. The patient was filled with hostility, rage and vindictiveness because of what his adoptive parents alleged had been done to his sexual organ ('the bird')."*

Schizophrenia is characterized by delusions, hallucinations, and

* From the Arieti reports written after his two examinations of Joseph Kallinger and stated again in an article co-authored with me in *Journal of the American Academy of Psychoanalysis*, Vol. 9, No. 2 (1981).

behavior instigated by these symptoms. Joe as an adolescent was clearly delusional about the alleged "castration," his basic and violent trauma. He was delusional, for example, when he fled from big-breasted women and "macho" men, when he stabbed photographs of breasts and penises, and when he planned to castrate the boy at the creek. He also had a delusion about the Kallingers' spying on him and being able to see what he did wherever he was and no matter how far away from them.

His grandiose plan to save mankind through his orthopedic experiments was a delusion of grandeur, an exaggerated idea of his importance to compensate for his feelings of worthlessness. The plan was part of his developing psychosis: paranoid schizophrenia. This psychosis characteristically involves, among other things, a retreat from reality with, as indicated above, delusion formation and hallucinations.

Joe also had hallucinatory experiences, if not actually full-fledged hallucinations, when he saw and heard God speaking to him and heard the voice of the demon. Hallucinatory too was Joe's childhood image of his penis on a knife as reflected in the living-room mirror. Joe's fantasies, especially the restitutional fantasies about knives, which were part of the violent trauma caused by "the bird" incident, also presaged schizophrenia. So did the first glimmer of cannibalistic feeling, the experience of being controlled by an outside force—by an "it" that manipulated him and dictated his behavior as if he were a puppet on a string, and by the belly laugh that had a personality and a will of its own. But the facial grimaces and the twisting and turning of the body, although indicating that Joe was mentally ill, were not symptoms of schizophrenia.

It used to be fashionable to claim that the mentally ill and the criminal are what they are because they have inherited a "bad seed." Clearly, in Joe's case, "the bad seed" is to be found not in nature but in nurture. Joe was physically and emotionally battered. He was deprived of his human dignity and made to feel worthless. For him there was no normal way out. As a child and teenager he played the victim in an unending drama of cruelty. He found, for a time, healthy refuge in the illusion of childhood fantasy and later on the stage. But, outgrowing the fantasy world of imaginary companions and denied the stage, he withdrew deeper into the psychosis that had preceded the stage experience.

Without the blessing of either the Kallingers or Hilda Bishop, Sr., Joe and Hilda boarded a bus and went to Elkton, Maryland. There they were married in the office of a justice of the peace with strangers as witnesses. They came back to Philadelphia and moved into a small Kensington apartment they had rented.

Joe, always an outsider, was now on his way, he thought, to having what he most wanted: "a large and loving family to belong to."

6 Love, My Season

"We're here!" Hilda said as the bus from Elkton, Maryland, pulled into a Philadelphia terminal.

"Hilda," Joe said as he looked out of the window of the taxi they took to their apartment, "I feel like the whole city has changed." Looking fresh and hopeful, the streets sparkled as if a shower of rain had washed the city with lustral water. The change was within himself, the washing away of painful memories. He took deep breaths of air that blew in through the open window of the taxi. He murmured to himself, "Love, love, my season."

Everything for Joe had a dreamlike quality as he and Hilda walked through the hallway of their apartment into the living room. Before his marriage, Joe had only felt in dreams that he was one with the rest of mankind and that he was like everybody else. Now the dream had become reality.

With water from the kitchen tap, Hilda filled the cut-glass vase, one of the wedding presents Joe had given her. She arranged the flowers—nine American Beauties from Joe. He kissed his wife on the cheek. "Lovely," he said, admiring his wife and the roses at the same time. "I don't know which is more beautiful, you or the flowers."

"*I* am," she replied quickly and giggled.

Their fingers interlaced, knees and thighs touching, they sat on the sofa. Joe poured drinks from a bottle of VO they had brought to the apartment the night before. Hilda turned on the radio. Dance music. She got up and danced, stepping and twirling, looking at Joe, her eyes bright with coy invitation.

Hilda sat in his lap and gently bit his ear. "Joe, let's make love," she whispered as she snuggled up against him.

Joe kept his eyes shut during intercourse. When it was over, he opened his eyes and stared at Hilda's naked body. He had never seen it before and had a sense of relief at her body's wholeness—that his fantasies of mutilation had not spilled over into reality to hurt his wife. He had wanted desperately to suppress these fantasies, at least this night, but, as in the past, they were there; a curse, he thought, that held him bound.

In spite of the fantasies, Joe was determined to put the memories of sixteen years of torture behind him and live the good life. But the next day when he came home from work, he found Hilda lying on the sofa. She had a glass of VO in her hand and she was watching TV. Joe felt a chill of apprehension pass through him, making him shiver. The house was exactly the same as it had been when Joe left that morning. Cartons of Hilda's personal belongings were still unemptied. The dirty dishes from last night's supper were still in the sink and unwashed; the bed was unmade, and Hilda's clothes lay rumpled here and there on a chair, on the sofa, hanging from an end table.

Hilda got up, kissed Joe, and said, "Let's go out to dinner." Joe said nothing about the apartment's being in shambles. But his dream of a perfectly ordered house in the suburbs—sparkling windows, immaculate kitchen, floors one could eat off—where Hilda and he would be surrounded by many children with spotless clothes and squeaky-clean hair, tottered for an instant.

The apartment became too confining to accommodate Joe's growing dream, and three months after moving into it, the young Kallingers moved to a house. It was two stories high, had three bedrooms, and was on Kensington's Masher Street. Stephen and Anna Kallinger had bought the house in their own name. Joe made the monthly mortgage payments to his adoptive parents. But Joe felt that the house was *his*—a castle where at seventeen he was king—because he knew that his adoptive parents no longer had power over him.

Joe was astonished by the way the senior Kallingers treated his wife and him. He had left their house after they had barricaded themselves against him because of his strange grimaces, snakelike movements, and belly laugh. They had taken extraordinary measures to make their adopted son impotent. After having discovered that he was dating Hilda, they had forbidden him to see her. But now they welcomed her in their home, where otherwise no guests came.

Recalling his feelings upon moving into the Masher Street house, Joe told me, "Call me blessed. In the house of Stephen and Anna I was a boy alone, but in *my* house I could bring a whole world of guests.

"I felt," Joe went on, "that I was no longer the boy who had been thrown into darkness. I was seventeen and a new sun had risen to shine on me: I was sure that I'd never commit any more reckless acts. No longer did a laugh roar out of my belly. Nor did my body twist and turn like a snake. Yes, you could call me blessed, for the past was a fragile shadow. I believed I had escaped the destiny I foresaw when I thought my life would end in disaster."

Out of the vast darkness of the past, Joe took his place in the luminous present. He was supporting Hilda and himself decently. He had bought her good clothes and had had her teeth fixed. His wife and he had added new pieces to the furniture they had brought from the apartment. They had fun roller-skating and going to museums. He listened patiently when she complained about his not being able to dance. He even tried taking dance lessons, but soon concluded that the beat of the music just wasn't in his feet.

Joe thought of himself as a better shoemaker than his adoptive father was, although Stephen was known throughout Philadelphia as a fine craftsman. Joe had his own following among the customers who brought their shoes to the Kallinger shop. They liked his warm, friendly smile as well as his superb skill with leather and rubber. Joe dreamed of opening a chain of shoe repair stores in Philadelphia's Center City, in New York, and in other large urban areas. Then he would have the house in the suburbs he had always wanted. He would drive a Cadillac, perhaps even send his kids to private schools. Hilda and the kids would live in style and would be proud of their husband and father. As a child he had been abused, but he was determined to raise his children with understanding and love. If he had to discipline them, he would. But never would he as much as raise a hand to them.

Eager to get ahead, Joe let it be known in shoemaking circles that he was looking for a new job. When a jobber told him of an opening in the Frank Grandee Shoe Repair Store on Girard Avenue, he went there during a lunch hour. Grandee offered him higher wages than he was getting from Stephen Kallinger. Stephen refused to match Grandee's offer, and Joe took the job. "Go elsewhere," Stephen had said, "and get more experience. But promise me you won't open your own store in this area. I don't want you to compete with me. Remember, *my* store will be for you. It is your inheritance."

To Joe, the Grandee store was but a small step forward toward the time when he would have enough money to launch his own chain of stores. He also wanted to lift himself into a cultured milieu. To this end he felt he should get a high school diploma and, if possible, go on to college. As a first step he registered for a course in American literature at Standard Evening High. Melville, Whitman, Dickinson, and especially Poe thrilled Joe. He felt that the darkness of Poe was in sharp contrast to his present existence, but carried echoes of the past he had put to rest.

Joe was not thinking of the past on August 9, 1955, the day that Hilda gave birth to a baby girl. Nor did he perceive the irony that his daughter was born in the same hospital where, the senior Kallingers had told him, he had been made impotent. Looking at his baby in her crib in the obstetrics ward, he felt oceanic, as if he could create new worlds and take God's place in the universe. But when Hilda and the baby (they named her Anna after Joe's adoptive mother) came home, there were times when Joe began to feel that the skinny girl he thought had set him free of the darkness of the past now had him bound in a new darkness.

Joe watched with dismay what seemed to be his wife's lack of maternal instinct. He recalls that Hilda refused to nurse the baby. When Joe came home at night, he often found the infant without diapers, her body and the bedclothes wet and smeared with excrement. The house was even messier than it had been before baby Annie's arrival, and Hilda even more restless than she had been before giving birth: Joe reports that she had to be up and going. Sometimes Joe and Hilda got a babysitter and went out together.

More often Hilda went out alone, and Joe was the baby-sitter. He recalls that usually she said she was going to her mother's or with her mother to a bar.

In the past Joe, wanting to preserve his dream of a perfect marriage, had largely suppressed his irritation at Hilda. But because of his anger at the way she was handling the baby, the old irritation flared up.

All through the marriage he had been exasperated by Hilda's slovenly housekeeping, poor cooking, and indifference to giving him a decent meal when he returned from a day's work. He had also been baffled by Hilda's mother. While he was dating Hilda, Mrs. Bishop had accepted him in her house with open friendliness, but after the marriage she had made him feel unwelcome. She also liked taking Hilda to bars while Joe remained at home. He hadn't faulted Hilda for this, because he knew she enjoyed bars and Joe and Hilda were too young to go into a bar with each other unless an adult was with them.

Joe and Hilda quarreled about religion. Shortly after their civil wedding, a priest married them on condition that Hilda, who was not Catholic, would take instructions for conversion. She didn't, but when Joe complained, her answer was "Fuck you!"

In May 1955, Hilda became pregnant again, and Joe hoped that the child would save the marriage. He was shocked when Hilda asked him for money for an abortion. An abortion threatened his family dream. An abortion, as he saw it, was murder. Though his fantasies during sex were destructive, he regarded the destruction of life, even fetal life, as evil. To be potent he had to have a knife near him while having intercourse. The thoughts and the knife, however, were part of his fantasy life, and his fantasy life remained quite separate from his moral values, among which respect for life was a high priority. The compulsion to kill that would spring from the fantasies and the psychosis of which they became a part had not yet developed.

He looked at Hilda coldly and said, "You will never get money from me to murder our child."

"If I had the money, I'd have the abortion without your consent," she replied.

"Behave yourself and have this baby," he said with an air of finality. ("Behave yourself!" was Joe's often repeated command.

The phrase had been directed at him in childhood. He used it to Hilda, and would use it again and again in later years.)

"You're crazy," she countered. "You have no business being a father. I didn't know it when I married you. But dammit, I know it now, all right, I know it now."

Crazy? Joe didn't think of himself as mentally ill, although at thirteen he had thought that his life would end in disaster and at fifteen he had seen alarming changes in himself. He wondered whether Hilda felt now about him the way his adoptive parents had felt when they had put the lock on their bedroom door and had told him that they didn't know him anymore because of his strange grimaces, strange gestures, and snakelike movements.

Never before had Hilda called him crazy. She had told him, however, that he had two personalities. One was the guy who was marvelous to her and gave her everything. The other she had described as a tyrant who wanted to dominate her and frightened her with his fierce angers and weird facial expressions.

Joe asked himself why, if he was so weird, had Hilda married him. But he tried to assure himself that he was neither crazy nor weird; that to Hilda these were just expressions; she had used the words loosely. His destructive fantasies while having sex, he admitted to himself, were weird, maybe crazy. But Hilda knew nothing about them. What could she have meant by crazy? The fantasies had interfered neither with his love for her nor with his being (in his own opinion) a good lover. But Hilda during the abortion scene hissed, "Sex with you is no good! Your penis is too small."

"How come you didn't tell me this a long time ago?" Joe replied angrily.

"I didn't want to hurt you."

The senior Kallingers had said that his penis would not grow. Now Hilda was saying it *had* not. On the rational level Joe thought her mockery of his small penis for the first time after all these years of lovemaking was absurd. But on the emotional level he believed her and felt that she had always found his penis too small but had not told him. For she had awakened the fears that the myth about "the bird" had engendered. He was once again trapped in the delusion that he lacked sexual power. He also felt worthless. The darkness of the past was blending with the new darkness of the present.

Each night when Joe went to bed he hoped not to be punished for having a small penis. By mocking his penis Hilda wore the mask, and became a persona, of Anna Kallinger, who had told him his penis wouldn't grow and who had often inflicted on him many humiliating and physically painful punishments. Joe had been afraid of his adoptive mother; now he was afraid of his wife in her role of the punitive mother. Although in Joe's delusional world Hilda was not transformed into Anna, yet, in moments of anxiety, he almost expected Hilda to speak English with a German accent and to end (or begin) her profanities with *Dummkopf*!

In September 1955 the marriage that Joe had thought was made in heaven became one spawned in hell. Whenever Hilda said "Go fuck yourself, Joe!" he imagined that he was writhing and howling on the mountain of the damned, his body twisting in anguish and horror.

"I was sure that I had licked the past, beaten it into the ground," Joe told me. "But when my marriage began to go sour, now and then I could hear the belly laugh and could feel my body moving like a snake. I tried to keep these things from Hilda, but I don't know whether I did. There was also something else: I not only came to doubt my sexual power, but began to see Hilda's naked body in the same way I had looked at the photographs of naked women when I used to masturbate into the hole in my bedroom wall in my adoptive parents' house. I really didn't want to hurt Hilda and certainly not our unborn child. But fortunately what I imagined vanished almost as quickly as it appeared. And I was alert to the bad signs in me. In the store I had continued working on my orthopedic experiments—my mission to save mankind. Now I also worked on the experiments to correct myself."

Joe began giving Hilda orders to shape up as a mother and housewife. She replied by laughing at him. She told him where he could go and what he could do with himself and his small penis. Besides, he was crazy, had no business being a father, and she just wasn't about to take orders from *him*!

They were in bed one night after a shouting match when Hilda suddenly sprang up and told Joe she couldn't bear sleeping near him. She said that he was like something she'd seen in a horror movie, the face "screwy and wifty. So fuck you, Joe. I wouldn't want to meet you in a dark alley in a flash of lightning." Hilda picked up her pillow and a blanket and walked out of the bedroom. Joe didn't try to stop her.

On January 12, 1956, in St. Mary's Hospital, Hilda gave birth to a son. They named him Stephen after Joe's adoptive father. Thinking magically, as he had when he first learned about this pregnancy, Joe fantasized that the baby Hilda *hadn't* wanted would restore happiness to the marriage. Joe had known happiness only twice: when he played Scrooge and during the first year of marriage with Hilda.

Anna Kallinger dropped in at Joe's and Hilda's from time to time to see her two grandchildren. She reportedly told him that Hilda often slept until noon, leaving the babies without food and in soiled diapers. Neighbors had also observed the soiled diapers and the lack of food. According to Joe, Anna also told him that Hilda fed the children only peanuts and soda pop. There was no milk in the house and no other nutritious foods.

Joe came home the night after his conversation with Anna armed for a battle with his wife. They shouted, threw things, got drunk, and shouted some more. They stormed at each other on many other nights. Their life had turned into a mutual temper tantrum. Many of their Masher Street neighbors felt sorry for the Kallinger babies, but most of their neighbors had little sympathy for Hilda and Joe.

Joe believed that he had become like everybody else, but the Masher Street men didn't like him because "he didn't mix with anybody." They thought him "a loner and peculiar." The women of Masher Street couldn't stand Hilda because her babies were "dirty and neglected" and she was a "flirt." Eyebrows were raised and tongues wagged when Hilda went to a nearby factory, as she often did, to flirt with the workers who were having their lunch outside.

On a night in late September 1956, Joe came home from work and found two-year-old Annie playing with her blocks alone in the living room and eight-month-old Stevie upstairs in the children's bedroom squatting in his crib unattended. Except for the rattle of Annie's blocks, the house was silent. Joe ran from room to room, but Hilda was gone.

For a few minutes Joe stood in front of his house, calling his wife's name. No sign of her. He went back in. Perhaps, he thought bitterly, she'd gone to the store for more soda pop and peanuts.

The evening wore on. Pacing up and down in his living room, wondering how much longer he'd have to wait for Hilda, Joe also remembered the many nights when at two or three o'clock in the morning he had heard a car pulling up in front of the house and the slamming of the car door. Then, as Joe puts it, "Hilda would stagger in, banging the front door closed, her clothes a mess, not even trying to sober up enough to look in on the kids."

It was getting late and Hilda hadn't come back. Joe wasn't sure what to do next. He went to the store, got some milk, fresh bread, and cheese, and rushed back home. He fed Annie and Stevie, then put them to bed. There was still no sign of Hilda.

In the morning, when Hilda still hadn't returned, Joe talked with some of his neighbors. After complaining about the ruckus he and his wife were constantly making, they told him that the previous afternoon Hilda had left with a man. Joe thanked the neighbors and, full of self-recrimination, went back into the house. "I had reason to resent the way my wife was handling things," Joe told me over twenty years later, "but it doesn't have to be one-sided at all. My wife stopped loving me and I believe that was mainly due to finding someone with more sexual power than I had to offer."

Two days after Hilda's departure, Joe noticed that Stevie's belly had become bloated and that his chest appeared to be sunken. A doctor said that he was suffering from malnutrition. Joe had never heard the word, but realized, after the doctor's explanation, that this had happened because Stevie had been fed pop instead of milk. The doctor prescribed a formula, gave Stevie shots, and checked him periodically.

The night that Joe had found Hilda gone he planned to stay home from work for a few days until he decided what to do with the children. A neighbor, however, had offered to take care of them while he was at work. After Hilda had been gone about a week, Joe placed Annie and Stevie with a family that boarded children in the suburbs near Norristown, Pennsylvania. From the lovely ranch house where they were living, he took Annie and Stevie home for weekends, cared for them, and continued Stevie's medical treatment. Hilda had not come back, and Joe decided that he was going to try to find her.

From Hilda's friends Joe learned that she was with her boyfriend, Hans Ibler, and that they were living together in Ibler's car. Each day after work, Joe, who had obtained the license number, combed the city of Philadelphia, looking for the car in which Hilda and Ibler were allegedly living. He kept thinking that perhaps Hilda's friends were just having a good time watching him, knowing that he was running around the city looking for a car in which nobody lived.

After two weeks of strenuous searching, Joe did find Ibler's car. It was parked in a secluded spot near a cemetery. Joe looked over the fence at the markers and tombstones and then he looked back at Ibler's car. He couldn't understand it. He assured himself that he could not have been so bad a husband and father that his wife would desert him and their children for a homeless man who had nothing better to offer Hilda than life in an automobile.

Scattered around the car and lying in the weeds were paper dishes, beer bottles, fragments of food, plastic utensils, and other signs of Hilda's housekeeping. Looking at the garbage, Joe saw that Hilda hadn't changed a bit. Quietly he walked up to the car and looked through the closed rear side window. Hilda was stretched out on the back seat. She was wearing a print skirt and blouse that Joe remembered having bought for her. The front seat was empty. Ibler was not there.

Hilda sat up with a start. "My God, Joe," she screamed through the closed window, "get out of here. Beat it! How did you know where I was?" Through the closed window Joe yelled back that Annie was crying for her mother, that Stevie was sick. He promised that there would be no more fights. Everything, he assured her, would be as perfect as it had been when he gave her the bouquet of American Beauties. Hilda shook her head. She said in a loud voice, "I'm *never* coming back to you, Joe, understand? I don't love you. You scare me because you're *crazy*. Now go away!"

Joe had a single explanation for the collapse of the marriage: Hilda abandoned him because she had found a man with more sexual power than Joe had to offer. He knew nothing, of course, about Ibler's sexual power. But Hilda's mockery of Joe's "bird" and her walking out had awakened Joe's small-penis delusion and he was filled with painful feelings of worthlessness and low self-esteem. Twenty years after Hilda had rejected him at the car that autumn night, he would tell Dr. Robert Sadoff, one of his defense psychiatrists: "My hernia operation *did* probably lead to the loss of my wife." This delusion, as evidenced in the aggressive acts of Joe's childhood, would also be the matrix of his crimes.

For the present Joe was a broken man, humble enough to hope that he might save his family dream by yet persuading Hilda to come back to him.

At the car Hilda had rejected Joe with hostile finality. With Hilda definitely gone, Joe thought that his hope of having a large family had been shattered, for he could not see himself coping again in a world which had so many overwhelming, big-breasted women and so few compliant, small-breasted ones. He had to have Hilda with him, although he didn't know how to get her back. Without her, his family dream would be lost forever.

One morning Hilda arrived at Joe's front door. He was certain that she had come home, but she told him that he had another guess coming. She had come for Annie and Stevie. The children were in the boarding home, but Joe pretended that they were inside the house.

"I won't let you near them," Joe said as he closed the door on his wife.

From inside the house Joe watched Hilda smash the windows in the door. She was trying to get in, but she never made it. What she did accomplish, without of course knowing that she did so, was to smash Joe's hope of a reunion.

The hope gone, Joe readily assented to the senior Kallingers' wish to sell the Masher Street house. They did so quickly, and ordered Joe to move back to *their* house. His family dream shattered and his spirit broken, he meekly followed the order and returned to the house that had been his prison in childhood and from which he had escaped to Hilda.

Joe was back in the bedroom where he had carved the hole in the wall, which his adoptive father had not bothered to plaster since Joe had left when he was fifteen. He had no temptation to use it, only a remembrance of the fantasies of slashing that had accompanied his masturbating into the hole and that had begun here. These were the fantasies that Joe had taken with him into his marriage to Hilda and that had never left him.

Joe tried to focus his thoughts on practical matters, like getting the church to annul his marriage to Hilda. After Visitation Church, where he had been regularly attending Mass and going to confession, had turned him down, he filed in civil court for a divorce. The court informed him that even though he had custody of Anna and Stephen, Hilda Kallinger had the right to see her two children twice a week. This meant that Joe brought the children from the suburbs near Norristown to spend weekends with him and on two weekdays each week to visit with their mother.

Joe was cool during the brief encounters with Hilda when he brought the children to see her. He was not cool, however, when he learned from little Annie that during the visits Hilda had taught the children to call Hans Ibler "Daddy." Hilda and Ibler were now engaged, and it was clear to Joe that Hilda was going to try to get custody of the children she had deserted.

Deeply agitated, Joe couldn't sleep, lost interest in eating, and stopped smoking. He had not yet reached his twenty-first birthday, but he felt as depleted as an old man. He had severe pain in both his temples, especially when he was working. Medication was effective at first, but by August 1957 the medicine proved useless, even when given in stronger doses. The doctor—the same Dr. Daly who had performed Joe's hernia operation—suspected a cerebral lesion and hospitalized Joe at St. Mary's on September 4, 1957.

The hospital ruled out a cerebral lesion as the cause of the headaches and, after eleven days, discharged Joe with a diagnosis of "psychopathological nervous disorder, anxiety state." According to the American Psychiatric Association's *Diagnostic and Statistical Manual of Mental Disorder*, psychopathological disorders are "physical disorders of presumably psychic origin." This means that Joe's headaches were physical symptoms resulting from emotional causes and that the doctors at St. Mary's thought of Joe's psychological distress as the direct outcome of his family crisis and the loss of his wife.

At the time it was impossible for the doctors to predict the long-range effects of Joe's loss of his wife. That loss, however, blended with the abandonments he had sustained in the past, intensified his delusions, and became an important psychological factor in his developing psychosis: schizophrenia.

A psychiatrist at St. Mary's explained to Joe that he had to lessen the stress in his life and that it was therefore essential for him to stop shouldering full responsibility for his two children. Joe admitted that being a single parent was difficult, yet he wanted desperately to keep Annie and Stevie with him. But the psychiatrist made clear that doing so would invite further psychological trouble. Afraid that if he let go the reins, Hilda would obtain custody, Joe continued to hesitate. He didn't want to trust his children to Hilda, who had walked out on them, nor to Ibler, who had run off with another man's wife. Joe felt that he was the more competent parent, because, except for the bus and bridge trips in the past, he had lived a clean life.

The psychiatrist's warning, however, had convinced Joe that even though he held on to his children, for the sake of his health he had to make some changes. He tried to lessen the stress on himself by putting Annie and Stevie in the care of the Catholic Children's Bureau. Under the new arrangement the children were placed in a private boarding home the bureau selected. Costs were reduced because Joe had to pay only half the board while the organization paid the other half. Responsibility was also lessened, for Joe was not allowed to take the children home for weekends or on visits to their mother.

Old stresses had been removed, but new ones had taken their place. Joe could not bear the agonizing loneliness of not having his children with him on weekends and the emptiness of not having anything to do with his free time. He no longer felt like everybody else and had no intention of dating—or even approaching—the big-breasted women who terrified him and whom he saw as dominating the world. In his delusional state he was certain that they would destroy him with their overwhelming breasts, smother him, enfold him in layer after layer of flesh until he was trapped—immobilized like a bug in amber. At the end of nightmares Joe, screaming and thrashing, would surface from a tangle of sheets that in the dreams were hordes of women who looked like Mae West; they attacked his naked, prostrate body, their breasts huge clubs pulverizing him, the nipples cutting his flesh.

The small-breasted women were too few in Joe's delusional world to make the effort of dating them worthwhile. Furthermore, he still hoped that *somehow* he would be able to bring Hilda home.

Joe had told the psychiatrist at St. Mary's Hospital that he had been "burnt" so severely that he would not look at women anymore. Soon, to fill the long, empty hours, Joe was spending at least one day and often two of every weekend with Annie and Stevie at their new home and in each home to which the Catholic Children's Bureau transferred them. He couldn't bear to be separated from them, for they were extensions of himself and the only remaining part of his lost dream of having a large family.

Joe's divorce from Hilda had become final on January 3, 1958. Some time later, on a Sunday morning, he lay on his bed in the room of his childhood and adolescence and reviewed the misfortunes that had befallen him. His adoptive parents were at church, but Joe had refused to go with them: The Vatican had excommunicated him because of his civil divorce. Nobody, of course, would have prevented Joe from entering his parish church, but he stayed away, the excommunication having angered him. It had hit him with the force of a fourth abandonment: First his natural and then his adoptive mother had made him feel worthless and unloved; then Hilda, his wife, who in his fantasies had become a punitive mother; and now the Catholic Church. Joe felt desolate.

Joe, lying on his bed, turned on his side and looked out the window. Sunday in Kensington was quiet and dreary. He thought of Elizabeth (Betty) Baumgard, whom he had met at the Norristown railroad station at Dekalb Street on a Friday afternoon in June 1957, while he and the children were waiting for the Philadelphia train to take them home for the weekend from the private boarding home where he placed them after Hilda had left. He was sitting on a bench and the children, in front of him, were playing with a big red ball. Annie threw the ball to Betty, a tall woman wearing dungarees and a blouse, who was sitting with her sister Patsy on a bench opposite Joe. Betty threw the ball back to Annie. Joe smiled and said, "Thank you." Stevie took the ball from Annie and threw it to Betty. She

111

threw it back. Joe smiled and said, "Thank you, again." They laughed and then began to talk.

On the train Joe sat behind Betty and her sister. Annie and Stevie kept running up and down the aisle. Then Annie, clutching the ball, climbed up onto Betty's lap, and Joe heard Annie say, "You're a nice lady. I'm going to let you hold my ball." Joe watched Betty, who was holding the ball with one hand and Annie with the other.

That girl, Joe mused, would make a good mother. But forget it, Joe. You were burned once.

Almost the same scene was repeated on many other weekends. For as long as Joe's children lived near Norristown, he met Betty at the railroad station every Friday afternoon. She was going from her home in Royersford to Manayunk, her birthplace, to spend weekends at the home of her aunt. From the Norristown station to Manayunk was only a fifteen-minute run, but during the week Joe found himself waiting for those fifteen minutes. And when he was taking the children back to Norristown on Sundays, he was delighted when at Manayunk Betty sometimes got on the train and he had an additional fifteen minutes with her.

One Friday afternoon at the railroad station, Joe, realizing that he had never been alone with Betty, asked her sister to do him a favor by taking the children to the lavatory. Alone with Joe for the first time, Betty asked him about Annie and Stevie's mother. Not wanting to go into the details about the collapse of his marriage and his impending divorce, Joe answered promptly, "She's dead." Upset that children so young had lost a mother, Betty began to cry. But Joe did not, at that time, change his story.

Joe remembered painfully how the train rides with Betty had ceased after Annie and Stevie left Norristown to live in a boarding home under the auspices of the Catholic Children's Bureau. In a letter to Betty he explained that circumstances would no longer bring them together, but that he hoped they would continue to see each other. After Betty replied that she would be happy to have him visit her at her aunt's house in Manayunk, he began going there frequently. He and Betty also exchanged letters. Betty's letters were written by her sister Patsy, because Patsy was the better letter-writer and Betty wanted to send Joe the best letters possible.

Unconsciously Joe had probably been wooing Betty from the time

112

he had first been alone with her and, not wanting to make a bad impression with the facts of his failed marriage, had told her that his children's mother was dead. Joe felt that there was something prophetic about the way a child's ball had brought Betty and him together. Again he began to see himself in a house in the suburbs, surrounded by a wife, Annie and Stevie, and many other children.

Joe realized as well that at no time had he accepted his living apart from Annie and Stevie as permanent. Shortly after Hilda had come to his door to take the children away from him, Joe had applied to the army as an orthopedic expert with the rank of captain. The army personnel officer told him that he was qualified and would be accepted on condition that he allow his children to be adopted and no longer be responsible for them. This he refused to do. He was strongly compelled to make a home for Annie and Stevie.

Now that Joe's divorce was final, he was glad that on one of his Manayunk visits he had already told Betty that his children's mother was not dead. He was happy that Betty, instead of having been angry at him for lying to her, had expressed her admiration for the time and money he was spending on his kids. Now, when he told her he was a divorced man and wanted to date her, she was joyous.

On their first date they went to the Ice Follies, and after that went out together almost every evening. It was five weeks, however, before he even kissed her on the cheek. But when he asked her to marry him, she promptly said yes. He gave her a diamond friendship ring that cost $80 and later a more expensive engagement ring.

Joe was in love with Betty and knew that she was in love with him. He was with her whenever he was not in the store or with his children. But apart from kissing, there was no sex. He was strongly attracted to this woman, who was five feet ten, taller than Joe. She was thin, angular, and flat-chested. He admired her gorgeous legs and was glad that her breasts were small.

Had she been large-breasted, he would have been afraid of her. After the experience with Hilda, he thought, however, that some flat-chested women were evil, others good. He still doubted his sexual power, but, believing through his characteristic magical thinking that the prospect of renewing the family dream would restore this power, he wanted intercourse. But when Betty demurely refused to have it before marriage, he respected her wishes.

On April 20, 1958—three months after Joe's divorce became final—Joe and Betty were married in Elkton, Maryland. He was embarrassed when he was asked to give his age, for Betty was two years older than he and he had told her that they were the same age. "Betty," he said, "step to the rear while I give this information." She didn't move and heard that Joe was two years her junior. "I knew," Joe explained as they were leaving the courtroom, "that you didn't like anyone younger than you, so I became older." He was then twenty-one and four months.

This time Joe made no attempt to follow the civil wedding with a religious one. Betty was Protestant and he had been excommunicated from the Catholic Church. In Joe's second marriage, as in his first, there was parental disapproval by both families. Betty's parents objected to her having a ready-made family. The senior Kallingers disapproved because, having gotten Joe back home and having paid for his divorce, they had hoped that at last they could keep him for themselves. Their exorcism of the demon from "the bird" had failed. But they had expected that as a single man Joe would take care of them in their old age, which had been one of the purposes in adopting him.

The court, satisfied that Joe could provide a home for his children, released Annie and Stevie to Joe and Betty. Joe's family dream had been restored, for with Betty he planned to have lots of children. But the traumas of the first marriage made it impossible for Joe to revive the illusion of health that he had had in the early days of his first marriage. Psychologically he started his second marriage outwardly serene and optimistic, but inwardly turbulent and apprehensive.

7 No Exit

Joe was desolate and in torment. He and Betty had just been married. They were on the bus returning to Philadelphia when two sailors, sexy and macho, grinned at Betty. She grinned back, then looked at Joe, who sat near the window. Across the aisle, the sailors' hard, masculine eyes challenged him. He looked away, watched the scenery rushing past as the bus drew nearer to Philadelphia. Bad memories awakened: humiliation and torture for sixteen years at the hands of his adoptive parents, their eyes, like the sailors' eyes, mocking his worthlessness. His first marriage and the family dream had collapsed. Now Joe had doubts about Betty: Would she be faithful to him; or would she walk out on him? And he had doubts about whether his family dream could be renewed in this second marriage.

Doubts about himself crowded in on Joe. He hadn't had sex since Hilda had walked out of their bedroom in the Masher Street house. In the empty house, lying alone in the big bed, Joe had had erections brought about by his fantasies of slicing and cutting. The erections, produced by the fantasies, had long ago—long before he married Hilda—convinced him that the demon had remained in his "bird." But, Joe wondered, could this demon that had given him the fantasies, and from them the erections, when he was alone in the bed in the Masher Street house, still make him potent with a woman lying beside him, still bring him the fantasies without which he could not have an erection? He didn't know.

Joe and Betty went directly from the bus to the house they had rented on Kensington's Janney Street. She made a good dinner, laughed, and told jokes. Joe ate lustily, praised Betty's cooking, talked about politics and love. They held each other and kissed. Then Betty washed the dishes and cleaned up the kitchen table. As they walked up to their bedroom, Joe checked to make sure that the penknife was still in his pocket.

As far back as the time of masturbating in the hole in his bedroom wall, Joe had discovered the connection between the fantasies that the demon gave him and a knife. He needed the fantasies so that he could have an erection. But when he held a knife in his left hand, he found that the knife prolonged the fantasies, which sustained his desire. Joyfully he discovered that the prolonged fantasies gave him multiple erections. And when his demon—his adoptive parents' epithet for abhorred sexual energy—became tired after Joe had had multiple orgasms, the fantasies stopped and Joe experienced detumescence, accompanied by either postcoital or post-masturbatory serenity.

While Betty was in the bathroom, Joe slipped the penknife into a small bookcase with sliding doors built into the headboard of their bed. Later, lying on his left side beside Betty, he caressed her with his right hand while he moved his left hand above her head. Very gently he opened the sliding door about five inches and, without removing it from the bookcase, squeezed the unopened penknife.

The fantasies came, and when they did not fade after his first orgasm, Joe knew that the knife and his demon had wielded their magic. A small knife, either a penknife or a straight knife, would always be in the bookcase of the headboard whenever Joe and Betty made love. She would never know it was there—to hurt or frighten her was not its purpose.

Joe's fears vanished. Both in bed and out of it Joe was warm and loving to Betty and she to him. She was proud to be the wife of a man whom she considered a handsome, intelligent shoemaker who gave her everything she wanted. She enjoyed making good meals for him, keeping their house in good order, and being a mother to Annie and Stevie, who had come to live on Janney Street after the marriage.

Joe was also an eccentric and exacting husband. He needed a sense of power not only during sex, but at other times as well. He had thought of himself as king at the beginning of his first marriage, but Hilda had overruled and dethroned him. Her flight to another man had also heightened Joe's adolescent trauma about his inferiority to macho men, and Betty had aroused Joe's suspicions by grinning back at the sailors on the bus. He vowed that he would not let Betty get away from him. In his second marriage he intended to be an absolute monarch whose wife would not take flight. He saw himself as a ruler who would govern his small kingdom with benevolence and firmness.

Betty was to have everything she needed and wanted, but he would immure her within the walls of their home and would not let her out by herself. So Joe didn't allow Betty to go anywhere without him, except to her job at a sweater factory before the birth of her children, or to the store. If she had someplace else to go, he went, too. He didn't dance, so she stopped dancing. The car she had before marriage he sold. He wouldn't allow her to drive because *he* couldn't drive and, as with dancing, he couldn't learn. He feared that while he was at work, Betty would drive away and never come back. Again Annie and Stevie would be waiting for him in a house alone.

Joe had a grandiose image of himself. But the same suspicions that made him want to be an absolute monarch also often made him withdrawn and reclusive. This was especially evident when he, the children, and Betty were weekend guests at her parents' home. He seldom left his room and even refused to do so for large family reunions. At one reunion he yelled to Betty out of a window, "Why don't you come up and stay with me?" When she came up, he thanked her. For his cry was not that of an imperious husband, but of a little boy frightened by abandonment.

Joe had not had a hallucination since he was fifteen, when a figure he thought was God appeared to him and ordered him to undertake his orthopedic experiments to correct himself and the world. Now, at twenty-two and a half, when things were going well, outwardly at any rate, Joe had a second hallucination.

Joe told me: "A figure in a black cloak and a witch's hat, also black and with white half-moons and stars on it, appeared to me while I was standing at my workbench. He pointed to other figures beside him and told me to watch them carefully.

"I did. To my surprise these other figures were of my adoptive parents and of me as a kid. We were at Neshaminy. I was helping them rake together fallen leaves in autumn. My father ignited a mound of leaves at the base with a match. The flames grew and spread. Hot, red sparks rose in the smoke. As I watched those flames that I remembered from my childhood I got a thrill.

"That scene was over. Another came. The second one was in the kitchen of our Front Street home. My father—I was just a kid—was standing directly behind me. He gripped my wrists and brought the fingertips of my right hand over the stove burner and then pushed them into the flame. I screamed and my father said, 'This will burn the demon thief out of the fingers that steal.'

"As an adult I was angry because my father was burning me as a child. But the flame itself brought joy to my heart.

"Then, Flora, that second scene cut off as suddenly as it came. I was alone with the creature in black who had flames gushing from his mouth. I couldn't decide whether he was the devil or one of the devil's spirits. Maybe, I thought, he was the demon that lived in my 'bird' or the demon my father said, when he was burning my fingers, he was driving out of my hand. I didn't know. I had never seen the demons, neither the one that lived in my 'bird' nor the one in my hand that made me steal the rolls of coins from my parents' closet when I was a kid.

"Before the figure in black, whoever he was, vanished, he told me something very strange and, I've got to admit, Flora, also very thrilling and exciting. He told me to go home at lunch and burn down my Janney Street house.

"I obeyed him. I don't know why. Burn my own house down! Crazy! But, like I said, it was thrilling and flames brought me a lot of joy. Fire gave me the same kind of sexual feeling I had from holding a knife in my left hand.

"Oh, what ecstasy, Flora," he went on, "setting fires brings to my body! What power I feel at the thought of fire—all my treasures in total ruin. Oh, what mental images fire brings. Oh, what a pleasure, what heavenly pleasure!" (Here the expression on Joe's face was beatific; his eyes looked at me as if he were having a transcendental experience.) "I see the flames and no longer is fire just a daydream. It is the reality of heaven on earth! I love the excitement of the

118

power fire gives me to burn up all that I own. This mental image is greater than sex. Oh, Flora, what a release, what bliss, what love, what . . . !" (At this moment, standing, Joe had an orgasm; a flush suffused his face, then he sat down on a chair, sweating and breathing heavily.)

After a few quiet moments, Joe sighed and smiled, like a child who in innocence has been caught doing something "naughty" and still wants to be loved in spite of his naughtiness. Joe went on in a soft voice: "I went home during my lunch hour. The house was empty, very quiet. No noise, except that I could hear my heart pounding with expectation and excitement. Betty was at her job. Annie and Stevie were at the day center where we sent them while Betty and I were at work. She picked them up at the end of the day.

"Alone in the house, I saw the figure in black again. The flames from his mouth were beautiful and really turned me on. Another demon was in my hand, not the demon my father said was there when he burned my fingers. *This* demon wanted to burn, to destroy my house, like a kid having a temper tantrum. He had no care.

"I walked into our shed connected in back to the rear of the house. In the shed we kept clothes belonging to everybody in the family. We had suitcases, tools, cans of paint and paint thinner in the shed. I took a pack of matches out of my pocket, lit the whole pack, and threw it into the can of paint thinner, which I'd opened. Whoosh! The flames shot up. I loved them, stood there watching them, getting myself turned on, you know. But I knew I couldn't stay there, so I hurried out of the house.

"I stopped at a fire-alarm box, reported the fire. Then I went back to the store.

"The shed burned completely. The house was partly gutted, although it didn't burn down. Some clothes and furniture were destroyed. That night and for several weeks we stayed—Betty, the kids, and me—at Betty's grandmother's house in Manayunk. After that we moved to a rented house on Kensington's Opal Street.

"The fire at Janney Street was my first fire. I collected nineteen hundred dollars in insurance money because nobody—not even Betty—knew how the fire started. The money couldn't pay for the anguish I felt *after* the fire. I'm no more Joe Kallinger," he said in a twisted but pathetic idiom. "I'm an arsonist. But I must admit I love fire! But I did this because I was ordered to do it by a force—maybe the devil—outside myself."

The house at 2039 East Fletcher Street in Kensington was not yet Joe's dream house in the suburbs. But when he moved there from Opal Street toward the end of the first year of marriage, he felt that this two-story red brick house came close. It was the most attractive house he had lived in. It had six rooms, a basement, a backyard, a patio, and a garden.

The senior Kallingers had bought it and kept the house in their name, as they had the house in Joe's first marriage. Joe paid the monthly payments to his adoptive parents. Yet, now as then, he felt that the house was *his*.

Having worked his way up from the Frank Grandee Shoe Repair Store and then through Kent Cleaner and Shoe Repair in Feasterville, a suburb of Philadelphia, he was working at this time in one of the best shoe repair stores in Philadelphia. In this shop, owned and operated by James Mahoney in the underground arcade in Center City, Joe was one of the highest-paid shoemakers in Philadelphia and had won awards for his work. He had gone as far as he could, short of owning his own shop and chain of stores.

At evening, when Joe came home from the underground arcade, he played with Annie and Stevie before they went to bed. On Saturdays and Sundays, as he watched them in the garden of their new home, he had a feeling of jubilation that the family that had been destroyed had been restored. This feeling of restoration became even stronger when Betty, who was pregnant when they moved to East Fletcher Street, gave birth to a baby girl at St. Mary's Hospital on March 16, 1959. They named the baby Mary Jo, Mary for her maternal grandmother and Jo for Joe.

Joe was with Betty when a nurse first brought the baby to her. "She's so ugly," Betty exclaimed upon seeing her daughter.

"I'm going to tell her the first words that came out of her mother's head," Joe teased. And when Mary Jo was six and beautiful, he playfully did just that. He had the same oceanic feeling from looking at this daughter, the first child of his second marriage, that he had had when Annie was born. He played with Mary Jo, coddled her.

As she would one day reminisce, "Daddy spoiled me rotten when I was little."

Joe tried to push the past away. In spite of the fire he had set at Janney Street, he thought he was well. But on July 25, 1959, when Mary Jo was four months old, the illusion of health stopped. He again had the severe pains in the temples that had led to his hospitalization at St. Mary's twenty-two months earlier. He told Betty that he was going to see Dr. Daly, but he never got there.

Instead he ended up in Hazleton, Pennsylvania, which is seventy miles northwest of Philadelphia, without knowing he was there or how he had gotten there.

Dazed and vague, lost and disorganized, Joe stood on the steps of St. Gabriel's Church at 121 Wyoming Street in Hazleton. He tried to shake off his confusion, but the church, the houses on the street, and the people walking in front of the church steps became figures running together incomprehensibly.

Joe huddled on the steps of this imposing gothic church of tan reddish brick with a fiery rose window above the front doors. A stranger to himself as well as to others, he saw passersby looking at him indifferently through fleeting side glances or stopping momentarily to stare at him.

He heard himself moan. Then a policeman talked to him and drove him to the Hazleton State Hospital, which was just a few blocks from the church. At 8:20 P.M., July 25, 1959, the hospital admitted him with no name for the records. The presumptive diagnosis was amnesia.

In the hospital, the doctors and nurses called Joe an anonymous Johnny. In his sleep one night, however, after he had been in the psychiatric ward for several days, he murmured a telephone number. A nurse called the number and spoke with Stephen Kallinger, who said he was the patient's father. Stephen told the nurse that he would come to take his son home on the day of his discharge from the hospital.

Before that discharge took place, however, there was a night when Joe, no longer amnesic, got out of bed, climbed a staircase, and found a closet on an unused floor. Locking the closet door, he sat down, hoping to die from suffocation. But a nurse who had found Joe's bed empty caught up with him before he could realize his wish to die. It was Joe's first suicide attempt, acted out through unconscious motivations, and totally unrelated to the facts of his present outer existence. Foiled in his attempt and returned to his bed, he remained with restrainers on him to keep him from leaving his bed, until the day of his discharge.

He was discharged nine days after his admission, with a final diagnosis made by the hospital psychiatrists of hysteria with conversion reaction. Hysterical neurosis, conversion type, as this condition is now called, involves a process of releasing through physical symptoms repressed psychic events, ideas, memories, feelings, and impulses. Dr. Irwin N. Perr, one of Joe's defense psychiatrists, reviewing the Hazleton Hospital records seventeen years later, believed that the Hazleton diagnosis was incorrect. According to Dr. Perr, Joe was suffering from dissociative hysteria rather than from conversion hysteria. Hysterical neurosis, dissociative type, as this condition is currently called, often involves alterations in the patient's state of consciousness or in his identity, to produce such symptoms as the amnesia from which Joe suffered in Hazleton. Dr. Perr maintained that the Hazleton episode was a type of dissociative reaction of a young adult who is reacting poorly to stress, a response that was predictive of future problems.

When an attendant brought Joe down to the main lobby of Hazleton State Hospital, Stephen Kallinger was waiting for him. But at home Betty was not waiting.

Betty knew nothing of Joe's amnesia nor of his hospitalization. She knew only that the day he left the house he had had a headache and said he was going to see Dr. Daly. When Joe had not returned, she called Dr. Daly's office. She was told that Joe had not been there.

The next morning, when Joe still had not come home, Betty took four-month-old Mary Jo and went to her parents' suburban house.

Betty thought that Joe had walked out on her. Joe, finding her gone, thought that she had walked out on *him*. This insecurity each of them felt belonged to a relationship that, although they still loved each other, had become tense. Betty, who was passive, childish, and good-hearted, submitted for the most part to Joe's domination of her. However, under the influence of her mother, Betty had gone back to her parents twice before in the four months since Mary Jo's birth.

The mother admitted that Joe was a good provider, but that was all she thought good about him. She had objected to the marriage in the first place, and was enraged by Joe's selling of Betty's car, his bizarre behavior at family reunions, and his refusal to let Betty out of the house unless he went with her. Yet both times that Betty had left Joe, he had been able to bring her back within a week by a single telephone call. He did so the second time by telling her that Hilda, who had come to see her children, was in the house. Jealous of Hilda, Betty had hurried home. In the Hazleton incident, however, Betty, who was pregnant with a second child, had not left Joe. She had simply taken flight to the only place where, in his absence, she felt safe. When he telephoned her, she came home promptly.

The Hazleton State Hospital psychiatrists sent a report to Dr. Daly recommending that Joe have follow-up psychiatric care, but no action was taken. The senior Kallingers, who had regarded Joe as a bad boy rather than a sick boy, had not recognized that he had emotional problems. Betty thought he was sound, and not even the Hazleton psychiatrists changed her mind. She had been furious when, before her marriage, Hilda had warned her not to marry Joe because he was "crazy." The only action Joe himself took was to increase his orthopedic experiments "to correct" himself. He had convinced himself that whatever was wrong with him could be "corrected" by a wedge in the heel of his shoe that would adjust the slant of his foot to harmonize with the functioning of his brain. His own—and the world's—problems could be solved by putting feet into shoes that had been fitted with the proper wedges.

Tense after Hazleton, he turned to bowling for relaxation. Each morning before work and again during his lunch hour, he went to a bowling alley. Bowling became a compulsion; he brought into his house on East Fletcher Street a twelve-foot-long, four-foot-wide bowling alley, a bowling ball, and a set of pins. He set them up in his and Betty's bedroom, the "alley" running from the party wall that separated Joe's house from his neighbor's, along the side of the bed to the opposite wall.

During the years he lived at East Fletcher Street, he bowled almost every weekday from four in the morning until it was time to go to work, and on most Saturdays and Sundays. Betty didn't mind the constant low thunder of the bowling ball rolling down the "alley" and the explosion when it hit the pins. At times she thought Joe a little strange, but she was good-natured about his "eccentricities," and never complained or threatened to leave after Joe had had a session with his bowling ball and pins.

But the neighbors complained, banged on the party wall, and called Joe "bananas," "goofy," and "crazy." He was insensible to their animadversions and bowled blissfully in his bedroom over a period of approximately six years.

Joe was also in the grip of his childhood compulsion for collecting discarded objects. "Trolley transfers and broken and battered motors had in childhood been a fascination of my life," he told me. "I was playing the role of adoptive parent to found treasures. I was looking for identity." By fixing the motors that he got from trash and making them work, he made them *his*.

Now at East Fletcher Street, where he had a home that was his, and where he was presumably realizing his identity through the fulfillment of the family dream, he was still in search of what other people had thrown away. Before the garbage trucks could pick up the trash lined along the curbs in front of his neighbors' houses, Joe would pluck from the heaps of garbage "found treasures" which he put into a little red coaster wagon and then took home.

He called his home at 2039 East Fletcher Street "the house of experiments" and filled it from the basement through its upper floor with his treasures: television sets, speakers, paper filing cabinets, record players, washing machines, folding cots, electrical motors, vacuum hoses, picture frames, garden supplies, an automobile cylinder head. He also accumulated various objects that captured his imagination in secondhand shops and at auctions. There was even an X-ray machine that he had purchased for $175 from the widow of a dentist.

Grandiosely struggling through the accumulated debris, Joe thought of himself as an ingenious scientist who could use the X-ray machine for his orthopedic experiments. He also considered himself a "super-repairman" and in this role sometimes dismantled a television set and salvaged its tubes or took apart a washing machine and saved the motor. He showed his methodical, organizing skill by carefully labeling each item in the house "junk."

"I got a feeling out of the junk," Joe told me. "I wanted to draw close to it. I went off on some of this stuff. But the junk gave me a feeling of closeness, of attachment, that I couldn't get with people."

On a night in 1963, Joe came home with an item even more surprising than battered motors and the bowling alley. He put it to me this way: "Let me take you from that chair you're sitting in and put you in a different world. I'm going to put you in Betty's shoes. All right?" Joe waved his arms theatrically and then pointed at me. "Now, you're my wife. No, don't punch me." He laughed, walked up and down. "You would have every right! I just put you in Betty's shoes. If you only knew what she had been put through, you would have every right to take a sock at me. It would be normal female instinct." He laughed again, then sat down and leaned toward me earnestly. "Now, you're Betty and you get this house fixed up as best you can with all the junk I've got all over the place. Betty is an excellent cleaner, so, Flora, you're in a sweet world of your own, where even each piece of junk has a place. So, you're all excited.

"Next week I come home one evening from work with a heavy finisher used in shoe repair. The finisher is twenty feet in length, five feet wide. On the finisher are brush wheels to polish shoes, and sandpaper wheels, and grinding wheels that shape leather for heels. And gigantic motors for them. Now, I place this in your living room. I've taken it apart and I'm going to make a jet finisher out of it. It is now ten to twelve feet long. Okay? I've also brought in a stitcher and it has two gigantic wheels on the sides. It's the heaviest piece of equipment in the shoe repair shop. I also bring in jacks on which a shoemaker fixes shoes. I bring in a scything machine that you scythe leather on. All the other contents that go with a shoe repair store are here.

"Now, you have this equipment in your living room. All of a sudden, I have destroyed you, Betty—I'm calling you Betty. I have destroyed your inner feeling of beauty. Then you complain a little bit to me, so I go and buy curtains and drapes. And I just leave enough room as a walkway, so that from the front door, you can keep walking into the kitchen. But, Betty, you have this big monstrosity of equipment in the middle of your living room. Every night when I come home, I don't spend it with you any more. I go right into this little workshop and develop my orthopedic heel adjustment work. I don't believe it's fair to do it while working for Mahoney. But getting back to you as Betty, you're trapped. Your beautiful home. You've got it, and it's lovely even with all my junk in it. And now your husband is destroying it. When I had a normal home, I destroyed it. Somehow, Flora, things that are normal for everyone else are abnormal for me."

I was moved by the scene he had painted, by his portrait of his wife and himself surrounded by the absurd junk in a well-furnished, attractive home. I felt momentarily as if I were in Betty's shoes. My toes were cramped, the sides of my feet hurt from hitting them against Joe's discards as I tried to move through "my" house as I imagined it while listening to Joe. But I was also in Joe's shoes, feeling the force of his compassion for Betty, helpless to act normally to put the compassion into action. I felt the paradoxes of his nature, the split in his personality that placed a family dream in one drawer, a feeling of being worthless and discarded in another, with no connecting links.

Somewhat later I learned about an absurd scene Joe had actually staged. He had come home from Mahoney's earlier than usual. Betty didn't see him come in, and he decided to play a practical joke on her. He went down to the basement, picked up some large lumps of coal, and flung them at the ceiling, one by one. He kept doing this until there were footsteps on the stairs and he heard someone say, "Put your hands up. You're under arrest."

"Don't shoot," Joe pleaded as he turned around and saw a policeman pointing a gun at him. "It's me—Joe Kallinger."

"I was scared, Flora," Joe told me, "and the officer was embarrassed. He was a neighbor and we knew each other. We went upstairs together and laughed about the misunderstanding."

Joe didn't know at the time how well his practical joke had worked. Betty had thought there had been a break-in. She called the policeman, who lived down the street. When he went down to the basement, he was ready to arrest the intruder who was robbing the Kallinger house.

The scene became a family yarn that both Joe and Betty liked to tell. That scene, however, had serious undercurrents stemming from Joe's childhood. Joe, having been denied play in childhood, was now playfully and prankishly pulling a ruse on his wife. Bringing with him frustration and rage from childhood, he was going to vent these feelings by throwing the coal at the ceiling. But in this scene there was

126

also a tinge of Joe's growing sadism that made him take pleasure in terrifying his wife.

Increasingly, Joe indulged in what retrospectively he called "my Fletcher Street destructiveness." In the kitchen he dug a hole supposedly to be used as an air-raid shelter but where he stored the overflow of junk. To hollow out the hole, he tore out an entire kitchen wall that connected that room to the foundation of the building. The hole was eight feet in circumference and extended eight feet beyond where the wall had been. "While tearing the wall," Joe told me, "I felt as if I were ripping up all the earth. Once you're turned on, you can't turn off. After it is over you feel like going to sleep." The feeling was similar to that sometimes experienced after sexual intercourse.

In late April 1963, Joe again saw scenes from the hallucination he had had on the day he set the Janney Street fire. The two childhood scenes appeared to him frequently: his adoptive father igniting a mound of leaves in Neshaminy and, in the other scene, putting little Joe's fingers in the flame from the kitchen stove's gas burner. But the figure with the witch's hat adorned with white half-moons and stars, and wearing a black cape, did not appear.

Blazing in space, however, were flames like those that had gushed from the figure's mouth four years ago. There was also a voice. Sometimes it was only in Joe's head; at other times he believed it came from outside himself. The voice had a single command: "Set fire to your house"—the same command the black-caped figure had given him.

But Joe hesitated. He was proud of his house at 2039 East Fletcher Street. For half a year it had been legally his, Stephen Kallinger having transferred the mortgage to Joe in October 1962. Although he would later take satisfaction in his "treasures in total ruin," he was—at first—reluctant to destroy them. Toward the end of May 1963, however, the reluctance disappeared and he could no longer resist the voice's command or his own desire for the bliss he would feel when he saw the flames consuming his "treasures."

Joe told me that he set fire to his East Fletcher Street house four times. Two were four days apart in May 1963, the third in August

1965. The fourth took place in October 1967, after Joe and his family had moved out. Joe said that the only fire he set to property not his own was at Mahoney's shop.

Joe was never publicly connected with the shop fire, but Richard Kimmel, a friend of Mahoney and later Joe's boss, told me that Mahoney had said that around the time of the fire Joe's behavior had become strange. Mahoney had come to think of Joe as a "mental case" and suspected him of having set the fire.

The first three fires that Joe set to his house at East Fletcher Street were classified as "accidental," and the October 1967 fire was the only one for which he was indicted and tried. He was acquitted because at the time of this fire, and only this one, he had no insurance on the house. He could not be charged with defrauding the insurance company. Gerald Gleeson, who as a lawyer had handled Joe's adoption and was now a judge, and Harry Comer, a state representative, were character witnesses for Joe.

The August 1965 fire, however, did have serious consequences. Joe had signed contracts for builders to restore his house, in exchange for which they were to receive all of the insurance money. He gave the builders the $15,000 he received from the insurance company. They wanted another $15,000 because they had replaced the back half of the house, which had been made of wood, with cinder blocks. When Joe did not pay, the builders took him to court. He tried his own case and lost; the builders got a judgment for $15,000 plus interest.

"From this point on," Joe told me, "the open judgment stagnated things for me, because there was no way I could move forward. I was cut off. The future was done. I wanted to build a chain of stores. That was over. From then on I even had to use my mother's and father's names when buying a house. Anything I owned could be foreclosed."

In the Hazleton hospital Joe had wanted, for the first time in his life, to commit suicide. Now the wish to do away with himself returned and became very strong. The open judgment against him had exacerbated his already growing psychosis.

BOOK THREE

Descent
into Hell

8 The Shoemaker's Castle

When Joe was a child, the house of his adoptive parents had been his prison. He was thirty years old when, in February 1967, he returned with his family to live there. Bad memories lurked in every corner. His hands trembled when he walked through the kitchen: With photographic clarity he remembered having his fingers burned over the stove. Inwardly he cringed from shame and frustration, for he saw in his mind's eye his adoptive parents sitting at the kitchen table and mocking him for wanting to be an actor, his adoptive mother flicking drops of water at him with her thumb and forefinger. In the living room he saw himself as a child sitting on his kiddy chair; intimidated, wondering, he had listened to his adoptive parents tell him for the first time how the demon had been driven out of his "bird." He even looked for the mirror over the staircase—although he knew that it had been taken down long ago—in which he had seen his penis hanging from a knife. That had been his first hallucination. As long as he lived in this house, to which he had been brought as a baby of twenty-two months and fourteen days, he would be haunted by these and other memories.

Outwardly he was triumphant on that day in February 1967 when he and his family, having had more than one residence since the East Fletcher Street fire in 1965, took possession of 2723 North Front Street (also known as 100 East Sterner Street). Stephen Kallinger had retired, and Joe, the heir to the store and the house, was now their owner. Outwardly, he had everything: his own shop and house, a wife and six children. Mary Jo was now eight. Joseph, Jr., with whom Betty had been pregnant during Joe's hospitalization in Hazleton, was seven. Michael Noel, now five and two months, had been born on Christmas Day, 1961. James John, who had arrived on December 8, 1963, was three and two months. Stevie, Joe's son by his first wife, Hilda, was eleven and still part of Joe's household. But Annie, Steve's sister, was not there.

When Annie was ten, Joe lost her to Hilda in a court battle. Long after Annie was gone, Joe kept her bed made, pretending that she would come back. He bought presents for her even when she wasn't with him. Joe kept them and gave them to her when she visited him on her birthday or at Christmas. But when she was twelve, she came to see him for the last time. She was now calling Hans Ibler "Daddy" and was presented to everyone, including Hilda's and Hans's children, as the Iblers' first child.

Brokenhearted over the loss of Annie, Joe had also been disquieted by the two miscarriages Betty had had between Joseph, Jr., and Michael. For in his normal state Joe abhorred the destruction of life even by nature.

Coming "home"—coming back to the house of his childhood—filled his mind with thoughts of destruction. The fantasies that in the past had accompanied sex now intermittently became unwanted thoughts at any time. Haunted by these thoughts and by the tortures inflicted on him in the past, he couldn't wait to get out of the house and into the store. For invariably the familiar hum of the finisher's three-horsepower motor had a peaceful and calming effect on him.

On some mornings, however, he had a hard time coming down to the shop. While Betty and the children were having breakfast in the kitchen in back of the store, he would be upstairs, pacing back and forth, trying to decide with which orthopedic experiment to begin his day. As other people required coffee to get going, Joe had to have his experiments. He often said that to him his experiments were more important than the morning.

Pacing was part of the experiment. All orthopedic changes, he believed, had to be the result not of theory but of practice. He had theorized and practiced during the fifteen years since the hallucinatory figure he thought was God had commanded him to save himself and mankind. After hallucinating the figure of the devil just before the Janney Street fire and after setting the fire, Joe had felt a new urgency about finding the right experiment to save himself. Now that he had moved into the house of his childhood tortures, the very environment that had spawned his psychosis, he was obsessed with making the shoe adjustments quickly. "Through the experiments," he told me, "I was trying to conquer the thing that was conquering me."

As he paced in his upstairs hallway, he studied his movements with care and precision. Returning to the bureau, he would then make adjustments in the shoe that the pacing had indicated were necessary. If the pad he had placed in his shoe felt a little too thick on one side, he would adjust it by perhaps as little as a sixteenth to an eighth of an inch in height to change the angle at which the foot rested in the shoe. If the pad threw his knee in a direction that was uncomfortable, he made an adjustment that would place the knee in a better position. He would call downstairs for the glue jar, pads, a piece of leather, a knife. Betty would bring up what he wanted, saying sometimes, "I wish I were a shoe so you would pay attention to *me*."

Minutely, fastidiously, like the perfectionist he was, Joe would slant the front or side of the pad with a knife. In the middle of the night Joe would wake up and start experimenting. On some nights he would dress and go out. A long walk became the test of how the adjustment he had just made would affect him when he was tired and his resistance was low. He hoped that the nocturnal "marathon" would show that the adjustment could overcome tiredness, that a long day could be followed by a long night and a long night by another long day. His goal was to achieve a power of endurance beyond what was then considered normal.

Joe felt lonely during these walks. To lighten the loneliness, he decided to take his children with him. Eventually, between the years 1967 and 1972, each of them and then all of them would be awakened on one night or another to go out with Joe.

The children tired too easily to be used as part of a test program, and other ways had to be found to keep them interested. Trash was the answer: the trash that had intrigued Joe since childhood. Now, while he tested his endurance, his kids became scavengers of garbage cans, looking at night for what by day other people had discarded. When the kids found something good, they took it home on the little coaster wagon on which Joe had brought his bowling alley to the East Fletcher Street house. As Joe watched his kids in their scavenging, they were for him "little Joe," embodiments of his inner child of the past. The illusion was the stronger because the children, especially Mary Jo, strongly resembled their father.

Joe also used the night to plan for the next day's horseracing, for horseracing had replaced bowling as his all-compelling hobby. He would send Stevie to Thirteenth and Market streets to buy the racing forms. The forms in hand, Joe would awaken Mary Jo, whose job it was to select the horses for the next day's races. From the time she was eleven until she was thirteen, Mary Jo, the racing form in front of her, sat at her little table in the living room and picked horses.

But Joe did not rely only on Mary Jo's choices. Before leaving for the track, Joe made orthopedic adjustments in his shoes. "If you can go out there," he explained to me authoritatively, "and you can have a perfectly relaxed body, you can communicate with the horses. You're at the same level. You feel the horses think and you think. And you win because you're in perfect harmony with them."

To finance the races Joe also turned his children into salesmen of various shoemaking products. Some were standard brands like Cavalier Shoe Color and Esquire Spray Dye. Others he developed himself. On one occasion he bought several truckloads of plastic bottles and filled some of the bottles with chemicals to be used for stretching shoes. At $1 a bottle the children sold the shoe-stretching liquid door to door.

The door-to-door selling, the horseracing, the nocturnal pilgrimages in quest of trash—there were times when Joe felt that he was pushing the children too hard. "What father," he asked me retrospectively and rhetorically, "sends his kids out with a duffle bag to knock on doors, begging for old shoes? I did that. What father finances his own hobby by his children's work? I couldn't stop myself. There was that thing again—it controls me, I don't control it."

Joe wasn't talking about the hallucinatory controls that had already been exerted upon him and that would grow stronger. The "it" in this case was the compulsion to dominate, as he had been dominated in his childhood. To be strong and all-powerful was his way of compensating for the feelings of worthlessness his adoptive parents had instilled in him.

As a child Joe had had to work full-time in the store. Now he was making his children work part-time for him. As a child he had not been allowed to go out to play or to bring friends into the house. Now as an adult he let his children play outside, but they couldn't bring friends into his house. In these respects Joe's treatment of his children had more in common with the bad memories of his childhood than with his family dream. Broken were some of the promises about being a father that he had made to himself when he was married for the first time.

But in other ways Joe was a good father, an involved father. In the Kallinger household he was the dominant parent and Betty a peripheral one. As the parent who invented games for the children, consulted with the children's teachers and school counselors, and took care of the children when they were ill, Joe was also a good mother.

But above all Joe was a father who through his children was re-living his own childhood. Each year, at one minute past midnight on December 11—the beginning of his birthday—he awakened the entire family for a party he gave himself. He had been giving these parties since 1962. Each year the ritual was the same. He shepherded his flock into the living room, which he had decorated with crepe paper. He distributed paper hats, horns, and index cards with party directions. There were cake, ice cream, cookies, and party plates for everyone. After saying, "If I don't have my party, you won't think of me," he sang, "Happy birthday to me!" (They did have presents for him, however.)

Comic on the surface, tragic in its implications, the scene was reminiscent of a constant childhood deprivation and particularly of Joe's reaction to it on his ninth birthday, when as he walked with Anna Kallinger to St. Boniface Church and School he had sung softly, "Happy birthday to me; happy birthday, dear Joe." Never had his adoptive parents given him a birthday present or acknowl-edged the day of his birth. "Every day is your birthday," Anna had chided as she itemized all the material things she and her husband gave their adopted son. As a husband and father, Joe was childishly struggling to get from his family the recognition that as a child he had been denied.

At times Joe found the memories of childhood so overwhelming that he woke up Mary Jo during the night to talk about them. Without dredging up the most painful and dehumanizing memories, he talked to his daughter of his having to stay in all the time as a child because her Grandma and Grandpa Kallinger didn't believe in letting him out to play. He said that instead of playing or having fun, he always had to do something constructive. He had to stay in the store when he was little. When he was old enough to learn shoe repair work, he had to come right to the store from school and stay there so Mary Jo's grandpa could teach him the business. Joe also told Mary Jo that her grandparents didn't believe in affection, never showed him that they loved him, and he often thought that they didn't. Joe told Mary Jo that he wanted to be wanted and that's why he wanted a big family. "So you're one in a part of it," Joe said.

Joe also awakened Betty during the night. Her task was to make him tea, sometimes as many as thirty cups in a single night. Betty told me that even while he slept, she would often be awake, listening to him "eating and chewing in his sleep." Psychologically, through his mouth movements and the movements of sucking, Joe was recapitulating the separation anxiety he had had when at a month old he was removed not only from his mother's breast but also from his mother. The chewing and sucking movements were also a substitute for other satisfactions, an indication of frustration and psychic hunger. The mouth also is a primitive means of knowing objects.* A child grasps objects and puts them into his mouth under a kind of primitive impulse. Joe, through these mouth movements, was simulating the putting of an object into his mouth and, by doing so, was regressing to early childhood. But some schizophrenics also have this primitive way of reacting.† And Joe, in the years after coming to live in the house of bad memories, was moving toward the onset of a full-fledged schizophrenic psychosis.

Betty and the children responded as the tides respond to the pull

---

* Silvano Arieti, *Interpretation of Schizophrenia*, rev. ed. (New York: Basic Books, Inc., 1974), pp. 428–429.
† Ibid.

of the moon to each of Joe's nocturnal compulsions. "It's like when we were younger," Mary Jo remembers, "Daddy would do fun little things that were weird. But as we got older, and the years went by, he'd do weirder things and it wasn't funny anymore."

Fun little things like waking the children up because he had invented a new game for them gradually yielded to things that weren't so funny, like waking them up at midnight, at two, three, or four in the morning, because he had decided that the cellar of the store needed cleaning. The children would have to dust heels and also the showcases. They would have to take inventory of the stock. As a shoemaker's child Joe had been a satellite executing the shoemaker's orders. Now Joe was the shoemaker, enforcing *his* will on *his* satellites.

As the years passed, the house that in childhood had been Joe's prison became his castle-fortress. Symbolically, however, he also made the castle-fortress the prison of Betty, the children, and himself. Here behind imagined prison walls he felt safe. He let nobody into the house because there was nobody he trusted (and because as a child he was not allowed to bring anyone there). He was afraid that an outsider would "get" to his children, "get" to his wife, and they would break out of the castle. He was afraid, too, that an outsider would discover his secret experiments. This was his kingdom. He was the king. That's why this house became what the friendly neighborhood shoemaker called "Joe Kallinger's castle."

Outside the castle was Kensington, no longer as serene as when young Joe had been brought there by Anna Kallinger. Even though Kensington still had its good families, its solid citizens, disaster and decay were in the air.

When the family moved to East Sterner Street, Stevie was eleven, Mary Jo eight, Joey seven, Michael five, and Jimmy three. As the years went by, Joe, working in the store, watched his children go out into the Kensington streets. He envied them their freedom, for, like the other Kensington kids, they "hung" with different cronies at different times. Like the others, instead of attending school, they would often go to the railroad to catch frogs, or would play under Silver Bridge. Sometimes Stevie, Joey, and Michael went "thiefing" for materials with which to make graffiti. One part of Joe, as he watched his children pass, was the father who disapproved of what they might—and, he suspected, often did—do on the streets. The other part, however, was the boy who had been a stranger to the streets on which his children cavorted. Now, by living through his children in his imagination, he made their capers his own.

A man divided, Joe was also a man in terror. Early in 1969, the Devil, who had commanded him at the time of the fires, began appearing frequently. The Devil demanded that Joe perform outrageously sadistic acts.

"Flora," Joe told me, "I had obeyed the Devil when I set the fires. Now I resisted. Since the orders were coming from the Devil, I didn't have to execute them."

Beginning in 1969, Joe was also subject to what he then called "unwanted thoughts." An extension of the old fantasies, these "thoughts" were now full hallucinations, although Joe did not recognize them as such. He heard voices that seemed to be coming from outside himself and were as real to him as the voices of the people around him. He saw images in full color. As the hallucinations became stronger, Joe, watching his children head for Silver Bridge, remembered that there, as an adolescent, he had performed two of his first acts of aggression. His boyhood premonition that his life would end in disaster, which had developed at that time, now came back forcefully.

As the terror grew, Joe put steel around all the cellar windows and heavy wire bars around the first floor. The prison that had been symbolic was now actual, or at least it had the trappings of incarceration. It wasn't that he or even Betty was actually afraid of someone's breaking in. Yet, almost as a forecast of things to come, he erected his own bars. With bars he felt secure. With bars he was unconsciously punishing himself for his "unwanted thoughts."

Fearfully, Joe began looking across East Sterner Street to the building facing his store where Harry Comer had his office. Comer was the district's state representative to the legislature in Harrisburg, had been a character witness for Joe in 1967 at the arson trial, and had known Joe as a baby. But Joe was now under the delusion that Comer, along with other men in the Comer office, had been engaged by the CIA to spy on Joe Kallinger.

One morning Joe got out of bed at four o'clock. From the open window of his upstairs bedroom he threw steel balls used in pinball machines at the large plate-glass window of Harry Comer's office, which was thirty feet away and directly across the street. One of the balls struck and smashed the window. Without having awakened Betty, Joe went back to sleep, hoping that the damage would force Comer to "brick up" his window and thus put an end to the spying. A few hours later he called Comer at his home to report the broken window. That afternoon he helped Comer board up the window. Now, Joe believed, the spying was over!

A week later, however, Joe looked across the street and saw that the boards had been removed and had been replaced by a brand-new piece of glass. Again he believed he was being spied upon. For two months, feeling that his every movement was being observed, suffering because he believed he was being watched by CIA agents, he took no action.

But, unable to bear the pressure, he again got up one morning at four and stood beside his open bedroom window. This time he had a line of steel balls before him on his windowsill. He picked one up, drew back his arm, and hurled it. But the ball bounced off the brick wall of Comer's office and hit the sidewalk with a sharp clack. Afraid that he might have been observed either by passersby in the street or by agents lurking in Comer's office, Joe withdrew for a few moments into the shadows of his bedroom. Then he picked up another steel ball from the windowsill and hurled it at Comer's window. This time Joe heard the glass fracture and the tinkling of shards as they fell to the sidewalk.

Again he telephoned Comer, helped him board up the window, and felt secure from spies. But again the boarding was replaced by glass, and Joe, for what he thought was his own security, had to break the window a third time. Then Comer installed a sturdy pane of glass that was divided into two sections. Joe gave up hope that he could keep the spies in Comer's office from observing him through the new window.

Joe now covered up the windows in his own store with dark screens. Behind them he hid from the dreaded CIA agents who inhabited Comer's office and spied upon him from across the street. The screens, cutting off light and air from the outside, forced Joe to work in a sealed area with artificial lighting and no ventilation.

He inhaled fumes from glue, dye, thinner, and other substances. He knew that the changes were harmful to him and that he was making his store almost unbearable to work in, but his delusion was stronger than his common sense. With his sallow complexion above his olive-green smock and black pants and his nose and throat painfully irritated from the fumes, he looked like a suffering recluse.

He felt that an alien force was manipulating him. When the Devil commanded him, he knew what the force was, and he didn't have to obey it; but at other times, as in the breaking of Comer's windows, the Devil had not appeared. Not knowing what to call this other alien force that was controlling him, Joe began thinking in phrases such as "the mind tells you," or "the hands and feet do." When these phrases came to him, Joe no longer felt that the mind within his skull, the hands with which he worked, or the feet that carried him were his own. Detached, separated from himself, he felt weak, defenseless, and persecuted. He was the hunted, and the forces that were hunting him made him feel like a wounded animal. He sought a dark retreat.

Under a full moon Joe walked toward East Hagert Street. He thought: In the wacky light of the moon witches dance on rooftops and demons squat and gibber. It can drive a man insane.

His shoulders humped, Joe now went into a slight crouch. The weather was mild. He wore dungarees, a turquoise sports shirt, and old shoes.

Hugging the walls of buildings, huddling momentarily in doorways, he avoided passersby, and hurried on his way to 1808 East Hagert Street, where that afternoon, April 2, 1969, he and his children had completed digging a hole twenty feet deep. It was now eight o'clock in the evening. He was returning alone, to use the hole for the first time.

Two months earlier, on January 30, Joe had bought the house at 1808 East Hagert Street in the senior Kallingers' name, to use as a warehouse and as a secret refuge for himself.

Three times a week for two cold months—February and March 1969—Joe herded his children into a large room of the frigid house on East Hagert Street. Thirteen-year-old Stevie, ten-year-old Mary Jo, nine-year-old Joey, seven-year-old Michael, and five-year-old

Jimmy ripped up floorboards and then dug into the damp earth. Joe supervised but didn't dig.

As the children went deeper, Joe put restraining strips of wood against the walls of the hole to keep it from caving in. At twenty feet they struck water and Joe told them that they could go no farther. Nine-year-old Joey, happy because the long project was over, screamed an obscenity of pleasure and made fun of his father and the hole. Enraged, Joe's face wrinkled with tension, his lips compressed. He screamed at Joey: "If you don't shut up, I'm going to bury you in that hole!" Joey leered at his father with a malevolent twinkle in his eye and raised his middle finger, while the other children snickered. Ignoring them, Joe placed a wide strip of thick wood at the bottom of the hole, just above the water level. Then he dropped a ladder twenty feet long into the hole for easy descent and ascent.

The long, arduous task having been completed, Joe shooed his children out of the house, locked the door, and pocketed the only key. 1808 East Hagert Street was off-limits to all except Joe.

"That house on East Hagert Street," Joe told me, "was a little niche that was all my very own where nobody could crowd in on me . . . where I drove myself into becoming the kind of man that simply pulled back from life as a mortally wounded animal that crawled into some dark retreat. The house had a multitude of sins. But that isn't what I was going to say. That house saw a multitude of experiments that I didn't complete at East Fletcher Street. The Hagert Street house was my private world. Like Thoreau's *Walden Pond*. I still remember that from my American literature course. That's exactly what that old place was. Exactly. Like a secret annex to my castle, it was a place to hide. In the castle I worked and ate and squeezed the knife when I made love to Betty. But in my secret annex I sought refuge where I could be alone with all my wild ideas and what I now know were hallucinations. No one else came there. I was the only one who had a key."

Joe's "secret annex" on East Hagert Street—what he sometimes called "the preacher's house" because of its previous occupant—was built of wooden boards and stood two stories high. Two high doors, made of wood over steel, opened inward to a long hallway. At the end of it was a door that led into the large room beneath which Joe's children had dug the hole; in the ceiling, twenty feet above the battered, buckling floor, was a skylight. The preacher had added the room to the house, building it directly over the backyard. Rotting stairs to the right of the long hallway led to the second floor. Beneath the original house, but not beneath the large room, was a rat-infested basement.

Battered, verminous, and rotten, this shade of a house became Joe's refuge from the possible consequences of his "unwanted thoughts," now his hallucinations. He didn't want anyone to know that there was anything wrong with him, and by now he felt instinctively that there was. One of his deepest fears was that if Betty found out, she would divorce him. That, he felt, had to be prevented at all costs. The marriage had again become solid.

Joe looked at his watch. It was now eight-fifteen, April 2, 1969. Before unlocking the left door of his refuge for the second time, he glanced once more at the full moon. A line of poetry he had once heard came to him: "The moon is a fragment of angry candy."* But it was not like candy now. Joe thought it was an angry skull bathed in nightmare milk, evil, like his own thoughts and visions. The eye-sockets were holes with disaster in them. He thought that maybe the universe was an old boneyard; that planets, stars, galaxies were really the glistening bones of all the dead hurled into the black sky by demons. Joe unlocked the door and walked down the long hallway into the large room.

Bolted three feet above the floor to a wall of the large room was a capacious bin. It was filled with scrap wood, old newspapers, and damaged bricks. Under the bin was the hole, twenty feet deep and four feet in circumference, that had been finished earlier in the day. Over the entrance to the hole and around it, Joe had placed boxes and boards so that it couldn't easily be seen by anyone who might break into his refuge. Alone in the large room for the first time, he removed the camouflage and climbed down the ladder.

He felt as if he were entering the depths of his own mind. The hole was not only part of his niche in this old house, it was also the womb of an imagined mother replacing the one who thirty-three years ago had given birth to him.

* The actual line from E.E. Cummings's *The Cambridge Ladies* is "The moon rattles like a fragment of angry candy."

Descending, Joe smelled the odor of earth, musty and dank, and felt the dampness closing in on him. Then his feet touched the thick wooden strip. Joe wished that he could have dug right through the planet to some faraway place on the other side where he would be at peace with himself. But the darkness of the hole comforted him. He thought of himself as a creature of darkness, a man of the night, an underground man.

"Flora," he told me, "there was no fear in the pit, in the hole that I built for myself, for fear had no meaning for me. The present became nothing, the world nothing. I lived only in my pit."

Even though he liked the darkness, he had brought a candle with him. He took it out of his pocket, stuck it in the mud wall between two retaining strips, and lit it. The weak flame rose unsteadily, tapering to a fine point. Fire excited him now as it always had. He knew it could also destroy him. The ghostly moonlight that streamed through the skylight made him turn back with revulsion to the hole.

Suddenly a surge of spoken words reverberated around him; unfamiliar and unfathomable, they sounded like a chant:

KRISTORAH, KYRIASTORAH KYRIEH MARIA KREH KRASTORAH
MARIA KRIASTOH KRIASTORAH MARIA KRIEHSTOH KYRIAH
KYRIEH ALA MARIA KRIEH KYRIASTORAH MARIA KYRIESTOH
KYRIASTORAH MARIA KYRIEH ALA MARIA KYRIEH KRIASTORAH
MARIA KYRIASTOR KYRIASTOH ALA MARIA KYRIEH ALA MARIA
AHKAB KAH MARIA KAH KYRASTORIAH.

Again and again the same words were repeated, but in different cadences and with varying inflections. To Joe this was an utterance without connection with anything he had heard before.

The voice was very close to Joe. He turned his body from side to side, looked up and down, tried to find the source in the wall of mud that enclosed him, in the ground beneath him, perhaps way down where his children had not dug. He could easily have gone up the ladder and gotten away. He remained in the hole, however, out of fascination, horror, and a curious sense of wonder about the sounds that had so strangely entered his solitude.

Turning from side to side, he hit the ladder, and for the first time he noticed that his arms were extended upward as if in supplication.

143

Astounded, he stared at his upstretched arms, wondering whether they were his, and then he dropped them to his sides. He placed his right index finger against his throat and felt a vibration as the chanting went on. He also realized that his mouth was open and that his lips were moving. He knew, at last, that the strange sounds were coming not from the mud walls of the hole nor from some mysterious place under the wood strip on which he was standing, but from within himself:

KYRIEH KYRIASTORAH KYRYAH KRIASTOH ALA MARIA KYRYEH KYRIASTORAH KYRYAH KYRIEH KRIASTORAH: The chant was rising in a crescendo of intensity. Although the meaning of the words still remained unfathomable, Joe could tell from the tone that the voice from within himself had become angry. He wondered whether the voice was angry at *him*! It seemed as though the voice were scolding him as a child who had done something wrong. Then the voice seemed to be *accusing* him, but not of deeds that he had done. It was accusing him of the deeds to which the "unwanted thoughts" might lead.

Over and over again Joe listened to the maddening repetitive chant: KRIASTORAH ALA MARIA KRIASTOH. Then at last the voice stopped. A smothering stillness hung over the hole of darkness. The candle flickered. Joe was shivering.

Whose voice was it? Joe asked himself. It was a question to which he thought he already knew the answer. He was convinced that although the voice had spoken with *his* tongue and had come from within *his* body, it was not the voice of Joe Kallinger!

Something is speaking through you, Joe told himself, just as at other times an alien force controls your hands and your feet. He remembered the spirits with whom he had communed as a child in the springhouse in Neshaminy and at the tanks in Kensington. Were the spirits talking to him, but this time *through* his body rather than from outside it? Or was the demon in his "bird" trying to tell him something? Perhaps the Devil was speaking to Joe through Joe's bones, nerves, and muscles. What had the words meant? He thought they resembled three words he had heard as a child in church: Maria, Kristos, and Kyrios. The tone of anger, however, had been clear. But who was angry with whom? Joe knew instinctively that he would hear the words again and that whoever had chanted the words—

spirits, the demon, or the Devil—*had* to be evil, for the "unwanted thoughts" had reached Joe's surface of awareness while the voice was chanting. His madness had spawned a private "language," the words of which had neither referents nor meanings, a symptom of paranoid schizophrenia.*

He climbed up the ladder into the large room. The ghastly moonlight silvered the battered floor. He looked up at the skylight and decided that he would cover it with canvas. He hated the moonlight.

Even though Joe was trying to resist the commands of the Devil, who appeared to him frequently, Joe knew that one of his reasons for having had his children dig the hole was to carve into the earth a passageway to Hell.

He thought of Hell as he walked home. In school, he remembered, there had been a great emphasis on learning the catechism, and from the catechism he had learned that Hell was one of the three rewards or punishments that one received immediately after the judgment on the deceased's spirit. The word hell, he had learned, meant *gehenna*, which, he thought incorrectly, was the word for *hole in the ground*. The new hole at East Hagert Street and the hole of the spring well were holes in the ground. Others, like the tanks in Kensington and the one in the East Fletcher Street kitchen, he thought of as holes above ground.

The streets of Kensington were silent. The weather was mild. When he got to East Sterner Street, he looked up at the moon, then at his house. It had the color of bones in the moon's dead light. He murmured, "This is my castle. May it be spared from evil."

* See S. Arieti and F. Schreiber, "Multiple Murders of a Schizophrenic Patient: A Psychodynamic Interpretation," *Journal of the American Academy of Psychoanalysis*, Vol. 9, No. 2 (1981), pp. 501–529.

9 Mutiny in the Castle

When Joe first descended into his East Hagert Street hole, he was already wandering in the dark night of psychosis. He was recoiling from the world. Awake, he often felt as if he were asleep and dreaming. Often the dream became a nightmare and the people around him nightmare figures. The world was becoming Joe's enemy. The delusion of persecution that had begun with Joe's thinking Harry Comer was a spy was growing, and Joe was becoming increasingly grandiose.

The spasms of madness that attacked him were terrifying. Each time he felt the onset of an attack, he retreated to his hole. By the light of the candle, he conducted assorted rituals, with masturbation and defecation as elements of the ritual, for the subconscious regards excreta and secretions of the body as gifts of power.

During one of these episodes, Joe, who saw himself as the king of the castle and all-powerful father, decided to deal with the delinquencies of three of his children. He made the decision immediately after he had excreted a large volume of feces, which, being part of the underground ritual, refreshed and invigorated him. The delinquencies of the children were real, but the way Joe set out to correct them was delusional and sadistic.

On a hot July night in 1977, Joe told me about the method of punishment he used on these three children. Over the scarred wooden table in the empty prisoners' infirmary of the Camden County Jail, I listened to Joe, his face earnest and sweating. His dark eyes looked beyond me into the past.

"Remember, Flora, I told you I turned my Front Street house into a prison. In the cellar I had three windows, one on the Sterner Street side, two on the Front Street side. Over both Front Street windows I had placed steel gates hinged to poles and locked to the wall of the house. Over the one window on Sterner Street I had bolted a flat steel plate. The bolts went deep into the wall. I'd covered them with cement."

Joe paused, then looked directly at me; the pupils of his eyes were blank and impenetrable.

"The cellar seemed the perfect place to punish and reform my kids. Working and living in the same house with them, I saw them more often than I had in the past. There were times I didn't like what I saw. I felt that my older kids, Stephen and Mary Jo, and Joey were rebellious and unruly. The boys got into street fights and I feared were also 'into sex' on the street. Mary Jo 'bumped' school frequently.

"Betty stayed on the sidelines. She was passive. She couldn't handle them. I had to dish out all the discipline. My older kids had become a torment to me. I wanted to correct them. But I didn't want to call it punishment. During my first marriage and until now that I was well into my second marriage, I hadn't believed in bodily punishment for my kids.

"One day in June 1969, I was in the hole and changed my mind about physical punishment. I've already told you what happened in the hole that made me change. I felt weightless and strong enough to do anything. Two months before that I had first gone down into my East Hagert Street hole to save myself. I now thought I was going to save my kids in the cellar of my Front Street home.

"I was sure that education was the right way to look at what I was planning to do. I was going to reeducate my kids, get them to come around and do things my way. So, lined up on the metal table in the cellar were a section of heavy rope, two feet of rubber hose, a box of straight pins, strips of leather, and a homemade cat-o'-nine-tails."

147

In my mind's eye I saw Joe's cellar with the shelves in the middle covered with skin-blistering leather soles, heels, straps, and other items. A few paces from the shelves, I imagined, was the metal table with Joe's "educational material," as he called it, all laid out, ready for class. In 1969 his three students were thirteen-year-old Stevie, ten-year-old Mary Jo, and nine-year-old Joey. The course lasted until 1972. Instruction was private, for Stevie, Mary Jo, Joey were taken down to the cellar—the "torture chamber," as they called it —one at a time, and no child ever witnessed the "instructions" that Joe gave to any of the others.

"I blamed myself for the children's behavior that I had to correct," Joe went on to tell me. "On the whole, I'd been a softie as a father. I had to get strict because I didn't want them to grow up bad. So my purpose was serious, Flora, just as serious as it had been with the hamsters I'd brought to my East Fletcher Street house experiments in 1964."

I asked, puzzled, "Were they pets for the kids?"

"No, Flora, they weren't pets for the kids," he answered grimly. "But they did have something to do with my *feelings* about my kids."

"Then what did you mean when you said you had gotten the hamsters for a serious purpose?"

"I meant, Flora, that they had a *lot* to do with my orthopedic experiments."

"Really?" I asked, astonished. "In what way?"

"Well, I'd already done over forty thousand experiments, most of them on myself, some on my wife and kids. I'd even talked the mailman into letting me put wedges into his shoes, so I did a few on him. But I'd never done experiments on animals before."

"What were you going to do to them?"

"I was going to make little shoes for their feet and little wedges to put into the shoes. I figured I'd get a lot of information that way."

"What kind of information about human feet would you get from experimenting on hamsters?"

"I believed I'd find that human life could be prolonged through strong, healthy feet that were well balanced by wedges in the shoes. People die more quickly if they have bad feet."

"They do?" I asked.

"Sure! Take a look at any old person's feet, like someone eighty or ninety years old. Those feet are *strong*, Flora; they've walked that person through a long life. Sometime let me look at *your* feet with your shoes off. I'll bet I could tell almost exactly how long you're going to live."

Without thinking, I looked down at my feet that had spent many thousands of hours keeping me upright to teach in front of classes and on the lecture platform. I wondered what my chances were.

"When we're not pressed for time, okay, Joe?"

"Okay. But there was something else I wanted to find out from the experiments on the hamsters. If you've got good feet, then your brain is in good shape, too. The feet control the brain. This means that if you've got durability and resistance in the feet, then you've got intelligence in the brain.

"I wanted to experiment on the connection between the hamsters' feet and their brains. If they listened to me and did what I told them, then I'd know that the wedges in the little shoes I'd have made for them were doing them good by giving them greater durability and intelligence. Then they'd be obedient to *me*, their master."

"Do you think, Joe, that blind obedience is a good measure of an organism's intelligence?"

"Look, Flora," Joe said with conviction, "I've always thought that if any living thing is obedient, it's intelligent. I *think* my kids were intelligent; anyway they had good feet. But they didn't *want* to obey me. I had to bring out their intelligence by reeducating them in my cellar. With the four brown hamsters, like with my kids, I was their master. I'd find out how intelligent the hamsters were by watching how quickly they listened to me.

"When I got them home to East Fletcher Street," Joe continued, "I saw that there was no way I could make shoes and wedges for my hamsters. Their feet were too tiny. But I knew I could go on with the second part of the experiment, the connection between obedience and intelligence, even without the shoes.

"To make sure I didn't get the hamsters mixed up—they all looked alike, you know, all the same color brown, same size—I put a name tag on the right rear leg of each one. I called them Winko, Popsicle, Jellyroll, and Humpty Dumpty.

"Then I put them into a large cage with a small wheel in it. I knew that the best way to test their intelligence and durability was on the wheel. If they had intelligence, they would listen to me; if they had durability, they'd listen and survive. To obey is one test of intelligence; to survive is another. Right?"

"Joe, how in the world did you expect the hamsters to 'listen' to you when they don't speak any human language? Did you train them by hand signals?"

"I spoke to them in English like I'm talking to you. I pulled up a chair right next to the cage and sat down. I told the hamsters everything I was going to do. It was very important to the future of mankind, I said, that they obey me. I told them their feet were too small for me to make shoes and wedges. But I promised to make them little hats and suits—even though I'm not a tailor—if they listened to me and survived. Flora, they understood every word I said!"

"What did the hamsters answer you?"

"Nothing! That was my second disappointment with them. First, I found I couldn't make shoes and wedges for their feet. Then I couldn't get them interested in my experiment. They didn't even perk up their ears when I told them about the hats and suits. But I knew they understood me, all right; they played foxy to throw me off my guard. They didn't listen, didn't seem to want to *get* it!

"While I talked, they *ignored* me. One would hop on the wheel and make it turn with the motion of his feet on the little rungs. Or they'd nibble food I'd put in the cage. One smart-ass kept eyeballing me with his little brown eyes; then he lay down in a corner and sulked. They were all boys, by the way. I didn't know how old they were.

"Finally, I realized I wasn't getting anywhere. I stopped talking and started the experiment. They'd listen to me now or they wouldn't survive.

"I got a pencil with an eraser on it and used the eraser end to force one of them—it was Winko—to get on the wheel and start trotting. I faced the wheel on its exit side, kept Winko moving by prodding him with the pencil. I wanted to see how long he could keep that wheel going around and around and around before he collapsed and died.

"But really I wanted him to *live*, Flora! If he lived, then my experiment would be a success by bringing out his intelligence and durability. I kept prodding him, *commanded* him to live. I said, 'Winko, stay alive no matter what!'

"I stopped to take a break. If I let Winko rest for too long, he'd get strong again. I didn't want that. The *best* way was the nonstop way. But *I* had to have a little rest. It was now two A.M. I'd been experimenting on Winko since four P.M.—except for a few short breaks. I hadn't eaten a thing because I was too excited.

"I was on vacation from Mahoney's shop during this time. I could work the experiment right through the night into the next day, then into the next night, and so on. I'd catch a sandwich from the kitchen, and an hour or two of sleep on the couch, which was in the living room near the cage. Then I'd get up to continue the experiment with the same hamster.

"The tags told me which one I had been working with. But dozing on the couch during a break, I'd worry that the hamsters might switch name tags with each other to confuse me, make me screw up my experiment.

"At three A.M. I went back to the cage, picked out Winko by his tag. I prodded him back into the wheel, kept him moving it around and around. He urinated, out of fear, I guess. So I commanded him to be brave, to stop urinating. But Winko wouldn't listen, wouldn't obey. A day and a half after I had started the experiment, Winko collapsed in the wheel and died.

"I felt terrible. I was like a parent to him. He hadn't listened to me, so now he was dead, no fault of *mine*, I thought. If he'd obeyed me, he could have gone on running that wheel forever, Flora, *forever*!

"Gently I picked up his furry little body. It was still warm. I carried him into the backyard, dug a hole, and buried him without marker or tombstone.

"Winko's three friends suffered the same fate: I prodded each one, in his turn, into the wheel. He ran the wheel around and around; then urinated and died.

"I had been a parent to all four of them. They disappointed me: Their feet were too small; they wouldn't listen to me when I sat at the cage and talked to them or gave them orders while they were running the wheel; and even though I told them not to, they up and died on me.

"By the end of six days, four little mounds of solid-packed earth covered Winko, Popsicle, Jellyroll, and Humpty Dumpty in my backyard. I got down on my knees, stayed there on the damp earth near their mounds a long time, prayed for their souls. I prayed that they would listen at least to God and behave themselves in that great golden cage beyond the stars. Amen, A-*men*, Flora!

"Then I went back into the house. I sank into the couch and slept for eighteen hours straight."

Joe took a deep breath and covered his face with his hands. Even though it was terribly hot in the jail, he was shivering.

"Joe, what would you have done," I asked, "if your experiment had succeeded?"

"Oh, I had great plans, Flora," he replied sadly. "I would have built a huge laboratory, with a big wheel in it for big animals like elephants and lions. Then I would've gotten human beings—convicts from prisons and crazy people from the funny farms—and run all of them through the experiment. I'd have had shoes and wedges for the big animals and the people.

"I would've found out how to keep people alive forever and ever and no one would *ever* die! That was God's commandment to me, when I was fifteen and He told me to do the experiments with the wedges and shoes.

"If we all had the correct adjustment of shoes to feet, there'd be no more wars. We'd know how to get along with each other, how to solve problems. There'd be no more hate, only love. No more sickness, no crimes, no one locked up in prisons and funny farms.

"I'd started with myself when I was fifteen, putting the wedges into my shoes to get the proper lineup of feet to legs to brain so that I could correct myself and conquer what was conquering me. The feet control the brain. They're God's magic gift to us. But we've messed them up, Flora, messed them up! If I could only take you through the world to show you the billions of sick, godless feet! *That's* why I've done over forty thousand experiments—not only to correct myself, but also to save mankind!"

When Joe awoke from his long sleep, he was suddenly appalled by what he had done. He had already destroyed inanimate things, but before the hamsters, he had never put a living creature to death. When Hilda, his first wife, had demanded money so that she could abort her second pregnancy, Joe had been horrified. He had refused to give her the money, told her to behave herself and to have their baby.

In those days, Joe had held life sacred; even death by natural causes, such as disease, old age, and Betty's two miscarriages, had seemed to him to be unnatural. He had felt that anything that was the enemy of life was cursed. But now in six days he had killed four little hamsters, and he knew that the Devil and all the other fallen angels were waiting to hurl him into the rotten mouth of Death's Hell.

In setting up what Stevie, Mary Jo, and Joey called "the torture chamber," Joe was giving evidence of the same combination of delusion and sadism that he displayed with the hamsters. With the hamsters the delusion was a scientific experiment; with the children it was parental guidance and discipline.

"With Stevie, Joey, and Mary Jo I wore the disguise of 'now you'll behave.' But now I realize that I took great pleasure in punishment that combined sex and sadism. I threw pins at Mary Jo's exposed body, and flogged Joey with my homemade cat-o'-nine-tails. I also brutalized Stevie, though I don't remember in what way."

It was the admission, perhaps the confession, of a man who, in talking with me about his past, had glimmers of its meaning.

At the time Joe inflicted the tortures he, of course, had no glimmers. He imposed his special brand of sadistic "instruction" whenever a child failed him by not making a sale during the door-to-door selling or, as in the case of Mary Jo, by not picking a winning horse. Torture was also meted out for what Mary Jo described as "doing stuff."

The "stuff" that Stevie, Joey, and later Michael did included, collectively, larceny in local stores, in a blind man's house, and from trucks, and the snatching of a purse from an elderly lady. "Stuff" also included running away, stealing signal flares and other property from freight cars in the railroad yard, stripping cars for spare parts, and setting fires to tool sheds and in the abandoned John Bromley

Sons factory. On July 3, 1971, Joey was arrested for shouting obscenities at a policeman who told him to stop dumping trash in the streets. Mary Jo smashed furniture when she had a tantrum, and often played hookey from school.

The children "bumped" school frequently, preferring the barbarous and lively education of the street to the inactivity of classrooms. Joey was on a cruise of schools: Sheppard to Daniel Boone to Douglas. Boone was for the worst kids in the city, and when Joey was there he was the worst kid in the worst school in Philadelphia. When he tried to get a male teacher fired, Joe sided with the teacher. The teacher was not fired. Joey lasted at Boone less than three weeks. He was sent to the Douglas School, an institution for the retarded and disturbed.

"Stuff" was also sex in a multitude of modalities and positions. Joe was distressed because Mary Jo was "dating" older boys, and Joey was having sex, both heterosexual and homosexual.

One afternoon, when Joey was eleven, he and Mary Jo, then twelve, sold "blow jobs" to fourteen boys on a roof that overlooked a Kensington playground. Mary Jo stood at the foot of the stairs that led to the roof and collected fifty cents from each of Joey's customers.

Some wanted their money back, claiming that Joey had cheated them by not bringing them to orgasm. Joey was an expert at making deals: He told them that the price of each appointment was fifty cents for the first two minutes, that it wasn't *his* fault if a few of them didn't "come." If they wanted more, they'd have to pay twenty-five cents for each additional minute.

Joe took Stevie, Joey, or Mary Jo—never more than one at a time—down to the cellar only after midnight. At exactly midnight of whatever day he had decided he was going to "reeducate" one of this crew, he had the hallucination of a huge clock emerging from smoky darkness pierced by flashes of lightning. Each hour on the face of the clock was represented by its proper Arabic numeral, except for the number twelve. In its place directly above the pointing hands was a white human skull. Joe listened to the clock's twelve slow somber strokes. As the last stroke died away, he looked at his watch: one and a half minutes after twelve; the clock was never late.

Then the image vanished, and Joe climbed the stairs, walked

154

down the hall, opened the door of the bedroom where the child to be "reeducated" was sleeping.

"The itch in the palm of my right hand was a signal that one of the kids had done stuff," Joe told me. "It didn't make any difference, Flora, whether that particular kid had done anything that day or not. I knew *all three of them* were doing stuff, including disobedience at home and foul-mouthing me and Betty and each other. 'Stuff' went on practically every day.

"But the itch was the signal for that particular kid on that particular day. I'd feel it on my right palm like a creeping thing and I'd hear the voice. It said Mary Jo. Or Joey. Or Stevie. I knew it was the voice of the Devil, who had appeared to me at the time of the Janney and East Fletcher Street fires. The Devil had reasserted himself in 1969. Although not present in April of that year, when I first descended the hole, the Devil had been a goading voice when two months later I started my program for reeducating the kids.

"At midnight I'd see the clock and the skull coming out of the smoke and darkness, with the lightning flashing. It was scary, Flora.

"I knew I was 'going out'—that is, ceasing to be the normal me— whenever I got the itch and heard the voice. I'd get a headache, then I 'went out.' I knew it was happening, but I couldn't control it. Again it was 'it' that controlled me.

"I was actually changed. My thinking became different. It wasn't like other people's thinking at all. My concern moved from visible things of this world to the world of invisible things when I got the itch and heard the voice.

"And that's the adventure, Flora. You're still Joe Kallinger. But you get this whole new way of thinking."

"Can you tell me, Joe, what the itch, the voices, the 'it' are that control you?"

"Ah, yeah," he replied in a soft voice. "Yeah. The itch, the voices, the 'it' are like—like, well, uh . . ." He hesitated, took a sip of water, then clasped his hands tightly in front of him, his eyes vague. "Like the spirits in January, yeah, the spirits in January."

In a stumbling whisper he repeated the phrase "spirits in January" three or four times.

Then we were both silent. I had not heard about the "spirits in

January" and didn't press him for a recollection that seemed to trouble him so much and that, I felt sure, he would talk about again. Furthermore I did not want the vagaries of the itch, the voices, the "it" explained in terms of the "spirits in January." I wanted something more concrete and understandable. He went on:

"I was becoming a whole system of signals, a private world unto myself. There was the chant that came from inside of me in the East Hagert Street hole. And the signal of the itchy right palm came soon after the hole.

"I wanted to be like everybody else," he said wistfully. "But what was normal for others was abnormal for me. The abnormal was *my* normal; delusions were real and reality was delusion. I'm just some kind of nut, huh, Flora?"

A few moments before Joe had talked almost incoherently about "the spirits in January." Now he was showing extraordinary insight. These shifts always amazed me, but they were part of the episodic nature of his madness. He was psychotic, but psychosis did not always block his intelligence and awareness. I learned that an insane person is not insane all the time.

The children did not think him insane, although they had of course seen a great transformation in him. He was only intermittently the father Mary Jo had described as "spoiling" her "rotten." The "instruction" had accomplished two things: Now the children always feared and sometimes hated him. The delinquencies the "instruction" was designed to remedy continued unabated and became more numerous. For the children stayed away from home as much as possible.

The seeds of the deteriorating relationship between father and children had been sown in the family's East Fletcher Street home. The roses in that backyard became symbols for me of what Joe had been saying of the normal perverted into abnormality by the "it" that controlled him and that he hadn't been able to define. In the autumn of 1964 he told Stevie, Mary Jo, and Joey to plant in the backyard roots of rose bushes that he had bought. Through most of the summer of 1965 Joe and the children took pleasure in the beautiful crimson roses.

But one afternoon in early August 1965 (before Joe's third East Fletcher Street fire), Joe and the children were walking among the rose bushes. Very suddenly Joe plucked a rose from its bush and tore the petals into fragments. His face became wrinkled with tension, his lips compressed, his eyes hard and cruel. He screamed a command, "Tear up the bushes, destroy the roses. All of them, understand, you kids?"

The children looked up at him in distress, did not move, could not comprehend the order he had hurled at them.

"Every last one of them right down to the roots. And watch out for the thorns!"

He took long strides in circles around the garden, crushing roses and bushes as he went. He pushed Stevie and Michael, looked ominously at Mary Jo. "You kids do as I say right now! I am the king. These flowers are my enemies. Destroy them!" He watched while the children obeyed his orders. "Pull out those petals! Rip them apart! Scatter them over the ground in little pieces!"

An hour later, the rose garden had been destroyed. The backyard was now a wasteland. Only the four grave mounds of the hamsters, which were nearby, were untouched. On them some fragments of petals had fallen.

The castle was the place where Joe thought of himself as a king. But the castle was also Joe himself.

In the cellar Joe inflicted punishments that made Stevie, Joey, and Mary Jo call it "the torture chamber." In the castle that was himself, Joe's psychosis inflicted torment on *him*.

But for three weeks in July, 1971, the torment lifted: the "torture chamber" was unused and Joe himself was free from hallucinations and unwanted thoughts. He was also sexually potent without the old reliance on fantasies of cutting and on a knife to squeeze. And he had an unaccustomed feeling of well-being, even of euphoria.

The three weeks began one night as Joe was about to close the store and Mary Jo appeared at his side. He thought it remarkable that, in spite of the "punishments" he had inflicted upon her, she still came to him just to chat. This assured him that the love she had for him had not died.

Leaning over the work table, she talked about things that he thought more properly she should be discussing with her mother. He listened, but said nothing. Memories crowded in on him, especially

157

of the comfort he had found in talking to her about the malignant memories of his childhood.

She was only twelve years and four months old, but as he looked at her dark hair and eyes, her comely Madonna face, her lithe figure in jeans and T-shirt, he had feelings about her that he had never had before.

It was growing late. It was time to close the store. In the gathering darkness Mary Jo seemed to him like a flower that has been looked at.

"Mary Jo," he said, "you're going to be a beautiful woman."

"Thanks, Daddy," she replied.

That night Joe thought of himself as a gardener nurturing a flower, and in delight he watched its petals open. Through the next three weeks the gardener rejoiced.

I had known nothing about the gardener and his flower when I talked to Joe about Mary Jo in the Bergen County Jail in 1976. But I sensed the intensity of his feelings for her.

A few days later I was with Betty when she returned home from visiting her husband in the jail. As Betty got out of the car, Mary Jo rushed up to her and asked excitedly, "Did you see Daddy?" Again I could see that there was a strong attachment between father and daughter. In the Hackensack court, spectators had marveled at how Mary Jo, having been abused by her father, could tell the press that, when her father was well, she wanted him to come home. The press didn't understand the strong attachment between father and daughter (nor Mary Jo's awareness that he had abused her because he was mentally ill). And I didn't really understand the relationship either until a year later when, at Camden County Jail, Joe talked to me about it.

"In July, 1971," he said, "we spent six wonderful evenings together in a period of three weeks. We did a lot of things, Flora, went out to dinner, just the two of us. One day, to celebrate the beauty of the previous night, I bought her a necklace; and I got her other presents not because it was Christmas or her birthday or she needed something. I bought them because during those weeks she had a very special meaning for me."

He paused, looked at me steadily, got up and paced. After a few moments in which he seemed to be plunged in recollection, he said,

"I broke it up when I realized that it couldn't go on. That's when I wished that she wasn't my daughter. But I couldn't tear her out of my heart the way I made the children tear up the roses at East Fletcher Street. I love deeply when I love. Too deeply. I take it too seriously, too deeply like everything else. It becomes part of an obsession. I have a terrible feeling that I wasn't any good in Mary Jo's life. Those three weeks were the greatest happiness I've ever known."

When Joe ended this relationship, he plucked up and destroyed the happiness of feeling and behaving like a normal man within an abnormal situation. During those three weeks he had not needed to squeeze a knife or to have violent and bloody fantasies to sustain his potency. During that period his personality had changed: he no longer felt incomprehensible rages, or the need to abuse his children or take refuge in his "dark retreat," the hole in the East Hagert Street house. He was free, during those three weeks, of unwanted thoughts and the hallucinations under whose spell he thought he was receiving commands from Hell.

Joe's happiness grew out of the delusion that a father and his daughter could freely "date" each other in a culture that condemns such a relationship. For a "normal" man—one who is not psychologically disabled—the happiness of a relationship with a wife or sweetheart has exactly the same qualities that Joe's relationship with his daughter had. The former, however, grows and flourishes with the approval of society. The latter could not.

He ended it. Morally it was right for him to do so. But in a very special sense, doing so was *wrong* for *him*. The tragedy was that the ending of this chapter of his life brought to a close a period free from hallucinations and sadism. Operating under a single delusion (with respect to his daughter), Joe had actually been happy for three weeks. The other aspects of his psychosis had been temporarily put to rest.

Joe had functioned well in maintaining a delusion; after he faced the reality of social mores, he slipped back into his old psychotic eccentricities. He reverted to having intercourse with the aid of the old bloody fantasies and the knife to support them. He also returned to a life ridden by hallucinations, unwanted thoughts, and the acting out of his sadistic impulses.

To save himself Joe worked obsessively on his orthopedic experi-

159

ments and made his lonely pilgrimages to his East Hagert Street hole even more frequently than in the past.

His mind continued to dwell on Mary Jo, at first nostalgically and tenderly. But in time he became angry because she was dating others. Toward these others, his jealousy flared. The boys she dated became his enemies; dark, persecutory figures even more threatening than the imagined CIA spies that in a delusion he used to think had inhabited Harry Comer's legislative office.

One night, as Joe was on the way home from his East Hagert Street hole, he saw Mary Jo walking hand in hand with a nineteen-year-old neighborhood boy named Freddy Prince. They were laughing and kissed each other on the lips. To avoid a confrontation, Joe retreated into a hallway.

The next day Joe noticed that Mary Jo was wearing a new necklace.

"Where's the one I gave you?" he asked.

"I have it, Daddy," she said. "But this one's new. Freddy-boy gave it to me."

Joe ripped the necklace off his daughter's neck.

Four days before Christmas, 1971, Joe again saw Mary Jo and Freddy on the street. Again Joe avoided them. At home he lectured his daughter about dating "older men" and ordered her to "quit" Freddy Prince.

Mary Jo knew that Joe objected to her dating Freddy not because of the disparity in ages but because, as she told me, "Daddy acted as if I were his girlfriend. He was jealous of any boy I dated."

Joe also wanted Mary Jo "to quit" the Strong family. Kensingtonians who lived only a few blocks away from the Kallingers, the Strongs made their home open to the Kallinger children. The Strongs had three children, two sons and a daughter: twenty-three-year-old Johnny, nineteen-year-old Willie, and thirteen-year-old Susan, who was Mary Jo's best friend. Joe was convinced that Mary Jo and Willie were lovers.

"I had no evidence," Joe told me, "that Mary Joe and Willie Strong were sleeping together. But I was sure of it. I didn't *really* know. But I knew."

For Joe, Willie Strong and Freddy Prince were the embodiments and extensions of past hatreds. They were the boys who, long ago

160

at the Howard Movie Theater, necked with girls while Joe sat alone. Even more important, they were Hans Ibler, the man to whom Joe had lost Hilda, his first wife. Joe also expressed through the mask of a father's disapproval the wrath he harbored in the delusion of being the betrayed lover of his own daughter.

"The Strong family was the source of my troubles not only with my daughter, but also with my sons," Joe told me in a combination of anger and sadness. "The Strongs turned my children against me."

Joe blamed the Strongs, but he also blamed himself for what he called "loose reins." He had tightened the reins when he began to take Mary Jo to and from school. He was repeating what had been done to him as a child. But by barricading his daughter against his "rivals," he was also expressing his surviving feelings of jealousy. He wanted to make sure that she didn't "bump" school to spend the day at the home of his enemies the Strongs.

New angers seemed to blend with old ones. Daily life became increasingly unreal and dreamlike for Joe. Sometimes he was fully awake and responsive to the requirements of the moment, but at other times his perception of reality was completely distorted by his delusions and hallucinations. He was often drowsy, and his speech patterns began to change. He often spoke with long pauses, invented new words, and rhymed inappropriately.

Voices came to him more frequently than in the past. He thought they came not from inside himself but from the external world. He could not distinguish them from those of people who actually talked to him. When he had set up the punishment area in his cellar, the Devil was a goading voice. But the voice had changed. It was no longer that of the Devil. "A force was manipulating me, Flora," he told me. "I didn't know what it was. But it had to be something other than myself."

On New Year's Day 1972, Joe, who was taking inventory of his stock in the cellar, looked up and recognized the large figure in a white light that had appeared to him twenty years earlier. Joe was then fifteen; now he was thirty-five. The figure spoke only one sentence:

"Joseph, *I* control you now!"

The light faded, the figure vanished. "When the voices came from the devil," Joe told me, "I didn't always have to execute the order.

But after 1972 they were coming from God, and I had to do exactly what I was told."

As Joe listened to the voice that he hallucinated was from God, he had a sense of power. For he was now under the delusion that God sanctioned and sanctified everything that Joe Kallinger did under His orders. Now that in his delusion he was carrying out orders from the Supreme Being, the Maximum Leader of the Universe, what was wrong for other people became right for Joe.

With this delusional rationale Joe became increasingly punitive with his children. But the children were rebellious: Mary Jo continued dating Freddy-boy Prince and visiting the Strongs, where she often spent the night. Joey would run away, then telephone Joe to take him back, and Joe would pick him up no matter where he was and bring him home.

On the afternoon of Saturday, January 22, 1972, Mary Jo and Joey left the house together and didn't return that night. When they were still gone the next morning, Joe didn't call the police as he usually did when just Joey was missing. He didn't call the Strongs because they were his enemies. But he also didn't call other friends of Mary Jo and Joey. He didn't trust anybody. Besides, Joe Kallinger, who took orders from God, wasn't going to ask for help from more mortals. At nine o'clock Sunday morning he got into a taxi and searched Kensington.

It was the old wanderlust that drove him onward. As a child he had wandered because of rootlessness; then he was searching for something of which he could become a part. He had picked up discarded objects on the way because he could be a parent to them, as later he had thought of himself as parent to the four hamsters.

Now he was looking for what was part of him, and he was afraid that he had lost. He had realized, or so he thought, his family dream by having six children. But in the punishment area in his cellar he had distorted and perverted that dream. As a result, the dream had shown signs of collapse. Now Joe thought there had been mutiny in his castle because Mary Jo and Joey had run away together.

As the taxi combed Kensington, Joe's paranoid suspicions and jealousies wrote the scenario of sex scenes he imagined Joey—and particularly Mary Jo—had been involved in since they had left home Saturday afternoon.

They were making a fool of him! It was his duty as a father, he told himself, to find Mary Jo and Joey and punish them so they would never run away from him again.

Joe could feel pain in his temples. It was the same kind of pain that had led to his hospitalization in St. Mary's Hospital and Hazleton State Hospital. His temples throbbed with the fury and despair not only of the present, but of a lifetime. The throbbing, like the primitive beat of a tom-tom, had a steady, compelling rhythm.

"I knew," Joe told me, "there was something inside of me that was going wrong. It was as if my brain were shutting off and unwanted thoughts—deviant thoughts, as I think of them now—had me in their possession.

"As soon as the mind gets back into the body, it rejects these thoughts violently. You have a broader outlook when normal. When you're in this narrow corner, your family, your work, the promises you made to customers have no meaning. You're running to get out and find this other world. You're walking in a blinded way. You have no direction."

Joe was still in this "other world" of hallucinations and violent fantasies after coming home from the morning's futile search. He paced away most of the afternoon, but toward evening he decided to go out again. A gun was not the weapon of the knife-ridden hallucinations and fantasies that were part of his psychosis, but he decided to take with him a .45 automatic with five rounds in it that, for security reasons, he kept in the store.

He put the gun in his belt and then put on his overcoat. He planned to use the gun as a tactical weapon to scare the mutineers, Mary Jo and Joey, into submission. Then he asked the members of the family who were home—Betty, eleven-year-old Michael, and nine-year-old James—to come with him. Unlike the mutineers, they had not rebelled against him and still represented his family dream. As the taxi cruised Kensington's narrow streets, he took comfort in their presence.

He had almost given up hope of finding the mutineers and restoring them to the family when through the taxi window he saw them coming out of the Midway Movie Theater at Allegheny and Kensington Avenues. Joe noted with loathing that Susan, Johnny, and Willie Strong were with Mary Jo and Joey.

The taxi followed as Mary Jo, Joey, and the three Strongs, unaware of what was happening, strolled along Kensington Avenue. When they neared Somerset Street, Joe asked the driver to pull up alongside the curb. After the driver had done so, Joe jumped out of the cab. Mary Jo, Joey, and the three Strongs saw him and ran swiftly away. Joe's children were running together, but the Strongs took a different route.

Joe told the driver to follow Mary Jo and Joey. He was angry at their obvious insubordination and also at what seemed to him a clear indication that they didn't love him. If they loved me, he thought, they would come to me and do as I say. But the children's obvious fear of him also pleased him, for it would assure their capture.

Twice the children turned back to see whether Joe was coming. The second time he had the driver pull up the cab alongside them. Joe got out and pointed the gun at his two children. Then twice he pointed the muzzle of the gun toward the open door of the cab, as if to say, "Go in."

Later Mary Jo told me, "From the *look* on Daddy's face, we were sure that if we didn't do as he said, he would shoot us!"

Joe followed Mary Jo and Joey into the taxi. Nobody spoke. "I couldn't believe it," Betty would tell me. "I never saw Joe use a gun before."

Winter darkness had fallen. The cab stopped. They got out. Betty and the children walked with jerky, nervous steps single-file into the house. They sensed danger.

Inside, Joe said to Betty: "Don't take off your coat. Go out and buy pizzas. Take Mike and Jimmy with you."

The street door closed. Joe stared coldly at Joey and Mary Jo. Tonight the palm of his right hand didn't have to itch, a huge clock didn't have to emerge from smoky darkness, and the hour didn't have to be after midnight. The roses in the East Fletcher Street backyard had been Joe's enemies. He had destroyed them. Joey and Mary Jo were his enemies now. He was no longer interested in inflicting pain for the purpose of "education." Tonight he wanted vengeance.

"The moment I saw Mary Jo and Joey with the Strongs," Joe told me, "I knew my children closed ranks with the enemy. Flora, I

164

could kill myself when I think of what I did after Betty and our two younger boys left the house when I told them to get pizza. Maybe you'll never speak to me again. That's why, even though you kept asking about it, I avoided—should I have said 'evaded'?—telling you.

"But I'm going to tell it straight. I can't remember *all* the details. Much of it seems vague, I remember what happened like bits and pieces of a dream. I remember the essentials. I remember them too well. I could kill myself."

I had heard the story from Mary Jo. I had read Mary Jo's and Joey's testimony at the trial. I had read the newspaper stories. Now I would hear the story from Joe.

"When we were in the cab," he said, sitting down, "I thought maybe I would have a court-martial. Their crime against me was great. But when we got home I received instructions from God. There was the same large figure in a white light that had come to me when I was fifteen—that had appeared again on New Year's Day, which was just twenty-three days earlier.

"I told Mary Jo to wait on the sofa-bed. I took Joey into the kitchen, sat him down in a red wing chair, and handcuffed his right hand to the handle of the refrigerator. To scare him I dropped a butcher knife on the floor. He screamed and cussed, but I was used to that. He loved his daddy when I was what he called his 'fun and games dad.' We would spray-paint the outside of his school together and go on other crazy adventures. Sometimes I made him a delegate to carry out my insane wishes. But the moment I showed him who was boss, he bad-mouthed me. No respect. Anyway I had him handcuffed. He was my prisoner. He could not get away. I could turn my attention to Mary Jo. That night she was the *big* enemy.

"She was sitting on the sofa-bed waiting for me, just as I'd told her to do. She knew better than to try to get away. That pleased me. Yes, she was clever. Both Betty and I regarded her as the most intelligent of our children. And beautiful. You know her, Flora. You know how beautiful she is. Striking. Yes, very striking. I seem to be hedging, getting away from my story.

"Well, I came up to her, right in front of her, and stood there looking down at her beautiful, frightened face. Vengeance moved inside me like electric power. I loved my daughter and I hated her.

We didn't say anything to each other. There was total silence between us. I could hear Joey in the kitchen straining against the handcuffs and shifting around in the wing chair. Every so often his cussing exploded right into the living room. It made Mary Jo jump, but *I* was as steady as a hangman's noose.

"In my hands I had a spatula I got from the kitchen and a rope from the cellar. On the floor right next to the sofa-bed I placed a little kerosene stove, all primed and ready to go, that I'd got from my store.

"In my pocket I had the switchblade knife I always carried. It gave me the same feeling of confidence I got from squeezing a knife during sexual intercourse. You remember it was only during those beautiful three weeks with Mary Jo that to feel at ease I didn't need a knife in my hand or a switchblade in my pocket.

"But on the night we're talking about, I took the switchblade out of my pocket and pressed the little button on the handle. The thin blade shot out, and I put the point against Mary Jo's neck. I told her that if she screamed, I'd stab her. I ordered her to take off all her clothes except her bra and panties. She did.

"I had never done anything like this before, but I sounded like a real criminal. Oh, yes, when I was a kid I did something like this on those bus trips and under Silver Bridge. But I got cold feet. Didn't do anything else.

"With Mary Jo I did. With the rope I bound her wrists behind her and her feet ankle to ankle. Then I placed the spatula on top of the kerosene stove. I guess it took about five minutes for the spatula to get hot. I waited. Mary Jo waited. She didn't know for what.

"I picked up the spatula. It was hot. A spatula isn't a knife, but I held it in my left hand, the knife-squeezing hand during sexual intercourse, what would later become the stabbing hand.

"I got on my knees in front of my daughter. I leaned toward her. She cringed. The voice of God was commanding me to burn Mary Jo. It had commanded me as soon as we came into the house.

"We have to burn to create, burn to purify. I hoped that when Mary Jo felt the pain from the spatula, all the pure cells in her body would rush to come back. I hoped that they would transplant into her body the original goodness that I believed Freddy Prince, Willie Strong and maybe others had driven out.

"I leaned toward her again. Her eyes were glassy. My left hand moved with the hot spatula to the inner part of her right thigh. The thigh was bare. The panties didn't cover it. I pressed the hot spatula against her bare flesh. I think she screamed. I said over and over again in a sort of singsong, 'You will never run away from me again.'

"When the spatula cooled off, I took it off her flesh and put it back on the stove to get hot. I went into the kitchen to deal with Joey. But I'll hold that for later. Let me go on with Mary Jo.

"When I came back to her, I pressed the hot spatula against her thigh again, in the exact same spot, about a little more than a quarter of an inch from her vagina. She was shaking violently. But she was lucky I didn't do what I started to do."

Joe paused and drank some water.

"I don't know how many times I reheated the spatula and pressed it against her thigh. I think it was only twice. Mary Jo says more. But suddenly I changed. The change seems to have come when I noticed that on the cold spatula there were a few pieces of burnt flesh. I took the spatula into the kitchen, washed it, put it back into a drawer. I went back to Mary Jo. I checked her wound: She had a circle of discolored flesh on the inside of her right thigh between three and four inches in diameter. I untied her hands and ankles. Then I went into the store to correct myself through my orthopedic experiments. I really needed correction *this* time."

We were silent for a few minutes. Then I voiced my perplexity.

"Joe, you wanted vengeance. But at the same time you wanted to purify her through burning. Why did you burn her thigh rather than some other part of her body?"

"So she wouldn't fuck," he replied.

"You mean the scar would last forever and embarrass her?"

"I wasn't thinking about forever. Just about the immediate time. The wound would be sore and would hurt. When you hurt, you can't fuck."

"But you told me," I said, "that you weren't really sure what she was doing with the boys she was dating."

"I also told you," he replied, "that I didn't know but I *knew*! I told you that I had to have my revenge for what she had done to me. She had conspired with the enemy."

"Did jealousy play a part?" I asked.

167

"A big part," he replied.

"Why did you say she was lucky you didn't do what you started to do?"

"I was going to put the hot spatula into her vagina and shove it right on up into her guts. Sizzle the badness out of her so that the goodness could come back. God gave me that instruction when He appeared after we came home."

We were both tense. He looked to see if I was angry with him. But though I was horrified, I knew the action against his daughter and son stemmed from the sadism reinforced by his psychosis. He had already admitted to me that he took great pleasure in inflicting pain.

"You believe what you're doing while you're doing it," he explained. "You believe it is right. It's a drive all its own. It's a force all its own. It is what it is at the time.

"But let me tell you about what I did to Joey. Like Mary Jo, he had joined the enemy. But what I did to him wasn't as dramatic as what I did to Mary Jo. I removed the metal head of a hammer. With the wooden handle I hit Joey on the hands, the face, all over. But mostly I struck his knees. With each blow I said, 'So you won't run away again!'

" 'Want to bet?' he snapped at me. '*I'm* the one who makes all the rules. You'll learn that, you fucker!'

"I wasn't surprised. He was always cussing me out. He deliberately did things to tease me and get on my nerves. I loved Joey, but I also feared him. I removed the handcuffs when I went into the kitchen to wash the spatula I'd used on Mary Jo.

"Well," Joe went on, "I freed Joey and Mary Jo. Then, as I've already said, I went into the store to work on my orthopedic experiments.

"I was frightened by what I had done. I was also frightened because this was the first time that I had put my fantasies and hallucinations into action. From the time I was twelve years old I had had fantasies about cutting open a woman's stomach or cutting off her breasts. In recent years I also had fantasies of sticking her with pins and of burning her with a cigarette or a hot iron. Mary Jo was a woman. I had burnt her with a hot spatula.

"From the store I went back into the living room to look for

Mary Jo and Joey. They were upstairs. I called to them. They came down. I gave each of them five dollars in coins. When I was a kid, I had stolen coins from my adoptive parents' closet to get rid of my loneliness by bribing kids to go to the movies with me—I paid for their seats. I guess I was doing the same thing with Mary Jo and Joey: bribing them to forgive and forget what I'd done to them, bribing them to love me. Anyway, we seemed to be friends again. Betty had called to ask whether she could come back home. I said yes. The whole family sat down to a late meal of pizza.

"But why did Betty leave me alone with Mary Jo and Joey? She shouldn't have trusted them to me that night. She had seen the gun I used to get them into the taxi. But she allowed me to be alone with her children. Why couldn't Betty save me from me?

"But I knew my orthopedic experiments couldn't save me, either. They were a failure. If they hadn't failed, I wouldn't have burned Mary Jo. And *I* failed, Flora. When I married at sixteen, I went out there to build a family. I had a family dream. And it failed. I failed.

"When I was fifteen, God had instructed me to learn to heal myself and mankind through my orthopedic experiments. I had tried to do both. But He had also ordered me to burn my daughter. I did. Then I knew I could not save myself. But I also knew that I could not save mankind. How could I save the world when I couldn't even save myself? That night I decided to destroy what I couldn't save."

10 The Naked King

The guard sat at a large desk with a small lamp on it. He watched over the fifty prisoners who slept on parallel rows of hard cots, head to foot, on the other side of the high section of wire mesh.

Joe Kallinger sat up on his cot. He stared through the wire mesh at the guard and couldn't believe it. During the day Joe had been at home, king of his turbulent castle. And now at night he was incarcerated in a dormitory of the Philadelphia Detention House.

I'm here because I'm unloved, Joe told himself. He looked up, hoping that the glowing hallucinated figure of God that had said to him, "Now *I* control you!" would appear in the Detention House to comfort him. But the Lord remained hidden from Joe. The only voice he heard was that of a prisoner nearby muttering in his troubled sleep.

I have nobody, Joe thought. No children, no wife, no mother, no father, no friends, no customers, no fellow shoe repairmen, no doctor, no minister, no God! Joe heard a chair scrape the floor. The guard got up from the desk, lit a cigarette, and paced slowly back and forth.

Joe decided that God was busy elsewhere, and no longer cared for His servant whom He had commanded to save mankind with the orthopedic experiments. They had failed, Joe Kallinger had failed, God had failed! Abject and depressed, Joe lay back on the cot. He put his forearm across his eyes while a deep shudder gripped his body.

"You will never run away from me again—never run away from me again—from me again—from me again!" Joe whispered. The words had the same rhythm that they had had exactly one week ago when he had pressed the hot spatula against the soft flesh of Mary Jo's thigh. Mutiny in the castle had led to a purge and a shift of power. The shift had led to his arrest on this night of Sunday, January 30, 1972.

This time not only Mary Jo and Joey but also Mike had run away from their father. They had gone to the combined 24th and 25th Police District, known as East Detectives, and had filed child-abuse charges against him. They had had him arrested and incarcerated in this place that smelled of disinfectants and stale sweat. Well, now the three of them could do whatever they damn well pleased! His castle was now theirs.

All week Joe had taken Mary Jo to and from school as usual, and had even had a conference at her school on Monday, January 24, the day after the burning. Mary Jo and Joey had gone out, seen friends, and had not been to a doctor about their injuries. Not once during the week had her father hurt Mary Jo. But Joey? Well, Joe had to admit to himself that during the week he had again handcuffed Joey to the refrigerator and had beaten him. Joe had never taken either of the two younger boys—Mike and Jimmy—down to the cellar. But this week Joe had hit Mike lightly with a belt.

Joe was horrified by his children's betrayal of him, especially Mary Jo's. In Joe's tortured mind, she had discarded him not only as her father but also as her lover. She had "sent him back"—to an institution—the way, when he was a child, his adoptive parents were always threatening to do. The feeling of abandonment he had had at St. Mary's Hospital when he was six years and nine months old he felt again in the Philadelphia Detention House at thirty-five.

Unable to sleep, Joe got up. He walked slowly down the narrow aisle between two parallel rows of cots toward the latrines that were in the back of the dormitory. They were wide open. Although he was alone, he could feel the inhibiting stares that by day he believed would assail him. As if he were being watched, and still under the small-penis delusion that had made him avoid public lavatories, he urinated not at one of the urinals, but by sitting on a toilet.

When he got up, he knew he was going to be sick. Leaning over the toilet bowl, he vomited in frustration and self-contempt. He slowly caught his breath and retraced his steps along a narrow aisle.

The next afternoon he was napping on his cot. When he awoke, he discovered in a pocket of his jumpsuit a large wad of toilet paper. He had no idea how it had gotten there. Another prisoner's silly joke? he wondered. Is this the way prisoners got their jollies? With the paper still in his pocket, he got off his cot and walked up to the wire mesh. He put the tips of his fingers on the strands of wire that formed the weave of the cage that imprisoned him. Gently shaking the metal strands, he thought that this was the kind of stuff behind which chickens and pigs were kept until they were slaughtered.

He imagined how his children would act if he were going to be executed. In fantasy, he could see them, waiting eagerly with the devilish Strongs near the place of execution. They would be making happy noises and throwing strips of leather and hammer handles into the air, Mary Jo leading them on like a cheerleader at a game. He could see Joey, avenged and triumphant, his spiteful eyes bright with hatred and exaltation, chanting, "I'm free! I'm free! I'm free!"

Pain throbbed fiercely in Joe's forehead. Objects on both sides of the wire mesh—the guard, his desk, the faces of the other prisoners, their cots—seemed to inflate like balloons. The ceiling light changed color from the hot white of illumination to cold blue and then to sea green. Nausea racked him.

A few minutes later, the objects returned slowly to normal size and the nausea stopped. The ceiling light did not change color. Joe walked to his cot. He ignored the other prisoners. The pain still throbbing in his head, he sat down on the cot and stared gloomily at the windows striped with steel bars.

This is the end, he thought. Everything is gone. The kids had me arrested. My business will fold up. I'll be ruined and bankrupt! My chain of shoe repair stores that I still hoped for after the judgment against me by the insurance company for one of the Fletcher Street fires—Joey would have succeeded me as owner and manager of this empire. Mary Jo would have become a lawyer. We would have lived in the suburbs together. Dead. Dead. Everything's dead and gone!

He took the toilet paper out of his pocket so that he could wipe the dampness off his face. He looked for a long moment at the paper. He put it back into his pocket, leaving a long piece of it hanging out.

172

He lit a match from a pack he had found on the floor. Cupping his hands, he carefully touched the paper with the flickering yellow flame. He then lit the whole pack, dropped it into the pocket of his jumpsuit, and waited.

He felt the heat on his skin. He prayed for a quick death.

"Hey, man, what the hell you doing?" one of the prisoners screamed at him. He grabbed Joe by the arm and pulled him out of bed, then slapped out the fire that had burned part of the jumpsuit. "You trying to kill yourself or something?"

A burly guard came up to Joe, who was lying on the floor. "What's going on?" he asked. "This ain't the Fourth of July, Kallinger!"

"It was an accident," Joe said.

"Sure!" the guard replied with sarcasm as he looked over the damage. "Follow me. Kallinger, you're a taxpayer's headache!"

Joe followed the guard, who continued to talk as they walked out of the cage:

"I think we'll just move you down to the front of the area to keep you out of trouble, keep our eyes on you. C'mon in for a body search."

In a small, private room the guard made his search and found nothing except the burned-out pack of matches. The guard called a medic to see whether Joe had burned himself. There was only a small, superficial burn on Joe's right leg.

Joe was moved into the first bed in the first row nearest the guard's desk at the extreme end of the dormitory so that he could be watched more closely. In Joe's file the guard wrote: "Suicide: High Risk."

Joe's first suicide attempt had been in the Hazleton State Hospital in 1959. This was his second. It was the result of what he regarded as his children's betrayal. But it was also the expression of his decision on the night he had burned Mary Jo's thigh. That night he had decided to destroy what he couldn't save.

Forty years! Thomas A. White, Joe's lawyer, told him that a conviction on the child-abuse charges could put him into prison for forty years.

The madness that had driven him to seek refuge in a hole, that had made him torture his children and want to kill himself, was no longer the enemy. It was replaced—temporarily—by the Common-wealth of Pennsylvania, its court and prosecutor, and by the Phila-delphia newspapers that had named Joe as an alleged child abuser. Convicted, he would spend the rest of his life in the slammer. The terror of the future made dim the horrors of the past.

Now Joe wanted to live. His fixed purpose was to win his case and to redeem his old outer life from the stigmata that had sullied it since his arrest. He wanted to walk out of the courtroom cleared of the charges and to read in the newspapers of his acquittal.

A guard removed the handcuffs. Joe sat down. On the other side of the desk in the City Hall office sat Dr. Francis H. Hoffman, chief psychiatrist of the Neuropsychiatric Division of the Philadelphia Court of Common Pleas. Joe, who had been a prisoner for a month and knew this was a pretrial psychiatric examination, felt that in this office he was about to confront one of his enemies. Behind bars for forty years drummed in Joe's mind.

"My children are one hundred percent lying," Joe replied. He now stood ready to deny the events of January 23 that led his children to have him arrested on January 30. Joe believed that anything he said at a pretrial psychiatric examination could be used against him in the court.

"The burnings and the beatings?"

"Not true! My daughter is lying!"

"Please tell me why you consider your daughter a liar. With a little more detail, please."

"You want examples?" Joe asked rhetorically as he leaned toward the doctor.

"There was the time my daughter and my oldest boy, Stephen, ran away. Nothing unusual for them to run away. Anyway, on this particular trip, they decided to make themselves look good. They tied themselves up in a freezer in the basement of an empty house not far from where I live. When the police found them there, the children accused some Puerto Ricans of tying them. That's the way the kids fooled the police and came out of their adventure looking like victims. That's their idea of fun. They were lying then. They're lying now."

Dr. Hoffman knew nothing about Joe's past or inner life. Yet on

174

the basis of this brief exchange, the doctor, as he later wrote in his report, was convinced that either Joe was "severely mentally ill or his children are the type that began the Salem witchcraft trials." He went on with the examination by saying, "Tell us about your health, Mr. Kallinger."

"It's beautiful," Joe replied. "I've never felt I was going crazy. I don't have a history of depression. I like life. My daughter is the one who needs help. I'm a sound person."

Joe had not been asked about going crazy, yet he had denied his old fear of madness.

"Have you ever thought you heard someone calling your name only to turn around and find nobody there?"

"Never!" Joe replied. In his report Dr. Hoffman later wrote that in denying a hallucination that is common to normal people, Mr. Kallinger had betrayed "paranoid defensiveness."

"No hallucinations or delusions?" the doctor asked.

"None."

"You were hospitalized in the psychiatric division of St. Mary's Hospital in 1958, weren't you?" Dr. Hoffman remarked as he glanced at a report on his desk.

"I was there for a rest," Joe insisted. "They put me in the psychiatric section. But I haven't seen a psychiatrist since."

Even when Dr. Hoffman asked whether Joe had ever had any seizure or period of unconsciousness, Joe did not talk about Hazleton.

Joe was glib about his relationship with his children. In the future, he said, he hoped the relationship would work out. He explained: "When one has kids, these things happen." And he asserted, "I'm emotionally healthy and quite average except that I'm a softie as a father."

When the doctor asked about sex, Joe was overwhelmed by agonizing memories that made him hesitate.

"Can you tell me about your sex life?" the doctor repeated.

"My sex life? There's nothing special about it. Married at sixteen and a half, divorced at twenty-two. Married again and living with the present Mrs. Kallinger for thirteen years. Happily. No problems. She's a good wife. I'm a good husband. A good provider. No cheating. Everything's beautiful."

Joe had concealed crucially significant memories. But to the trained ear of the psychiatrist, the intensity of Joe's denial and his paranoid defensiveness had made the concealment a revelation in itself.

During the interview Albert Levitt, a clinical psychologist, had sat to one side, listening but not participating. After the interview he administered a series of psychometric and projective tests. Psychometric tests have to do with mental measurement—the measurement of intelligence, mental traits and abilities, and the speed and precision of mental processes. Projective tests are used as a diagnostic tool in which the test material is so unstructured that any response will reflect a projection of some aspect of the subject's underlying personality and psychopathology. Among the most common projective tests are the Rorschach (inkblot) and the Thematic Apperception Test (TAT).

The tests indicated what has already been described in these pages: that Joe had problems caused by "sexual difficulties" and that there were times when he wasn't sure he was like other men. And, as Albert Levitt put it, "there seems to be some distrust as it concerns the female figure."

The distrust that Joe had developed in the past was now anchored in Mary Jo, who had exiled him from his castle, and also in Betty's weakness. Betty was warm, good-natured and loving, but she was also self-centered, childish, and passive. She could not discipline the children, and when they hurt themselves or were ill she became hysterical. As Joey told a court, "When we cut ourselves and are bleeding, Mom runs around in circles when we're bleeding." She leaned on Joe and did not perceive the necessity, as he put it, "to save me from me." He was the dominant force in the family partly out of inclination but also because Betty's withdrawal and passivity forced him into dominance.

The tests also revealed that Joe was able to make only superficial contact with other people and that he did not know when to advance toward them and when to withdraw from them; that he felt both inadequate and impotent; that he was riddled by suspicion and torn by tension. The tests disclosed, too, that his ideas were "morbid" and that he was primitive in his perceptions. Again the tests re-affirmed what has here been noted.

Joe showed the primitiveness of a man traveling the route of symbols—the Devil, for example—that for him were real. With his children he had also displayed a primitive sense of the power of the father with respect to the family. In Joe the components of Jung's collective unconscious—"the racially inherited psychic materials present in the individual unconscious"—seem to be much closer to the surface than they are in persons who are not psychopathologically disabled. His digging a hole deep into the earth and his obsession with fire were primitive manifestations. In a primitive way he was also an underground man, a man of the night, and, as he sometimes called himself, a creature of darkness. He was, in short, a twentieth-century anachronism.

The morbidity the tests revealed was a reflection of the unhealthy mental state that had evolved from the transformation of a sensitive child into a destructive adult who still maintained in a part of himself the early sensitivity.

The Hoffman examination and the Levitt testing involved some three hours of intense work. Then, wanting an opinion by another psychiatrist, Dr. Hoffman took Joe to the office of Dr. Alex von Schlichten. For thirty minutes, this new doctor asked Joe questions that went over some of the same ground that Dr. Hoffman had covered. Dr. Hoffman, who had remained with Joe, listened very closely to everything that was said. Joe was asked to leave while the two psychiatrists conferred with each other.

Dr. von Schlichten, who had been called upon to check the work of his boss, Dr. Hoffman, agreed that the child abuse with which Mr. Kallinger was charged had probably taken place and that it was rooted in his mental illness. The important finding, as far as these examinations were concerned, was that Mr. Kallinger was seriously ill. The finding was strengthened by Albert Levitt's test results. Noting the difference between the inner and the outer Joseph Kallinger, Levitt observed that his "overt thinking tends to have a paranoid and defensive quality and he seems to be functioning in a pathological condition which may be a major mental illness." Levitt also stated that Mr. Kallinger's condition "builds up pressure to do something serious."

Dr. Hoffman wrote that he had concluded, in consultation with Dr. von Schlichten, that "at the present time Mr. Kallinger is best

177

seen as suffering from a schizophrenic process, probably of the paranoid type."

Each of the doctors, under oath, signed separate documents classified as "certificates of the physician," stating that Joseph Kallinger was "mentally ill" and should be evaluated for a "schizophrenic process and dangerousness."

In March 1972, Hoffman, von Schlichten, and Levitt had arrived at essentially the same diagnosis later made by Dr. Silvano Arieti (on February 22, 1980, and March 9, 1981) and by Dr. Lewis Robbins (on December 11, 1981, Joe's forty-fifth birthday). Both Dr. Arieti and Dr. Robbins had the benefit of the biographical facts here presented. The City Hall examiners, however, knew nothing of Joe's biography. The results were the same. Retrospectively, Dr. Arieti determined that at the time of the City Hall examinations, Joe's psychosis was already full-blown: Joe was psychotic before he committed a single criminal act, including the child abuse for which at the time of the City Hall examinations he was awaiting trial.

The City Hall doctors stated that Joe was not competent to stand trial, but that he should be under observation for sixty days at the State Maximum Security Forensic Unit, which was F Block at Holmesburg Prison, for a more detailed evaluation.

Like the arms of an octopus, F Block and the other cell blocks of Holmesburg Prison jut out from a large circular central hallway. Housing prisoners who are under psychiatric examination, F Block is a mixture of prison and madhouse.

At about eleven o'clock of his first night on F Block, on March 6, 1972, Joe was awakened by a scream. When he opened his eyes, he saw one of his two cellmates, a big fat heavy prisoner of about thirty with long, messy black hair, hopping back and forth from one end of the cell to the other like a crazy ape. The man was flailing his arms, thrashing in all directions. Then, stiff with fear and leaning against the bars of the cell, he pointed at the rear wall and raved, "He's here again!"

"Who?" Joe whispered at the cowering figure.

In the darkness Joe could barely see the outstretched arm, the fat torso squeezing against the bars, one foot cocked back against them as if the raving man wanted to propel himself clear out of the cell.

"Look! The window. He's coming through the window," the man growled.

Joe looked at the rear wall. He saw only the cold concrete of the prison. Then he looked up quickly as if to reassure himself that the slanting skylight in the ceiling, the only window in the cell, was still there.

Joe looked back at the fat man. Like a caged animal scared into flight, he began moving from side to side in rapid but stumbling steps from one end of the bars to the other. The cell was only nine by twelve feet, with a double-decker cot along each side wall, the space between them only the width of one of the cots; so that the fat man's movements along the bars, his bulk bumping against them as he moved from side to side, made Joe think he himself was caged in a zoo.

Joe could not see the fat man's face, and he didn't know whether the prisoner who slept in the cot above the raving man was awake.

Pulling himself away from the bars, the fat man paced the length of the cell. His words became incomprehensible. Joe realized that the man was raving in Spanish. But one word, uttered piercingly over and over again, was in English. The word was *bear*.

Almost every night the young Puerto Rican would rave in terror about the bear. They have everything here that you can think of, Joe observed. All kinds of nuts like this man who sees a bear. All kinds of criminals. They have murderers here, too. This fellow who sees the bear threw his baby through a window. His own child! Who ever thought that Joe Kallinger would be dumped with murderers?

The physical setting also depressed Joe. He had to kneel to wash at a spigot in the cell wall under which there was a bucket on the floor. To get hot water, Joe had to walk from his cell to the shower. A wooden shelf on one of the walls of the cell swarmed with roaches.

Roaches even shared the prisoner's food. Joe, who always enjoyed a legal fight, wanted to sue. He learned, however, that other inmates had initiated a suit against Holmesburg the previous year and that the case was pending.

He also wondered what he could do about the man who saw the bear and almost got Joe and the other cellmate to see it with him.

Report the guy? Men here were expected to be nuts. That's why they were under observation.

Joe thought bitterly that he was supposed to be a "nut," too. That's why he was here. But he didn't think of himself as being one and did not connect his hallucinations with that of the man who saw the bear.

Most of the time Joe wished to be out of this place, where men were beaten and chained, and to be free; but there were times when the suicidal impulse was also strong, times when he had dreams and dark fantasies about the children who had imprisoned him.

Joe learned from Thomas A. White that the examination at City Hall had been damaging. That is, damaging to Joe's return home. But White, who was also Harry Comer's lawyer, also said that he and Comer hoped that the findings at City Hall would be overturned at Holmesburg.

The Holmesburg evaluation of Joe for a schizophrenic process, dangerousness, and competency to stand trial rested with Dr. Norman C. Jablon, the head of the forensic diagnostic unit. Since 1965 he had been evaluating prisoners both in terms of their competency to stand trial and their classification with regard to the recognized psychiatric disorders: neurosis, psychosis, or personality disorder.

In making a final evaluation of Joe, Dr. Jablon referred to the dossier that staff psychologists had prepared about Joe and his wife and children. The doctor also had the reports of the police investigation, family court records, and Joe's medical file, including the findings of Hoffman, von Schlichten, and Levitt. Presumably there was also the record of Joe's suicide attempt in the Philadelphia Detention House.

From his own examinations of Joe and from the reports about the family, Dr. Jablon concluded that the prognosis was poor for Kallinger to function as an emotionally healthy father and husband. Kallinger couldn't cope with his environment or his children, and, according to the report of Charles Gallun, a counselor for the facility, Mrs. Kallinger couldn't cope either. "From all appearances," Gallun had reported to Dr. Jablon, "Mrs. Kallinger seems to have been a rather inadequate mother. She is reported to be completely subservient to Mr. Kallinger and takes no responsibility for the

180

household." Reports from school personnel, psychologists and psychiatrists, had clearly indicated that, as Gallun summarized them, "the mother is an extremely weak individual who abdicates responsibilities and decision-making to her husband."

"It appears," Dr. Jablon wrote in his report of May 9, 1972, "that it would be rather important to involve Mr. Kallinger in family counseling should he be released from incarceration. It also seems imperative that from what we have learned of the family situation, *all* of the family members should be involved in counseling as well. It is hoped that the court might be able to provide the means for such plans to be put into effect."

Dr. Jablon also observed in his report that Mr. Kallinger was suffering from paranoid attitudes, schizoid involvement, "at least the beginnings of a thought disorder," unrealistic thinking, and a condition that suggested psychopathology. Dr. Jablon also wrote that Joe's emotional reactions didn't relate to the situation in which he found himself, that he giggled inappropriately, that there was an evasive quality about him, that he projected blame on others.

After noting these symptoms which relate to psychosis, Dr. Jablon diagnosed Joe as nonpsychotic—as suffering from "an inadequate personality," a subdivision of "personality disorder." Despite the symptoms, Dr. Jablon informed the court: "There is no reason to expect that Joseph Kallinger would require institutionalization or hospital treatment at the present time." The doctor also declared Kallinger as competent to stand trial.

"Diagnostically," Dr. Jablon explained, "Mr. Kallinger does not present a clear-cut picture." The doctor reasoned, as he later testified in open court, that Dr. Hoffman and Dr. von Schlichten had not been sure, either. If they had been, Dr. Jablon maintained, they could have submitted a final report that Kallinger was not competent to stand trial and they could have recommended that he be committed to a state hospital for treatment. Instead they had sent Kallinger up for a diagnostic workup.

Dr. Jablon also explained in open court that his diagnosis was less serious than that of Drs. Hoffman and von Schlichten. "Usually," Dr. Jablon said, "the evaluation at City Hall is more serious than the one made at Holmesburg." He further explained that the reason for this "is that the City Hall examination is closer to the time of the prisoner's arrest when the tensions and pressures are greater." Passed unnoticed was the fact that underlying symptoms that are masked at other times may surface under tension and pressure. Also unnoticed was that in October of 1972, seven months after first examining Joe and five months after the Jablon evaluation, Drs. Hoffman and von Schlichten did a second examination. Their new conclusion was: "We continue to view Joseph Kallinger as suffering from a major mental illness."

They recommended that Kallinger be committed to Philadelphia State Hospital to avoid a recurrence of the behavior that had led to the child-abuse charges.

"Personality disorder" is one of the recognized psychiatric diagnoses. Although less severe, it may have many features of a psychosis. In Joe's case, it was incorrect in terms not only of his symptoms, but also of his day-to-day behavior. Even though he was psychotic, he made the decisions in the family, was the strong parent, and was highly effective in his work as a shoemaker. Actually he was what family therapists call "overadequate," dominant, all-powerful within his special sphere—a king in action as well as in fantasy. It was not inadequacy that made him burn Mary Jo's thigh or that in the Philadelphia Detention House made him try to kill himself. These acts sprang from what Hoffman, von Schlichten, and Levitt had characterized as the onset of a major mental illness and of the psychosis that Dr. Arieti established as full-blown between 1969 and 1972.

Joe, still fighting the possibility of forty years behind bars, had told Dr. Jablon, "I want to get back to my business." The doctor had replied, "That's the right spirit to have." Joe thought that Dr. Jablon was on Joe's side and was triumphant that the Holmesburg findings had set aside those of the City Hall examiners. The doctors at City Hall had sent Joe to Dr. Jablon's unit for a diagnosis based on more detailed study.

"I had assurances that I would not be sent to prison," Joe told me. "Judge Robert Williams had been the original judge, but my friends succeeded in having the case tried before Judge Edward J. Bradley. 'I can work with Bradley,' my lawyer told me. I knew the lawyer could work with Judge Bradley because Harry Comer could work with Michael Bradley, a powerful Democratic Party ward leader who was the judge's father.

"My lawyer came to see me at F Block a week before the Jablon report of May 9, 1972. He said there would be a delay in getting to court, but that the delay would work to my advantage. He assured me that I would be back in my store before school opened to get the return-to-school trade."

What actually happened is not clear. However, Deborah Glass, an assistant district attorney in the case, told me that she had been warned that the case was "something of a hot potato and that Judge Bradley was predisposed to let this man [Kallinger] out on bail." Judge Bradley refused to be interviewed on the subject and the court administration kept me from interviewing Dr. Alex von Schlichten and Albert Levitt. (They were part of the team that diagnosed Joseph Kallinger as suffering from a major mental illness and that recommended that he be hospitalized.) For, after Dr. von Schlichten had made arrangements for the interview, a court public relations officer telephoned me to cancel it. Dr. von Schlichten and Albert Levitt, who were eager to talk with me, had no choice but to abide by the administrative decision.

If Harry Comer went to any trouble on behalf of Joe, we may assume it was because of their longtime friendship. Comer's legislative office was across the street from Joe's store and home, and Comer knew Joe from the time Anna Kallinger first brought Joe home from St. Vincent's. Comer had been a character witness for Joe in the arson trial at which Joe was acquitted. By displaying Comer posters in the shoe repair store Joe beat the candidate's drum with customers and generally helped in Comer's legislative campaigns. The two men helped each other.

On Tuesday morning, June 6, 1972, Joe sat in a small room on the sixth floor of City Hall, waiting for his trial to begin. Through the old-fashioned hallway with its high ceiling he could see three figures, one behind the other. The first was strutting and arrogant, the second shapely and graceful, and the third lithe with swift movements. Joe recognized Joey, Mary Jo, and Mike.

Minutes later his children reappeared in front of the open door and peered into the room. Joe smiled at them, but they did not smile back. They were whispering to each other, giggling, and it seemed to Joe that, staring at his handcuffs, they were gloating. Three times they came back to stare and to gloat over the king they had dethroned.

"I felt I was the prisoner not of the Commonwealth but of the children," Joe told me. "I had come to see them as gods—total gods. They had power over me. I was afraid of them."

Ten minutes after Joe saw the children, his trial began.

Joe pleaded not guilty and waived a jury trial. Judge Bradley reminded him of his right to such a trial and said that he could still have one. But Joe replied, "Your honor, I would want to rest in your hands."

Rep. Harry Comer, a character witness, testified to Joe's "excellent reputation" and to the fact that the Kallinger children kept the neighborhood in "a continual turmoil." He recalled that he had often advised Kallinger to move his business away from his home "because of the continual interruption from the children and others in the area."

As witnesses for the Commonwealth of Pennsylvania, Mary Jo, Joseph, Jr., and Michael Kallinger dealt with the events already described.

The judge ruled that in respect to Mary Jo, Kallinger was guilty of cruelty to a child and aggravated assault and battery; he was not guilty, however, of assault and battery with the intent to maim. In the case of Joseph, Jr., Kallinger was guilty of cruelty rather than of aggravated cruelty, and of simple assault and battery rather than aggravated assault and battery with intent to maim, as had been charged. Michael Kallinger's charges were dismissed.

Joe had been found guilty on most counts. But Judge Bradley explained: "At this point the matter is not an adversary proceeding. It is for the best possible outcome."

The judge was saying that he was not concerned with punishing Kallinger, that the real issue was to do what was best for all the members of the Kallinger family.

The judge pointed out that Kallinger had threatened no one except his family, and that "the whole family relationship" was more important than whether or not Kallinger ought to be in prison. The judge also said that he would feel more sanguine about sending

Kallinger home if Joseph, Jr., and Michael were not going to be there. (Mary Jo was living with her maternal grandparents.) But before making a decision about reducing Kallinger's bail or sentencing him, the judge ordered the District Attorney's Office to conduct, through the Department of Public Welfare, a thorough investigation of the Kallinger family.

Bail imposed on the day of Joe's arrest was $75,000 on all counts. Actually, in Pennsylvania a defendant can make bail by paying 10 percent of the amount of bail. But, not being able to raise the $7,500, Joe had been taken to the Philadelphia Detention House. He now returned to Holmesburg Prison to await "the best possible outcome."

The bail hearing took place on August 24, 1972. The investigation Judge Bradley had ordered had produced no results: The wrong agency had been notified; the wrong persons had been subpoenaed. Instead of being referred to the City of Philadelphia on the basis of child care, the Kallinger case had been put into the hands of the Commonwealth of Pennsylvania as a matter of welfare.

Thomas White, Joe's lawyer, insisted that the snafu had been a deliberate attempt on the part of the district attorney, Arlen Specter, to keep Kallinger in prison.

Whether or not the snafu was deliberate, prison was where the prosecution wanted Kallinger to be. Like the senior Kallingers, the prosecution thought of Joe not as "sick" but as "bad."

At the trial (June 6, 1972), when Judge Bradley said that Kallinger had been a danger *only* to his family, James Bryant, an assistant DA, disagreed. He cited a case of child cruelty involving Pasquale Munio. The boy had thrown orange peels into the Kallinger shoe repair store. Joe had run after Pasquale with a gun. The case, which was to have been heard in May 1971 before Judge Glancey of the Municipal Court, Philadelphia, had been dismissed because Kathryn Munio, Pasquale's mother, who had pressed charges, had not shown up for the hearing.

Judge Bradley didn't have the data he felt he needed to make an informed decision about bail or sentencing. He postponed sentencing, but said he would make a decision on bail at this hearing. Deborah Glass, the assistant DA who called Joe "a walking time bomb," opposed the lowering of bail. The Judge asked Betty

Kallinger whether she would like to see bail reduced so that her husband could come home. After she had said yes, Judge Bradley reduced bail on all counts to $5,000. A condition was that the court's Probation Department should supervise Joe while he was out on bail.

On January 17, 1973, after Joe had been home on bail for five months, he appeared in court for sentencing. He received a suspended sentence with regard to Joseph, Jr. For the burning of Mary Jo's thigh, he was put on four years' psychiatric probation. He was required to report to the Community Mental Health Center at Episcopal Hospital. After an interview that lasted for five minutes, the interviewer told Joe that there was nothing wrong with him. Joe reported this to his probation officer, who wrote to the Community Mental Health Center and got the same reply. That was the end of psychiatric counseling for Joe, but he remained on probation.

The "best possible outcome" would have been for Joe, who was psychotic and dangerous because of the psychosis, to have been placed in a mental hospital for treatment. Drs. Hoffman and von Schlichten, in doing a presentencing examination of Joe while he was on bail, had reaffirmed their original findings. These findings were never sent to the Community Mental Health Center. The two psychiatrists had specifically suggested that Joe be sent to Philadelphia State Mental Hospital. Judge Bradley could have acted not on Dr. Jablon's diagnosis that Joe was not psychotic, but on the second Hoffman–von Schlichten report that he *was*. But at the time of sentencing, while Deborah Glass argued for either incarceration or the placing of Kallinger in a mental hospital, Judge Bradley resisted Ms. Glass's argument.

Judge Bradley said, ". . . barring the episode of the kind for which Mr. Kallinger goes on trial, the children are somewhat better off if he is there, rather than not there, in terms of the fact that he does provide a livelihood and also in terms of the fact that he does give some form of supervision, which otherwise would be absent altogether. The question is, should it be a disposition to remove Mr. Kallinger or permit him to remain at home? As I say, I am not convinced by any means that having him removed would be an improvement for the children or the general home situation. There is no dispute that he is, in terms of economics, a good provider in the home. Otherwise the children and mother and the family would be without support at all, and apparently the children would have less supervision than they have when he *is* there. I am led to the conclusion that the disposition has to be one which will permit Mr. Kallinger to be at home providing a living and support for his family."

At each juncture of Joe's life, when psychiatric intervention might have been possible, it did not take place. When he was fifteen and first gave evidence of snakelike movements, a gothic belly laugh, and other symptoms of mental illness, Anna Kallinger, instead of taking him to a psychiatrist, filed an incorrigibility complaint. At twenty-two Joe had been hospitalized in the psychiatric ward of St. Mary's Hospital, but the psychiatrists there did not see the signs of serious mental illness.

At the Hazleton State Hospital, where Joe was amnesic and attempted suicide, the doctors did recommend follow-up care, but no action was taken by Joe himself or by anyone close to him. When the City Hall doctors diagnosed for a second time the gravity of Joe's psychosis and recommended hospitalization, the hospitalization did not take place.

In 1972 and 1973 Joe had a reasonably good chance of getting well or at least of having his psychosis controlled through medication and therapy. He was denied that chance because Judge Bradley ignored the second Hoffman–von Schlichten–Levitt report recommending hospitalization and acted instead on the report of Dr. Jablon which stated that "There is no reason, however, to expect that [Joseph Kallinger] requires institutionalization or hospital treatment at the present time for psychiatric reasons." Dr. Jablon did recommend that, if Kallinger were released from incarceration, he and his family should have family therapy.

The consequences of Dr. Jablon's conclusions against hospitalization or hospital treatment were the more unfortunate because he himself had noted in his report of May 9, 1972 some of the symptoms of serious psychopathology and had written that "Diagnostically, Mr. Kallinger does not present a clear-cut picture." While making the diagnosis of "inadequate personality," Dr. Jablon cited symptoms that were psychotic or at least prepsychotic. Among these symptoms were tangential and autistic-like thinking.

Affixed to the diagnosis itself was the statement that "His [Joseph Kallinger's] tendency toward withdrawal and his inability to express hostility, even when appropriate, suggest schizoid involvement. His over-evasiveness and suspiciousness suggest some paranoid attitudes." And Dr. Jablon wrote: "The prognosis is poor for this patient to be able to function as an emotionally healthy father and husband."

The Jablon diagnosis that Joe was *not* psychotic and was suffering from a personality disorder, would set a diagnostic pattern with which many later psychiatrists concurred, and later prosecutors used to their advantage. In 1976 and 1977 Dr. Jablon himself would publicly repeat and defend this original diagnosis that Joe was a sociopath.

"Flora," Joe told me as he looked at me sadly over the scarred wooden table in the Camden County Jail infirmary, "in Holmesburg something really deep was happening inside of me. At the time I wasn't really aware of what it was. I didn't know how far it would go."

11 The Total Gods

"The guard walked beside me out of the prison toward the main gate, where Betty was waiting outside. The sun was hot and bright, hotter and brighter than I remembered. I'm not crazy about the sun, Flora, too much brightness for an underground man like me; but the lights inside a prison are dull, and daylight doesn't get in very much through the narrow barred windows; also there's this inner darkness a prisoner lives with, almost like his soul has been put into storage with his clothes and other personal belongings.

"That morning, August 26, 1972, Betty had gone down to City Hall to pay the ten percent of the five thousand dollars Judge Bradley had reduced my bail to from seventy-five thousand dollars. All Betty had to do was to pay five hundred dollars. Now in the afternoon she was going to take me home.

"The gate opened. I shook hands with the guard, who wished me luck. He smiled, and suddenly he looked human, not like a guard anymore—the first time, I think, I'd seen anyone smile in six months and twenty-six days.

"My own clothes felt strange on me when Betty and I put our arms around each other. I had forgotten how a woman's clothes feel under my hands, how the soft, clean skin of a woman feels to the touch. My hands had been batting cockroaches to death, turning dirty handles of water spigots, pulling scratchy blankets up over my body on the hard mattress—there's nothing sweet and feminine in the slammer.

"Betty and I got on the bus to go home. The soft seats and the movement away from the jail felt good. I squeezed my wife's hand. I was back 'on the street.' I was free!

"But *was* I free? As we rolled along, I watched people walking, going in and out of stores, just doing their thing. That was pleasant. But then I got to thinking about *my* thing—my shoe repair store—and the pleasure curdled into fear.

"I was only out on bail. It had been my dream to walk out of Judge Bradley's courtroom cleared of the charges, but that hadn't happened. The newspapers had printed that I had been found guilty on most counts. I was a criminal!

"I couldn't believe it. *Me*, a criminal? I was thirty-six years old. I'd had no prior convictions. I was not like the men I'd met in prison. *Their* lives were filled with crime. No! Crime was their *life!*

"I had to think of something that would change the verdict of guilty, otherwise customers would stay away and my business would be ruined. Nobody wants to do business with a criminal. And although the date of my sentencing was five months away, I could be sent back to the slammer at any time if I didn't keep my nose clean, or my kids put in another complaint about me.

"Betty went back to her parents' house the day she brought me home, as she had told Judge Bradley she was going to do. That's where Mary Jo was living; and Joey, Mike, and Jimmy were staying there until school opened up. I was furious because I was going to be alone during the first week and a half after coming home. But there was nothing I could do about it.

"I sat in my shop and did a lot of thinking about how to get my business rolling. And I got familiar again with all my tools and machinery. I hadn't forgotten how to use them, the old skill was still in the fingers, and I enjoyed touching my tools as if they were old friends, getting to know all about them all over again. I turned on the finisher, sat back, and just listened to its music, music I hadn't heard in six months and twenty-six days: the whine of the electric motor, the drive belt hissing, the shaft turning in its bearings. Prison music is like nothing else in the world: the sounds of Chaos and Old Night—guards cracking orders, mutterings and screaming nightmares, skittering and crackling sounds in the cold stone walls, thud of fists on prisoners' bodies, gates slamming closed.

"Everything was in my shop just as I'd left it, except there were no customers' shoes. Without them, my shop was like a mouth without teeth.

"In prison I'd written a promotional letter about the shoe repair pickup and delivery service I planned to start when I got home. I sent five hundred mimeographed copies of my letter to the offices of lawyers, judges, and legal services throughout the city. The letter said that the Kallinger Rapid Shoe Repair Pickup and Delivery Service would pick up and deliver to the offices on the same day.

"By the time I got home, a few orders had already trickled in, and I was hopeful. At the beginning Betty would have to handle the pickups and deliveries; then I was going to get a truck and a delivery man. But I did a lot of thinking about the business, because a trickle is not the same thing as a flood of orders. Remember, Flora, I was a *criminal*, so I also did a lot of thinking about how to remove the stigma."

Joe decided that to do this he needed a powerful plan. It would have a good chance of succeeding, he felt, if it involved Joey, Michael, and Mary Jo, whom he had dubbed "the total gods" because they had overcome the king of the castle by sending him to jail.

Joe felt dethroned as he sat alone in the castle's living room after Betty left for her parents' house. He was as afraid of Joey and Mike as they would be of him when upon their return with Betty they would tiptoe fearfully into the house. At Joey he was also angry. For, while at Holmesburg, Joe had received anonymous letters about how Joey was looting the East Hagert Street warehouse.

Joe saw his adoptive mother, now seventy-five, come in. When he had taken over the shoe repair business and the East Sterner–North Front Street house, Anna and Stephen had moved into the house they owned next door, at 102 East Sterner Street.

The contact Joe had had with the senior Kallingers had remained strong; the influence they exerted on him had for the most part become weaker. They had adopted him to inherit their business and take care of them in their old age. Both purposes had been fulfilled. The business was Joe's, and after having retired, Stephen often helped

Joe with the shoe repair work. Joe and Betty nursed the senior Kallingers when they were ill and were solicitous of them in other ways as well. Stephen had died in 1971, and at the moment of death, Joe was rubbing Stephen's feet to prolong his life.

Whenever Joe and Betty quarreled, Anna sided with Joe, Stephen with Betty. When Joe and Betty had taken four-month-old Mary Jo to a Boston hospital to be treated for an ear problem, Anna took care of Annie and Stevie, the children of Joe's first marriage. Hearing that Joe was thinking about settling in Boston, Anna fainted. After Stephen had revived her, he telephoned Joe to come home. Joe did, and the second purpose of the adoption continued to be fulfilled.

The children of Joe's first marriage had been named for the senior Kallingers, and for this reason Anna doted on them. She was cooler to Joe's and Betty's children. Talking with Joe on the day he returned from Holmesburg, Anna shook her head, clucked her tongue, and declared that it was a great shame that a father couldn't even punish his children anymore in this crazy world without being sent to jail for it. In the old country, she went on, shaking her finger in the air, this would never have happened. There, parents were respected and feared; but here in this *gottverlassen* country the kids run wild.

On a visit home from her maternal grandparents' house while Joe was in jail, Mary Jo had shown Anna Kallinger the scar. Anna had said angrily to her granddaughter, "Ach! It's nothing. A tiny crinkle in your skin, and for this you put your father away? I suppose now you are worried that the boys won't like you because you got this little *Puptzich* on you, eh? Your father should have burned the other thigh, too! You are a very bad girl to do this to your father, who loved you and worked hard for you. *Ja, meine Enkelin!* You understand, you boy-crazy good-for-nothing?"

The Kallinger Rapid Shoe Repair Pickup and Delivery Service was beginning to grow with a few small orders every week, but not many of his old customers had come back to Joe. As good a shoemaker as he was, he was also a criminal, and this was holding up the recovery of his business. Joe looked at the shelves where he stacked shoes to be worked on. The shelves were almost bare, except for one pair of shoes from a judge, another from a lawyer in Center City. The plan had to be put into effect *now*!

After supper, he called Mike and Joey into the shop.

"Sit down, boys," he said invitingly with a big smile.

Joey leered at his father. Mike mumbled something indistinct. Joey was skinnier and shorter than his brother, and his hair was darker than Mike's. Mike had buck-teeth, but otherwise looked much like Joey; still, Joey looked much more like his father than Mike did, although both boys had sandy hair, while Joe's hair was jet black.

Joe noticed that they had gotten thinner. Too many cheap TV dinners, he thought. He noticed also that their clothes were old and worn, their sneakers scuffed and dirty.

In the pre-Holmesburg days, Joe would have issued an order and his kids would have snapped to to carry it out. But ever since the mutiny in the castle, he had lost his authority as a father. He knew he had to appease these "total gods," that he had to bring them around so that they would work not against him but for him. He knew that they could send him back.

"What's up?" Joey asked.

"Yeah, what's up?" Mike echoed.

"We're busy. Let's have it, man!" Joey ordered.

"Yeah, let's have it," Mike demanded.

It wasn't going to be easy, Joe thought, looking at his two sons, but he had to try. Otherwise the future would be a disaster.

"Look, boys . . ."

"We're looking," Joey and Mike said in unison and pretended to look attentively at a spot on Joe's shirt.

Joe looked down and laughed. "No, you guys, I don't mean look at my shirt. I mean, well, a lot has happened between us, right?"

"Right!" Joey replied. He blew smoke rings. Mike nodded his head knowingly and sucked on his buck teeth.

"But *I* say," Joe went on doggedly, "forgive and forget. I know you love your daddy. . . ." Joe waited for a reply, but Joey and Mike were silent.

". . . that you love me," Joe persisted, "and your daddy loves *you*. That's how families should be, anyway."

Joey and Mike were silent.

"There's something I want to ask you, something I want you boys to do—and your sister, Mary Jo, too. It's for the good of the Kallinger family."

Joey, who was by habit fidgety, got up from the seat. He walked up and down the shop, looking at his father.

"Well, what's it all about?" Joey asked.

Joe halted Joey with his hand on Joey's bony shoulder. Joe looked at the thin face, the suspicious, distrustful eyes.

"Okay, this is it, fellas," he said. "There's only one way I can get this business back to where it was before I was sent to Holmesburg, when I was making a good living and we were eating steaks and drinking milk, not like now when we're eating welfare dinners. There's only one way back to the good old days, and that's if I can get my name cleared of the charges for which I'm going to be sentenced in five months. People don't like to take their business to a guy like me who's been convicted of a crime. Like I said, I've got to clear my name!"

Joey and Mike looked at each other.

"What's that got to do with us?" Mike asked.

"I'm asking you, Joey and Mike—and your sister, too, you can call her up at Grandpa's and ask her—I'm asking you three kids to go back and tell the court that the child-abuse charges you all accused me of and on which I was convicted are untrue!"

"What's in it for us?" Joey asked.

"Plenty!" Joe replied. "Good food, good clothes, nice restaurants, movies, trips on weekends, pocket money, and you name it. Look at my shelves, you guys. Look at them! Practically empty, right? Hardly a pair of shoes on them. Without those shoes coming in here for me to work on, we'll be on welfare payments the rest of our lives, and *you* guys can go whistle to the winds for good times and dollar bills, because your daddy won't be able to give them to you— if the business doesn't recover. And like I said, the only way it can recover is if I clear my name—and you and your sister can do this for me by recanting before the court."

Joey lit a cigarette. Silence.

"Don't tell me right now," Joe said. "Please just think about it, then let me know. Okay?"

"Okay. We'll think about it and let you know," Joey said.

Joey, who was twelve, and Mike, who was eleven, talked over

their father's request in their bedroom. Joey wanted his father's business to recover because, as he and Mike agreed, life was no fun without money, steaks for supper, and trips on the weekends. Mike didn't like Joey very much—he was foul-mouthed and disagreeable—but he went along with Joey with respect to their father's request just as he had gone along with Joey and Mary Jo on the day they reported their father to the police for child abuse.

But for Joey, as Carol Dwyer, his teacher at the Douglas School, told me, there was a more important reason: He had been proud that his father owned a business and that the Kallingers were middle-class. This, as Joey had told Mrs. Dwyer, made him feel superior to kids whose fathers worked for other people in stores or factories.

Mrs. Dwyer described to me how Joey would ask his classmates what their fathers did for a living. If the answer was that the other kid's father worked in a hardware store or in a hat factory, Joey would brag that *his* father owned and operated a shoe repair store, that he made a lot of money and that he was the best in the business.

Joey, according to Mrs. Dwyer, was openly scornful of the lower status held by many of his schoolmates. Many times this led to fights; but win or lose, Joey walked away proud that he was the son of a man who owned his own business, wasn't bossed around by anybody, and made all the rules in his own shop.

The two brothers also decided that recanting would be fun. That they would be perjuring themselves didn't occur to them. Even if it had, they wouldn't have cared, for telling lies was an important part of their way of life. The fun would come from lying to adults, whom they hated and distrusted, and from the glorious hullabaloo their recanting would probably cause in the court and in the community of Kensington, and even perhaps throughout Philadelphia. Furthermore, they wanted to see their names and pictures in the newspapers and on TV again. Money and good times were sweet, but so was notoriety.

They put in a call to their sister, Mary Jo, who was thirteen, and told her what Daddy wanted them to do and what they would get out of it. Mary Jo agreed eagerly, for the good life appealed to her, too. Having a little fun at the expense of the authorities, who were always trying to make life tough for kids, was worth all the recanting in the world.

An hour after Joey and Mike had walked out of Joe's shop, they returned and told him that they and their sister, Mary Jo, had decided to recant the child-abuse charges.

By manipulating his children Joe had taken the first step toward recantation. The recantation hearing itself would not take place, however, until a little over a year after the sentencing of Joe on January 17, 1973, to four years' probation, which meant that he would remain at home rather than being sent to an institution. The tragic events that would occur during those four years were the result of his being at home and not of the recantation. Yet if during his so-called psychiatric probation he had actually received psychological help he might have faced some of the problems that were destroying him instead of working deviously with his children to hide the facts of his psychotic abuse of them.

Joe had learned during his trial and incarceration about what lawyers call "after-discovered evidence"—evidence uncovered after the conclusion of a trial that can reverse the verdict. Joe knew that in addition to the children's recantation, he needed evidence. It was, in fact, on the basis of after-discovered evidence that on November 31, 1973, Joe's lawyer, Arthur L. Gutkin, filed a motion for a new trial in the child-abuse case.

Joe knew, however, that in his case no such evidence existed. He therefore asked Joey to help him create it. Before his arrest, Joe had kept the instruments of punishment in the cellar. The day after he had come home, he removed them. The cellar now was where, after the store was closed and supper over, Joe and Joey went for the purpose of creating after-discovered evidence through backdated entries in four diaries: a brown, a black, and a blue diary and in another later known to the court as the Ben Franklin book.

To Joey the father with whom he was playing the diary game was a "fun-and-games dad." It was the same father who, on an antic high (induced wholly by inner forces), had suggested that Joey and he spray-paint the outside of Joey's school, and had accompanied him when he did it one morning at the crack of dawn.

In the cellar Joe and Joey, bound in a conspiratorial closeness, worked on the diaries over the course of fourteen months: September

196

1972 to November 1973. Except for a few interpolations of his own, Joey wrote what Joe dictated.

Among the entries to be used as after-discovered evidence were: "My sister Mary Jo Kallinger asked me Joe K. last January 30, 1972 to go with her to the police to put my father away because he would not let her go out with boys. I said I did not want to go. She begged me to go to the police. She told me what to say. I did not want to lie but Mary Jo Kallinger said that it would be all right once they put dad away. Mary said we could do what we want. She said I could fuck all girls all I want and she could go with the Strong boys all she wants and cut school, there being nobody to stop her, and we could make lots of money selling dad's merchandise in his ware-house and keep all his money. My dad, you were a nice dad."

"Mary Jo put Dad away and I had to help her. She made me say that she was crying so the cops would believe her when she told them dad hit her with a hot egg turner which I knew he did not hit her with. I should not have said my dad was hitting me with a handle because he was not. I think he's a great guy, he always tries to help me when I have a problem and I love him. I think my sister is a liar."

". . . We are going to the police and have my dad locked up. I am going to tell them all lies about my dad and say he handcuffed me to the ice-box and beat me. Then they will put him away and I can make fun. I can't wait until tomorrow." (This entry was dated January 29, 1972.)

"While dad was away, I was glad then that I lied to keep him in jail because I now could do what I want. It was easy to get the judges to believe my lies about dad. Anything I said they believed."

By May 2, 1973, Joe thought he had enough after-discovered evidence to get himself a lawyer to file a motion for a new trial on the child-abuse charges. That day he wrote a letter of which he sent three thousand Xeroxed copies to lawyers not only in Pennsylvania but also in New Jersey and New York. He received fifty answers, but chose lawyers he met through another source.

197

John Fareira, Administrative Assistant to the Superintendent of School District 5, had been one of the people who believed in Joe's innocence despite the verdict. This had been true of many of the children's teachers. As Carol Dwyer, Joey's teacher at the Douglas School, put it to me, "Mr. Kallinger was the most cooperative and concerned parent we had. When I called him, he always came right over. He's intelligent, articulate, well dressed, businesslike, and knows important people. He was not at all the sort of man you'd suspect of abusing his children."

Fareira called Joe and gave him the telephone number of Kenneth F. Hoffmaster, president of the Philadelphia Parents' Organization, which investigates false accusations of child neglect and abuse against parents. Joe phoned Hoffmaster, who came to see Joe and help him with his case. In July 1973, Joey, Mike, and Mary Jo gave statements of recantation to Mr. Hoffmaster. When Joe showed him the May 2 letter to lawyers, Hoffmaster suggested that his own lawyers, Malcolm W. Berkowitz and Arthur L. Gutkin, might be interested in representing Joe. On November 31, 1973, after interviewing all the Kallinger children and reading Joey's diaries, Gutkin filed a motion for a new trial, based on after-discovered evidence.

Joe proceeded with the filing of the motion, even though by that time his business had improved well beyond his gloomy predictions at the time of his homecoming; it was no longer as important as it had been for Joe to clear his name for business reasons. By working a twelve-hour day he had gotten his family off welfare two months after he had come home. His life had also improved in other ways. A month after leaving Holmesburg he had joined the Kensington Assembly of God, a fundamentalist Protestant church, and found comfort in the affiliation. He had not belonged to a church since the Roman Catholic Church had excommunicated him thirteen years earlier.

There was also comfort in knowing that three months after his homecoming Betty had become pregnant and that in August 1973 he would be father to his seventh child.

Now both Joe and "the total gods" wanted his name cleared, even though business was no longer the primary motive. The kids enjoyed the game. Joe felt that business or no business, he could not live with the stigma of being labeled a criminal. So, wearing the mask of innocence with his lawyers, with Mr. Hoffmaster, and with Joe's friends among politicians and educators, he hoped that the court would also think him innocent. He proceeded with deliberate intent to make the court think this. Yet at the same time he was still under the delusion that he had not abused the children, but had tried to "educate" them. That was why he believed it just for him to be freed of the child-abuse stigma.

In June 1973, the diaries that had begun for the purpose of developing "after-discovered evidence" now also had an additional *raison d'être*. They became the means by which Joe delegated to Joey some of his own wishes and fantasies. When Joey went out on the streets to which as a boy Joe had been a stranger, Joe had his son take with him a hidden microphone and a small tape recorder to record his adventures. By listening to what Joey had recorded, Joe, without leaving his shop or house, was able to satisfy the wanderlust that he had had at Joey's age—and still had. In this way the inner child in Joe experienced both the normal adventures of which he had been deprived and the abnormal adventures for which the deprivation and other aspects of his grotesquely abnormal childhood had created a festering need. Some of the adventures, as lived or imagined by Joey, or fantasized by Joe, also made their way into the diaries.

"Before Joey left for the day," Joe wrote me on June 12, 1977, "I injected my feelings, my impulses and personality into him. In the morning I gave him my personality for the day to preform [sic] my personality. The finished product at the end of the day would be a combination of my injection and Joey's abilities which could lead to the wonder lust [sic], to a surprise and the awaited outcome either by writing in the diary or listening to a tape."

"Wonder lust," a neologism or invented word typical of a schizophrenic, was also symbolic of Joe's lust for wonder in a milieu that cramped his imagination. "To *preform* my personality" was a transformation of "perform," and carried the overtone of the forming, the shaping, of Joey according to his father's psychotic needs.

The diaries report that Joey set six railroad fires, a fire to a big house, and a fire around one of his lovers. There are also frequent references to sadistic-sexual intentions and experiences that are exactly like the content of Joe's own sadistic-sexual fantasies. "The fires were Joey speaking," Joe told me on July 14, 1977. "But the entries about sex were mine. A normal father would not have been permissive about the fires and certainly wouldn't have dictated about cutting off a girl's nipples. But I was a normal father only some of the time."

In November 1973, the month during which a motion for a new trial on the child-abuse charges was filed, Joey got into trouble that Joe hadn't delegated. Joey was a runaway for fifty-six hours because he was having an affair with Thomas Black, a thirty-four-year-old homosexual. Joey, at Joe's insistence, became the juvenile complainant in a morals charge (involuntary deviant sexual intercourse with a minor) against Thomas Black. In this connection Joe and Betty took Joey to see Harold Balger, a Juvenile Aide Division officer of the police department's Morals Squad. The next day, November 17, 1973, Joey came to Balger's office alone.

When Joey walked into the office, he was carrying two big bags of candy. Alternatingly sullen and childlike, he demanded that Balger arrest him and lock him up. Joey explained that he didn't want to stay home anymore for two reasons. One, his father, reminding him that he was a runaway, didn't allow him out of the house and made him sit on the steps leading to the second floor *all the time*. Two, his father kept telling him not to get upset because of this punishment and the problems Joey had at school and on the street. Joey also told Officer Balger that he had "punched at" his father and had then come over to the office to be locked up.

Balger refused.

But before Joey left the office, Balger asked whether the child-abuse charges he had made against his father a year and a half earlier were true.

"No, that isn't true," Joey replied. He was angry at his father, but he was standing by his promise to recant.

"Why did you make these untrue charges?" Balger asked.

"I don't know," Joey said.

"Are you sorry you did it?"

"No," Joey replied, "I'm not sorry."

Joey also unofficially recanted the child-abuse charges to Anthony Medaglia, a probation officer. Joe had filed an incorrigibility petition against Joey. While interviewing Joey about the petition, the probation officer asked how Joey got along with his parents.

"Fine," Joey said.

"Isn't it true that your father assaulted you?" Officer Medaglia asked.

"No," Joey replied. "My sister and me made up this story."

Joe, apparently a normal father on the side of law and morality, was in the police car when Balger and other Morals Squad officers arrested Thomas Black. Both Joe and Joey attended Black's preliminary hearing at Family Court. Thomas Black was later tried and sent to prison.

In the course of the prosecution of Thomas Black, Joey got into a fight with a police officer and kicked him in the testicles. Joey was arrested.

The arrest was serious not only because Joey had assaulted a police officer, but also because in the past two years he had had three previous adjusted cases. On July 3, 1971, Joey, who was then eleven, had been arrested for shouting obscenities at a policeman who told him to stop dumping trash in the street. On May 11, 1972, while Joe was in Holmesburg, Joey, then twelve years old, had been arrested for larceny of a railroad car, RSG (receiving stolen goods), conspiracy, and vandalism. On April 4, 1973, Joey had been arrested for vandalism on railroad property, trespassing, and conspiracy.

Detained on a charge of runaway and incorrigibility, Joey was court-committed to Philadelphia's Youth Study Center, then to a psychiatric facility of Philadelphia General, and after that to Eastern State School and Hospital in Trevose, Pennsylvania. Eastern State is a hospital for emotionally disturbed children, most of whom are court-committed for serious offenses.

Robert J. Donovan, M.D., a neuropsychiatrist at Youth Study Center, speculated that Joey's "hostility may be born of the sadistic treatment to which he may have been subjected" and observed that he "seems to be at war with the world." Dr. Donovan's diagnosis was "runaway reaction of adolescence" and "passive-aggressive personality." The doctor's prediction was: "As [Joey] gets older, these tendencies could become dangerous to others as well as to himself."

At Eastern State School and Hospital, Robert H. Falkenstein, a psychologist, reported, "Joseph, Jr., appears to lack interest in the psychology of others, but is involved in an overly close, hostile-

201

dependent, love-hate relationship with his father." When Joey was in that hostile-hate phase, he wrote in a diary: "I'd like to drown my dad—or burn him in lots of fire." That was one of the times that Joe was not with his son during the diary-writing. But when Joe read these lines, he was not surprised. "Flora, Joey and I went in and out of loving each other. It was like our emotions went through a revolving door."

At Eastern State, Joey was restless, unhappy, beaten by other patients, and a terror to staff and patients alike. He was diagnosed as suffering from "schizophrenia, latent type (pseudopsychopathic) with sociopathic and sadistic features, and acting-out tendencies." Joe was never told about the diagnosis of schizophrenia.

Joey looked forward to his weekends at home. On his second weekend he and some friends wanted to get on a train, as they often did, just for the thrill of riding around without paying. They made their way to the roof of a three-story building with a barbershop on the ground floor. The building was on Harold Street, but the roof ran parallel to the el station at Kensington Avenue and Harold Street.

To get to the el station the boys had to jump from the roof to the station platform. Joey jumped first, but he did not land on the station platform. He fell three stories onto the barbershop yard. The police took him to Episcopal Hospital. The doctors said that he had a break in the part of his right foot where the ankle joins the two bones of the lower leg. The break was severe and the prognosis poor. Joey's leg was put into a cast that went from behind his toes to his right hip. Joe took Joey from Episcopal to St. Mary's. When Joey finally returned to Eastern State, he was on crutches and his right leg was in a cast.

On Friday, March 15, 1974, Joe took Joey, who had a one-day pass, to a Philadelphia doctor. Joey begged his father not to take him back to Eastern State. Joe pointed out that Joey was court-committed and had to go back, but Joey escaped from Joe and hobbled into the woods opposite the hospital.

Joey returned to Philadelphia by bus. He spent that Friday night and most of Saturday riding trains. At 10:15 P.M., Saturday, he presented himself to Lew King, the night city editor of the *Philadelphia Bulletin*. Another editor called Joe to say that Joey had surrendered to the *Bulletin* and was safe. Joe came to pick Joey up. They embraced and clung to each other. Tom Gibbons, a *Bulletin* reporter, drove Joe and Joey home. The next morning Joey returned to Eastern State. His weekend visits were restricted because, as a hospital social worker put it, it was essential to "help Mr. Kallinger to realize that Joey's manipulation of him hurt father and son."

Joe continued to fight vigorously on behalf of his son. At the end of February 1974, the battle revolved around Joey's cast. Doctors to whom Eastern State sent Joey after he complained of pains in his right leg removed his cast, but the pains came back while he was on a weekend at home. Doctors to whom Joe took Joey put the cast back on and said he needed it for an additional six weeks. The cast stayed on even though the Eastern State medical department believed that the decision to remove the cast had been correct. During the conversations about the cast Joe also complained that Joey had come home in a "deplorable condition" and that even though it was raining heavily Joey was wearing neither a coat nor socks. Now Joe devoted his energies to having Joey, who had been court-committed to Eastern State, returned home. Finally this happened as a result of a court hearing on May 6, 1974.

When I asked Joe about Joey and Eastern State, he wrote a lengthy letter on the subject, which is an important contribution to our understanding of the tragic love-hate relationship between Joe and Joey.

"I'm going to write down the thoughts that are flowing to your final question on the phone," Joe wrote me in his Thanksgiving Day letter of November 25, 1976, "the why in my battle against Eastern State. Well, yes, I was a loving father, so loving that neither Heaven nor Hell could stop the forces within this man. My son Joey's cry for help was the march to fight, a fight that would later be a battle by one man against the forces of modern times—meaning law institutions, doctors, sociologists, social workers, attendants and the very Court that put my son into Eastern State, the Morals Squad that started the action and the whole juvenile structure. All of these, this man—Joe Kallinger—would take on and nothing could stop him. My love was so strong I would at the end win and did—a victory that left scars and brought amazement to many. But my son was my love. What he did to abuse me mattered not and my abuse of him mattered not to him.

"He [Joey] had faith in me and I would not let him down. We were close. I loved and that love was a knight in shining armor or the prince in any story, and I knew myself to be just that. On condition that he receive out-patient treatment at Philadelphia's St. Christopher's Hospital for Children, Joey was returned to my custody after a juvenile court hearing on May 6, 1974.

"What in my childhood you ask, Flora, was connected with my feelings and attitudes toward Joey. I think I know. No one was my prince. No one rescued me. No one could I depend on or I would not be this way."

In late February 1974, "the total gods" testified on the motion for a new trial at a hearing before Judge Bradley in Courtroom 443 of the Court of Common Pleas. They said that their testimony at the trial had been untrue and that they were ashamed of having had their father arrested.

On February 19 and 20, Joey came to the courtroom from Eastern State. He was on crutches and was accompanied by deputy sheriffs. Lawyers for both the defense and prosecution read excerpts from his diaries. Joey stood firmly by them.

February 20 was Joey's fourteenth birthday. Joe brought him a dozen cupcakes, but because of the Eastern State rules Joey couldn't accept them. At the end of the day's session, however, while Joey was waiting for deputy sheriffs to take him back to Eastern State, Joe leaned over his chair, kissed Joey on the forehead, and said, "Happy birthday."

Joey came home in May 1974. When he visited the Douglas School, he was disappointed, according to Carol Dwyer, to find that Chow-Chow, the kitten he had found and cared for in his classroom, was no longer there. When he talked of Chow-Chow, Mrs. Dwyer told me, he showed the same gentle side that he had expressed when in August of 1973 he had announced in class, "There's a new baby in our family, Bonnie Sue."

Since Joe's homecoming from Holmesburg in August 1972, he had been more concerned with the external world of immediate realities than at any other time since his psychosis had become full-blown. But he was also laboring under the most serious delusion that had yet beset him. After he had burned Mary Jo's thigh, he had realized that his orthopedic experiments to correct himself and heal mankind had been a failure. In his hallucinations God then ordered him to destroy the world he hadn't healed and saved.

In Holmesburg Joe had hallucinated the presence of God, the voice of God ordering him to destroy. For approximately a year and a half after his homecoming the orders had not come. But in the winter of 1973–1974, at the very time that Joe's lawyer was filing a motion for a new trial based on after-discovered evidence and at the same time that Joe encouraged Joey to press charges against Thomas Black, and later fought Joey's battle against Eastern State, Joe started to act on his grotesque and hideous delusion, spawned by hallucinations of God, to massacre mankind.

That winter of 1973–1974, Joe, following orders he thought were coming from God, was determined to destroy mankind, to kill with a butcher knife every man, woman, child, and infant on the face of the earth. For this purpose, he launched a crime partnership with his son Michael, one of the "three total gods." Joey had been Joe's delegate in Kensington to act on Joe's unexpressed wishes. Joe thought of Michael as a delegate in the suburbs for the same purpose. Joey went out alone, but Joe went with Michael.

With Michael Joe had what he called "a companionate delegation." Whenever the order came from hallucinations of God, Joe and Michael took buses to other parts of Pennsylvania and to New Jersey, where they got off at random in strange towns whose names they didn't know. This happened approximately twice a week. Michael would then break into houses while Joe waited for him at the bus stop, walked ahead, or sat on a bench. While Joe waited outside, Michael committed two dozen robberies from the winter of 1973 to June 1974.

On a beautiful June day in 1974, Joe and Mike walked to an old country road in New Jersey. While Joe sat on a rock by a stream, Mike went down the road and broke into a house. Joe looked away from the sparkling water of the stream toward the dusty road. The road was empty.

The stream reminded Joe of the one near the old bungalow in Neshaminy where as a child he had had happy fancies about the butterflies. The bungalow was now his, but the happy fancies that had surrounded it no longer existed. Here beside the sparkling water in New Jersey he remembered the boy he had taken to the stream near Neshaminy to castrate. That had not happened. His thoughts now, as he made these exploratory forays into the suburbs under what he hallucinated as orders coming from God, were also of castrating and destroying. He had not told Michael about "God's order" or world massacre, yet he knew that the time would come when he himself would have to take action, though he was not ready yet.

Joe looked up and saw Michael walking down the road. Under his left arm was a jewelry box. Michael vaulted the fence easily, and with challenging, unsmiling eyes walked down the embankment to where Joe was sitting. Michael stood above Joe with the jewelry box still under his left arm.

"From now on, Dad," Michael said, "you'll have to go in with me!"

"Why is it necessary?" Joe asked.

"That's the way it's going to be," Mike answered.

"Mike, you want me to be in danger?"

"Well," Mike challenged, "you come in with me or I won't go in again."

"Okay, Mike," Joe replied fearfully.

"Flora," Joe would tell me, "when Mike challenged me, it was like my heart stopped. I had never entered a house illegally. Mike was living in a world of three-karat diamonds. I knew that robbery was only a way to get ready for world massacre. I was afraid to start going into houses. But Mike had said that *from now on*, I had to go in with him. He didn't say I had to go in with him *that day*. I hoped that there wouldn't be another command, that God would not continue to challenge me to destroy mankind."

Joe's first break-in and entry was in a Pennsylvania town. He felt that he had to learn what Mike already knew. Mike was Joe's strength and courage. They walked along farmland, then went into a farmer's house, and Mike started ransacking the rooms. Joe followed, feeling as if he were in the dream he had had as a child about bars shaped like half-moons, roofs merging, and the people on the roofs becoming his friends. In the dream Joe had tried to find his way back into the house and felt like an intruder.

Joe followed Mike, then began to help him. They took a large coin collection and left. Walking with Mike along a dirt road, Joe became dizzy, his head hurt, he saw lights. When he got back home, he went to his workbench. But the tools didn't come down to the spot they were supposed to reach. His coordination was off.

After Joe's first illegal entry, he and Mike went to many Jersey towns that Joe later forgot, and became, as he put it, "wastepaper by the wayside." He did remember that he and his son broke into and entered houses in the Pennsylvania towns of Lansdale, Norristown, Conshohocken, Bryn Mawr, Ardmore, Upper Darby, Broomall, Wayne, King of Prussia, Swarthmore, Media, Willow Grove, Hatboro, and Doylestown.

Each time Joe came home from a suburban foray he hoped he would not go out again. But when the hallucinated order from God to go out with Michael returned, Joe would say to his son, "Let's go!"

When the command Joe received was very strong, he and Michael sometimes left the house before six in the morning. But when the command was less urgent, Michael went to school and met Joe at a prearranged place. Then Joe called the school to say, "Michael is needed."

There were times when Michael called Joe to ask, "Are we going?" If the command hadn't come, Joe would reply, "Not today." If it had, Joe would say, "Meet me at Bridge and Pratt." That's where they took the elevated to the bus terminal.

As I sat with Joe in the Camden County Jail infirmary, he said ruefully, "Michael didn't have to go with me. He could have gone to the police. He had been that route before. If he was afraid to go alone, he could have gotten Joey, a friend, or a teacher to go with him. Or he could have called my probation officer. I'm not saying Michael started this, but if he had said no, that would have been the end of the whole thing. He was my strength, my courage, the heartbeat of the whole operation.

"Flora, Flora," Joe chanted, "why, *why* did Michael endanger me?"

12 The Test of Strength

Sunday, 4:00 P.M., July 7, 1974. The shop was closed, the shades drawn, but Joe was at his workbench, Michael standing beside him, watching. Joe held a handcutter, a then newly patented tool for cutting heavy materials, in his left hand. He squeezed the handles and the thin blade cut through the heel of a woman's shoe. Like a head chopped off at an execution, the heel fell onto the tiny metal "table" attached to the handcutter. That excited Michael, and he said to his father, "Let's go!"

Joe put the handcutter and a roll of black tape into a small plastic bag. He put the bag into his pocket. Father and son went out of the shop.

The day was sunny, the temperature was in the high eighties. For nine months Joe and Michael had been walking aimlessly through many miles of suburbs, but today they were staying in the city. This walk was going to be different: Before it was over, their first victim would be lying dead in an abandoned factory.

On my June 17, 1977, visit with Joe in the empty infirmary of the Camden County Jail, he told me:

"Mike said 'Let's go!' because we were on the same wavelength. Mike was a magnet for my thoughts, Flora, he grabbed them and held onto them just like a magnet attracts and holds iron filings.

That made me feel secure with Michael, for it was a crazy world I was falling into—it was even crazier than the one I lived in before my incarceration in Holmesburg Prison.

"In that summer of 1974 I knew I had to destroy the world, to kill every man, woman, and child in it. That was God's command to me. Almost every day I heard His voice: 'You must destroy what you couldn't save with the orthopedic experiments.' Sometimes God would remind me of the hamsters and Mary Jo. He'd say, 'The destruction of the hamsters was the beginning. You continued by burning Mary Jo's thigh, only you were *going* to shove the hot spatula up into her vagina and guts, but you chickened out and burned only the soft flesh *near* her vagina. Now the time has come for you, with Michael's help, to kill three billion people.' I heard a lot of talk like that from the Lord in the summer of '74.

"Kill three billion people! A big order from God, Flora, a big order! And it had to be done! But how was I to begin? My mind, ever since I was twelve, has been full of pictures of cutting sexual organs, both male and female. I used this thinking through the years mostly so I could be potent first with Hilda, then with Betty. But I can see now that it had another purpose: *Without* the images, which brought me erections, I couldn't obey God's command. With them, I could.

"But I didn't know how to kill. I didn't know how to kill. Except for the hamsters, I'd never killed a person or an animal. This was war, God's war. I was His general, Michael was my second-in-command, both of us against the world for God!

"Flora, I've never been in a war. I was just a little boy during World War Two. Later, Korea and Vietnam were just names and pictures in the newspapers to me.

"I had been a fearful child. Now I was a fearful adult. But Michael wasn't afraid of anything, had none of the fears I had at his age. In the summer of 1974 he was twelve and a half. I needed someone who was cold and fearless to help me kill three billion people. And I needed someone I loved and trusted. That was Michael: He didn't have a nerve in his body and he was my beloved son. Also I knew that my penis wasn't as large as his, so he would have the power I didn't have. Michael became my strength and courage.

209

"I couldn't do it without him, so on June 26 I made a direct appeal: 'Mike, I have a strong desire to kill people and you're the one to help me.' Michael didn't wait one second. He came out with it loud and clear: 'Glad to do it, Dad!' We had a close, heart-warming father-and-son relationship.

"I didn't tell him about God's command. Maybe he wouldn't have believed me, would've thought I was out of my mind and maybe refused to help me.

"A week and a half went by. We hadn't said anything more about this, but at three o'clock in the afternoon on Sunday, July 7, I told him that I wanted to find someone to kill today. 'Good, Dad,' he said. 'I'll help you.' I went on working, even though the shop was closed. Michael was watching me work with the cutter and just as I sliced off a heel—it was about four o'clock—he said, 'Let's go!'

"We walked without knowing where we were going to end up. Michael said, 'I'm going to pick out somebody!' I said, 'We'll see.' There was something in me pulling back from what I knew had to be done. But because I depended on Mike so much, it was like he had me under a spell. I knew I'd do anything Mike did. I'd do what *he* wanted.

"And who would believe that? Here I am, the father, but the son, Mike, is the power. And except for my penis, I'm bigger than him. Michael was just four feet ten, skinny as they come, with long brownish blond hair waving around his shoulders that made him look almost like a girl, so frail-looking you'd think a wind could blow him over. But he was good at sports, like I'm not. I always encouraged him in sports because that was something I couldn't do. But Mike *was* sort of sickly, Flora, with that asthmatic cough of his.

"Well, it was around six-thirty when we stopped in front of the Mann Recreation Center on Fifth Street and Allegheny Avenue. Just outside the building is the swimming pool, and although it was late, there were still a lot of people at the pool, mostly kids.

"We spotted a short, skinny, dark-skinned boy, about nine or ten years old. He was wearing sneakers. His shirt and dungaree shorts were ragged. He was standing by himself, playing with a cigarette lighter. He flipped it on and off, on and off, over and over, on and off. There was something strange about the way he did that.

210

"Mike and I watched the kid for a few minutes to make sure he was alone. He'd flip the lighter on and off, then take a few steps, stop, flip it on and off again. It was weird. Nobody came for him, so Mike went up to him. From the kid's accent, I guessed he was Puerto Rican. When Mike asked him where he lived, he said only a couple of blocks from the swimming pool. When he gave Mike his address, I recognized it as a mixed neighborhood of whites and Puerto Ricans. Mike asked him his name and looked up at me, winked, and slightly nodded his head as if to say, let's get this one. The kid said that his name was José Collazo.

" 'We need some help in moving some boxes of ribbon,' I found myself saying to José. 'Will you help us?'

"Why I thought of ribbon I didn't know. Why I was looking for a reason to take him with us I did know. If the kid had started screaming and struggling in public, we'd lose our first victim in world massacre.

"José hesitated. 'I have to be home by nine,' he said.

" 'You will be,' I told him.

" 'We have these boxes of ribbons, see,' Mike added, very friendly. 'We'll pay you to help us, okay?'

" 'Okay,' José agreed. 'But I have to be home by nine.'

"We left the recreation center. José put the lighter into his pocket. I knew that not far away was an abandoned rug factory. I decided we'd kill José there.

"We walked along the streets, then up steps to a small black footbridge over the railroad, down steps, and again along the streets. There was little conversation; all I can remember is that José said that he was in the third grade. As we walked along, I was outside nearest the curb, Mike was inside, and José was between us. He seemed to be comfortable next to Mike, who was about José's age.

"When Mike and I left the store, I was not a willing subject to my own thoughts. I was frightened, but I knew what *had* to be done. But after Mike had nodded at me, telling me that he had selected José to be our first killing, I was no longer afraid. The Lord of Hosts was with us.

"However, if we failed this first time—if our strength failed us and we couldn't kill José—then we would always fail. But if we succeeded, the rest would follow: Mike and I would knock over three billion people like they were ducks in a pond. On this Sunday evening would come our test of strength.

"It took us less than a half hour to get from the swimming pool to the abandoned rug factory at Hancock and Westmoreland Streets, where we were taking José.

"We walked in. The inside of the factory was pitch-black and we couldn't see where we were going. I asked José for his lighter and, with the lighter to light our way, Mike and I started to go up a long flight of rusty steel steps. But this time José drew back. 'I have to go home,' he whimpered. Now his voice had a different ring from his 'I have to be home by nine.' The ease he had felt in the street crumbled the minute he was inside the factory and saw that it was an abandoned place.

"When José said that, we made him walk up the stairs by holding his arms tightly. Again he was between Mike and me, but now he didn't walk voluntarily. He wiggled a little on the way up to the landing but didn't really try to break away. He just kept saying over and over again, his voice sounding more frightened each time, 'I have to go home.' He didn't scream.

"We reached the landing. It was very small—sort of like a little balcony. Kids used this place to play, and empty soda and beer bottles were strewn around. We felt our feet hit against them as we moved about. There was hardly room enough to walk in. The landing didn't seem to lead anywhere and we felt as if we were hanging in space. With the help of the cigarette lighter I inspected the area. With my penknife I cut the black wire of an old electric fan that I found. Because of the darkness, José couldn't see me cutting the cord.

"I was nervous. I had put the lighter in my pocket while I was cutting the cord. I took the lighter out when the cord was cut. But the lighter fell out of my hands, fell down the stairs. I didn't try to get it back.

"It took less than a minute to cut the cord. While I was doing that, Michael began undressing José. There was no rough stuff. The undressing was nice and pleasant. After it was over, the boy sat nude on the steel floor with Michael holding him down by the shoulders. Michael had placed José's clothes in a neat pile right near where he had been stripped. Then we put him flat on his back and with one section of the cord we bound his hands in front of his body and then with the other section we bound his ankles.

"When I touched him, the only thing I felt was my fear. He struggled a little, but was too scared to resist. The room was dark and odorless. There wasn't even the dusty smell you might expect from an abandoned place, nor the sweat you'd expect to smell from a kid who had taken a long walk on a hot night and was then terrified by what we were doing to him. But there was sweat on me. I could feel it dripping from my forehead, hands and nose.

"Michael took one of José's socks from the pile of clothing, put the sock in the boy's mouth, and then taped the mouth with the black tape I had brought from the store and had slipped to Michael just after I'd cut the cord. The gag was tight.

"I took the handcutter out of the plastic bag and gave it to Michael. This tool is heavier at the top than it is at the point where the handles are connected to the sharp blade.

"Michael was kneeling on the floor. He leaned over José, and tried shoving the top and heavier part of the handcutter into the boy's rectum. It didn't fit. We needed something thinner. Michael then jammed the bottom part of the handcutter into the kid's rectum. He struggled and tried to yell through the black tape. His whole body was writhing, but he couldn't get out much of a sound. I held him.

"After pulling the tool out of José's rectum, Michael turned him over. He was light. There was a little thud, the sound of his thin body rolling over and hitting steel. The kid was now flat on his back. I didn't notice if he was breathing. Michael leaned over and placed José's penis on the tiny metal table that was attached to the handcutter. Michael squeezed the two handles and the steel blade came down on the penis—just like a guillotine chops heads off.

"Michael handed me the handcutter. It was too dark to see anything. I could feel that about half an inch of penis was stuck on the table. I removed the piece of flesh, put the handcutter into my pants pocket, and put the flesh into the plastic bag in which I had carried the tool. Michael never knew that I'd saved the flesh.

"Michael and I untied the boy. I was pretty sure he was dead. We never heard him panting for breath, and he maybe died because of suffocation. Or maybe because the tool cut up his rectum. Whatever killed him—the gag, the cutter, terror—Mike and I did what we had planned to do. We'd passed the test. The rest would be easy. God's will be done! Amen, Flora!

"José hadn't even cried. We picked up his clothes—shorts, sneakers, underwear, shirt—and left the factory, the clothes in a bundle under Michael's left arm.

"I was a little disappointed because it had been too dark in the factory to see blood. I wanted to see blood. My thoughts were drenched in blood: blood gushing out of human bodies, blood flooding the cities, staining rivers and oceans, blood boiling in a huge pot with morsels of sexual organs in it that quiver while bubbles pop and splash.

"But I knew there'd be plenty of blood at the end of the world massacre, so I cheered up and put my arm around Michael's shoulders—Mike, my second-in-command, my courage, my son. Without him, I couldn't have passed the test.

"Michael and I didn't agree on only one thing—at first. I wanted to destroy the victims' sexual organs. I had almost castrated a boy at the creek near Neshaminy when I was twelve and a half, and three more times I'd tried to destroy sexual organs. The urge died off and didn't come back until I was a father. Now I wanted to make Mike a delegate for what I had *not* succeeded in doing when I was his age. I wanted him to do what *I* hadn't been able to do.

"But Mike just wanted to stab the victim, to plunge the blade into his heart. I don't know why, Flora, but Mike agreed to do it my way. So everything worked out as planned: Mike cut the boy's penis as easily as falling off a log.

"We walked through the darkness straight down Hancock Street to the dead end of the railroad. Wildly I threw José's sneakers into the railroad embankment. The rest of his stuff we dumped into an open empty boxcar in the railroad scrapyard. I threw the black tape into a culvert between the curb at Second Street and the scrap yard. We kept the handcutter.

"We went toward Lehigh Avenue, but took a detour so as not to go directly into Front Street. We didn't say much, and we hadn't talked much in the factory, either.

"We got back to the store about nine P.M., five hours after we'd

214

left it. Michael went upstairs to his room. 'Goodnight, Dad.' 'Goodnight, Michael.' It was a warm goodnight. The test had brought us even closer together than before. Mike and I were now fighting God's war against the world. It was going to be easy, like shooting ducks in a pond.

"Alone in the store, I took the cutter out of my pocket. It smelled of poop. I wiped it and put it back on the bench where it belonged. I took the flesh out of the plastic bag. It was half an inch, as I'd figured back in the factory. I put it back into the bag, which I put into a drawer of the workbench.

"The next day the piece of dead penis gave off an odor, so I sealed it in a square of plaster of Paris an eighth of an inch thick. Although this trophy was small, I could *imagine* that an entire penis had been amputated and the testicles cut off. In the factory, Michael had acted out my castration fantasy, so that I had the same feeling of release as if I had done it myself.

"For a week I kept the square piece of plaster of Paris in the store near my workbench. After that I stored my trophy under the planks of the wooden floor of the large room in which I had dug my hole at 1808 East Hagert Street. But after two weeks I could smell the stench rising up through the wooden floor. I threw the plaster-of-Paris square down a sewer four blocks from my Hagert Street house.

"Why did Mike and I kill this kid? Why José? Why a *kid*? Well, Mike chose him and I went along with it. Picking José for our first victim seemed to me at the time as right as going to church on Sunday. A few days or a week after killing José, I remembered the incident only as pieces of a dream, although God's command to me was coming in almost daily from Heaven.

"Flora, it's only during the past few days talking to you here in Camden County Jail that the memory of Michael and me killing José Collazo came back to me in a violent rush. For years it hasn't been with me at all. It seemed like just another horror story in the newspapers. I remember talking to Harry Comer about it; we both said it was cruel and shocking. A man was arrested for the crime, and Comer and I talked about him as we did about anything else. I was just another outraged citizen, Flora. The man was released and the story died off."

"But," I asked, "why should you make this dissociation? You didn't feel guilt because you were acting under God's command and thought that what you were doing was right."

"Yeah," Joe replied. "That's the mystery, the hell of the whole thing. Whole periods of my life, whole episodes, are wiped away. There is still so much I haven't told you. I *know* there is. But I don't know *what* I haven't told you. You may not believe me, but that's the way it is."

"Joe," I replied, "I wouldn't believe you if I hadn't written a book about a woman—Sybil—who couldn't remember many whole stretches of time from the age of three and a half until forty-two. She suffered from hysterical dissociation. What accounts for your time lapses, I think, is schizophrenic dissociation."

"Call it what you like," he said. "But the fact is that there is an awful lot I don't remember. Until just a few days ago, the murder of José was one of those episodes. Now that I remember, I wish I could forget. The kid was minding his own business, and we killed him. He didn't scream. He didn't make a fuss. He was a sweet kid." (Here Joe giggled, and then began to cry.)

"Flora," he continued after he had calmed down, "I chose Michael as my partner—my second-in-command—because he was so cold and never showed emotion. But after we had killed José Collazo, I was scared because I knew Michael could really do it—really kill people without losing his cool. Even God's orders could not remove my fear. Mike took pleasure in that Sunday's outing. He felt like a big shot and his voice showed excitement. I knew that the combination of Michael and me was going to be the terror of the world. But I was frightened, Flora, really frightened. While Mike and I were walking back from the abandoned factory where we'd just killed José Collazo, I said to Mike as we approached our house, 'We're going to murder others.' And Mike replied, 'Good!' "

The outside door of this jail on the sixth floor of the fourteen-story white granite county building closed behind me—until tomorrow night, when I would be coming back.

"Late tonight," the elevator man said.

Late, I thought, because I had had a first-row orchestra seat at a private—in fact exclusive—showing of a horror story. It was the

story of a cold-blooded, senseless, altogether unmotivated murder—
at least from the point of view of the relationship of the murderers
to the victim. But it was also the first full-blown expression in tragic
action of Joe's psychosis that is being traced in this book.

On this hot June night, as I stepped into my car, I felt a cold chill.

13 The Last Song

Early on Sunday morning, July 21, 1974—exactly two weeks after Joe and Michael had killed José Collazo—Joe saw, as if on a movie screen, a boy being thrown off a mountain and falling to his death.

At the moment the boy hit the ground and the frail body was shattered, Joe, lying in the sofa-bed in the living room, had an erection.

He believed that the Lord was again sending him the command to kill, but in pictures rather than in words. Joe started to masturbate, but without pleasure. In the past month he had ceased to be potent even with the old images of slicing and cutting. No longer potent, he had moved from Betty's room to a sofa-bed in the living room. Thinking the move only temporary, Betty had acquiesced.

Now Joe thought of Betty upstairs, but without excitement. Not sexual desire, but the command to kill and the bloody thoughts the command implanted had made Joe's penis hard. He buttoned his pajama pants and sat on the edge of the sofa-bed.

"You must get *him* up there," the Voice of the Lord ordered. "Up there where it's high. Throw him off the edge of the cliff. Make sure the place you choose to kill him is so high that falling will mean certain death!" Now the Lord's command was in words.

Up there? Where was that? Joe wondered. Who was *him*?

Joe saw the boy limping toward the edge of a cliff. He had a malevolent twinkle in his eyes. Looking at Joe, the boy said, "You stop picking on me, motherfucker, or I'll get you locked up again." It was Joey! He was cussing out his own daddy! One of the three "total gods," he was trying with his mean eyes and devilish words to send Joseph Kallinger back to the slammer!

To *destroy* him! Joey had kept the diaries. In one of them he had written, "I wanna drown my Dad—burn him in lots of fire." Joey's message was clear; and the son's death wish for the father incited the father's hallucination of *his* death wish for his son.

"You will find the name of a high place in a brochure on the small table beside the sofa-bed," the Voice of the Lord instructed.

Joe, still sitting on the edge of the sofa-bed, reached for the travel brochures. He had picked them up a few days ago at Tourist Information in Center City because he had wanted to take Mike, Jimmy, and Joey on a day's outing. After looking over the brochures, he selected one and replaced the others on the table.

Joe read the brochure slowly and carefully. He looked for the high place about which the Voice had told him. It was ten miles from Wellsboro, Pennsylvania, a place called Grand Canyon. He read: "Located in beautiful north-central Pennsylvania, the Pennsylvania Grand Canyon has become one of the fastest-growing tourist meccas in the East. Thousands are awed each year at the majesty of this 50-mile-long gorge. At Leonard Harrison Park Lookout, Pine Creek flows through the canyon 1,000 feet below. But a visit to Canyon County offers more than the beauty of the canyon itself. . . ."

Joe closed the brochure and put it back on the table. One thousand feet below, Joe mused. A body falling from Grand Canyon into the gorge would be destroyed.

The eyes. The foul mouth, Joe thought. The look of the Devil! That's Joey. . . .But I love Joey. I worry about him all the time. How can I kill him?

"You must destroy what you love," the Voice of God commanded.

"But I've never thought of killing *Joey*!" Joe replied. "The whole world, three billion people, okay, but Joey . . ."

"Joey is a thorn in your heart, Joseph. He's a homosexual, too."

"But he's my son," Joe whimpered.

"Destroy this son! Even though you love him, you must kill him,

219

because he's possessed by the Devil, a spawn of Satan that went through your body into Betty's when you laid her to produce Joey. Kill Joey! I, the Lord of Hosts, command you, Joseph Kallinger!"

"All my battles were fought for Joey. I rescued him like no one rescued me when *I* was a kid. I'm Joey's knight in shining armor. When things went wrong for him, I was there. I'd put my arms around him and kiss him. I never abandoned him. When he ran away, I took him back."

"Back?" asked the Voice sardonically. "Did you say *back? That's* a laugh! Joey can send *you* back! Back to prison, Joe, back to prison for violation of probation. Remind you of anything, eh, *mein Kind? Ja?*"

"Sure! When I was a kid, my folks threatened to send me back to St. Vincent's. All the time. But Joey loves his daddy. We've been together since May. Even if he didn't love me, *I'm* the boss because I have a weapon over Joey: I can send *him* back to Eastern State. He was released in my custody, and I can send him back."

"Joey helped to destroy your orthopedic experiments," the Voice persisted. "You had to take time from the experiments because Joey was always getting into trouble or running away. If you had spent more time on the experiments and less time worrying about that Devil's spawn, they wouldn't have failed, you wouldn't have burned Mary Jo's thigh, the three 'total gods' wouldn't have sent you to Holmesburg. And you would have been the savior of the world. But now you must destroy it."

"I was shaken by what I was being ordered to do," Joe told me on July 4, 1977, in our familiar infirmary niche in the Camden County Jail. "I asked Michael to come into the store with me for a minute. He had already told me that he wanted to kill his brother. Michael hated Joey. 'I can't stand Joey!' Michael often said. There were times I couldn't stand Joey, either. He drove everybody up the wall. But I loved him and liked him so much. I closed the door. I said, 'Mike, we're going to Grand Canyon today.'

" 'Never been there,' Mike replied.

" 'I know that,' I said. 'But we're going today—you, Jimmy, Joey, and me.'

220

" 'Why you telling just me?' Mike asked.

" 'Because . . .' I hesitated. Then the Voice spoke for me: 'When I woke up today, I knew I had to kill Joey.'

"Michael didn't seem to recognize that there had been another voice. He just looked at me, frowning a bit, sucking his buck teeth. Fear rose in his eyes, Flora, real fear. Michael, the Cool, was capable of being afraid. Although Michael had said many times, 'Let's get *rid* of Joey!' I could sense what he was thinking. 'This is the family. If Dad could do it to my brother, he could do it to me.'

"Looking at Michael, I thought how wrong that was. He was the heartbeat of the whole thing, of all my plans to kill. I was nothing without Michael. From the time we began our partnership in the winter of 1973–1974, Mike had been to me like a seeing-eye dog to a blind man. Every other member of the family could have been killed—anyone except Michael. Without him my strength would have faded away. If anything happened to him, it would be like my heart had stopped. I needed Michael to help me destroy the planet Earth.

"I said, 'Mike, it's okay.'

"He seemed to change when I said that. Fear left his eyes and the old coldness returned. The eyes were cold when Mike asked: 'How we gonna do it, Dad?'

"I explained that Grand Canyon was a high place. Mike got the point right away. 'We'll throw him off a cliff,' Mike said. His eyes, always glassy, seemed more so than at other times.

" 'Maybe, Mike,' I replied.

" 'Why maybe? Let's get *rid* of him *today*!'

"I thought to myself, imagine saying that about your own brother. It's so unnatural. I didn't say anything to myself about killing your own son. That would have been too cruel. I think that *now*, but I didn't think that *then*."

" 'Why maybe?' Mike asked again.

"Flora, I don't know why I said 'maybe.' Perhaps it was because, in line with the thoughts I usually had, I wanted to mutilate my son sexually instead of throwing him off a cliff. Remember, that's how I planned to kill three billion people—through destruction of their sex organs. Or maybe it was because I loved Joey and didn't want to do what the Voice commanded. 'Well,' I said to Mike, 'we'll see. Who knows what the day will bring?' "

After breakfast, Joe walked into the shop, where Michael, Jimmy, and Joey were waiting. Joe took the Brownie camera off a glass shelf and then took money out of the cash register. He gave each of the boys two dollars and pocketed the rest.

"You kids ready to go?" he asked.

"Shit, yeah!" Joey replied, lighting a cigarette. "If we don't get going *now*, something's going to flatten the mountains and they'll look like pancakes. It sure took you long enough to get dressed!"

Joe watched Joey lean insolently against the street door of the shop. The cigarette dangled from the corner of his mouth. Joe again saw Joey's body falling from a cliff; then he heard the cracking of Joey's bones, the tearing of his skin as his body bounced once or twice before flopping to rest, limbs twisted, his face smashed like a bloody rag doll. The picture changed: He saw Joey's battered and twisted body lying among those who made up the great mountain of the damned, so high that it could be seen over the horizon. The invisible demons, who flew in eternal patrol around the mountain, were cutting off Joey's penis and testicles with their flaming knives.

"Why are you just standing there, Daddy? What are you looking at? Let's go!" Joey screeched.

"Listen, Joey . . ." Joe began.

"C'mon, Daddy," Michael said. "Don't listen to him—not now, anyway. Let's go!"

Joe watched Joey limping eagerly ahead of Jimmy and Mike, who were running in circles and pretending to be airplanes and birds. "I'm a big bird flyin' over a mountain," Mike said as he circled and dipped with his arms outstretched.

"All right," Joe said, "let's stay together now and don't go running off getting lost. We'll have more enjoyment out of this thing if we stick together. Right?"

Joey still jauntily limped ahead, however, and sang to himself softly: "We had joy, we had fun, we had seasons in the sun/But the hills that we climb are just seasons out of time." Joey thought about

222

his good dad—the "fun-and-games dad." He stopped walking at the Frankford Elevated Line station to wait for his father and brothers.

"How long'll the bus ride take?" Jimmy asked as they walked up the steps to the elevated platform at Kensington Avenue and A Street.

"Two or three hours, I guess," Joe replied.

"Are we gonna do a lot of climbing?"

"I don't know, Jimmy. Maybe," Joe said.

Though Jimmy had reservations about climbing, all three boys were excited about going exploring.

A chubby boy with bushy blond hair, who had just come onto the el platform, walked toward them.

"Where you goin', Marty?" Mike asked.

"Gonna have Sunday dinner with my grandma," replied Martin Slocum, one of the kids with whom Mike "hung."

"Shit, that ain't *nothin'*," Joey said. "*We're* gonna climb a high mountain. I bet it's the highest mountain in the whole of Pennsylvania."

"Where's it at?" Martin Slocum asked with awe.

"Grand Canyon," Joey replied. "Ten miles from some place they call Wellsboro. We're takin' a bus."

"You're lucky, Joey! I wish *my* dad would take me places like Grand Canyon. But he don't take me noplace."

"Hey, the train's comin' in," Mike yelled.

Joe walked grimly toward the ticket window in the bus terminal at Thirteenth and Arch Streets. He wanted to turn back; he felt panic churning his stomach and found it difficult to breathe, as if he had a vise around his chest. But he couldn't stop now.

"Four round-trip tickets to Wellsboro," Joe told the agent. "When does the bus leave?"

"In eight minutes," the agent replied.

Joe walked slowly away from the ticket window. The boys wanted to go to the rest room, so Joe went with them to the one on the Arch Street side of the terminal, the opposite end from the ticket area.

They stayed too long in the rest room and missed the bus. Knowing that he couldn't kill Joey unless he got to Grand Canyon, Joe felt relieved; but he also felt a great urge to kill his son, which he hallucinated God had commanded.

Still feeling the strong urge to kill Joey, he went back to the ticket window, where he learned that he could wait until one o'clock for the next bus to Wellsboro or go to Hazleton, where he could change for Grand Canyon.

After a brief discussion with the boys, Joe bought tickets for Hazleton.

In the Hazleton station, Joe asked a ticket agent about the Grand Canyon connection from Hazleton, but the agent told him that on Sundays there was no bus making that run.

The boys were disappointed. Joe said, "Well, how about visiting the mines?" He knew that he could kill Joey as easily by throwing him down a mine pit as by pushing him off the top of Grand Canyon. Joe said, "We'll go to Grand Canyon next week."

"Great!" Joey said sarcastically. "But I wanted to see Grand Canyon today! Balls, Daddy. Did you have to fuck this up? Who wants to see some old mines when we could be standing on top of Grand Canyon?"

Joey rolled his cigarette with his tongue from the left corner of his mouth to the right. He inhaled a large amount of smoke and blew it in Mike's face.

"Stop smoking for a minute, will you? Your butts are killing me with this cough. You're a pain, Joey, you know that?"

"And you're just a *goody-goody*, Mike Kallinger. You're not worth a fuck." Joey made a fist with his right hand and raised the middle finger at Michael.

"Joey, be quiet," Joe ordered. "Jimmy wants to say something."

"I bet the mines will be fun," Jimmy said. "Better than hanging around this creepy station doing nothing."

Joe went back to the ticket window and asked the agent for the way to the mines. After having listened to the directions, he gathered his sons from different points in the bus station to which they had wandered.

Joe was angry at himself for having decided to go to the mines. In spite of the Voice's command Joe was fearful of what might happen when he and Joey stood near the edge of a pit. As he opened the door of the station and walked onto the streets of Hazleton, Joe heard Joey's scream trailing away as his body picked up speed falling down a mine shaft toward the center of the earth.

On Sundays only tourists came to the coal mines and slate pits that surround the city of Hazleton. Once as fertile as the surrounding mountainous country covered with pines, birches, and aspens, the land was now scarred by strip mines, and deep holes pocked the surface of the ground. Many flat-topped cones of slate and clay, wide at the base, narrowing as they rose, sat among the pits. Scattered throughout the area were power shovels, drills, trucks, and cranes, their motors silent. In the cloudless sky the afternoon sun burned into the wasteland, and the silence deepened the desolation.

Joe and his sons walked along a footpath that wound among the holes and the cones. Joe stopped beside one of the highest and looked up. The mound had a gentle slope and did not seem difficult to climb.

"Okay," Joe said as he walked along the base of the cone, "we're going up this pile and see what's on top." He was no longer interested in the deep holes.

Joe found a rocky footpath that went up the flank of the cone. The large number of flat rocks and the path's gentle ascent made the climb easy.

Less than halfway to the top, however, Joey stopped walking. He and Jimmy were behind Joe and Mike.

"Hey, Dad," Joey called.

Joe stopped climbing and turned around.

Joey sat down on a rock. He said, "I'm pooped—I'm not going any farther. That's it!"

"Your ankle bothering you?" Joe asked.

"Naw, I'm just tired."

"How come your brothers aren't tired?"

"I'm not interested in them."

"Okay," Joe said, "we're going without you."

"Fuck you, Daddy!" Joey got up from the rock, gestured with a thrust of his hips, his hand rubbing his crotch, and sat down again.

"C'mon, Jimmy," Joe said, "let's leave him."

225

"Up yours!" Joey snarled. He stayed on his rock and angrily watched his father and brothers climb away from him.

A few minutes later, Joe heard Joey yelling, "Hey, Daddy, wait up for me!"

Joe saw Joey climbing toward him. The sound of his voice and the slap of his boots on the rocks were disquieting. At the same time Joe realized that the afternoon was quickly passing and that he had better get moving if he was going to kill Joey today.

Joey lit a cigarette and blew a few smoke rings. Then he spat on the ground, smiled, and said, "I decided to catch up with you 'cause I don't wanna miss the fun. But I walk when I wanna walk, get it?" He scowled and went on seriously, "Nobody tells me what to do. I make all the rules."

Looking at his son, Joe remembered a line from Joey's "dear-dad" diaries: "I wanna drown my dad—burn him in lots of fire."

Suddenly Joe was hallucinating. He saw himself as an adult lying on the floor of the cottage in Neshaminy. He was on his back, cruciform and naked. Over his body Joey was throwing dry branches and brittle leaves that he ignited with a match. The branches and leaves crackled as Joe's skin burned and shriveled. The reek of burning flesh and muscle filled the cottage. Joe raised his head from the floor The lower half of his face was burnt: fragments of charred skin hung from jaw and cheekbones. Only his eyes were alive with pain, while beneath them his skull grinned. Joey watched him from an old beach chair on which he was reclining. His eyes were merry. A cigarette dangled from the corner of his mouth. He hummed softly to himself, "We had joy . . . we had fun . . . we had seasons in the sun. . . ."

The images of the hallucination vanished.

Joe shivered under the hot sun. His body trembled; sweat poured over his eyes. He was thirsty; his lips were parched; his spittle was bitter. He wished that he had taken canteens filled with water.

"What's the matter, Daddy?" Joey asked. "Now *you're* the one that's tired, huh?"

Shaking him gently by his shoulders, Joe answered quietly, "No, I'm not tired, Joey."

He looked at Mike and Jimmy. It would have been better, he

thought, to have left Jimmy home. Then Joe looked upward. The Voice of God boomed in his ear that on the top of the mound he would find the right place to kill Joey.

The top of the mound was a wide plateau with a few heavy rocks jutting from the flat surface. Scattered around were many small rocks, all made of fine-grained bluish-gray slate formed by the compression of clay and shale. The sun beat heavily on the plateau. The treeless surface was without shade.

Joe and his sons sat on the ground to rest. They squinted against the harsh light. Joe picked up a few small rocks, dropped them, and wished again for water. His shirt and pants were sodden with sweat.

"I gotta go piss," Jimmy said.

"Go piss over the other side, see what it looks like," Mike said.

"Okay." Jimmy walked to the other side of the plateau. "Wow!" he yelled, "Sure looks different than the side we came up. It's straight down!" He picked up a small rock and threw it, watching it arc far out, then plummet to the ground.

Joe walked up to Jimmy and looked over the edge. The drop was vertical. This was the place to kill Joey; there was nothing to break his fall.

Joey was standing a little way from Mike, who was carefully watching Joey. Joey cupped his hands around his mouth: "Joeeeeee Kaaaaaallinger, Joeeeeee Kaaaaaallinger!" Joey lowered his hands and waited for the echo. He frowned. Then he yelled again, "Joeeeeee Kaaaaaallinger!" No echo came.

"Shit!" he exclaimed. "No echo, no sound. Like this place is real *dead*!"

"I didn't trust Daddy when he started taking pictures of me and Joey," Jimmy Kallinger told me on March 19, 1978. "Daddy's lips buckled and got tight, like they always did when he snapped out.

"Me and Joey were out on the edge of the rock. Joey was behind me on the tip, almost into empty space. Daddy said:

" 'Move back a little. I want to take your pictures.'

" 'A little more,' Daddy said.

" 'That's fine.'

227

"Then Daddy started taking pictures. He had Joey move in different poses. He also asked me to pose, but not so much. Me and Joey were on the tip of the rock. Michael was with Daddy, but only Daddy took the pictures.

"I was scared, man. Joey was too, I think. But he was brave, you know. I admired Joey for being brave and for standing up to Daddy. But on the tip of that rock Joey mostly did everything Daddy was telling him."

"I didn't trust myself," Joe told me on August 9, 1977. "I was taking pictures of Joey and Jimmy on the edge of the top of that high slate mound we'd climbed—on the edge of the plateau. I was telling them to move closer to the tip—Joey closer than Jimmy. I didn't trust myself because I didn't like the way I had looked over the edge to see whether Joey would be killed if he fell. And I had been thinking about killing Joey on and off all day.

"Mike was standing next to me while I was taking the pictures. I had no idea of what he was thinking. We had talked about killing Joey in the store that morning, but we hadn't said anything about it after that.

"While I was taking pictures, Mike touched my arm to get my attention. He said, 'Dad, lemme throw a rock at Joey.'

" 'Go ahead,' I replied.

"Joey was standing right on the tip of the edge. I knew he would lose his balance if the rock hit him. If the rock hit him, he had to go, but I told Mike, 'Go ahead.'

"This frightened me. Something was pulling me back from killing Joey, Flora, but I was also trying to follow God's command. It was a struggle, a real struggle.

"I did know that I didn't want Jimmy to see Mike throw the rock. I didn't want a witness. And I didn't want Jimmy to see his brother kill his brother. So I said, 'Jimmy, come this way. I want to take your picture back here.' I took him to the other side of the plateau and made sure his back was turned to Mike and Joey. Mike waited while I did this.

"I was facing both Mike and Joey. I saw Mike pick up a rock with a jagged end and a circumference of about nine inches. Mike aimed

228

the rock at his brother. I saw the rock flying through the air, heading for Joey. Then I saw the rock miss him and go over the edge.

"I took another picture of Joey and acted like nothing had happened. Then I saw Mike walking over to Joey. What was Mike up to? I wondered. Was Mike going to push Joey? I didn't know. I did know that I no longer wanted Joey to be killed. The desire was gone. Totally gone. Like when a full cup becomes empty and dry. I no longer wanted my son killed.

"So I went to where Joey and Mike were standing. Mike, looking down, was saying, 'I'm not afraid to jump.'

"It seemed like Mike was challenging Joey to do just that. So I said, 'C'mon, Joey. Come off the edge. It's time to go, anyway.'

"Joey did as I said. Then we walked down the cone. On the way I heard Joey say to Mike, 'What were you trying to do, kill me?'

"I didn't like the sound of that. It came too close to what might have happened. And I was glad Joey said that to Mike—not to me.

"I wanted to kill Joey when I left home that morning. The Lord had told me that early on in my world massacre, I had to kill a member of my own family as a sacrifice. I had to prove that my family was no better than anyone else's family. That morning, when I saw the scenes of Joey falling, I knew he was the one to be sacrificed. My cup was full of the desire to kill Joey; the cup was full of blood.

"In the bus terminal I had wavered. Joey was my own flesh, my child. I wanted to save him. This feeling kept coming between me and my desire to follow the Lord's command. But the command— and, yes, my *own* desire to do the Lord's bidding—made me want to kill my son.

"On the slate mound my cup was very full. Then the feeling of a normal father came back and the blood drained out of the cup. The same thing had happened when I was twelve and a half and planned to cut off the penis of another boy. I couldn't do it, even though the boy was standing right in front of me and naked from the waist down. I ran away. But at that time I was not under the command of the Lord. *Now* I was!

"I didn't know whether the Lord knew I was drawing back. He probably did. The Lord knows everything. I was afraid He'd think

229

I was a traitor and punish me. I was scared. But killing Joey was far from my thoughts as we walked down the mound in Hazleton and headed for home. The desire had been washed away like an ugly stain. The cup was dry!"

At 5:45 A.M. on Thursday, July 25, 1974, Joe heard an explosion. He got out of bed, turned on the lights, and went from room to room on both floors of the house and into the store. He found no cause of the explosion and no signs of damage. Glimmers of sunrise were coming through the window. In the street only a police car went by slowly, quietly.

The Voice of the Lord came to him, and he turned from the window in terror. Not since Hazleton had the Voice revealed the All-Powerful to Joe. The fear of God's anger, of divine punishment, swept through Joe's body.

Even though Joe was frightened, he could hear the Lord's words distinctly: "You ran away in Hazleton," the Lord said. "You're not going to run away now. The explosion you heard was in yourself. It was a sign that you are getting ready to blow something up." The Voice became silent.

Joe did not know what the "something" was. But he thought of the Niehaus parking lot where large interstate trailers and containers stood side by side. He kept thinking about the trailers: their dark interiors, their spaciousness, how easily they could be destroyed by fire or explosion. A flame from a match igniting a flammable liquid could set fire to a trailer. It could be done before anyone was at work on the parking lot.

Barefoot and in pajamas, Joe went up to Michael's room to say, "Let's go!"

Ten minutes later, Joe stood next to the customers' side of his store. Mike, attentive, was facing him.

"What we tried to do on the slate pile didn't come off, right?" Joe asked.

"Right, Dad."

"At the end, on top of that mound in Hazleton," Joe explained, "I didn't *want* anything to happen to Joey. Yesterday you told me you wished we could have killed him on the mound. I promised you another chance. Well, I'm going to keep my promise today."

"Swell, Dad!"

"So look, Mike," Joe went on. "Let's give Joey some gasoline and get him into one of the trailers on the Niehaus lot at Mascher and West Lehigh. He'll start smoking a cigarette and he's sure to slosh some gasoline around while he's smoking—Joey's pretty dumb about things like that. The gasoline'll catch fire, the trailer will go up in flames and Joey with it. How *about* that, huh?"

"Super!" Mike said.

Mike went upstairs to wake up Joey.

Joe hallucinated: Joey's limbs torn from his body, his inner organs shriveled from the heat, his skin in flames, his head a burning ball of flesh and bone and hair, sending out screams of agony. . . .

Joe's lips widened into a maniacal grin. From his stomach came a rolling, roaring laugh, the belly laugh that had belched out of him for the first time when he was fifteen. Now, as then, it had a will of its own. From Joe's mouth came peals of laughter, like a huge glistening snake quickly uncoiling itself, coil after coil, out of its hole.

Suddenly the laughter stopped.

Joe roused himself and gathered the stage props for the trailer caper: a five-gallon can of gasoline he had bought to take to Neshaminy for the cottage lawnmower, a flashlight, safety matches, three empty half-gallon spring-water bottles made of glass, and two extra-large supermarket shopping bags. He filled the bottles with gasoline and left them uncapped. Into one of the shopping bags he put two of the gasoline bottles, and into the other bag the third gasoline bottle, the flashlight, the cigarettes, and the matches. The two shopping bags were sitting on the counter when Mike and Joey came into the store.

"Man, it's hilarious!" Joey yelled as he came up to Joe and leaned against the counter. "Dad, this idea's a beaut! Are we going to go over to the trailers right now?"

"Yep," Joe replied as he handed Joey the bag with the two bottles of gasoline. "You and Mike are going over *now*. I'll wait here. Mike'll come back for me." Joey lit a cigarette.

"Put out that cigarette, Joey. You better not smoke with gasoline around."

Joey crushed the cigarette in an ashtray on the counter. He began swinging the bag.

"Stop that," Joe ordered. "The bottles aren't capped. You want to get gasoline all over the street?"

"See you later, alligator," Joey said to Joe as he walked into the street.

"I'll catch up with you, Joey," Mike called.

Joe gave Mike the bag with the matches, the flashlight, the cigarettes, and the third bottle of gasoline.

"I don't want Joey lighting a match on the way over there," Joe explained. "We don't want anything happening on the street."

Joe went upstairs and stood at the window of the middle bedroom. It was the room where as a boy he had carved a hole in the wall and had had his first fantasies of destruction.

Joey won't be back anymore, Joe thought as he watched Mike and Joey walking in the direction of the parking lot. The prospect of Joey's destruction by fire in a trailer, Joe told me on August 9, 1977, during one of our last sessions in Camden County Jail, "gave me a feeling of excitement, a thrill, an erection. It was the same kind of excitement I had when later I used a knife for torture. But I didn't have any desire to masturbate while watching Joey walk to his death. When the erection was over, I left the window, got dressed, and went down to the store to wait for Mike."

For Joe, an erection no longer had anything to do with erotic pleasure—an erection had become the expression of the pleasure of murder. Ever since he had evolved the plan for global massacre, murder through sexual organs had replaced the fantasized mutilation of sexual organs as a stimulus to potency.

Later Mike told Joe the story of what happened in the trailer and Joe told it to me.

"Joey and Mike picked a trailer close to a wall. On the trailer there was a container. In case you don't know, Flora, cargo is placed in the container and the container is unloaded from the trailer at docks, railroads, wharves.

"Joey climbed into the container through the rear door. As soon as he got inside, he took the gasoline bottles out of his shopping bag and put them in the front part of the container. When he came back to the rear door, Mike gave him the shopping bag with the cigarettes and matches. Mike told Joey that he was going to get me and we would come to help with the caper. Mike shut the door, but couldn't lock it. He was too short. So he wedged an empty twelve-quart steel milk case between the trailer and the wall. He found the case on the parking lot. Anyway, when Mike told me this I said, 'Okay. Whatever you did was right.'

"We went up to the middle bedroom and looked out of the window. Mike pointed out the trailer. We kept watching it, not talking, but just waiting.

"After a while we saw smoke. It was very black and rushing out of Joey's trailer!

" 'Good,' Mike said. 'He's dead.'

" 'Yep, I guess so,' I said.

"It seemed so, Flora. But I had no thrill, no erection. *Now* I didn't want Joey to be dead. It was like Hazleton in the end. Like, on the slate pile, the cup was empty.

"But in Hazleton I was able to save Joey from *me*. Now I couldn't do anything if Joey was dead. I had delegated Joey to kill himself. And that smoke made me think that this was my last delegation to Joey.

"Mike and I went down to the store to wait for news."

Joe and Mike sat tensely in the while-you-wait booths. They heard fire-engine sirens, for at 6:38 A.M. the local firehouse had received a telephone call about the fire on the Niehaus parking lot. Two minutes later Company 31, Platoon A, Battalion 06 of the Philadelphia Fire Department arrived at the scene.

In the silence after the wailing of the sirens, Joe heard footsteps, their rhythm uneven and familiar, coming toward the store. Puzzled, he got up and waited for the bell to ring; but instead the door was thrown open.

"I guess that fire got started kind of early," Joey said as he stood framed in the doorway. "I was waiting for you guys to come over."

Joey limped through the doorway, past his father and into the store. He stopped in front of Mike.

"Are you okay?" Joe asked.

Without answering Joey raised himself to the top of the counter and sat down. "Dad, you sit in the booth next to Mike, and I'll tell you all about it."

Joey told what had happened after Mike left him in the trailer. He smoked incessantly and shot lighted cigarettes at the bottles of gasoline. Then he sloshed gasoline on the floor and shot cigarettes at the gasoline. When flames singed the bottom of his pants, he hurled himself at the door with all his might. The trailer door opened and the empty milk case Mike had placed against it was shoved aside. Outside the trailer, Joey rolled on the ground to get the fire out of his pants. Once this was done, he went to Sam's Luncheonette, where he telephoned the fire department and reported the trailer fire. Then he came home.

At 3:00 P.M., Sunday, July 28, 1974, the Voice awakened Joe from a deep sleep. Earlier that morning he had started out with Mike and Joey for Grand Canyon, but on the train to the bus terminal he had decided against Grand Canyon. The Voice of the Lord had led him to a building under construction as a place to kill Joey.

On the pretext of taking pictures, Joe and Mike got Joey to lie face downward on a scaffold a foot above their heads. They wedged Joey between a ladder and planks—in exactly the right position to cut off his penis. But Joe couldn't do it. The cup had run dry.

Joe put the switchblade knife back into his pocket. He and Michael removed the planks from Joey's back and told him to come down from the scaffold.

Joe told his sons that now they were going to the bus terminal to make reservations for the afternoon Wellsboro bus for Grand Canyon. After buying the tickets, they went home.

Joe had fallen asleep on the sofa-bed, and had slept through bus time.

Still wearing the trousers and shirt he had worn in the morning, he sat up in the sofa-bed and listened to the Voice, which had awakened him.

"Killing Joey is right," said the Lord. "This morning you failed because you thought it was wrong. You should have cut off his penis while he was on that scaffold. So think again, Joe, think again, and gird up your loins like a man."

Joe hung his head. He did not answer. In the morning at the scaffold he had fought the Voice, fought it again in the afternoon by falling asleep; even though he had made reservations, Joe had not taken Joey and Mike to Grand Canyon.

"Find a hole. Kill Joey in it. Joey is a demon, he is filled with evil. And he's a fag: His body is dirty from arming and legging it with other boys, from taking their dripping penises into his mouth, taking their hard bones up his ass. Ugh!"

"It's going to happen this afternoon," Joe replied.

"Today, Joey; tomorrow the world," the Voice went on. "You and Michael, your second-in-command, will commit global massacre. You'll kill every member of the filthy human race. Then you'll wipe out your family, what's left of your whole rotten crew. Finally, you'll kill Michael, then yourself."

"I want to die," Joe whimpered.

"You will, Joe, you will. You'll commit a glorious suicide. But first you've got to know something about that mysterious fellow Death. You and Mike got a good start with José Collazo."

"With who?"

"The kid by the pool, Joe. Don't you remember him?"

"No."

"Well, it doesn't matter. There are so many to kill. But you and Mike killed José. *That's* what's important. You proved you have good stuff in you, Joe. Use it!"

"Kyriastorah kyrieh maria kreh," Joe chanted.

Whenever he uttered these sounds, Joe was filled with energy. It was an oceanic feeling that made him aware of what he liked to call his superhuman powers.

Suddenly he was on the summit of the highest mountain in the world. He looked about him from horizon to horizon. A keen wind was blowing. He walked to the edge of the summit and looked down. Swarms of people, very tiny, were rushing about in cities, across farmlands, and in boats on oceans. They were his enemies.

He pointed his finger at one of the cities. Immediately a hurricane destroyed it. He shook his fist at the ruined city—the survivors died horribly from hunger and disease. He turned slightly and pointed his finger at the farmlands. Huge black tornadoes danced across

235

acres of wheat and corn. Farmers, housewives, horses, cows, pigs, children on their way to school, buses, automobiles, trucks, entire farms were all sucked up into the maws of the tornadoes.

Joe turned again and puckered his lips at the oceans. Monstrous waves with thick rain sank ships, inundated solitary islands, ripped from their foundations the buildings of seaports.

Joe looked up. Scudding across the sky were black clouds; the wind now carried the stench of bodies rotting in the cities and farms.

Maybe I've become the demon that wasn't cut out of my "bird" by Dr. Daly, Joe thought. The demon grew; it's no longer *only* in my penis, but I'm bursting at the joints because the demon's taken over my entire body. Now *I'm* the demon.

A knife of lightning split the exact center of the summit. It flung rubble around and dust into the air. The stench of putrid flesh vanished. Joe shook dust and particles of rubble from himself.

As the thunder rolled through the dark sky to the horizon, a figure with the face and body of Joe Kallinger appeared just above the spot where the lightning had struck. A pure light enveloped the figure. Its posture was noble: It wore a shirt and pants made of fire with flecks of opal and turquoise swirling in the flames. On its feet were slippers of mother-of-pearl with golden clasps studded with rubies. On the back of the flaming shirt, written in letters of immutable ice, was the sign: *The Kallinger Rapid Shoe Repair Pickup and Delivery Service.*

The likeness of Joe Kallinger looked around scornfully at the debris, and with its hand fanned away from its face motes of dust.

"I stand before you," the figure said, "in the heavenly form that you will take after you have committed suicide. You are not a demon. *Now* your powers are superhuman, but hidden by that sick and earthy [sic] body that you carry around like a condemned man. After your death you will cast it off and be God. You will rule the universe."

With the grace of a dancer, Joe's likeness glided above the rubble a short distance toward Joe. The radiance of the figure was now a cocoon of light that enveloped the entire summit. Beyond it were the low-scudding clouds and darkness.

"But the time grows short," the figure said. "You must bring Michael into your store and talk to him. Show him the power of

236

your resolve to kill Joey today. On this death trip you must take four chains, four locks, and four keys. Remember: *Be* the figure you now see before you—the god you will become through your suicide after you have destroyed the world."

The hallucinatory scene vanished.

Joe was still sitting on the edge of the sofa-bed, musing over his "vision," when Michael walked into the living room, turned on the television, and sat down to watch the program.

At the scaffold, Mike had called Joe a coward. Mike was disgusted because Dad had chickened out. He wanted nothing more to do with his gutless, spineless father.

But Joe knew that once he had spoken with Mike, his son would have a different opinion.

"Mike, I'd like to have a word with you."

Reluctantly Mike turned off the program anu came over to his father. Truculent and scornful, he stood silently in front of Joe.

Joe said, "Let's go into the store."

In the Sunday stillness, Joe asked, "Where's Joey?"

Mike made a small jump to the top of the counter, near the cash register, and sat quietly for a few moments before he answered his father. Then he said, "He was sitting outside, but he took off. Said he'd be back at six because you were going to take us out to dinner and the movies. To make up for not going to Grand Canyon, he said. I guess he's around someplace."

Joe sat down in one of the while-you-wait booths. He leaned forward, his hands clasped together, his face earnest and determined. "Mike, I've got to tell you something."

"Look, Daddy, if you got me in here to talk about this morning, well, I'm not interested. So forget it, man!"

Joe took a deep breath. He knew that without Mike he couldn't kill Joey no matter how insistent the Voice had become.

"Mike, this afternoon," Joe said slowly in a quiet, trembling voice, "Joey goes down the chute, out of the world—finished!"

Mike raised his eyebrows. He gave a short, derisive laugh.

"I'm not kidding, son," Joe said. "But you must help me. I can't do it without you."

"I was ready to cut off Joey's cock at the scaffold, Daddy, but you

237

wouldn't give me the knife. You said it wasn't right." Mike gave another derisive laugh.

Suddenly Joe's lips lost their sensuous shape. They puckered, the way they always did when Joe was ready for sadistic action. Seeing this, Mike said, "Okay, Daddy. I'll help you this afternoon. But if you mess it up this time, we're not partners anymore."

"I won't mess it up, Mike."

"Where we gonna kill him?" Mike asked.

"You go find Joey now," Joe said. "I'll meet both of you in the OK Restaurant on York. Then we'll find a place."

Joe washed his hands and face, sleeked his hair with VO5, and changed to a fresh pair of black trousers and a clean white shirt open at the collar. Then he went to the cellar. On the floor in a corner were chains with which he had chained his eldest son, Stephen, to a bed. He took four of these chains up to the store.

Into bags used for carrying shoes Joe put the chains and four locks and keys. He took a camera and three flashlights with him, and left through the store door.

Betty, who was sitting on the Front Street steps, thought Joe was sleeping.

Joe met Mike and Joey on York Street, in front of the OK Restaurant. They went in and sat at a window booth in the back.

Joe and Mike sat on one side of the table, Joey on the other. Over hamburgers and cokes Joey reminded his father about Joe's promise to go to Grand Canyon *next* Sunday, but Joey predicted, "You'll fuck up again. I know you." Joe repeated his promise to take the whole family out to dinner that night and said that in the afternoon he and the boys were going to take pictures.

"That's why I brought chains," Joe said.

"Wow! That's super!" Joey exclaimed.

Joey always loved to pose in front of a camera. One day he put on handcuffs for a photograph taken of him and some friends. The friends were pointing at him wearing the handcuffs.

Joey lit a cigarette. He said, "Dad, give me money for the juke-box."

Joe hesitated.

238

"Let him have it," Mike said. Then he whispered in Joe's ear, "C'mon, it's his last time."

Joey was looking at the list of records on the selection control. "Hey, Dad, they have my favorite."

"Here," Joe said.

Joey put the coin in the slot, then sat back and listened to his favorite pop-rock song, "Seasons in the Sun." Terry Jacks sang, "We had joy, we had fun, we had seasons in the sun; but the hills that we climb are just seasons out of time."

Joey sang, too. So did Joe, who rarely sang at all. He sang very softly, the words scarcely passing his lips. Mike just listened.

At the line "Good-bye, Papa, please pray for me, I was the black sheep of the family," Joey said quietly, "That's me, the black sheep."

On July 28, 1974, the north side of Market Street, extending from Eighth Street to Tenth Street, was a demolition area. Buildings and shops had been partially or completely torn down.

A half hour after leaving the OK Restaurant, Joe, Mike, and Joey turned away from the paved streets of Philadelphia to walk on this rough ground of dirt made muddy in many places by broken water lines.

Scattered over the entire area were broken bricks, cement blocks, pieces of steel, fragments of glass, plumbing fixtures, bottles, cans, and crushed cigarette wrappers. Here and there water had collected in puddles that reflected the clear summer sky.

To Joe the bricks and pieces of steel were like broken images in a dream. He felt as if he were floating, yet, prodded by the Voice that had come intermittently after Joe had left his house, he knew where he was and why he was here.

Joey had hurried into the demolition area ahead of Joe and Mike. He explored the site and began to fill his pockets with treasures. In one of the puddles he found a crushed small bouquet of wax flowers. He shook the water off them and stood up, waving the bouquet in the air.

"Hey, you guys, look at this. Man, if I could get a whole bunch of these *new*, I could sell them from door to door and make lots of money, huh?" He looked at Joe and Mike.

"Yeah, fine, Joey, fine," Joe said. He walked on, trailed by Mike. Long ago Joe had given real flowers to his adoptive mother for Mother's Day. She had looked down at him and said, "Ach, Joseph, such nonsense! They will die. For these things that die, you waste money." Anna had thrown the flowers away.

Joe watched Joey limping among the rubble, digging, picking up, examining, discarding, pocketing, like a scavenger. Joey's slim torso was bent over his thighs as he crab-walked among the trash, his face close to an old twist of electrical wire, almost sniffing it, like an animal. A flower-animal, Joe thought, that will be thrown away this afternoon somewhere below the rubble.

Joe knew that underneath were foundations that had not yet been exposed by the wreckers. On this site, Joe was sure, he would find an entrance to an underworld of cellars, pipes, stairways, storerooms, and secret doors. The air would be musty and dank, like the air in his East Hagert Street hole.

"Hey, Dad," Joey yelled, "why don't we take pictures with the chains you brought along right here?"

"No, Joey," Joe replied, "we'll save the chains for the last picture, the best one. But we'll take a few pictures here."

Joe felt at home on the demolition site. He remembered the little red wagon that they used to take when he and the kids went exploring in garbage cans and trash heaps. Joe wished that he had it with him now, so that a few of the unwanted objects scattered throughout the area could find a home in his cellar.

Joe heard Joey call again. "Hey, Dad, come here. You too, Mike."

Joey was standing in front of a huge gap that exposed a long lunch counter in a large room that had been a novelty shop called Goldman's.

"What's in here?" Mike asked.

"I don't know yet. Let's look around," Joey replied.

Joey was disappointed. The room had been stripped. Only the lunch counter was here; the merchandise and the fixtures had been removed and the outside wall had been demolished. Even the floor was bare, without rubble.

The front room had been stripped, but Joey discovered a large iron door in the back of the room which was partly ajar. The dark-

240

ness beyond was mysterious. Joey pushed the door open, and Joe saw in the gloom and dust the landing of a circular steel staircase.

"I'm going down," Joey said.

"You want to go too, Mike?" Joe asked.

"Okay."

"All right, Joey," Joe said, "let's go down and see what's there."

On the landing of the staircase they turned on their flashlights. Clutching his bouquet of wax flowers, Joey led the way into the underground. Slowly they walked down the circular steel steps. Mike was behind Joe.

"This looks good," Mike said.

"Could be. We'll find out," Joe replied. Joe knew that he and Mike had the same thought: This might be the place they were looking for to kill Joey.

Descending, they noticed that the farther down they went, the wetter the steps became. After they had completed another turn of the circular stairway, the steps were under water and seemed to spiral down beyond the range of their flashlights.

They stood looking at the large pool of stagnant water into which the staircase now led. They knew that if there was another landing, it was inaccessible.

"Wow!" Joey said. "I'm going wading."

Joey sat down on the step, rolled up his trousers to his knees, took off his sneakers and socks, and dangled his feet in the pool. The stagnant water was warm and slimy.

Joe and Mike stood a few steps above Joey. They played their flashlights on the walls, the staircase, and the water. The staircase had no projections on which they could hang Joey with the chains, and the surrounding dank walls were bare and smooth and sweated moisture.

As they searched for a proper spot with their flashlights, Joe and Mike saw a large steel platform that extended from a wall to the staircase. The wall was at a right angle to the stagnant pool of water. In the wall was a window frame without glass.

Standing against the wall near the edge of the platform was a ladder about six feet high, with six round rungs. The steel platform was about five feet above the pool.

Joe and Mike examined the ladder. Joe nudged Mike with the bag of locks and keys. Mike shook the bag of chains. They rattled.

"This is *it*!" said Mike.

"Yeah, yeah," Joe replied with awe in his voice.

Below, Joey was splashing his feet in the water and singing softly, "We had joy, we had fun, we had seasons in the sun."

"Get him up here," Joe ordered.

"C'mon up, Joey," Mike called. "We're going to take pictures."

Joey dried off his feet with his handkerchief and put on his socks and sneakers. He left his trousers rolled up to his knees. His bouquet of wax flowers was still tucked into his belt. He walked up the stairs by the light of Mike's flashlight.

Joey looked around. "Shit! It ain't light enough to take pictures."

"Well, we got plenty of light from the flashlights," Joe said.

"Okay. But I don't wanna come out on the film looking like something you stuck in a barrel of ink."

"Don't worry, Joey; you won't," Mike said.

Then Joe said, "Joey, come over here near the edge of the platform. See this ladder leaning against the wall? Well, go up two rungs, then turn around and lean your back against the rungs."

His back against the ladder, his arms and legs pressed against the ladder's sides, Joey giggled when he saw Mike take the chains out of the bag.

Joe was afraid that the flowers in Joey's belt would get in the way of the chains. He threw them into the room on the other side of the window frame.

"Hey," Joey yelled, "why did you throw my flowers away?"

"Later on, Joey, I'll get you more flowers," Joe said.

Mike gave the chains to Joe, who secured Joey's ankles and wrists to the ladder. Then Mike put a lock on each chain and snapped them shut.

Joey giggled again. "Daddy, this reminds me of the time I had handcuffs around my wrists with some guys watching me on the street, and somebody took my picture. We got that shot at home, right?"

"Right, Joey," Joe answered.

Joe nodded to Mike. Each stood now on one side of the ladder, the pool of water on their right. Joe gave a last look with his flash-light at the chains and locks, reassuring himself that they firmly bound Joey to the ladder.

"Which one of you is going to take my picture?" Joey asked.

Mike, who now had the camera, looked up at Joey and smiled. "I'm going to take it."

Joe and Mike turned the ladder the space of a right angle so that Joey was facing the water. Then they pulled the ladder a few feet from the wall against which it had been leaning. Joe put his hand on top of the ladder; Mike reached up as far as his arm could go. They held the flashlights in their free hands, the beams playing over the surface of the pool.

"Hold it!" Joey said. "Are you guys moving me to another spot? You'd get a real good picture if . . ."

Joe and Mike pushed the ladder over the edge of the platform.

At the moment the ladder went out of Joe's hand, he had an erection. Energy coursed through his body; he felt invincible and close to the stars and the universe. He watched Joey and the ladder hit the water five feet below the platform. They made a large splash and went under the surface. The ladder, Joey chained to it, bobbed up and lay on the slimy surface. It quivered and rocked gently among the ripples.

In his penis and throughout the rest of his body, Joe had the ecstasy of a murdering orgasm, a divine fire, radiant and pure.

Under the ladder Joey wiggled. He turned his face up between two rungs. His sodden hair was over his forehead and eyes. Around his nose and mouth were lumps of wet, black dirt and slime.

"Daddy, help me," he called in a weak voice.

Then Joey turned his face back to the water and was still.

Joey's call for help roused Joe from his ecstasy.

"Mike, I'm going down to Joey!"

"Balls! I'm staying here," Mike replied. "I'm not going in that filthy water."

The ladder floated a few feet to the edge of the pool, bounced gently off, and drifted slowly to the opposite edge.

Joe left the platform and went down the staircase until the water was up to his chin. The light from Mike's flashlight illuminated the surface. Joe tried to pull in the ladder. Seeing Joe do this, Mike rushed down the steps.

"I'll hold you," Mike said, "but I'm not going into the water."

Mike stepped down and held Joe's right shoulder while Joe pulled in the ladder. When Joe had put the lower part of the ladder on a step, Mike released his grip. The step was covered with water.

"I'll help you with the locks, but I won't touch Joey," Mike said.

I'm feeling cold arms and legs, Joe thought as he removed the chains. And cold feet like my father's on his deathbed. Joe remembered that he had tried rubbing his father's feet to bring him back to life. He was unable to do so and blamed himself for not having perfected his orthopedic experiments.

Joe handed the chains to Mike, then touched Joey's hands and face. He wasn't breathing. Joe checked Joey's pulse and pulled up his eyelids.

"He's dead," Joe said.

"Now get him off the ladder and let me have it," Mike replied.

Joe lifted Joey off the ladder. He held Joey with one arm and with the other handed the ladder to Mike. Mike went up the platform with the ladder and the locks and chains.

Joe held Joey to his chest for a moment, then gently placed him on the nearest step.

"Let's get out of here," Mike called from the platform.

"I'm in no hurry," Joe said.

Mike rushed from the platform down the steps to his father.

"C'mon, get out of the water," Mike ordered. "It's up to your chin."

"I said I'm in no hurry, Mike."

"This is what we wanted, wasn't it?" Mike's voice rose in panic. "There isn't *anything* you can do for him. He's dead, *dead*! So c'mon!"

Joe did not move. He kept looking at Joey's face. He hoped that Joey would open his eyes and speak to him. His face was so lifelike.

Joey's death was right, Joe told himself, a sacrifice that had to be made.

Mike went back to the platform and threw the ladder into the flooded room. He picked up the bags with the locks and chains.

Mike called from the platform, "We have to get out of here. We'll get caught."

Joe slowly turned. Before walking up the circular staircase, he looked again at his son lying on the step.

Joe knew that at last he was on the road to godhood.

14 Case Number 4003-74

Joe's clothes were sodden with filthy water, but he didn't know that. As he and Mike left the demolition site with the bags of chains and locks in their hands, Joe forgot the descent on the circular staircase, the stagnant pool, the killing of Joey, and his own immersion in the slimy water. And even though Joe was aware that Joey was no longer with him and Mike, he was neither distressed by Joey's absence nor curious about where he might be.

By a process of dissociation characteristic of some schizophrenics, Joe's psyche was protecting him against pain and guilt—the same process by which he had forgotten the killing of José Collazo.

Joe and Mike went directly home. Their exertions underground and the heat of the summer afternoon made them sleepy, so they were silent during the ride on the el and until they reached Kensington.

Mike stayed out to play. Betty was still sitting outside the door leading from Front Street into the living room, and didn't see Joe come into the house through the store door. He went upstairs, took off his clothes, which appeared to be dry and clean to his distorted perceptions, took a shower, and got dressed.

Betty called up to him from the foot of the stairs.

"Joe, you said you were going to take us out to dinner."

"But Joey isn't here," Joe replied. "We'd better wait until he gets back."

246

Betty sighed. "Joey told me he was going to be home at six. It's almost seven."

"We'll eat here, then," Joe said. "We'll have pizza. I'll send Mike for it."

Joe went downstairs and out the Front Street door. He called Mike and gave him money to buy pizza.

During supper and afterward, Betty, who thought her husband had been in the house all afternoon, kept repeating, "Joey told me he'd be back at six because his dad was going to take us out. I know he didn't run away this time—he doesn't say he's going to be here when he runs away."

At 11:00 P.M., Joe called the 25th District of the Philadelphia Police Department to report Joey missing.

Joe concentrated on the details of a private investigation. On the workbench in his store he had a tape recorder on which he recorded leads about Joey that were brought to him by customers, housewives, and neighborhood children. On a chair near his bench was the store telephone, which he was using as a hotline for tracking clues from people all over the city who had read the Kallinger family's plea for help.

Joe worked with the Morals Squad, which was investigating the case; but he also left his shop to explore the streets, vacant lots, and abandoned houses, not only in Kensington but also in Richmond and Fishtown.

During the first night after killing Joey, Joe had a dream. He dreamed that he, Mike, and Joey were walking on a demolition site. Then suddenly Joey vanished. When Joe woke up, he believed that the dream had been sent to him by the Lord, who was instructing him to look for Joey on the demolition site at Ninth and Market Streets. Joe did not remember that the Lord had ordered him to kill Joey.

In the morning, before he opened the store, Joe, with Mike at his side, went to the demolition site. Joe had brought his camera and took pictures of old landmarks. Ninth and Market seemed eerily familiar, as if Joe were having a moment of *déjà vu*. Beyond that, he had no memory.

Acting upon the Lord's command that Joe believed had come to him in the dream, Joe, with Mike, returned to the demolition site every morning from July 29 to August 9, before opening the shop. Mike did not refer to the murder of Joey. He was evidently acting out of the already established pattern that father and son never talked about a crime once it was over.

One morning at the demolition site, while Mike wandered off to a street corner, Joe watched the trucks of the Hawthorne Hauling Company coming and carrying away parts of razed buildings. The longer Joe watched, the stronger his impression grew that he had seen Joey here on the Sunday that Joey had "disappeared."

Whenever Joey ran away, he had telephoned Joe. This time he hadn't. Joe had faced, as he had already tried to make Betty face, the possibility that Joey was dead.

"I want to know," Joe asked a man who was directing the Hawthorne trucks, "if you found any *body* here."

"No, I didn't find no *body*," William Facison, an employee of Advance Security, replied.

"Are you *sure*?"

"No, I'm not sure. But I'll check."

Facison assigned someone else to detail the trucks and made a telephone call to the Coroner's Office and reported to Joe that a *body* had *not* been found. Facison then called the 6th Police District. Again the results were negative.

Joe found Mike. Going home, Joe thought the possibility of Joey's being dead was no longer merely a panicky speculation.

The body of the white male lying on the slab was five feet seven inches in height and weighed seventy pounds. It was dressed in blue-and-white-patterned socks, blue-red-and-white-checkered trousers with a brown belt, black-and-white sneakers with the name "Dug" and the number "74" on one toe and, on the other, an undecipherable set of initials. It also had on a brown short-sleeved shirt.

The body had been removed by OME (Office of the Medical Examiner) personnel at 6:15 A.M. on August 9, 1974, from the sub-basement of a building on the demolition site at Ninth and Market streets. It was taken to the morgue, where it was received by E. Woerle of the OME and designated as Case Number 4003-74.

The OME did not suspect murder. But the police department evidently did. For at 10:30 A.M., Detective Paris of the Homicide Division arrived at the morgue to gather information about the deceased.

At 11:30 A.M. the deputy medical examiner, H.E. Fillinger, M.D., made the pronouncement of death. He recorded on the Certificate of Death that the cause of death was undetermined and the manner of death unknown. At the same time, a postmortem examination was begun and disclosed that the body was in a partial state of putrefaction.

The identity of the deceased, like the cause and manner of death, was undetermined. The news media worked with the police department and the OME to discover who Case Number 4003-74 had been.

On August 12, a homicide detective named Ed Funk indicated that it was likely that Case Number 4003-74 had been Joey Kallinger, age fourteen, of 2723 North Front Street, reported missing on July 28. At 5:45 P.M., OME Investigator James A. McGovern interviewed Kallinger. Homicide Detective Daniel Rosenstein had taken Joe in an unmarked police car from the store to the morgue.

Joe gave facts, according to the OME's Certificate of Identification, relative to the circumstances of death. The form also states that "data was supplied by informant personally" and that he did not view the body. He did, however, see photographs of the body.

Joe's statement, signed by him and certified by James McGovern, appears in the Certificate of Identification as follows:

> We reported him missing to the 25th District on July 28, 1974 at about 11 P.M. He was last seen by his mother at about 2 P.M. that day.
>
> He was being seen regularly at St. Christopher's Hospital psychiatric unit for about six weeks prior to being missing. He was at Eastern State School in Trevose, Pa. He had been at the Mills Building because of incorrigible behavior at school.
>
> I have six other children. He was our fourth child.
>
> I identify the trousers as those of my son. There was a singe mark on the left bottom which made the cloth stiff. He has the same kind of sneakers [that were found on the corpse] and the shirt looks the same.

"They lock the door behind you in the morgue," Joe told me three years later at the Camden County Jail. "You feel trapped—much more trapped than in prison. I felt they were maneuvering me. Officer Rosenstein made it a word game.

"I made the identification through the pants charred in the trailer. I saw photos of Joey's body, but not the body itself. The police asked, 'Did your son go around with pants up to the knees?' I didn't remember ever seeing Joey's pants that way.

"Flora, when the police took me to the morgue, I didn't remember anything about Joey's death. I told you about it three days ago. But until just before that I remembered nothing, Flora, *nothing!*"

Even in official quarters there had never been any certainty about how Joey died. When Joe told me about the killing, he did so not in answer to any question from me, but spontaneously. He took hold of a ladder that happened to be in the infirmary, and vividly acted out the details of how he and Michael had chained Joey to the ladder and then dropped the ladder into the stagnant pool.

I didn't believe Joe when he said that he had no memory of the killing until three days before telling me about it. Because of my skepticism I reminded Joe that in the Bergen County Jail about a year earlier, he had told me, "Joey probably died from drowning." I asked him what he had meant by that statement. He replied, "Only that drowning seemed probable from the facts I got from the police and the OME."

But I believe Joe now. My belief, actually my conviction, is based on psychiatric insights into schizophrenia: Joe is a paranoid schizophrenic, and his dissociation from the killing of Joey and also of José Collazo is as much a part of his psychosis as were the killings themselves. Dr. Arieti and I agreed that Joe was telling the truth when he said he did not remember the killings. We also agreed that the long hours of talking with me had unsealed the memories, bringing them from Joe's subconscious, where they remained latent, into consciousness.

Joe could not understand why he, as the father of the deceased, was taken from the morgue to the Police Administration Building—the Roundhouse, as it was called.

Nor could he comprehend why he was not allowed to telephone his wife about the identification of their son's clothes and why at the Roundhouse Detective O'Brien asked him the same questions that he had already answered fully to investigating police.

That night, in a telephone interview, Joe told *Philadelphia Bulletin* staffer Thomas J. Gibbons, "I've just come back from the morgue and I identified Joe's [Joey's] clothing. The pants that they showed me were the same exact pants down to the char mark" (from the trailer caper). Joe also told Gibbons that the morgue officials had said that the body had broken bones in a foot. "Joey had that," Joe explained. "That came when he jumped off a roof in January. He still limped from that."

The front-page *Bulletin* article, bylined by Gibbons and Naedele, ran on August 13 and noted that Joe Kallinger had said nothing about what had caused Joey to run away on July 28.

"One of the happiest we've had" is the way Joe described Joey's last week to William Storm of the *Bulletin*. "I took Joey and my son Michael on a hiking trip through the Pennsylvania mountains. We took a bus to Hazleton, then camped out and hiked. We saw quarries and coal mines and enjoyed each other's company."

Joe had forgotten not only the murder itself, but also the attempts at murder that had preceded it.

Kensington believed that Joey had been killed in a homosexual assault. Rumor had it that he had driven off with a man in a red Pinto. Another rumor was that a man who had promised him a job in a car-wash had driven away with him in a late-model green sedan. Some people said that a twenty-three-year-old man had killed Joey; others, that Bobby Vane—a friend of Joey's who had lived in the East Hagert Street house while Joe was in Holmesburg—was the murderer.

Joey had actually talked with Bobby just before going to meet Joe at the OK Restaurant. Of the Kensington "suspects," Bobby Vane was the only one who was also a police suspect. The police held him, but he took a lie-detector test and was found innocent.

Only the Philadelphia police suspected Joseph Kallinger. These suspicions were the reason they had taken him from the morgue to the Roundhouse on August 12. But they had not informed him that he was a possible suspect in connection with Joey's disappearance and death.

Neither the police nor anyone else suspected Michael Kallinger.

* * *

251

Friday, August 16, 1974. Stony-faced and rigidly calm, Joe sat in the first row of a large room in the C.J. O'Neill Funeral Home. In their seats on his right were Anna Kallinger, Mary Jo, Stevie, Jimmy, and Michael. Michael had wanted to stay home, but Joe insisted that he attend his brother's funeral.

Betty's seat on Joe's left was empty. She stood before her son's casket and stared at the place where Joey's face would have been visible if the casket had been open. She looked, disbelieving, at the flowers on both sides of the casket and at the wreath in the middle. She murmured to herself, "How do I know it's Joey? I don't know *what* they got in there."

Joe left his seat and stood beside her.

"I won't believe it until I see him. *Anybody* could be in there, Joe, *anybody*."

"I know it's Joey. I was down at the morgue."

"That doesn't mean a thing," Betty said. "Maybe you're all trying to kid me, and tonight Joey's going to walk back into my house."

"Betty, I saw his clothes, *his* stuff, Betty. They showed me photographs."

"How come they don't let us see him? How come they closed the coffin?"

Joe couldn't tell her about the photographs. In them Joe had seen the shriveled scalp and part of the skull. The gummy eyes looked like the empty ovals on the face of a statue. Gently Joe led Betty back to her seat.

The Reverend Anthony A. Marinacci, pastor of the Kensington Assembly of God Church, approached the lectern.

"Because of what we know about the life of Joseph Michael Kallinger, Jr.," he told the twenty-five mourners who had come to Joey's funeral, "we shall make no observations about him, but we shall try to support and strengthen the family."

After the sermon and Bible readings, the funeral cortege drove to the six-grave family plot of the senior Kallingers in Whitemarsh Memorial Park. As hymns from the stately bell tower drifted among graves, trees, and mausoleums, Joe and Betty stopped at Stephen Kallinger's grave. Things happened when I was a kid, Joe thought, that I can't forgive. But if I could have prolonged Dad's life, I would have. I feel as bad for Joey as I did for Dad. But for Joey I could do nothing. I don't even know how he died.

Joey's casket lay on the ground beside an open grave. Reverend Marinacci was about to begin the service when Anna Kallinger went up to the grave. "Steef," she cried, "I want to lie near you, but that Joey took my grave from me." She shook her fist at the casket.

After the service, Anthony Marinacci spoke comforting words to Betty and Joe. When he left them, Joe took Betty's arm and said, "Time to go, Betty."

"It isn't Joey," she whispered harshly.

"Joey's better off, Betty, and we're better off," Joe said as he led Betty away from the open grave.

"Don't talk like that," she said, her face dashed with tears.

They walked toward the cars in the roadway. Betty said, "You didn't even cry, Joe. You didn't even cry. You were the only one that didn't cry, and I'm never going to forgive you for that."

She walked ahead of him.

15 Dead End

On a Thursday morning, September 26, 1974—a little over a month after Joey's funeral—Joe was awakened between three-thirty and four by the insistent ringing of his doorbell. Wearing a robe, he went into his store, switched on the light, and opened the door. He faced two detectives and two uniformed policemen.

"What is it?" Joe peered sleepily at the men standing before him.

"You're wanted at the Roundhouse for questioning about the disappearance and death of your son, Joseph Kallinger, Jr.," one of the detectives said.

"Again?"

"Yeah."

"But I went through all that last month. I answered every question in the book."

"Lieutenant O'Neill wants to talk to you," the other detective said. "So get dressed—now!"

"I'm not going, that's all!"

"You're going," the first detective said, "whether you like it or not."

"I won't go!"

In August the police had not told Joe that he was a suspect; now they didn't tell him that he had become the prime suspect. It seemed clear to Joe that they were harassing him, and he felt sure that it was because of a Complaint in Trespass filed by Malcolm W. Berkowitz

254

and Arthur L. Gutkin, the lawyers who had represented Joe in a motion for a new trial on the child-abuse case. The complaint described Joe's arrest and imprisonment in 1972 as false. The three counts of trespass were against the Law Department of the City of Philadelphia; Policewoman Caristo, née Baker, of the police department's Juvenile Aide Division; and Philadelphia Police Commissioner Joseph O'Neill. The contention was that in the 1972 child-abuse trial Joe had been convicted because of his children's perjured testimony *at the request of the police.* Policewoman Baker had made the arrest and had written the complaints the children signed. The children claimed that in the complaints she exaggerated what they said.

Joe let the police into the store, then telephoned Arthur Gutkin.

"The phone call woke me up," Gutkin told me four years later. "Joe said, 'The police want me to go with them. They don't have a warrant for my arrest, but they're taking me in anyway.'

"Then a detective got on the phone," Gutkin continued.

" 'Is Joe under arrest?' I asked.

" 'No,' the detective replied.

" 'No,' I said, 'so you won't take him in, right?'

" 'I have my orders from Lieutenant O'Neill to take him in, and I'm going to take him in.'

"Joe got on the phone again and asked, 'Do I have to go?'

" 'No,' I replied. 'But I can assure you, Joe, that if you *don't* go, they're going to *take* you. It's unlawful, but they're going to take you anyway. You'd better go. Don't do anything. Don't make any statements till I get there.' "

Gutkin, who is Jewish, had been looking forward only to a day of fasting and prayer, for the police had come to Joe's house on Yom Kippur, the Day of Atonement, the holiest day in the year for Jews. But Joe's urgent voice over the telephone forced Gutkin to go to the Roundhouse. He had a strong feeling that the police hoped that because of the holiday Joe's lawyer would not show up.

From the air the Roundhouse looks like a pair of gigantic handcuffs. In fact it is made of two round three-story buildings connected by a corridor. As Joe entered the lobby, the two detectives were in front of him and the two uniformed policemen were in back.

Joe, who was not under arrest and not manacled, was certain that he was at the Roundhouse not because of any crime he had committed, but because the police were retaliating against him for suing them. In his tortured mind, Joe believed that the police were his enemies. They replaced in his fantasies the "total gods" who had wanted to destroy him.

As he walked through the lobby toward one of the Roundhouse's cylindrically shaped elevators, Joe didn't know that he was going to be interrogated in one of the Homicide Division's interrogation rooms by Lieutenant James F. O'Neill, who was convinced—even though he didn't have evidence on which to indict Joe—that Joseph Kallinger had killed his son Joseph, Jr. O'Neill was playing hunches based on instincts developed during fifteen years of police work. O'Neill was a shrewd, savvy cop and was proud of his record in the Philadelphia Police Department.

In Squad Room 104, early on the morning of September 26, 1974, O'Neill was standing at his desk. A heavy smoker, he had a cigarette between his thin lips. His trench coat was open. He was wearing a plain navy-blue suit, slightly rumpled, and a paisley tie with regimental stripes. As always, he had his revolver strapped to his right side. He unbuttoned the top buttons of his shirt and yanked his tie down three-quarters of an inch, a characteristic gesture.

Waiting for his men to bring in the prime suspect in the killing of Joseph Kallinger, Jr., O'Neill mused that a father who abused his children could also kill them; and he didn't believe that the three Kallinger kids had told the truth when they recanted their accusations against their father at the hearing on February 19, 1974. O'Neill could smell that they were lying. He hadn't spent all those years on the force just sniffing roses.

He could smell something fishy in the fact that a few weeks before reporting that Joey was missing Kallinger had purchased life insurance on Joseph, Jr. He did not know about the Metropolitan Life Insurance Company double indemnity policy that in the case of Joey's accidental death would pay Kallinger $24,000. But he did know about the John Hancock Mutual Life Insurance policy that in the case of Joey's accidental death would pay Kallinger $45,000.

* * *

An officer told O'Neill that Kallinger had been put into an interrogation room. Lean, hard, and spoiling for a fight, O'Neill threw back the bolt of the heavy wooden door that was flush with the wall in Room 103. He opened the door and walked into a small, windowless room. An officer closed the door behind him and bolted it from the outside. O'Neill and Kallinger were alone.

Sitting on the hard wooden chair at the bleak wooden table, Joe heard the door slammed shut. He forced himself to turn and look at O'Neill. He wanted to run, as when he was a kid he ran under the bed when his adoptive father came after him to welt his skin with heavy leather soles. There was no place to go. Dead end. Both times. Joe felt his stomach tighten as he watched O'Neill go around the end of the table. He had heard that O'Neill was a tough cop who never got tired. Joe wondered whether other cops were watching him through the mirror built into the wall.

"I'm Lieutenant O'Neill." The cop pulled out a chair opposite Joe and sat down. He leaned across the table, pointed his index finger at Joe. The nail was trim and clean, the finger steady.

"Listen to me, Kallinger. You killed your son Joseph, Jr. You had forty-five thousand dollars' worth of insurance on him. While I'm a police officer, you're never going to get that money. And you're never going to get out of here, either. Get it?"

Stunned, Joe leaned back in his chair.

"My God," he said, "is *that* what you brought me here for?"

"Cut out the crap, Kallinger. You know you killed him, *we* know you killed him."

"Look, I'm a shoemaker. I never killed anybody."

O'Neill lit a cigarette. "You're not going to get away with this," he said in his gravelly voice.

"I've heard about innocent people accused of murders. But this is the first time I've seen it. Where's the evidence?"

"Don't tell me how to do my job. I want to know where and exactly when you killed your son."

"How could I do such a thing?"

"You tell me." O'Neill's lips were tight, his jaw muscles moving. Joe thought O'Neill was going to bite him, sear his brain with death rays from his cruel eyes, or squash him between his lean muscular hands. Beneath his chair a bottomless hole was beginning to suck Joe down into everlasting torture.

"Kallinger, if it takes me the rest of my life, I'm going to see you pay for killing your son. Understand?"

"I want to talk to my lawyer," Joe said. He was shaking.

"No!" O'Neill replied, banging the flat of his hand on the table. "You talked to your lawyer from your home."

"That was before I was taken into custody. I want to talk to him now."

O'Neill got up. He crushed the cigarette under his shoe. With a short, angry movement of his leg, he kicked the butt toward the wall. His eyes were slits between the lids.

"Will you sign a confession, Kallinger?"

Joe shook his head.

O'Neill started to take his hand out of the pocket of his trench coat.

He's going to hit me, Joe thought.

Then O'Neill said, "Shit!" He walked to the door, knocked on it. Outside someone threw the bolt, and O'Neill left the room.

Again the door was bolted from the outside.

Arthur Gutkin believed that Joe was innocent. He knew that his client was being detained illegally in the Roundhouse by Lieutenant O'Neill. Gutkin walked into Homicide Squad Room 102. He was very angry with the police, because they had violated Joe's civil rights. Gutkin identified himself as Joseph Kallinger's lawyer. Gutkin was tough and assured, but civil.

The door of the interrogation room was bolted behind Gutkin from the outside. He saw the mirror built into the wall and guessed that it was a two-way mirror through which he and Joe would be watched. Even though he couldn't see any apparatus, he was sure the room was bugged. Gutkin and Joe would keep their mouths shut. No point in saying something that might make matters worse. Gutkin went up to the wooden table where a burly detective, who was watching Joe, sat opposite him.

"Hello, Art," Joe said.

"Hi, Joe," Gutkin replied.

Gutkin greeted the detective and said with a cold smile, "You boys made me choose between God and my client!"

258

"We were hoping you would choose God!" the detective answered, giving Gutkin a hard look.

Now Gutkin knew that he had been right in thinking the police had chosen this day so that Joe could be interrogated without a lawyer.

Joe and his lawyer sat behind the bolted door for almost four hours. They were silent most of the time. Each believed that an innocent man was being outrageously detained.

O'Neill came into the room twice during those four hours: once to accuse Joe again of having murdered Joseph, Jr., and once to ask Joe two questions: "Do you want to make a statement?" and "Will you take a lie-detector test?" Joe looked at Gutkin, who shook his head and whispered "No" for both questions. This was what Joe expected. He knew that the lawyer didn't believe in lie-detector tests. And Gutkin didn't want Joe to make any more statements. Back in August 1974, he had told Joe, "You've already told the cops all you know about Joey's disappearance and death. You don't have to do another thing."

Between 9:50 and 10:00 A.M., the burly detective returned to the interrogation room. "You can go now," he told Joe and Gutkin.

O'Neill slouched in the chair at his desk. A dead cigarette hung from his lips. He was frustrated and disgusted, but he couldn't just grab Kallinger and throw him into a cell. O'Neill knew that he had no evidence. He was sure that he had had Joey's killer within his grasp.

He knew he would probbaly catch hell from the media if reporters found out how he had gotten Kallinger into the Roundhouse at four o'clock in the morning. Someday O'Neill was going to get Kallinger, but for today, September 26, 1974—so near, so far.

Joe and Gutkin sat at a table in the Horn and Hardart cafeteria on Market and Fifth streets, just a few blocks from the Roundhouse. Joe told Gutkin everything that O'Neill had said to him before the lawyer walked into the interrogation room. O'Neill not having had any evidence, Gutkin wondered on what ground the detective was so certain that Joe had killed Joey. The insurance Joe had bought on Joey's life? But many people have insurance on their kids' lives and don't kill them. Joe had gotten insurance on Mike, Jimmy, and Bonnie as well as on Joey.

"Joe, I think you've got a case here," Gutkin said. "The police violated your civil rights by taking you to the Roundhouse without a warrant and by forcibly detaining you in the interrogation room."

"This case would be separate from the Complaint in Trespass, wouldn't it?" Joe asked. "I mean the complaint against the city and the cops because that policewoman wouldn't let my kids withdraw the child-abuse charges the night I was arrested."

"Yeah, Joe, it would."

"Okay, Art, I want you to start this suit as soon as possible. I'm not going to let these people harass me anymore."

The traffic was moving slowly as Joe started home. On the back of a passing truck was a small carousel. Just behind the mane of one of the wooden horses, a boy's head bobbed up and down. The right side of the face and head was covered by hair; the head was in profile, so Joe couldn't see the left side. Although there was no wind, the hair rose slightly and settled, as if ghostly hands were gently dropping it and picking it up. Joe wondered what the boy was doing on the carousel when it wasn't open for business.

Near the end of the block the traffic began to move faster. Joe kept looking at the boy's head and walked quickly to keep up with the truck. The hair was light-brown, silky and long, like Joey's hair. Joe felt queasy and coughed. He tried not to think about Joey.

Twenty minutes later Joe got off at the Huntington el station and walked to East Sterner Street. He was glad to be back. The only place in the world where he was safe and comfortable was at his workbench in the shop. Here nobody accused him of having killed Joey.

Walking up the path to the shop, Joe felt as if he had been away a long time. He was eager to put on his olive-green smock and feel in his hands leather and the tools of his craft. He looked forward to throwing the electrical switches that would activate his equipment. Then he would feel powerful and creative. He knew that some people thought him the best shoemaker in Philadelphia, the king of cobblers in his own city. Joe's home was his castle, his shop was his throne room.

Walking up the steps to the shop, Joe saw the boy he had seen half an hour ago on the truck at Market Street. Still in profile, his head bobbed at eye level between Joe and the shop door. Joe wondered how the kid had gotten here. Then the boy turned his head until the front of it was facing Joe, and he saw a cascade of dense, silky brown hair. In the middle of it a part formed; the hair separated and hung thickly at both sides of the head. Gleaming with moisture were the empty whites of the eyes. Over the forehead, without brows, and over the cheekbones, thin, pus-white skin was tightly drawn. In the center the skin was flat and smooth, without nose, nostrils, or mouth. The outlines of the jawbones met in a round, fleshy chin.

Joe ran off the steps in panic. Halfway down the path he stopped and looked back to see whether the boy was still there. The boy was following him. The eyeballs appeared between the lids, small discs of brown cork surrounded by tiny veins like red worms in the white fluid. The eyes looked at Joe with loathing. He was about to throw his keys at the face when he saw that the head had nothing beneath it: no neck, no limbs, no torso. It had moved by itself.

Joe threw the keys and the head vanished.

Betty, who had been minding the store while Joe was in the Roundhouse, came out and stood on the steps.

"Who's throwing things at the door? God, Joe, I'm glad you're back. I don't mind being your counter girl. That's my job. You say I'm a terrific counter girl. But being in the store all these hours without you is something else. Why are you throwing your keys around, anyway? Everybody'll think we're nuts!"

Trembling, Joe picked up his keys from the steps and went into the shop. He locked the door and put a chair against it. Then he rushed to his workbench, took a heavy hammer, and stood looking at the door. After a few minutes, Joe went into the kitchen and asked Betty to make him a cup of tea.

"Jesus, Joe, you look awful! What did they do to you down there?" Betty asked.

"More harassing. O'Neill thinks I killed Joey. He tried to get me to sign a confession."

"Oh!" Betty screamed. "That's terrible, Joe, *terrible*! My God, O'Neill and his men are devilish people, Joe. Accusing you of killing Joey when Joey isn't dead!"

261

"Joey's dead, Betty—dead. You'd feel better if you'd accept it."

At his workbench Joe sipped the tea slowly, grateful for the tea's warmth and for the sweetness of the sugar.

He was very tired. He was tired every day, but even more so today. He had been awake since the police had come for him early in the morning. But he couldn't go to bed now. No matter how bad things were, he had to keep the shop going.

Since the winter of 1973–1974 and even more since the previous spring, Joe's delusions, hallucinations, and accompanying feelings of depletion had often prevented him from working with his accustomed energy and dedication. This was true even when he didn't go into the suburbs with Michael.

Joe took off the shelf an old pair of shoes he had fixed many times. He knew their owner; they were like old friends. Still feeling a trembling within himself, he tried to work. He was about to rip the worn sole and heel off the left member of the old pair of shoes when he heard a voice, light and high in pitch, a young boy's voice.

"My name's Charlie."

Under a shelf of stacked soles and leather, the head, its face covered by the hair, bobbed gently above Joe.

Joe felt as if he were sinking into a huge, bottomless hole. His heart pounded wildly. He couldn't move. He was powerless.

He tried to raise his arms, as if to touch the head, but it whisked itself away to the French door. The ends of the hair were rising and falling with the movement of the head, suspended in the air.

"You have no mouth. How can you talk?" Joe asked. He felt feverish and desperate.

The hair parted. "I can talk. Look." The voice came as if from a loudspeaker. The brown eyes stared at Joe.

"What do you want? Where do you come from?"

Charlie didn't answer. He kept staring at Joe.

"Why don't you answer me?"

Slowly the hair covered the face, like a curtain on a stage.

"Very funny!" Joe screamed.

Betty's voice came from the kitchen: "Joe, who you talkin' to out there?"

"Listen," Joe said to Charlie, "that's my wife. She'll see you. Go away, for God's sake!"

"Don' worry, Joe. Betty will never see me. No one else will, either. Only you."

"How come you know my wife's name?"

" 'Cause I belong to you and you belong to me," Charlie replied.

The hair parted again. Charlie's brown eyes looked once more at Joe, but this time with hatred.

Terrified, Joe said, "I never did anything to you. Why are you bothering me? I can't live this way. I can't!"

Joe buried his face in his hands and sobbed. When he looked up, Charlie had vanished.

Charlie appeared frequently to Joe during the next two years. The first appearance, on September 26, 1974, was not, in my opinion, by chance. On the morning of that day, Lieutenant O'Neill had accused Joe of having killed Joey. Even though Joe did not consciously remember the killing, his subconscious probably reacted to O'Neill's accusation by creating Charlie, a figure of symbolic retribution.

I conjectured that Charlie was a distorted image of Joey's head bobbing up from the filthy, stagnant subbasement pool, and crying through the rungs of the ladder to which Joe and Michael had chained him, "Daddy, help me!"

Joe killed under the force of a powerful hallucination and a powerful delusion that made him think wrong was right. His murder of his son was unconnected with insurance or other immediate, worldly concerns. Joey was a sacrifice on the road to Joe's paranoid concept of his own godhood.

16 Retaliation

Joe thought the police were out to get him. He believed that they were harassing his family and waging a hate campaign against him, and he became obsessed with the desire to avenge himself.

In the two months since Joey's body had been found, Joe thought himself subjected to a Hate Kallinger campaign by the Philadelphia police. O'Neill felt instinctively that Kallinger had murdered his own son. The police wanted to protect society from Joe, who did not know that he had killed Joey and did not think the police had any reason to regard him as dangerous. He was terrified by the irregular tactics they used against him, their brutalization of his family, and he looked upon the police as his enemies. Bursting with vengeance, he was determined to strike back.

Joe's need for retaliation was that of a man who felt that the police had brutalized him, but it was also an expression of Joe's "inner child of the past."* An "inner child of the past" lives in all of us and influences our thinking and behavior. People who have been subjected to extreme parental punitiveness are often motivated by an intense desire to get back at or to get even with the world.

From October 4 to October 13, 1974, Joe staged six episodes through which he sought to make the police "look bad." He also

---

* This concept is explained in W. Hugh Missildine, M.D., *Your Inner Child of the Past* (New York: Simon and Schuster, 1963).

planned to use their treatment of him in the course of these actions as further evidence of his already initiated civil-rights case against the City of Philadelphia and the Philadelphia Police Department.

The first of these episodes took place on Friday, October 4, 1974, nine days after Lieutenant O'Neill's interrogation of Joe and the first appearance of Charlie. That Friday Joe told Mike to stage a fall in the Kiddie City store on East Erie Avenue and to pretend that the bump he already had on his forehead as a result of a street fight that afternoon had been caused by the fall.

Having accompanied Mike to the store, Joe waited on a bench outside until he saw an ambulance stop in front of the main entrance to Kiddie City. Then he went home to receive a call from the Frankford Hospital, to which Mike had been taken.

Joe was certain that the police would not believe that Mike had gotten the bump in Kiddie City and would accuse his father of more child abuse. Joe wanted the police to interrogate him so that he would end up as the innocent and injured party.

Joe went to the hospital, where a doctor told him that his son had fallen in Kiddie City and had a bruise on the forehead and a small concussion. The doctor told Joe he could take Mike home and to wake him up during the night to see whether his eyes were functioning properly.

Mike's eyes were all right, but at 4:30 A.M., Sunday, October 6, he vomited three times. The vomiting was evidently due either to tension or to injuries resulting from Friday's street fight.

Joe took Michael to St. Christopher's Hospital for Children, which was closer to the Kallinger home than was the Frankford Hospital. Dr. Deborah Price, who did not know about Michael's actual fight or his alleged fall, did know that Kallinger had been found guilty of child abuse in 1972. She suspected that more abuse had caused Michael's concussion. She therefore filed a child-abuse report with the Department of Public Welfare.

Joe did not permit DPW to follow up on the St. Christopher's report, and the agency requested "that the court investigate urgently the living situation of Michael Kallinger." A hearing was called at the Juvenile Branch, Family Court Division, of the Court of Common Pleas. Joe attended the hearing, but the case was dismissed because the records of Frankford Hospital clearly indicated that

Michael's concussion was the result of a fall in Kiddie City. The police had not become involved in this first retaliatory episode.

On the Sunday Dr. Price examined Michael at St. Christopher's, October 6, 1974, Joe staged the second episode of his retaliation against the police. "I took Mike to St. Christopher's," Joe told me on July 15, 1979, "because he was vomiting. But I also took him to establish a basis for the amnesia we planned for the second round of my retaliation."

The "second round" began as a family outing with Mary Jo horse-back riding and Mike riding a pony on the bridle path of Juniata Park. Later Joe and Mike went into the woods. Joe had told Mike to disappear from the woods, then go to Camden, New Jersey, where, feigning amnesia, he was to check into a hospital. Joe would report Michael as missing and demand a manhunt. But Mike suggested that instead of going to New Jersey, he hide in Anna Kallinger's basement.

After Mike had left for East Sterner Street, Joe went to the stables to wait for Mary Jo and to telephone the 25th Police District. He reported that his son Michael, who had disappeared from Juniata Park, was missing.

While Mike was in Anna Kallinger's basement, the police hunted for him in the park with police dogs. Actually the police were hunting for Michael's body. They thought Kallinger had killed another son!

On Monday, October 7, Mike was still in the basement while his parents and his brother and sisters were detained and interrogated about his disappearance—Joe at East Detectives, which is the combined 24th and 25th police districts at Front and Westmoreland, the rest of the family at the Roundhouse.

While Joe was being questioned at East Detectives, Charlie floated through the wall opposite Joe, directly behind the captain's chair. Charlie bobbed over the captain's head and at eye level stopped close to Joe. His hair was gathered at the sides of his head; his brown eyes beamed with jolly malice.

"Every cop in the room," Charlie told Joe, "would love to see you in your coffin!" Joe put his hands over his eyes and sighed. A detective reprimanded him for not staying awake.

Now Charlie was between Joe and the captain. To see the captain,

266

Joe had to move his head, but Charlie moved every time Joe moved, blocking Joe's view. Joe had to lean over to see him—to the left, to the right, and back again.

The captain finally asked Joe what he was trying to look at—and it was just too damn bad if Kallinger was impatient, because the team of officers, headed by the captain, was going to keep Kallinger in this room until the situation got straightened out.

Charlie eyed the captain murderously, then swiveled back to Joe. "Give this guy hell, Joe!" Charlie said. Without thinking, Joe hissed, "Shut up, Charlie!" Hearing this, a detective at the far end of the table boomed, "*What* did you say, Mr. Kallinger?"

"That pig thought you told *him* to shut up," Charlie said. "Oink-oink-oink."

Charlie bobbed up and down a few times and then floated toward the glass of the closed window. Floating, Charlie sang, "We had joy, we had fun, we had seasons in the sun . . ." and then vanished into the bright sunshine on the other side of the closed window.

After five hours of interrogation by the team, Joe was told he could leave. Charlie was waiting for him, bobbing in the breeze about five and a half feet above the sidewalk. The pus-white skin, the scornful brown eyes, the hair gathered in overlapping strands at the sides of Charlie's head made Joe wonder whether Charlie had come from God or from the Devil.

"You want me to go away, Joe, don't you?" Charlie asked mockingly. "But I'm *never* going to leave you. One of these days I might appear and just never go away again. Wouldn't that be nice?"

Joe looked at Charlie with disgust but didn't answer.

"Well, don't worry about that today. I don't feel like going back with you to that smelly old shoe repair shop. But I'll be around when you do more exciting things than hacking away at shoes. And you're going to do plenty, Joe, *plenty*!"

At the Roundhouse a detective warned Betty "to lock your bedroom door at night because you might not wake up in the morning. You seem to love that child," he added, pointing at fourteen-month-old Bonnie, the Kallingers' youngest daughter. "What if you came home from shopping and found her drowned in the tub and your

267

husband did it?" Betty replied that if her husband were someone she feared or who beat her or the children, she would not have lived with him for seventeen years.

"Your father," another detective told Mary Jo, "had three thorns in his side. One, Joseph, Jr., is gone. Now there are two more to go." By the remaining two, the detective of course meant Michael and Mary Jo, who, with Joseph, Jr., had pressed the child-abuse charges.

To ten-year-old Jimmy, still another detective said, "Your Dad is a maniac who kills his own children. And you, James, are *next!*"

Noting that Bonnie had purple patches on her hands and arms, the detectives ordered a physician to examine her. The detectives were certain that the patches were the results of beatings that Joe Kallinger had inflicted. In fact, Bonnie had been born with a rare congenital condition for which she was still under treatment and which caused the purple patches.*

The police had warned Betty, Mary Jo, and Jimmy, each of whom was in a different interrogation room, that Joe was going to kill them. In doing so the detectives were employing a strategy for breaking down their resistance, for the police believed that the family knew more than they were telling about Michael's disappearance and Joey's death.

Although the police were intuitively correct about the murder of Joey and in thinking that Joe was dangerous to society, the brutal tactics they employed against Joe and his family were without justification. They also thought that Joe had brutally killed Joey for insurance money; they did not—and could not—know anything about Joe's deeper psychotic motivations.

That night, while the family was trying to relax from the grueling interrogations, Joe told Mike that it was time to go to Camden, New Jersey, and be found. Wearing the same clothes he had worn when he had "disappeared" from Juniata Park the day before, Mike left for Camden. As Joe had originally planned, Mike was to feign amnesia and get himself admitted to a hospital.

---

* The medical name for Bonnie's condition is *cutis marmorata telangiectatica congenita*. It is a condition contracted congenitally (in the mother's womb) in which the patient's skin becomes marbled (*marmorata*) as the result of a chronic dilation of the capillaries and other small vessels.

At 9:45 P.M., after being told by telephone that Mike was in the emergency room of Cooper Hospital in Camden, Joe went to pick him up. From Camden Joe telephoned the East Detectives Division to report that he had found his son and was bringing him home.

At 11:00 P.M., Joe and Mike arrived home. Five minutes later two detectives, who had already been there, came back. They insisted on seeing Mike so that they could report he was alive. At 12:30 A.M., Joe had to awaken him because two uniformed policemen had come to confirm what the detectives had seen. In pajamas and logy with sleep, Mike stood before the two police officers. The police left, with a warning to Joe to keep track of his kids after this.

Round three of Joe's plan for retaliation against the police began at noon on Sunday, October 13, 1974. Joe had brought Mike and Jimmy to the East Hagert Street house in order to trap the police into breaking the law and possibly into falsely arresting Joe.

Joe took a roll of beige masking tape, some wood, and a small Sony tape recorder into which he had inserted a sixty-minute cassette. He set the Sony for record and securely taped it to one of the front doors. Then he delegated Mike to go out and call the 24th Police District from a public phone booth. Mike was to say that someone had broken into 1808 East Hagert Street.

After Mike came back Joe went out, but before doing so he instructed Mike to tape a long, narrow, and very thin strip of wood to both doors. Joe wanted the police to kick in the door and break the law. The tape recorder was set for record because Joe wanted to get it all on tape.

At 12:30 P.M., Mike and Jimmy, who were sweeping the East Hagert Street office, heard the police banging at the outside doors. The police warned, "Open the door or we're going to break it down." Mike and Jimmy went to the door and said the police couldn't come in. One of the policemen kicked the door in, and four uniformed men entered the hallway and surrounded Mike and Jimmy. Three officers then searched the house, but the officer who remained at the entrance told Mike and Jimmy to "beat it" or they would be arrested.

Mike and Jimmy did beat it. They saw their father on the corner of East Hagert and Emerald. Jimmy went home, but Mike and Joe went back to the East Hagert Street house. The policeman at the entrance didn't want to let them in. He reminded Mike that he had told him to beat it. He wanted to know who Joe was.

"I'm his father and this is *my* house," Joe said. "What are you officers doing here?"

"We got a call," explained an officer who had just come down the stairs.

"Terrific!" Joe chided. "Some nut calls in and you all come running. Looks like you broke in here, too. I'm calling my lawyer."

"We could arrest you for interfering with police work," another officer said. "What's your name?"

The first officer took out a pad and pencil and began to write.

"Joseph Kallinger."

"*The* Joseph Kallinger?" the second officer asked, his eyes opening wide.

"Yeah, there could only be one," the first officer said. He made another note in the pad.

"Very funny," Joe said.

"Sure is," replied the first officer. He went on writing in the pad. Then he looked up.

"What's your kid's name?"

"Michael," Joe replied.

"Michael," the officer repeated. "We know about you, too. Lost and found, huh?"

The police continued to keep Joe and Mike from entering the house until the second officer, who had gone to check with a neighbor, came back to say, "This place *is* Kallinger's."

That night after supper Joe took Mike and Jimmy to Independence Mall in Center City, hoping to catch the tail end of the fair and carnival Philadelphians call Super Sunday. Joe also had a plan that, if properly executed, would result in the false arrest of his sons and himself. As part of the plan Joe was carrying a large paper bag into which he had put a cluster of human bones wired together. These were bones that he routinely used to demonstrate to customers how arches work (they were a standard product used by shoemakers), but he knew that because the bones had come from a human being, they would arouse police suspicion.

Super Sunday was over and the streets deserted when Joe, Mike, and Jimmy got to the mall at 7:15 P.M. Mike and Jimmy scavenged among puffs of cotton candy and tattered balloons. Then Mike went to a public telephone and made an anonymous call to the 6th Police District. He reported that a man carrying a bag of dope was walking with two children on Independence Mall.

At 7:30 P.M. seven police cars pulled up to the curb. Fifteen officers got out of the cars. "Remember what I told you," Joe cautioned his sons. "When you get arrested, don't say one word, not even your name." Then Joe stepped ahead of his sons. He wanted the bag of bones to be conspicuous.

A police officer snatched the bag from Joe, opened it, and looked for dope. Instead he found the bones. He took them out, juggled them lightly in his hand, then held them between his thumb and forefinger, as if the bones were a bunch of grapes. All the officers looked hard at the dangling bones. After the officer who was holding them had put them slowly back into the bag, he looked at Jimmy, then at Mike, and asked, "Where's your mother?"

The boys didn't answer. The officer's face was taut, but Joe was enjoying himself. He went on enjoying himself when he was put into one paddy wagon, his sons in another, and they were taken to the Sixth District station house.

When Joe tried to phone Gutkin, a policeman dragged him away from the phone and handcuffed him. The second time Joe made the attempt, he was subjected to a body search and then put into a cell. Although Joe was going to prove that this arrest was false, it was now as real as the cold hard cot in his cell, and the handcuffs that had made his hands swell. He hated himself for having imposed this suffering on Mike and Jimmy.

A series of unexpected developments followed.

Joe and his sons were transferred from the Sixth District, which is part of the Central Division, to Central Headquarters. The transfer was made so that Joe could again be interrogated about Joey's death. He refused to answer any questions.

At 9:20 P.M., Arthur Gutkin, whom Joe had not been allowed to call, arrived at Central Headquarters. Betty had called Gutkin after the Juvenile Aide Division of the Sixth District had called her to say that her sons were in custody. Gutkin got Joe, Mike, and Jimmy out of their cells and got Joe's handcuffs removed. While the lawyer and his clients sat together in the detectives' room, Joe was asked whether he and his children would take a voice graph. The answer was no.

At 10:20 P.M. a lieutenant came into the room. He was carrying a large paper bag with the bones in it. The police had sent the bones to a hospital for analysis, and the hospital had reported that they were old bones. The police now believed that Joe was telling the truth when he said that he used these bones in his work. The lieutenant handed the bag of bones to Joe.

Outside the station house Gutkin told Joe that the false arrest would become part of the civil-rights case. So would the brutalities and indignities. Gutkin didn't know that while the brutalities and indignities were real, the arrest had been contrived by Joe.

Joe felt that the world was darkening around him. This was true of the outside world in which the police were brutalizing his family and himself. It was also true of Joe's inner world. As the delusions and hallucinations became more powerful, Joe moved closer to putting his plan for world massacre into action.

BOOK FOUR

The Massacre
of Mankind

17 A Gift for Bonnie

A little over a month after the six episodes of retaliation, Joe, asleep on his sofa-bed, dreamed that he was walking down a long corridor with a crystal wand in his left hand. At the end of the corridor an iron gate, with bars shaped like half-moons, stood closed. Joe waved his wand and the gate opened.

He saw before him a straight road that led through a valley of enameled fields. On rows of sweet-smelling flowers gaudy butterflies frolicked; songbirds circled and dipped in their flight over the valley. On both sides of the valley were snow-covered mountains. The sun was shining, the sky was blue. Far away was a one-story house with a fence around it. Joe knew that was his destination this November 22, 1974.

He had not gone far along the road when a shower of golden shoelaces fell from the mountaintops. From the sky singing angels glided down. They sang:

"Joe Kallinger, master shoemaker and God of the Universe. O Healer and Destroyer, we sing your praises. Hallelujah!"

Joe looked up. High above the flowers the angels made wide turns and gentle undulations in the sunlight, which glinted off the tips of their wings. Descending, they stirred the air over the fields as they flew toward the mountains. Then, spiraling upward, the angels vanished in the white light of the snow.

In ecstasy Joe waved his wand. He spread his arms wide. A great

275

explosion shook the ground and destroyed the flowers. Fog shrouded the valley. The headless figure of a naked woman stood in the middle of the road. Fog drifted around her. A demon with a huge, tumescent penis was squatting where the woman's head should have been.

The woman's breasts were enormous. From her nipples a doll-sized man with the wings of a bat and the head of a frog hung by his hands. He was trying to put his penis into a large cavity in the woman's body that exposed the internal organs from the top of her hips to the bottom of her rib cage.

Sitting among the coils of intestine was Bonnie, Joe's fifteen-month-old daughter. Glistening with body fluids, she slapped the little man's legs and peered out at Joe.

Bonnie slid out of the cavity and jumped nimbly to the ground. She, too, was naked. Her arms, legs, and back were covered with purple sores. She passed her hands gently over the sores and looked sorrowfully at Joe. Then she pirouetted on the ball of her right foot, turning faster and faster until Joe saw only a revolving blur.

He said, "Bonnie, when you grow up, those awful sores will make you go round in circles, like now. You won't have any friends. You'll wind up talking to yourself. But I'm going to cure them."

At the moment Joe made the decision, he found himself standing outside the fence of the house that was his destination. He looked for a gate. There was none. Joe tried to climb over the fence. It changed into a squirming, hissing wall of snakes.

Joe waved his wand. The snakes disappeared. He was walking along a passageway. On the walls were eyes; they looked at him and blinked. The passageway forked into three directions: up, down, and straight ahead. Joe didn't know which one to take. He waved his wand again, but it shriveled into a small, dried penis with a red rose on a stem at the end of it. He threw it away.

Hearing the sound of fire, Joe peered into the passageway that went straight ahead. It led into a great plain. Through the murky air Joe saw people with arms like the branches of trees. Waving to and fro, the branches were burning with a fire that did not consume them. Around the ankles of the people were iron bands with chains sunk deep into the earth. Joe heard fierce groaning and wailing, curses and shouts from twisted mouths:

"I'm chained and I'm dying."

"Nobody cares!"

"Hey, a little help, huh?"

"I'm burning!"

"Burning! Burning! Burning!"

Fingers of flame snapped at the people's heads. On the ground empty shoes were dancing to the sound of the wailing and groaning, turning and shagging to the infernal music. Now and then a shoe kicked somebody in the leg. The burning arms of branches, trailing sparks, swept down in anger, but the shoe scampered safely away.

Joe looked into the passageway going up. He saw the head of Jesus impaled upon the point of a butcher knife. Blood was dripping from the neck. No sound came from Jesus' moving lips. Behind the knife and the head of Jesus were psychedelic colors flashing on and off along the passageway, until the distance brought them together into a pulsating dot of light.

Then Joe looked down. He saw suspended from the ceiling of the descending passageway a rose window with the face of Lucifer, King of Hell. The face changed slowly into the shape of a delta covered with short, curly, dark hair. A raunchy voice came from the delta:

"I know what'll cure Bonnie."

"Tell me," said Joe.

"Take my fluid, mix it with your semen and with perfume. Put the liquid on Bonnie's sores."

The delta was repeating these instructions when Joe woke up.

The borough of Lindenwold in the County of Camden, New Jersey, is fifteen miles from Philadelphia. It is a terminal from Philadelphia for the High Speed Line Railroad. In 1974 the population of Lindenwold was almost 19,000. Children played and adults walked in shady woods and open fields. Lindenwold was an average-income suburban community. In 1974 nobody there suffered from poverty. Everybody thought his home was secure against assault.

Early Friday morning, November 22, 1974, Joe and Mike arrived in Lindenwold by the High Speed Line. They wandered through the streets until they came to 4 Carver Avenue, a house that looked promising. It belonged to Wallace Peter Miller, a New Jersey state trooper, and his wife, Karen.

Mike broke the small glass pane next to the doorknob and

opened the door. Only the Millers' dog was home. Joe was disappointed: The dog was a male, but even if it had been a female, canine vaginal fluid did not have the magical medicating properties that Joe believed human vaginal fluid had and could not be used on Bonnie's sores.

To keep it quiet, Joe and Mike fed the animal food from the refrigerator. In the bedroom they found a large blue suitcase. Into it they put a camera, jewelry, and pennies that they took from a five-gallon glass water-cooler tank. Then they left.

They were going to walk the streets until they found the right place: a house with a woman in it. Joe wanted a woman nubile and healthy, who would have plenty of vaginal fluid, and sexual organs that would look beautiful mutilated and bathed in her own blood.

Approaching godhood, Joe knew that he had the power to slaughter all the people on the planet Earth by destroying their sexual organs. The best way to global extinction, Joe believed, was by hitting them where they lived, those organs of bliss and ecstasy. With the butcher knife he was carrying in a large brown paper bag, he intended to cut off the penises and testicles of all men, the breasts of all women, and then to slice open the women by making a downward slash from the soft flesh above their hairy deltas to the rear of their vaginas. If a woman had been in the house he and Mike had just left, she'd be dead now, Joe thought.

A house with a woman in it, alone, defenseless: That, Joe decided, would be a good start in the killing of three billion people. Not only was Joe going to kill her, but before he did, he had to force her to spread her legs so that he could rub her genitals with a Kleenex tissue, which would soak up some vaginal fluid. Then he would put the soaked tissue into one of the rubber gloves he had in his back pocket. The fluid, mixed with Joe's semen and a few drops of perfume, would be the magic with which Joe was going to cure Bonnie of her hideous purple sores. He remembered the mysterious delta that had instructed him to get the vaginal fluid.

The blue suitcase was heavy and Joe was tired. He wanted to lie down by the side of the road and sleep, a long sleep, about two million years. Joe knew that he was going to be God someday, but even God needed a rest. The Creation had not been an easy job.

Mike was on the alert for a likely house. Joe remembered the host of angels who had called him Healer and Destroyer. He wasn't sure where he had been when the angels sang his praises or where he had seen the delta. He didn't even know whether he had seen them earlier in the day, or on the day before, or the week before, or perhaps last year, or in some former life.

Hallelujah! the angels had sung. Hallelujah! the crowd had yelled after Joe had fed them. He had been sitting on a barren hill in a parched land. A great multitude were coming up the hill toward him. They held plates in their hands. Cracked from starvation, their mouths opened and closed like the mouths of fish out of water. Gray dust covered their heads and ragged garments. A little boy with a basket was sitting beside Joe. In the basket the boy had only five loaves and a couple of fish. With these, Joe had fed the ragged multitude. And there had been some left over. Hallelujah!

Joe didn't know when he had performed this miracle or where the parched land was. Nor did Joe know the little boy with the basket. He had vanished. He was dead. Lord have mercy on us sinners. In that wasteland the little boy was better off dead than alive. Hallelujah!

Mike had gone behind a tree to urinate.

Joe waited. He switched the suitcase to his left hand, the hand of power that he was going to use to exterminate mankind, the hand that defended Joe in his battles against Lucifer. Joe had to admit, though, that Lucifer, aided by Joey, had destroyed Joe's orthopedic experiments; old Lucifer, King of Hell, who flashes the fancy lights of evil before men's eyes, had won the first Battle of the Shoes. But there would be other battles, Joe knew, and he, Joe, would win them.

Zipping up his fly, Mike came out from behind the tree and said, "Let's go!"

Snug under Joe's left armpit was the brown paper bag with the butcher knife in it. He wouldn't dare carry it under his right armpit, for the right arm was not the arm of power. Joe thought about the head of Jesus impaled upon the point of a knife, blood dripping from the neck. He knew that if he, Joe, were on his way to godhood, then Jesus would be His Son. Had he cut off that head whom millions worshiped and begged for mercy? If so, then Joe Kallinger, master shoemaker and God-to-Be of the Universe, had killed His own Son. Joe stopped walking, horrified.

"What's the matter, Daddy?" Mike asked.

"Nothing. Just thinking, that's all."

Mike said, "Let's try that house across the highway. It's all by itself on that corner lot. Over there, see?"

"Okay, Mike," Joe replied. "Go up to the door, find out what's what inside. But if a woman isn't in there by herself, we're not going in."

Joe knew that he had two godlike duties to perform today: He had to take fluid from a woman's vagina and had to activate his plan for killing everyone on the planet Earth. He checked his equipment. Into the brown paper bag he had put the butcher knife, and also rawhide laces used in boots. In the right-hand pocket of his overcoat he had rubber gloves, and in the left, a needle attached to a syringe, both wrapped in tissues so that he wouldn't prick himself.

He intended to insert the needle into an artery of his victim and with the syringe withdraw all her blood. Then he would slice off her breasts and cut through her hairy delta. But first, of course, he had to take the vaginal fluid for Bonnie.

Mike was talking at the door of the corner house with someone indistinct.

"Long time no see, Joe. Not since our little talk with the pigs at East Detectives. Remember?"

Bobbing in the air at an angle of forty-five degrees above Joe's right shoulder was Charlie.

"This isn't the time to come around bothering me, Charlie. I'm busy. I've got to watch Mike."

"Joe, you old horse's ass! Chickenbrain! Fucker-up! You're a real laugh, you know that? If you're going to be God, then I'm the Holy Ghost and I'm going to fuck the Virgin Mary. Wow!"

Joe knew it was no use. Charlie left when he wanted to, and no amount of bad-mouthing from Joe was going to make him vanish.

"Here's your chance, Joe: Get into that house and kill her!"

Charlie's eyeballs disappeared, leaving only the red-veined whites of the eyes. Laughing, Charlie did a slow fade, going out like the last ember of a small fire. Only his laugh lingered for a few seconds.

Mike came back and said, "Daddy, there's a woman inside. I think she's alone. She's a little woman, I think, in a white sweater and slacks. Not much meat on her. You can knock her over with spitting on her, so she isn't going to keep us out. You want to go in now?"

"Go back, Mike. See if you can find out if she's got any money in the house. Try to make sure she's alone. Ask her for change of a dollar."

Mike jogged across Carlton Avenue, the tassel on his cap jiggling up and down.

Joan Carty closed the storm door, which gave onto Carlton Avenue. The inner door was open and latched to the wall of the living room. Winter had come in sunny and mild.

Joan had opened the storm door slightly for the boy in the plaid coat and the woolen cap with the tassel. He had long sandy hair. Holding up a small box with the top off, he had asked, "D'ya want to buy any tie clasps?" No, she had told him, her husband didn't wear tie clasps. Was there anybody home he could show them to? No, Joan had answered. The boy, whose face was thin and pale, had walked away.

Joan went into her kitchen to straighten things up. Then she turned on the television in the living room. *The Price Is Right* was on, but she was eager to see a soap opera she watched regularly. It was *Another World*.

Having turned down the sound of the TV set, Joan talked on the telephone with a friend and kept her eye on the screen. She heard a knock on the door but went on talking. The knocking continued. She asked her friend to hold on. The boy who had tried to sell her tie clasps was holding a dollar bill close to the window of the storm door.

"D'ya have change for a dollar?" he asked.

"No."

"You have *any* change? Pennies?"

"No. I have only tens and twenties."

Joan closed the door. She told her friend that they would talk later and hung up. While waiting for her soap opera, she did a few things around the house, then went to the cellar and carried upstairs the litter pan that belonged to her Siamese cats, Tascha and Benjy. Holding the pan, she pushed open the storm door.

On the other side of Carlton Avenue, Michael was standing on the sidewalk with his father, who was watching the Carty house. Joe was unable to decide what to do.

He was scared, and wondered whether to break in or to go wandering through Lindenwold until his courage returned.

But early that morning, having just awakened from his dream about the valley and the forked road, Joe had been full of murderous energy. Awake and lying on the sofa-bed, he had had a fantasy about a planet of corpses, with everywhere the stench of death:

Through the blood-stained windows of his shop, Joe looks once more at East Sterner Street, now silent and strewn with corpses, their sexual organs destroyed.

Joe fantasizes that in cities and fields all over the world the dead are rotting, rats feasting on them. In the blood-red oceans sharks gorge on the dead. Above deserts, vultures circle and cry, gliding down through the burning air on wings too dark to reflect the sunlight. With his arm of power wielding the butcher knife, Joe, with Michael's help, has killed all the people in the world by destroying their sexual organs. Only he and Michael are alive. Hallelujah!

In his fantasy Joe opens for the last time the door that leads to "in back." Pale and still, his slain children lie on the living-room floor. Only Joey is missing. He lies under the green grass of White-marsh Cemetery. Joe fantasizes about exhuming Joey's corpse and bringing it home, so that his children could be together in death. He decides against it because Joey met death not by destruction of his genitals, but mysteriously, beneath the surface of Ninth and Market streets. Joey belongs to a bygone era: B.G.M., or Before Global Massacre. He is not among the three billion blessed dead that Joe has slain with his divine butcher knife.

On her back in the midst of the children lies Betty, Joe's wife. Her small breasts are severed from her body. A long, deep wound runs from her navel through her hairy delta. The living-room floor, crimson with blood, glistens with her internal organs.

Then Joe looks lovingly at his children's dead, twisted bodies. Bonnie has one thigh modestly over the other, partly hiding the vertical slash, her sores like fat purple tendrils growing around her arms and legs. The hands of James and Stephen clutch at their bloody crotches. Daubed with blood are Mary Jo's long, delicate hair and comely Madonna face, the lids covering forever the dark, erotic eyes; her small shapely breasts hang from her chest by shreds of skin, blood dripping onto the floor.

Joe remembers the euphoric three weeks he had with Mary Jo when she was twelve. He has an erection. But it is getting late. Joe plans to kill Michael and himself before nightfall.

He calls Michael into the living room. He opens Michael's fly. With the veteran butcher knife in his left hand, the hand of power, Joe hacks off Michael's penis and testicles. Michael dies.

Joe drops the butcher knife onto the floor. Now dull, pitted, and stained with universal blood, the knife will never be used again. With tenderness and respect, Joe looks at the knife and knows that he stands alone on a planet of human corpses.

From a five-gallon can sitting in the corner of the living room, Joe pours gasoline over himself and ignites his clothes. The incineration of his body releases his soul. Rising with the smoke, it drifts to heaven, bringing Joe Kallinger to his apotheosis.

From his throne in heaven Joe sees all he has slain made whole, their souls—the celestial images of their earthly bodies—exalted and perfect. On Joe's right sits Joey; on his left, Michael. Bonnie plays with comets, her skin as clear as moonlight; in jewels and gorgeous robes Betty, with a gleaming set of new teeth in her mouth, now Queen of Heaven, dances before the adoring angels; and Mary Jo, Stephen and James, speeding among the sparkling stars, explore Daddy's heaven, moonflowers on their wings.

Now, in Lindenwold, Joe saw the woman Michael had described walk out of her house, carrying a large pan. She was wearing a white turtleneck sweater, brown corduroy slacks, and old bedroom slippers. With quick, dainty steps she crossed a side street into a wooded area. After emptying the pan, she went back into her house, closing the storm door behind her.

She was just what he needed today, Joe thought. In his hallucinatory state Joe saw Joan Carty's breasts as huge and pendulous under her sweater. Actually, her breasts were small and well shaped. Joe was filled with rage by her short, trim hair and the erotic swaying of her hips under the clinging slacks. He knew he was going to terrify her with cruel sex, get her vaginal fluid, drain the blood from her body, cut off those swinging breasts, and then slice her open. For Bonnie he would be the Healer. But for this evil blonde, he was the Destroyer. Hallelujah!

He and Michael crossed Carlton Avenue and left the suitcase, stolen that morning, in the wooded area where Joan Carty had emptied her pan. Then they crossed the side street and walked toward the steps of the Carty house.

Joan Carty took the pan to the basement, washed it out, and filled it with kitty liter. Then she came up and looked at her kitchen clock. Time for her two daughters to have their afternoon naps. First she went into the bedroom of the one-year-old. The baby had fallen asleep in the playpen. Without waking her, Joan put her into the crib. In the other bedroom the two-year-old was playing with her toys. Joan put her to bed.

Having had nothing to eat since breakfast, Joan went into the kitchen, took lunchmeat and bread out of the refrigerator, and placed them on the counter. It was not yet time for her soap opera. As she was opening the wrapper on the loaf of bread, Joe knocked on the door.

Joe looked at his reflection. He noticed the fancy scrollwork on the door window. The scrollwork cut the reflection into disjointed sections, but Joe felt that he probably looked respectable. His dark overcoat and suit had recently been pressed. He straightened his silver-gray tie and gave himself a poor man's shine by rubbing the front of each shoe against the back of his trousers.

Perhaps the woman would think that he was a truant officer or a probation officer with a delinquent child on his hands. He was holding Mike, who pretended to be scared, by the arm of his plaid coat. She would wonder why he was holding the boy and would open the door to hear what the man in the dark overcoat had to say. Then Joe and Mike could charge into the house. He knocked again, much louder.

Joe saw her walk through the shadowy living room. She didn't open the storm door, but looked at Joe and Mike through the window.

Joe smiled at her. He looked questioningly at Michael and then back at her.

"Has this boy been trying to sell you anything?" he asked softly. He knew that the woman could not hear him unless she opened the door. She opened it about an inch.

"Has this boy," Joe repeated in a normal voice, "been trying to sell you anything?"

"Yes, tie clasps," she answered.

Joan thought that the boy with the tassel on his cap was now under arrest and that the man in the dark overcoat was a detective. She felt uneasy about them—the boy seemed to be playing at being scared. The man's smile seemed forced, his eyes without light, the eyes of a corpse. His manner was somehow false; behind his question to her about the boy, there seemed to be something else that he had wanted to say, something that might scare her and corrupt the calm, secure atmosphere of the day.

She noticed the brown paper bag. His left hand was around it like a claw; the curled fingers were parted and his arm under the coat sleeve seemed to be rigid. Frightened, wishing her husband, Harry, were home, she started to pull the door closed, but Joe grabbed the handle and yanked it toward him. Joe and Mike burst into the house. Thrown off her balance, Joan stumbled toward the wall, then cowered against the inner door. Joe flung her down onto the living-room carpet. Mike pulled the storm door closed. He locked it, then closed and locked the inner door.

Naked, Joan Carty lay on the bed. Her legs were spread, her wrists and ankles bound by the bootlaces to the bedsprings. Joe had taken off her clothes and gagged her lightly. Over her head he put a pillow case.

Mike came into the bedroom with a suitcase he had taken from the Cartys' basement. Joe gave him the butcher knife. He told him to hold the point against the woman's body.

"Use it if she gives any trouble," Joe said.

"Right!" Mike replied. He sat down on the edge of the bed and pressed the knife point, without breaking the skin, against Joan Carty's thigh.

Joe opened the suitcase and filled it with cash and jewelry from the bureau drawers and from the two night tables. He glanced at her wallet and learned her name. Then Joe gestured to Mike that they should leave the bedroom. He shut the door so that Joan Carty could not hear them. In the living room he said to Mike, "Go on ransacking the place as you've been doing. But stay out of her bedroom. I want to be alone with her for a while, get it?"

"Daddy, can I fuck her?"

"No."

"Aw, come on! I thought we were partners."

"I've got to do this alone."

"Why can't I do it when you're finished?"

"That's the way it is, Mike."

"You doing it to her isn't fair to Mommie!" Mike said, his voice rising. "I won't forget this, Daddy!"

Joe walked toward the bedroom.

"At least we'll *kill* her together like you said, no?" Mike asked.

"Yeah," Joe replied.

Mike was right behind his father when Joe walked back into the bedroom.

"I said stay outside," Joe growled. "Behave yourself!"

Joe closed and locked the bedroom door.

After Joe had finished tying Joan Carty to her bed, he saw in the corner of the bedroom the figure of a man turned partly toward the bedroom wall. Joe could see only a part of the left side of the face, but he knew he was looking at his double. The figure was the same height as Joe, the color and dress of the hair were exactly like his, and the figure's dark overcoat was the duplicate of the one Joe was wearing.

Facing the man was the figure of a nude woman. Her features were vague, her face unidentifiable. Her mouth was open in a silent scream. Moving in and out of her stomach was a large knife, which the man was holding in his left hand. His arm was bent at the elbow and was going back and forth, back and forth. The two figures made no noise; no sound came from the woman nor from the knife as it tore into her body. Blood poured from the wound and fell over the woman's thighs and legs and onto the rug. Her long black hair disappeared into the daylight as if the strands ended in an invisible world.

Joe knew that the two figures were both a sign and a holy vision. He sucked power from them and from the thrusts of the knife into the woman's stomach. Joe had an erection, which was another holy sign. As long as he had the vision of the two figures and his erection, Joe knew that he was going to consummate in this bedroom what he believed would be the first killing in his plan to exterminate the world. He had no memories of José Collazo and Joey.

Joe stood at the foot of Joan Carty's bed. His penis remained tumescent as he watched the left arm of his double thrust and withdraw over and over again, back and forth, back and forth, like the arm of a robot. Blood from the phantom woman's wound spread slowly over the floor.

Joan Carty hadn't made a sound. The pillowcase over her head prevented her from watching Joe and Michael. The bootlaces bound her arms and legs to the bed. Now and then her shapely legs quivered. She changed the position of her head on the pillow every few minutes, turning her head to the right or to the left, or raising and then dropping it, as if to move at all was futile. Joe's illusion that Joan Carty's breasts were huge and pendulous, when in fact they were shapely and firm, made him think of them as white flat sacks with little pink knobs on the ends that rose and fell as she breathed.

Joe put his needle and syringe on the bureau. He took off his overcoat and folded it quickly over the back of a small chair near one of the night tables. Standing at the side of the bed, he unbuckled his belt. He dropped his trousers around his ankles.

Then he got on the bed with the butcher knife in his left hand. He was naked from the waist down, his trousers still rumpled around his ankles. His penis erect, he moved toward his victim like a pilgrim in ecstatic expectation waddling on his knees toward a holy shrine. Joe also kept his eyes on the two figures in the corner of the room.

As Joe was about to put his erect penis into his victim's vagina, the figures vanished. At once his penis became limp. Despairing and inwardly wailing, Joe looked down at his "bird": It had shrunk, and

287

now nestled in his pubic hairs. Only the wrinkled, pointed head, ugly and small, was visible; from the nest its little eye peered out, still looking toward Joan Carty's hairy delta.

On the bed Joe squatted on his haunches. He laid the knife across his naked thighs. The two figures had vanished, Joe believed, because the demon who lived in his "bird" had at that moment abandoned him.

Joe trembled and sweated. He looked at the space where the vision had appeared. It was empty. He looked over the side of the bed at the rug; the blood, too, had vanished.

Joe brought the knife up to Joan's chest, but when he placed the tip of the blade against her cleavage, he knew that he could kill neither this woman nor any other human being without the power from the vision. His left arm could not thrust the knife into her body.

The cleavage was the wrong spot, anyway. Joe's mission was to kill by destroying sexual organs. Thrusting the knife into the bony substance between the illusory pendulous breasts would be cheating. With the tip of the blade he traced patterns of circles and squares without breaking the skin.

He looked again for the vision. The space was still empty. He dropped the knife onto the floor.

Although unable to kill his victim, Joe knew that he had to get her vaginal fluid. Against her pubic hairs he rubbed the head of his penis. The "bird" extended a bit, and, after some more rubbing, it weakly squirted a few blobs of semen onto Joan Carty's pubic hairs.

Immediately the "bird" shrank back into its nest.

Then Joe leaned back so that he could get his hand into the rear pocket of his trousers, where he had put the rubber glove after he had taken off his overcoat.

With the glove on his left hand, he put his forefinger into his victim's vagina and took out a small amount of vaginal fluid. Then he turned the glove inside out and put it back into his trouser pocket. The perfume would come from a bottle Mike had taken from the top of the Cartys' bureau.

Joe got off the bed and put the butcher knife back into the large brown paper bag. Then he got dressed and combed his hair. He put on his overcoat and told Mike to take the Cartys' suitcase into the living room. He put the needle and the syringe, still wrapped in tissue paper, back into an overcoat pocket.

From the bedroom door he looked at Joan Carty. He had not untied her, and had not put anything over her except the pillow case. She was silent and still. Joe felt that she was listening to every move he made.

Sex for its own sake had not been the purpose behind the assault on Joan Carty's house and person, but even though he had not been able to sustain his erection, Joe didn't want her to think him unmanly. As he was about to close the bedroom door after him, he said, "You just aren't my type, Joan, that's all. G'bye."

Mike was waiting in the living room.

"Pick up the suitcase and let's go, son."

The storm door slammed shut. Joan Carty lay quietly and listened.

Mike wanted to get the suitcase from the wooded area, but Joe said they would come back for it the next day. They returned at seven the following morning, and picked up the suitcase without being apprehended even though the Lindenwold police were looking for them. Joe's willingness to come back to the scene of the crime shows that he didn't expect to be caught. He felt, at this point, that he was above the battle because he was on a mission from God.

Joe and Mike got home from Lindenwold around 5:45 P.M. After supper Joe went upstairs to the bathroom and took a box of gauze pads from the medicine cabinet. From the kitchen he got a shallow pan of water. He took the gauze and the pan of water into his shop. Then he picked up Bonnie from her playpen in the living room and carried her into the shop. He put her on the large wing chair near his workbench, where she often sat and played while he worked.

Bonnie was Joe's pride and joy, but her skin looked as if it had been stained with an indelible purple pigment by an insane tattoo artist. Dark-purple stains were broadcast not only over her arms and hands, but also over her back and legs. Joe loved Bonnie very much, and his heart was broken.

When she was born, the doctors had said she would "outgrow

it," but she hadn't. Joe had been with Betty in her hospital room when newborn Bonnie was brought to her for the first time. It had been a moment of horror for both parents—"the worst moment of my life," as Joe often said. He decided to sue the hospital for having given him a purple baby. They gave the baby the middle name of Sue, Joe having already settled on Bonnie as her first name.

He took Bonnie to local dermatologists. They said they couldn't help her. He sent dozens of weirdly spelled letters to specialists all over the United States and overseas. Written in his strange, looping script, the letters pleaded for a cure.

A dermatologist at an Ivy League university advised Joe to take Bonnie to local clinics and hospital radiation departments. Joe had already taken Bonnie there. Many of the specialists didn't answer Joe's letters.

Joe then went to medical libraries, where he spent many hours trying to read the technical journals and textbooks on dermatology and hematology. Groping among the big words in the texts and journals, words derived from Greek and Latin, he understood only that the cause was unknown and the condition incurable.

Joe finally convinced himself that doctors had been trained in hell and were sent into the world by Satan to tyrannize the sick and to terrif' the healthy. He decided that during his global massacre, he and Mike would send all the doctors to a remote island in the ocean. Joe and Mike would then tie the physicians, both males and females, to crosses, destroy their genital organs, peel the skin off their bodies, and then throw bucketfuls of salt soaked in hot vinegar over the exposed muscles and nerves. Joe laughed out loud at the prospect.

Bouncing her legs against the back of the wing chair, Bonnie gurgled with happiness. She was happy that Daddy was laughing.

He took the rubber glove out of his back pocket and laid it on the workbench next to the pan of warm water and the box of gauze. The Cartys' suitcase was under the counter. He opened the suitcase and took out the perfume bottle Mike had taken from the top of the Cartys' bureau. He shook out a few drops of perfume into the open rubber glove, which he held in his left hand. Then he took some gauze pads from the box and soaked them in the water. With the pads, Joe scooped out of the glove some of the mixture of semen

290

and vaginal fluid. These had dried up, but Joe believed that he could make them effective again with the warm water. The odor of the perfume mingled exotically with the familiar odors of glue and shoe leather.

"Daddy's gonna get his little precious all well," Joe said to Bonnie. Fascinated, she watched as Joe rubbed the gauze over her legs, hands, and arms. When he had finished, he buttoned Bonnie's dress. Then, standing in front of his workbench, he chanted slowly to himself:

"Kyrieh kyriah maria kreh kriastorah kyrieh kyriah maria kreh."

Hearing these sounds for the first time, Bonnie laughed and threw the rubber heel she was playing with onto the floor. Joe picked it up. She threw it down again. Joe again picked up the heel. They played until Bonnie tired and fell asleep in the wing chair, holding the rubber heel in her hand. Joe carried her into the bedroom, where he put her gently into her crib.

Joe applied the strange mixture of semen, vaginal fluid, perfume, and warm water to Bonnie's skin for the first time on November 22, 1974. On Tuesday, November 26, he looked for signs of improvement but saw none. He applied the mixture again, and once every evening thereafter, until he made the last application on Monday, December 2. The stains on Bonnie's skin were as disfiguring as they had been on the first evening in the series of applications.

Joe picked up his lip knife from the workbench and drove it into the rubber glove, slashing wildly downward, and then threw the glove against the window. On the wing chair Bonnie, wide-eyed, watched her father in his rage. It wasn't the daddy who loved her and made her laugh. His face had changed. She began to cry. Joe picked her up and called fifteen-year-old Mary Jo. Mary Jo took Bonnie from Joe's arms, and walked quickly back into the house, shutting the door; not since the night he had burned her thigh had she seen the dark look on his face and the puckering of his lips.

The Lord had abandoned him, Joe thought, left him out in the cold with a baby whose face was beautiful but whose limbs and back were disfigured by purple stains. He was like Job in the Bible: despised and afflicted.

"Hey, fuckup, I thought you said *you* were God—or were going to be God. I guess you can't make up your mind, right?"

Charlie's head was on the seat of the wing chair. His hair was parted, the ends of it waving gently as if stirred by a soft breeze. The fierce brown eyes looked up scornfully at Joe.

Joe turned his anger on himself for having taken Bonnie to the local clinics and hospitals. He had expected the doctors to release Bonnie from the curse that disfigured her. He believed that instead of treating her, they had shown contempt for him and his daughter, telling him that there was nothing they could do for her.

"Riffraff," Joe muttered to himself, ignoring Charlie, "all the doctors are riffraff. I'll get them on that island in the ocean and they'll learn, all right, they'll learn what suffering is. When I become God, there won't be any more suffering. Because everybody, including me, will be dead." Joe laughed softly to himself.

"Stop talking to yourself—you sound silly," Charlie said from the seat of the wing chair. "Tomorrow you and Mike get out there in the streets again, go to and fro in them, walk up and down in them, and find a house. Break in there, and this time do what you didn't do in Lindenwold. Kill them! Look over there, in the while-you-wait booths."

The figures that had appeared and faded in Joan Carty's bedroom had returned. The left arm of the man went back and forth, back and forth, the knife in his hand moving in and out of the woman's bleeding stomach. Joe felt power surge quietly through his body.

Now Joe knew that he would redeem himself in his own eyes by killing everybody in the world; and at the end he would slay his own family. He would kill even his precious Bonnie, she, too . . . only in Heaven would she be radiant and pure, her skin cleansed of the hideous sores.

He called Michael into the shop. Mike had just come back from the Lighthouse, where his basketball team had won a game. He was sweaty and excited. Joe put his hand on Mike's shoulder and said quietly, "We're going out tomorrow morning, son. Early. And we'll go some place farther away than Lindenwold."

"Yeah? So?"

"Tomorrow our victim dies!"

"Yeah, Lindenwold was a flop, all right."

Standing in the while-you-wait booths, Joe's double was still stabbing the nude woman with the knife. Blood was cascading over the woman's thighs and legs and spreading over the floor of the shop. Through their pantomime, the double and the woman were spurring Joe to murder.

"Okay, Daddy," Mike said, "let's go out tomorrow. But if we don't kill anybody, I won't go out with you again."

"Let's go back inside, son. It's getting late."

As they walked toward the doorway to "in back," Joe heard Charlie say, "Give them hell tomorrow, Joe!"

Joe turned for a moment. He saw that blood washed over the floor of the shop from wall to wall. Tomorrow, December 3, 1974, was going to be a good day.

18 House Parties

They listened for sounds. There were none. Like a small cat stalking and finding no threat of danger, Mike slunk through the long, elegant living room into the hallway and up the stairs.

Joe went to the picture window in the living room to watch for the blond woman he had seen leave the house and drive away. He had had a hunch that she would soon be back. After a few minutes he walked from room to room. When he saw that the breakfast-room table was set for four, with green straw placemats and white china dishes, he knew he had been right in thinking the blond woman would not be gone long. He went back to the picture window.

Joe knew that the main business of the day was to get on with world massacre by killing in this house; that the secondary purpose was to mutilate eyes. It was now 11:25 A.M. All morning—at home, on the bus, and since arriving in Susquehanna Township, Pennsylvania, at ten o'clock—Joe had seen his double using his thumbs to gouge out eyes or pouring into eyes lighter fluid from a can. The eyes were those that had accused Joe: from the teacher who had accused him of stealing the missal to Lieutenant O'Neill, who had accused him of killing Joey. The hallucination had been so strong that Joe had put into his brown paper bag absorbent cotton and lighter fluid.

Joe felt triumphant, elated, and very much at home. As a child he had felt like both an intruder and a prisoner. Legally he was now an intruder, but instead of being a prisoner, he was going to retaliate against his childhood by making the blond woman and the other three people for whom the breakfast table was set *his* prisoners.

"The beautiful homes I saw in suburbia," Joe told me on June 30, 1977, "were something I wished I had. You remember I thought of building a home of my own in the suburbs after I got my chain of shoe repair stores. You remember what happened, Flora. Well, I still felt I belonged in the suburbs. I was jealous of the people who were there."

At the same time that Joe was responding to what he believed was God's command through the hallucination of the double he was giving vent to the resentment that came with his defeats.

At 11:30 A.M. Joe saw the blond woman get out of her car, reach for her packages and books, then close the car door. When she started walking toward the red front door of this two-story white brick house on Susquehanna Township's Green Street, Joe went into the hallway. He wanted to be there when she opened the door.

She opened the door and walked in. At once Joe grabbed his prisoner and pulled her into the hallway and onto the floor.

"If you scream, you're dead," he said in a quiet, even tone as he pointed his butcher knife at the center of her left cheek. In the other hand he held a gun, which, although not the weapon of his fantasies and hallucinations, was used for commanding obedience.

Helen Bogin didn't scream. She asked, "Why must you do this?"

Joe removed the knife from Helen Bogin's cheek and pushed her forehead against the bottom of the staircase. He pressed her head down. Michael, who was standing beside Joe, held both her hands behind her.

"Take what you want and get out of here," she said. "I'm having guests."

"Just keep quiet," he ordered. Then he asked, "How many are coming?"

"Three." This confirmed what he had seen in the breakfast room.

"Get up," Joe said. "Walk up the stairs."

She pulled herself to her feet and asked, "Why aren't you working at an honest job? Why isn't that child in school?"

"Lady," Joe replied, "we need a fix."

In saying this he was playing a cops-and-robbers game. He wanted his victim to think he was here just to steal, and he knew that many thieves stole to get a fix. He himself didn't need one—the "trips" induced by his psychosis were enough.

Joe held Mrs. Bogin's hands behind her back and pushed her up the stairs. Mike followed after picking up her books, packages, and large shoulder-strap bag. Upstairs Joe left Mrs. Bogin with Mike, who now had the gun, and went alone into her son's room.

The room was spacious and had twin beds. Joe walked past the bed near the door and stopped at the other one from which he removed the bedspread and sheets. Then he flung the mattress, the spring, and the bed frame to the floor, flipping over the metal frame so that its legs were up. For he knew that, like the double, who hadn't left him, he was going to have the exquisite pleasure of burning out eyes. The job would be done on the bed frame so that the mattress and sheets wouldn't catch fire. Joe went into the hallway for Helen Bogin.

A few minutes later he had her lying on the upside-down bed frame. The bridge of her nose, her head, her hair, and her eyes were covered with several layers of two-inch-wide adhesive tape. Between the blindfold and her eyes there was absorbent cotton, the same kind of cotton that the double had used and was now using. Moistened with lighter fluid, the cotton burned out the eyes of the double's victims, and the flame, shooting up, set their hair on fire.

Joe took the can of lighter fluid out of his brown paper bag and was about to tip the can when the double vanished. Joe put the fluid back into the bag.*

"I had everything set up," Joe told me on September 6, 1980. "The cotton, the lighter fluid, and everything. And I didn't do it. The cup ran dry."

I looked at Joe silently, thinking about the other times his cup had run dry. This had happened in the Carty house in Lindenwold, New Jersey, just eleven days before. It had happened with Joey in Hazleton, at the scaffold, and even when Joe saw the smoke from the trailer. But I knew that in the Bogin house as in the Cartys', the cup ran dry because the hallucination from which Joe derived murderous energy had vanished. Joe lost the erection that the

---

* The cup had run dry even before the double's first appearance.

hallucination had engendered. The psychosexual basis of his crimes was clear.

To Joe I said, "When you say 'the cup ran dry,' do you mean that your wish to kill, or even to destroy in lesser ways, suddenly leaves you?"

"Yes, Flora, that's the way it is."

"Do you need a hallucination to do these things?"

"Well," he said, "I didn't know anything about hallucinations at the time we're talking about. But now that I do know about hallucinations I can see that that's the way it was."

"Were you sorry when the cup ran dry?"

"No, because when it did, the desire was gone. I felt silly, though, that I had gotten everything set up and then nothing happened."

After Joe had put the lighter fluid away, he kneeled beside the upside-down bed frame to which Helen Bogin was bound. She had been lying on her stomach. He turned her on her back. He tied her ankles spread-eagled to the bed frame. Into her mouth he put a man's handkerchief and on her lips adhesive tape. After tightening the bonds on her ankles, he said, "Don't worry. I'm not going to hurt you. But I *am* going to show you what could happen if you don't behave!"

He pulled up her tan turtleneck undershirt and her brown print button-down outer shirt. Her white bra had hooks on the back, but he pulled it down from the front.

He kept her right breast covered, but exposed her left breast. He did this for a reason: He was going to amputate the left breast and take it home with him as a trophy. With this in mind he moved the butcher knife to the left of the nipple at about the center of the breast. As he did so, he said, "This is just a sample of what will happen to you if you don't behave yourself." But instead of cutting further as he had planned, he pulled up the bra, pulled down the two shirts, and arranged Mrs. Bogin's clothes neatly. "I don't want your friends to see you in that condition," he said.

Mrs. Bogin told me about the cutting of the breast and testified about it at the preliminary hearing and the Harrisburg trial. Both times she quoted Kallinger's comment about what would happen if she didn't behave herself. She told me that she was afraid of infection, and at the trial when asked with what the defendant had cut her, she said, "It was a knife. I didn't see it but I presume it was the same knife I saw downstairs, which worried me because it looked so rusty and dirty."

"I couldn't cut off the breast," Joe told me. "But after I had gotten her dressed, I decided to kill her. That was why I was there. I was planning to cut out her insides and walked toward the lower part of her body. I needed a directive from the double. He had come into the room while I was working on the breast, and, no longer concerned with eyes, was doing what he had done in the Carty house. But suddenly he was gone and, unable to kill, I left the room. There had been something about the double that seemed different this day. He still looked exactly like me and, though I knew I was not God yet, the double seemed to me like the Supreme Power."

A half hour after Joe had pulled Helen Bogin into the hallway, he opened the front door for Ethel Fisher Cohen, the first of the bridge-luncheon guests to arrive. He swung her around, pushed her against the wall, and with one hand held her arm behind her back. With his other hand resting on her shoulder, he placed the knife against the right side of her throat.

"Did you come alone?" he asked.

"Yes, sir," she replied.

"You're lying to me," he said. "Where are your friends?"

"Look at my car."

He told Mike to look. Mike said the car was empty.

"Did you see the blue car that I drove?" Joe asked. "Did you see where I parked it?"

He was testing her, but he was also fantasizing about the car he never had.

"Where's Helen?" Ethel Cohen asked. "I saw her keys in the door."

"Upstairs," Joe replied. "I want you to see your friend. Keep your head down. Walk toward the steps."

"Yes, sir."

Thelma Suden was the second guest. The door opened. She

stepped into the hallway. A hand grabbed her by the back of her neck, pulled her to one side. Joe warned, "You scream and I will kill you."

"I'm not going to scream, sir," she replied.

"You look up and I will kill you," he warned again.

"I'm not going to look up, sir."

Still holding her by the back of her neck, he took her upstairs.

Annapearl Frankston was the third guest to step into the hallway. Joe grabbed her and placed his gun at her head. She screamed.

"If you scream one more time," he warned, "I'll kill you."

Michael walked up the stairs. Joe, holding his hands over Annapearl Frankston's eyes, followed. When they reached the top landing, Mike was standing outside the bathroom door. Joe removed his hand from Mrs. Frankston's eyes and said to Mike, "Show her the knife I'll kill her with."

Mike displayed the butcher knife with which Joe intended to destroy mankind.

All three women, like Helen Bogin, were fashionable, middle-aged, upper-middle-income suburbanites, and prominent in the Jewish community of Susquehanna Township. The township, which is just north of Harrisburg, the capital of the Commonwealth of Pennsylvania, is also where many leading Harrisburg businessmen, lawyers, prosecutors, and state officials live.

Joe took Ethel Cohen to see what he called "your friend Helen." The portion of Helen's face that was visible through the blindfold was white. Her body was inert.

"See?" Joe said. "She's perfectly all right."

He leaned over Helen Bogin and ordered, "Move your head."

She did.

He led Mrs. Cohen across the hall to the bedroom that belonged to Mrs. Bogin's daughter. There he ordered Mrs. Cohen to lie with her face against the floor and her hands behind her back. Mike took a black wire hanger out of the closet and stretched it into a single long piece of wire. With it Joe bound both of Ethel's wrists. When he told her that he was going to put a gag in her mouth, she said she couldn't breathe through her nose. He agreed not to use a gag, but warned that if she screamed, she would be harmed. Then he flipped her coat over her head.

When he took Thelma Suden to the second floor, he showed her "your friend Helen" and then her friend Ethel. He put a black shawl over Mrs. Suden's hat and ordered her to lie down on the floor next to Ethel Cohen. He pulled Mrs. Suden's hands behind her back, and with wire from another coat hanger, tied her wrists and feet. She begged him not to take off her sunglasses to tape her eyes because she had poor vision. He put the adhesive tape away. He helped her to her feet, carried her into a small closet, and put her inside. She asked him to take off her sunglasses and to leave the closet door open. He honored both requests.

After Joe had left the room, Michael came in and threatened, "Open that door one more time and you're going to come to harm."

He slammed the door shut and barricaded it from the outside with a heavy bureau. Joe came back and told Mike, "Don't do that. They're intelligent women. You don't have to do that to them."

Joe removed the bureau and opened the closet door.

He showed Annapearl Frankston her friends Helen, Ethel, and Thelma. After that, he took Mrs. Frankston to a little alcove between the stairs and threw her down on the floor. He tied her hands and ankles, taped her eyes and mouth, and told her, "I'm not going to rape you."

The hallucination that had been stilled after the encounter with Helen Bogin had returned as Joe was walking down the stairs to open the door for Annapearl Frankston. He had placed a gun at her head because the double, the Supreme Power as Joe now thought of him, coming up the stairs as Joe was going down, had been holding a gun. Upon observing this, Joe had exchanged weapons with Mike. Joe had asked Mike to show Mrs. Frankston the butcher knife because the will to slaughter had come back just as Joe and Mrs. Frankston reached the top of the stairs.

After leaving Mrs. Frankston in the alcove, he went to the master bedroom to plan his next moves. But before doing so he looked at the jewelry Mike had put into a zippered canvas bag that belonged to Mrs. Bogin. There were the jewels Mike had taken from the drawers in this room, along with Helen Suden's and Annapearl Frankston's diamond engagement rings and wedding bands that Joe had removed from their fingers.

Joe knew that the jewelry was worth a lot of money. Yet he also knew that he was going to rip the stones from their settings, store the stones in the finisher in his store, and throw the settings into the Delaware River, as he had done with the Carty and Miller jewels and with those he and Mike had stolen from houses since the winter of 1973–1974. In his finisher he had stones and cash that by the end of the "crime spree" amounted to $600,000.

In this house he had taken $700 from Mrs. Cohen's wallet, and that was only the beginning. He had to admit that he seemed like a thief, but he didn't think of himself as one. A thief, he reasoned, would have a fence, and a car to make the loot easier to carry, and he wouldn't throw much of the stuff away. Above all a thief would not be saving the precious stones and much of the cash to finance world massacre. A thief wouldn't have a double to help him. A thief wouldn't be acting under the command of the Lord.

Joe thought of the rolls of change that as a boy he had taken from his adoptive parents' closet to bribe other kids to go to the movies with him and be his friends. The kids had gone with him to the movies, but had withheld their friendship. Having wandered far from the rolls of change in the closet to the diamonds in the canvas bag, Joe thought of his four women prisoners as "friends."

On November 17, 1978, in a poem entitled "Power," Joe wrote that as a child and an adult he longed for a friend but never had one. Then came these lines:

> My love turned to hate,
> My hate to torture:
> My life became cold
> For I hated those
> Who had what I wanted all my life:
> Love, tenderness, understanding.

Then he described the day when he "became full of Power" and, blaming the world for his losses, raided homes that

> Looked like that's where I
> Belonged.

He concluded with:

> ... for Power had become
> My friend, so opposite to what
> A friend should be.

His hate having turned to torture, he concentrated on the logistics of slaughtering the four women. First he had to have them in different locations. Thelma Suden remained where she was. He put Ethel Cohen in a closet on the way to the attic and moved Annapearl Frankston from the alcove to the bathroom. Then he returned to Helen Bogin to ask again for the closet key she had refused to give him. She still refused, and he told her that he was going down to the basement to get some tools, perhaps an ax, to break open the closet.

The women remained bound and alone, listening to their tormentor descending the stairs. They knew, as Ethel Cohen put it, "that he was in a position where he was a king. He had absolute power. We were doing what he wanted, and he could do to us whatever he pleased."

Downstairs, Joe was looking at the green straw placemats and the white china dishes on the breakfast-room table. It was almost two hours since he had been in this room, but he had felt a strong compulsion to return. Even when he told Mrs. Bogin and Mike that he was going to the basement, the breakfast room was where he knew he had to come.

He was in the room only a few moments when he saw his double—the Supreme Power—striding toward him. Joe was tempted to greet his double, but refrained. They had never talked to each other. Joe backed away as the double passed him, and then he sat down at the table.

The table and the objects on it were real, but just as real to Joe were the double and the four phantoms of Mrs. Bogin, Mrs. Cohen, Mrs. Suden, and Mrs. Frankston. Delighted and entranced, Joe watched the double strip the four women. Joe did not wonder by what mechanism the women he had left bound upstairs were now in the breakfast room. Nor did he question why the double was performing upon them the actions that Joe himself had planned. But not knowing that the women, like the double, were phantoms,

Joe accepted the ways of God, which were not the ways of men; if the Lord wanted the double to kill the four women instead of having Joe himself kill them, then Joe was just as content to sit and watch. Joe did not know that he was hallucinating.

When the phantoms of the women were naked and lying on the floor, the double kneeled and slashed off their breasts. He neatly put the eight breasts into plastic bags, and then guided his knife, the double of Joe's butcher knife, downward from where the breasts had been to the vaginas, the hairy deltas of the dream Joe had had before going to Lindenwold.

Pushing his hands into their open bellies and slit vaginas, the double ripped out hearts and lungs, small and large intestines, fallopian tubes and livers. He also dredged up bean-shaped kidneys, stomachs looking like thick-walled muscular sacs, vaginas that resembled tubes, and pear-shaped wombs. Ovaries, each the size and shape of a shelled almond, slipped almost unseen among the larger organs into a huge tin can.

Still kneeling, the double cut out the eyes and tongues, and cut off the ears. One by one he severed four heads from their bodies, and then wound the hair around the foreheads. The double put the entrails into pans for baking. He put the eyes, ears, tongues, and ovaries into Pyrex dishes. Making several trips, the double carried the pans and Pyrex dishes to a stove. The sounds of cutting and sucking and of women's screams seemed to Joe the opening bars of world massacre.

Wearing an apron of fine linen over his suit, the double came back from the stove. He was carrying two deep, gold dishes, which he put on the table. Joe thought a faintly succulent aroma was coming from the stove.

Coming back from his third and last trip to the stove, the double was carrying a sterling-silver platter. Onto it he put the four heads, each head facing a point of the compass: north, south, east, and west. Into the mouth of each head the double put a shiny red apple. Lying in the center of the four heads, the featureless face looking toward the ceiling, was the head of Charlie! The double put the platter of heads onto the table.

Joe looked intently at Charlie. The hair parted slowly, and the pupils dropped down into the slimy, red-veined whites of his eyes.

Charlie looked mockingly at Joe and winked. Joe didn't wink back and didn't smile. He was taking enormous pleasure in the sights before him, which corresponded to a fantasy he had had ever since he had decided to massacre mankind. The only one Joe didn't like to look at was Charlie, who was always a "bad scene."

Ignoring Charlie, Joe looked with delight at the ragout of organ meats on the silver platters; the dark rich gravy of blood, the hors d'oeuvres of marinated eyes, ears, tongues, and ovaries. The food looked tasty, but Joe had no desire to eat. He knew, from his fantasy, that the feast was reserved for someone else.

The scene before Joe being an hallucination, time was telescoped and space twisted and compressed, so that objects that in reality could not be juxtaposed were placed side by side or in close proximity. The red front door of the Bogin house now stood near the wall of the breakfast room.

A key turned in the lock of the red door. Joe watched his double grab a tall man as he came through the door. He wore an expensive-looking tweed suit and carried a leather briefcase. Joe thought him a wealthy executive and knew that, because he had a key to the front door, he was Helen Bogin's husband. Joe had never seen Mr. Bogin in real life, nor had he seen a photograph of Mr. Bogin in the house. His features, therefore, were indistinct and cloudy. Joe watched the double strip and blindfold him and lead him to the beautifully set table.

The double tied the man's chest to the chair, but did not bind his arms or hands or tape his lips. It was with these that Mrs. Bogin's husband would partake of the feast that the double—now the Perfect Waiter—would serve.

Mr. Bogin ate with relish the savory dishes the Perfect Waiter placed before him: the hors d'oeuvres of eyes, ears, tongues, and ovaries and ragout of organ meats soaked in a hot gravy of blood and lymph. But he did not know the name of the animal he was eating, did not know whether it was veal or pork, cattle or lamb. When he had had enough, the husband wiped his lips with a napkin that the Perfect Waiter had placed in his lap. At the same time, the blindfold was removed. With delight he looked at the platters and dishes, but recoiled in horror when he saw the four heads on the sterling-silver platter, with Charlie's head in the middle.

Observing the husband, the Perfect Waiter, with the combination of obsequiousness and authority characteristic of a classic maître d'hôtel, took Mr. Bogin into confidence. The husband's eyes became glassy, his pallor deathlike; his stomach retched. From the mouth of what had been Mrs. Bogin's face, the Perfect Waiter took an apple and gracefully handed it to Mr. Bogin, who looked up in agony, screamed, and fainted. His body, tied to the chair by his chest, canted over to one side and was still. His napkin fell to the floor.

The Perfect Waiter kicked away the linen napkin and seized the butcher knife. He was again Joe's double. To the strokes of the knife fell first the husband's testicles, then his penis, and finally his head. As the knife severed the head, his screaming stopped in midflight. The double put the penis into a plastic bag that was beside the bags in which the eight breasts had been stored. The head and testicles he carried to the already crowded table. By skillful re-arranging, he placed the heads of the husband and wife side by side. Then the double put the testicles in the husband's mouth and closed his eyes.

This final tableau in Joe's hallucinatory vision, especially when the husband's testicles and penis fell to the strokes of the knife, was deeply etched in the childhood scene that was the matrix of Joe's psychosis. When, during that scene, his adoptive parents alleged that his penis would never grow or get hard, the seeds of his symbolic castration were sown. Later he was filled with hostility, rage, and vindictiveness because of what had allegedly been done to his penis. The hostility led to mechanisms of defense by which he felt justified in mutilating as part of world massacre the penis of every male on earth. Knives restored to Joe as an adult the power of which as a child he had been told he had been shorn by the surgeon's knife.

When Joe witnessed the final tableau, his penis became erect. Not wanting the double to see him that way, Joe rushed from the table and to the kitchen door. Opening it, he chanted: "Kristorah kyrieh kyriah maria kreh kyrieh kyriah maria kreh."

Joe came back to the breakfast-room table. Looking again at the testicles in the husband's mouth, Joe thought, as he told me on September 6, 1980, "that my adoptive father had no balls, never stuck up for little Joe. I felt that the testicles in the head on the

305

breakfast-room table were big Joe's way of getting even with his father.

"I wanted to tell my father: 'Here are your balls, eat them!' He wasn't there, so I told that to the head of the dead husband. I added, 'They're no good to you now that you're dead!' "

Joe shot a parting glance at the five headless corpses, then at the six decapitated heads on the table. Hallelujah! Joe thought. No more false starts. My global massacre has begun. Five dead is a good start.

Mike was standing at the top of the stairs. He was carrying the large canvas bag with the jewels. In his pocket Mike had about half of the cash taken from the four women. In his pockets Joe had approximately the other half. According to Mrs. Bogin, the total loss in both jewelry and cash was $20,000, $10,000 of which was hers, and $10,000 that belonged to her three guests.

Joe motioned Mike to come down.

"Let's go," Joe said as Mike came down the stairs. "If we don't hurry, you won't get to the Lighthouse on time."

Looking up toward the bedrooms, Mike started to ask, "Aren't we going to . . . ?"

Joe opened the front door, then closed it. Charlie was floating outside. When the door was shut, Charlie was in the hallway, just in front of Joe.

"Fucker-up!" Charlie intoned shrilly. "You think killing five people in one day is enough when you have to kill three billion? At that rate it'll take you six hundred million days to destroy the world. So get going, man! On to the next house. Keep working or you'll be dead yourself before you kill them all!"

Until fifteen days before Christmas, the cup was empty. There were no commands from God, and Charlie did not appear.

On Tuesday, December 10, 1974, the cup was full again. Shortly after 3:00 P.M. Joe and Mike broke into a house in Homeland, a wealthy suburban enclave of northern Baltimore, Maryland.

"I had only one thing in mind," Joe told me on August 9, 1979. "The pleasure of soft spots. I knew I could not stop the knife that plunges into soft spots, for it's in a magic spell and must continue until no life exists. I wanted to plunge to satisfy Charlie and my

306

double: They would get great thrills when I plunged my knife into the soft spots. But I myself have no power."

In this Homeland house Joe got his victim—Pamela Jaske—ready for slaughter. Then he found himself removing from her wrists and eyes the handcuffs and blindfold. The will to kill his victim had dissolved with the departure of the double.

Joe now wanted not to kill her, but to have sex with her. Pointing a gun at her head, he ordered her to perform fellatio on him. It was what the boys in the tank had done to him when he was eight years old.

Joe came to orgasm and felt macho and normal. His erection had sprung from murderous thoughts, but his orgasm had been evoked by the first sexual desire he had had since leaving Betty's bed five months ago. And the double having disappeared, the cup was dry.

At home that night—the eve of Joe's thirty-eighth birthday—he staged his traditional "Happy birthday to me" celebration. In the days that followed, as the delusion of world massacre became stronger, Joe made plans to speed up the process. He and Mike would take planes to places as far-flung as Miami and Peking, Los Angeles and Moscow. He also went frequently to his "dark retreat," the hole he and his children had dug long ago deep into the earth.

He went to the hole shortly after dawn on Monday, January 6, 1975. The double and Charlie were clamoring for him to go out that morning and get on with the slaughter. But the jobber came to the store on Monday, and Joe wanted to be there. Caught in the agonizing conflict between the dictates of delusion and practical necessity, Joe went to the hole where he intended to stay until it was time to open the store. The chanting, the candle, and the masturbation could not appease him. He went home, changed into good clothes, and woke Michael.

It was a little before 9:00 A.M. when Joe and Mike arrived by bus in Dumont, New Jersey. Again they found a house, entered, and bound their victim, Mary Rudolph, to her bed. This was the only time that Joe permitted Mike, who had asked for sex in Lindenwold and Homeland, to have sex with a victim. Joe told the victim that he was sending in his son and that she was to do whatever the boy wanted. Joe left the room. Mike removed some of his clothes, then mounted the victim. He apparently intended to rape her, but couldn't. After ten minutes he left the room.

This had followed Joe's own experience with Mrs. Rudolph. He had an erection induced by murderous thoughts, but which he released through oral intercourse. In the afterglow of orgasm he felt serene.

During fellatio in Dumont Joe warned his victim not to put her teeth into his penis. His castration fear was at work; he was afraid that his victim would castrate him as the double had castrated the husband in the final hallucinatory tableau. On a retaliatory mission to kill by destroying sexual organs, Joe felt that his own sexual organ had to be preserved.

In his tortured mind Joe regarded fellatio as a way of humiliating his victims. By doing so he felt that he was evening the score of his own past humiliations. Fellatio in Homeland and Dumont, like the ghoulish, cannibalistic banquet in Susquehanna Township, was also a retreat from murder, the appeasing of the conflict about killing that underlay Joe's actions ever since the cup first went dry. The knife held in his left hand at the victim's throat was also Joe's weapon of power.

What happened in these places, including the Kensington of Joe's childhood, was only a prologue to the tragedy that occurred on January 8, 1975, in the small New Jersey town of Leonia.

19 The Hunting Knife

Leonia, New Jersey, Wednesday, January 8, 1975, 2:20 P.M. On
the bedroom floor of a two-story tan stucco house two nude women
lay on their backs, their knees bound tightly against their breasts.
They were blindfolded and heavily gagged. On the floor beside each
woman was a bloody Tampax. The room was filled with the rancid
odor of menses.

The two women were the mother and aunt of a little boy who
was also nude and lay on the floor near them. A man with dead eyes
like black marbles had stripped and bound him. When the boy
screamed, Joe, the man, said, "Roll over and pretend you're asleep."

His feet spread and one hand on his hip, Mike pointed a silver-
plated gun at the boy and the women.

2:35 P.M. On the first floor of the two-story house, a man lay
face-down in front of a fireplace. He was fully dressed. His ankles
were bound with green cords cut from a Venetian blind, and his
wrists with his own belt. Over his head was a woman's coat.

Parallel to the man and nearer to the center of the living room
were two women who also lay face-down. Side by side, the women
were bound to each other at the wrists and ankles by two Venetian-
blind cords. Like the man, they were fully dressed, and had coats
over their heads.

The younger woman looked through the narrow space between the carpet and the edge of the coat. She watched a boy's sneakers and a man's loafers move briskly back and forth, appearing, disappearing, briskly returning to the living room. The older woman was breathing heavily. Hearing this, Joe said, "It's okay, Mom. Everything's going to be all right."

2:45 P.M. A black Volkswagen parked in front of the tan stucco house. A slender woman, whose name was Maria Fasching, turned off the ignition, put the key into the pocket of her imitation fur coat, and stepped gracefully out of her car. She was five feet two inches tall, had brown shoulder-length hair, brown eyes, and a round face with full lips. She was engaged to be married, and, already a licensed practical nurse, she looked forward to becoming an RN.

A militant women's libber, Maria Fasching was famous among her friends for her battles on behalf of the weak and downtrodden. She would always try to rescue someone a bully had attacked, and she could not tolerate racists.

Maria thought of herself as a "free spirit." She resisted anything that she considered a restriction on her freedom. She cared for cats that had been hit by cars and for birds with broken wings.

Today, Maria Fasching was on the four-to-midnight shift at Hackensack Hospital, and she wore her nurse's uniform under her coat. In the morning Maria's friend Randi Romaine, who lived in the stucco house, had called Maria and asked her to drop over for coffee. The two women had not seen each other for a long time, for, between hospital duties and preparations for her wedding, Maria's schedule was full.

At first Maria said that she couldn't visit because she had to go to a wake. The wake, however, was only for an acquaintance. Randi and her twin sister, Retta, had been Maria's friends since they were all in the first grade. Besides, Maria was eager for news from Randi about a junkie they both knew who was doing time in prison. Finally Maria changed her mind. She didn't go to the wake, but drove her Volkswagen to the two-story tan stucco house at 124 Glenwood Avenue, the house of Mr. and Mrs. Dewitt Romaine.

* * *

310

Just two days earlier, on January 6, 1975, in Dumont, Joe's desire to kill had been deflected to fellatio. Since then, the double and Charlie had been clamoring for slaughter and mocking Joe for his failure to kill not only in Dumont, but also in Homeland, Susquehanna Township, and Lindenwold. This morning he had started to go back to Dumont, but had shifted his course instead to this nearby town.

When Joe and Mike stepped onto the screened porch of the Romaine house, Joe's hallucinations of killing were full-blown.

Joe and Mike saw a young woman, a little boy beside her, standing in the hallway to which the porch door led.

"She must've seen Mike and me through a window," Joe told me on July 17, 1977, in the Camden County Jail. "We didn't even have to ring the doorbell. Mike was right behind me, and I started to push my way in. But she grabbed my wrist and fought me. She wouldn't cooperate. The kid started screaming, so I pointed the gun at him and he screamed some more. Then the woman let go of me. They both looked scared to death, which was good. I wanted them that way. I put my hand behind her head, grabbed her by the hair, real hard, and turned her around.

" 'Upstairs and close your eyes,' I commanded.

" 'My grandmother's an invalid upstairs in her bed,' she answered. 'Leave her alone. She can't do anything to you.'

"Then she said she was taking the kid with her. I didn't object. She lifted him off the floor. We started up the stairs, and I told her to go into one of the bedrooms. I didn't like the bedroom she picked, so I pushed her, with the kid in her arms, along the hall into another bedroom. She said it was her sister's room. She put the kid on the bed. I let go of her hair, and she turned around.

" 'Close your eyes,' I said.

"Then I ordered her to get undressed. When she wouldn't cooperate, I stripped her myself, then commanded her to lie down on the floor. I told the kid to stay on the bed and be quiet.

"Meanwhile, Mike was checking Grandma in the small bedroom. He came back and said she was lying in her bed without moving a muscle. She'd be easy to kill. He helped me tie the women, then the boy. The kid was so scared he seemed as if he was going to shake himself to pieces.

"I was just about to go into the small bedroom to kill Grandma when the doorbell rang. Mike stayed to watch the women and the kid—I could tell they were mother and son. I went downstairs and opened the front door. Another young woman was standing there. I got her in quickly, told her to close her eyes, and rushed her upstairs. She opened her eyes when we got into the purple bedroom and asked hysterically, 'Are they alive?' The kid's mother grunted, and she could see the kid was alive by his movements. At my command, she stripped, then Mike and I tied her up on the floor near the other woman—her sister. Then we gagged and blindfolded her.

"The women's knees were tied up against their breasts, and the undersides of their hairy deltas were exposed. I could see a little string hanging out of each woman's snatch, all red with blood. I was going to slice through their twats the way the double did in the Bogin house. But I knew I'd never do a good, clean job with those things stuck up there, because they'd get in the way of the blade of my hunting knife.

"So I grabbed the little strings and pulled. That's what you call logistics: Everything must be in the right place at the right time. And this was the wrong time for the two women to have Tampaxes. I didn't want to do nasty things to these women, but I had to get rid of a big obstacle to killing them. The Tampaxes could mess up my plan for global massacre."

Joe decided Grandma was going to be first, then the kid, then the kid's mother, and finally the aunt.

Knife in hand, Joe was halfway down the hall to Grandma's room when the doorbell rang again. A voice was calling somebody frantically. Joe couldn't make out the name. Mike rushed out of the purple bedroom to the banister and leaned over the stairs to see what was going on.

"Mike," Joe recalled, "was pointing the gun in the direction of the front door. I thought maybe we'd come into a family reunion. But that was good, because the more creatures we could get under one roof, the more we could kill at one time and speed up the plan, like those Nazi death camps that killed all those creatures one after the other. Before God commanded me to destroy mankind, I used to think those concentration camps were shocking. But I thought differently after I'd begun to receive the Lord's commands. Those camps! *That* was organization!

"I took the gun from Mike and told him to hold the knife. He followed me almost all the way downstairs and stood near the bottom landing. Mike held the knife like he was ready to use it.

"I opened the door, with the gun pointing outward. There were two women, one old, one young, and a big guy, over six feet and heavy. Wow, I thought, this guy is going to be trouble. I put the gun to the big guy's head and got them all inside. I told them to act cool.

"Mike closed and locked the house door. The three creatures stood in the middle of the living room. The older woman said something about the old lady in the small bedroom, but I didn't pay much attention to her. The young woman didn't say anything. The two women looked scared and confused, and the big guy was scared shitless. I had other thoughts, but I told them that this was just an ordinary robbery and they wouldn't get hurt if they behaved themselves and did what I told them.

"Well, Mike put the knife in his belt and helped me tie them up after they had got on the floor, face-down. They cooperated. We also got them blindfolded, but we didn't take their clothes off.

"I knew that I had to change my plan from first killing the creatures upstairs to killing the big guy first. Although he didn't put up any fight or even say anything, I didn't want to take any chances with him. I was better off with him dead as quickly as possible.

"I took the knife from Mike and walked toward the big guy. Just as I was going to turn him over and unfasten his belt so I could get his pants down to cut off his penis and balls, the doorbell rang *again*! I got his belt off in a hurry and bound his wrists with it. No time for the pants. The cords, I could see, weren't tight enough, and using his belt seemed to me the quickest way to secure him. I ran to the front window. A young woman was standing on the porch steps by herself.

"I put the knife down, went out, and opened the porch door. She had a smile on her face and a warm look in her eyes. I figured she was about the same age as the two young female creatures I'd got tied up inside, one downstairs, the other next to the kid's mother upstairs.

"Her name was Maria Fasching, but I didn't know that at the

time. I smiled back to keep her cool until I could get her into the house. She must've thought I was company, a friend of the family. Maria Fasching said:

" 'Hi!'

" 'Hi! Come on in,' I answered, very friendly.

"I led the way into the living room. Inside I got behind her and closed the door quickly. I didn't want her running out, starting trouble that would mess up my plan for world massacre.

"I said, 'Just do what you're told, and you won't get hurt.'

"Well, Maria Fasching stood there for a few seconds and looked at the three creatures tied up on the floor. Then she turned to me and knew I wasn't company. Her warm smile was all gone. She looked at me with anger in her eyes.

"I put a hard expression on my face to fight her mean look. She said, almost spitting the words at me:

" 'You don't belong here. This isn't your place. Get out!'

" 'Be quiet,' I answered and pointed to the man on the floor. 'Just lie down across his legs. Right now, understand?'

"But she wouldn't cooperate.

" 'Don't you know, whoever you are, that Mr. Romaine is in the hospital with a bad heart attack? Mrs. Romaine's mother is an invalid in her bed upstairs. My God! Don't they have enough trouble without *this*?"

"Flora, I didn't know about this guy's heart attack or their troubles. And I didn't care about it, either. They weren't even people to me. They were just a few creatures that had to be destroyed during my mission of global massacre. That's all that meant anything to me. I didn't want to hear anything about the creatures' feelings or troubles or about any stuff that would stop me from killing everybody on this planet.

"Maria Fasching started to walk to the three creatures on the floor, like she was going to untie them. I blocked her way. Mike took a few steps toward Maria. The silver gun dangled by the trigger guard from Mike's finger, and I just kept the hunting knife in the palm of my hand, the blade pointing at Maria. You'd think that'd get her to behave herself and cooperate, but she just glared at me and Mike, and said:

" 'Get out! Now! Both of you!'

314

"Nobody moved.

"I said:

" 'Get down crosswise on the man's legs.'

" 'Get out!' she said again in a low, harsh voice.

"Mike twirled the silver gun around his finger, the way they do in westerns, then he snapped the handle into the palm of his hand and closed his fingers around the metal, his first finger on the trigger. He extended his right arm all the way out and sighted along the barrel, which pointed at Maria Fasching's head. Mike had that killer look on his face and wanted to waste her right there on the spot. He kept glancing at me for the okay to shoot.

"Maria Fasching stood very still, looking at Mike. She was trembling. I could see the hairs of her coat and a loose button shaking. A line of sweat beads was on her upper lip, with dampness on her forehead. She brought the palm of her hand over her mouth and let out a sob; then her body slumped, like all the piss and vinegar had drained out of her. The next minute she was getting on her knees— I thought she was going to pray—then she eased herself down on top of the big guy's legs in the way I'd told her to do, so that she was at right angles to the man creature.

"Now Maria Fasching was behaving herself, Flora; it could've been easy for her if she'd cooperated with me in the first place, right?

"While Mike and I were tying her up, she said softly, almost begging:

" 'Don't make it too tight.'

"She asked the man:

" 'Am I hurting you, Jeffrey?'

" 'No, you're all right,' he answered. His voice sounded funny, muffled the way it was with the coat over his head.

"After we'd tied up Maria Fasching at her ankles and wrists, I put her coat and blue woolen jacket over her head so she'd be muffled like the other creatures.

"Just as I dropped the jacket over her, I looked up and saw something moving between me and the front window of the house. A hunting knife, just like the one I had with me, was floating in midair. The handle was brown, like mine. The blade was four and a half inches, also like mine. It was pointing at the ceiling, and stuck on the tip of the blade was the little head of a very small penis. I knew it was *my* penis. Blood oozed down the sides of the tiny shaft and dripped onto the carpet. There were no balls, just my penis.

"Next to the knife was Charlie—that bad scene. He floated toward me, stopped about a foot away at eye level. His hair was over his face and waved back and forth a little, like a soft breeze was at it. Then the hair parted in the middle, and there was that same face with no nose or mouth, just his fierce brown eyes staring at me.

" 'Do you see it hanging there on the point of the blade?' Charlie asked.

"I nodded yes.

" 'Do you get the message?'

"I got the message, but I didn't know what to do with it. That sure *looked* like my penis hanging there.

" 'You must cut it off, Joe!' Charlie ordered.

" 'My own prick?' I asked, feeling panicky.

"I could never do *that*! Global massacre was one thing, but this was something else.

"I stood very still and looked again at the bloody penis hanging from the tip of the hunting knife that floated in midair between me and the living room window.

"Then off to my left I heard voices. Many voices, like many gods. They were laughing. I turned, and behold! I saw figures of people, like pictures in frames, one picture right after another, in a line that curved from one end of the living room almost to the front window, side by side, not one behind the other.

"The laughter suddenly stopped. In the first frame, furthest from the window, Betty was looking at me, mocking me. She said:

" 'Joe, you remember we were making love one night, and you put your thing inside me, moved around some, and then you screamed and pulled out? You rushed off to the hospital because you thought your penis got broke inside me. But you didn't break it in me, Joe. You cut it off!' Wild laughter from all the figures in the frames."

I knew this was a true incident except for the cutting which was part of Joe's perpetual nightmare.

Joe continued, "Betty pointed to the bloody penis on the knife. She said:

" 'You had a small penis, Joe. That's why you kept me in the house all the time. You were afraid I'd run off and find a bigger

316

one! How about that, Mom?' Betty asked her mother, who was in the next frame.

"My mother-in-law gave me a reproachful look.

" 'Joe,' she said, 'I cut your thing off. I told you I'd do it because you kept getting my daughter pregnant all the time!' "

I knew that this had been her threat, made in jest; that when she had made it, Joe, thinking his mother-in-law was serious, had hidden in his room and locked the door.

"In the third frame," Joe went on, "was Joey, my dead son. He was pointing at the penis on the knife and jeering:

" 'My prick's bigger than *yours*! Yeah, and Stevie's is bigger than yours, too; so are Mike's and Jimmy's. We *all* got bigger pricks than you!'

"Hilda, my first wife, was next. She was smirking at the tiny penis on the knife. She said:

" 'Wow! It's *real* small, and I never had any fun with your little cock in me. Some lover *you* were! Why do you think I ran out on you, huh? I needed *real* loving from a stud.'

"In the fifth frame was my daughter, Mary Jo. She looked at the penis on the knife, then smiled sweetly at me.

" 'Daddy, remember when I was twelve years old? We had good times together for three weeks during the summer. Just you and me alone, enjoying each other. It was beautiful, Daddy, and I'll always love you. Always!'

"My adoptive parents were in the sixth frame, with me at six and three-quarters in my little kiddie chair. I was sitting there naked. They were looking at my penis. They were very serious and chanted:

" 'Small, small, small. It will never get hard. Always soft because the demon was cut out of it. You'll always be a good boy and a good man, never get into trouble. You will be the new Adam in the new Garden of Eden and there will be no funny business with the apple tree, *ja*?'

"Naked little me got up from the kiddie chair and looked in a mirror and there was my little penis on a huge lip knife.

"In the next frame was me again, but when I was eight years old in the tank with three older guys. One of them was holding a knife at my throat, another was giving me a blow job, and the third one was jacking off. I was scared. That was my first experience with sex,

317

and maybe I should've cut their cocks off. Maybe I wouldn't have wanted to after that.

"In the eighth frame I saw myself when I was twelve years old. I was kneeling on the bed in my bedroom and masturbating in the hole I cut in the wall. On the bed near my knees were pictures of nude men and women. With one hand I was jerking off; with a knife in my other hand I was slashing the breasts and penises in the pictures. This made me feel powerful. Inside the circle of the hole in the wall there were teeth. The teeth were biting my penis. I knew that the part about the biting didn't happen when I was twelve. It was new.

"In the last frame I saw myself at the age of thirteen and a half. I was jumping off a bus and luring a kid about my own age down to a creek. Me—Joe Kallinger at thirteen and a half—had a lip knife and stripped the kid right near the water. Little Joe was going to cut off his cock, but didn't do it. Little Joe ran away; he didn't want to castrate the kid the way his own adoptive parents had castrated him when they told him his penis would never grow or get hard.

"After the last frame, I brought my hand to my crotch. I was terrified. At the same time all the frames and pictures vanished, along with the penis and the knife. Only Charlie was still floating in midair. I looked at his fierce brown eyes; we were eyeball to eyeball, Flora. He was challenging me.

" 'Cut off my own cock?' I asked.

" 'Not yours, *Dummkopf*. The big guy on the floor. *His* cock. Aren't you supposed to be killing by cutting off cocks and tits and slicing through hairy deltas? Or maybe this little show we just had here scared you out of it, huh?'

" 'Nope,' I answered.

" 'You're not chickening out as you did in Lindenwold and those other places?'

" 'Hell, *no*! I was just going to do it to the big creature when the last woman creature rang the doorbell. They're all going to die. Before I leave here, there's going to be wall-to-wall blood in this house. Global massacre's my thing. You know that, Charlie.'

"Well, Flora, I was always an underground man: the basement where I sometimes tortured my kids, the hole in the East Hagert Street house, my dark retreat. I thought I could kill in the basement of this house, but I had to see what it looked like. So I went down-stairs."

Having walked from the large basement area into the boiler room, Joe thought for an instant of releasing all the oil and burning his eight victims to death. He dismissed the thought, for his special mission as a delegate of God the Destroyer was to kill through the destruction of sexual organs. He went back to the basement where the destruction would take place.

The basement windows bothered him. Although he believed that to kill under God's orders was right, he feared, as he had in other houses, that what was right for him would be regarded as wrong by those who did not understand his mission. Deciding to do a cover-up job on the windows, he went upstairs to get sheets and blankets.

Fifteen minutes later the basement, its windows shrouded, was as dark as dusk. Feeling secure, Joe went upstairs to get his first victim. Coming toward Joe on the staircase was the figure of himself at the age of twelve and a half that he had seen earlier in the frame. His twelve-and-a-half-year-old self was pursuing a boy to castrate at the creek. In the living room Joe went directly to the fireplace where he had left "the big guy," as Joe called him.

"I stuffed a handkerchief in his mouth," Joe told me, "taped his ears and nose, kept the coat over his head. I rolled Maria Fasching off him (I didn't know her name at that time) and took him down the creaking stairs to the boiler room.

"I sat him down and tied him to a water pipe. I secured the bonds of his ankles and wrists with wire, put his hands behind his back, and tied them to his legs with a tight cord. I pulled his trousers down to his ankles, his undershirt up to his neck, and his undershorts to his knees.

"There he was: about six feet three, broad-shouldered, plenty of weight on him, sitting hog-tied with a coat over his head and his pants down. I had him the way I wanted him with his penis and testicles exposed.

"I gave his testicles a poke with the point of my hunting knife and said, 'If you move, your balls are going to move.

" 'Don't try anything,' I warned as I walked to the door. 'I'll be watching you.'

"His penis is small but larger than mine, I thought as I closed the boiler room door behind me. Then the voices I had heard earlier were saying, 'Small, small, always small!

" 'Small, what a fall, no ball, you better crawl, small' went round and round in my mind. 'The big guy doesn't know he's going to die, eat a pie in the sky, don't cry, die!' " (Joe, like other schizophrenics, often rhymed as he was talking.)

"I left the big guy in the boiler room," Joe said, "and started to go upstairs to get my first delegate. Charlie was floating toward me.

" 'Chicken!' he sneered through his mouthless face. 'What happened? Your cup run dry again?'

" 'Wrong,' I replied. 'The cup's very full. The big guy has his pants down. His penis is exposed and ready for cutting.'

" 'So?' Charlie asked.

" 'Well,' I explained, 'my delegate is going to castrate and kill him.'

"Flora, I don't think I convinced Charlie. But this was the way I knew it had to be done. I was God's delegate, and here in this house I was going to choose *my* delegate. My mission was to kill through the destruction of sexual organs and that's what my delegate was going to do for me.

"I wasn't interested in straight killings. If I were, I could have used the gun I had with me. But the gun was for the purpose of reducing my victims to submission. I never had any intention of killing with a gun. Mike, who didn't understand that I planned to kill *only* by destroying sexual organs, had asked me upstairs, as he had in the Bogin house, whether he should shoot anybody. Of course I said no.

"They had to be devoured sexually, everybody in this house. No. No. I don't mean rape. I didn't make any sexual advances to any of the women in the Leonia house. Upstairs Mike had asked if we were going to have any sex. I said no. He had asked me in Lindenwold and Homeland, Baltimore, whether *he* could have sex with the women. I said no. In Dumont I felt I had to make it up to him and I let him mount the woman there. But there was to be no sex in this house. If I wanted to rape these women, I could have done it right where they were. I didn't have to take them to the basement." (Joe *had* to kill with a knife because, as already stated, a knife was the weapon of his restitutional fantasies and hallucinations. The knife restored to the adult Joe the power that the surgeon's knife had symbolically removed from the child Joe. It is a psychological truism that fear of castration leads to aggression, and this was true of Joe.)

Then Joe was silent. His dark, blank eyes seemed to look beyond me at some infernal vision that very likely would have fascinated Hieronymus Bosch. What a Bosch canvas *that* would have made, I thought: Joe and Mike, dressed in Dutch peasant clothes, fifteenth-century, walking among their mutilated victims. Dancing around Joe and Mike would be a circle of devils with flaming knives in their claws, the famous Bosch knife with the nick in the blade in Joe's left hand, blood dripping from the point.

Joe breathed softly, then looked at me and smiled. He went on.

"When I got back to the living room, I had to choose my first delegate. The women upstairs? No. They were tightly bound. Down here? Yes, their bonds were light. I looked at the three women on the living-room floor. Two of them were tied to each other. Maria Fasching was tied only to herself.

"I chose Maria Fasching. It was completely impersonal, like flagging one of three taxis all able to take you where you want to go. I didn't choose Maria Fasching because she was young or beautiful. She was chosen because it was easier to get her up from the floor. Logistics again, Flora.

" 'Okay,' I told her, 'I'm going to take you downstairs now.'

"She let me help her up from the floor.

" 'You tied the cords on my ankles too tightly,' she said.

" 'No, that's all right,' I replied.

"All right, tight, night, no fright, bite! Like a top the rhymes went spinning in my head. I couldn't stop them. Bite!

"Charlie was floating around me. He was echoing the sounds I wasn't saying out loud. I was afraid he would be overheard.

"I guided Maria Fasching to the basement door and down the stairs. I was behind her, my hands on her shoulders. Again the stairs creaked.

" 'The cords are going to cut off the circulation in my legs,' she complained. 'Can't you loosen the ropes a little? I can't walk. The ropes are too tight.'

"I knew the electrical cords I had on her were really quite loose.

So I ignored her complaint. After a few more steps we were in the basement. We walked a few feet. She complained:

" 'My legs are killing me. You said you weren't going to hurt us.'

"The rhymes were still spinning in my head: bite! I turned my delegate around so that she was facing the boiler room where I had prepared the big guy for her. I removed my hands from her shoulders and took off her coat and jacket. I stood in front of her without blocking her view of the boiler room. I had heard her call the big guy's name: Jeffrey.

" 'You're facing the boiler room,' I told her. 'Jeffrey's in there. You are to chew off his penis or I'll kill you.'

" 'Kill me,' she replied. 'I don't care to live.'

"My left hand swung out and plunged the hunting knife into the right side of her neck—a soft spot. I had an erection. She screamed. The hand plunged the knife a second and a third time, still on the right side of the neck.

" 'More, more!' Charlie shrieked. 'Stab her *more!*'

"The hand thrust the knife into the left side of her neck, once, twice, three times. I had an orgasm, the energy of the Lord.

" 'I'm choking,' she cried from a standing position. 'You're drowning me.'

"Down went the knife to just below the nipple of her right breast, to below her armpit, to the middle of her back, and then again to her neck. The hand knew where to stab. It knew the death organs.*

"But just as the hand got to the middle of her back, Mike was on the basement stairs yelling:

" 'Someone's loose!'

"Mike grabbed me by the arm and pulled me to the stairs.

" 'One of them got away,' he told me. 'She's outside screaming. Don't you hear her? Get your coat.'

"I wasn't in a hurry, Flora. I had done to this delegate what the double had previously ordered me to do with all the women victims. And I still had to cut off her breasts and her ears, to cut out her eyes and tongue as the double had done in the Bogin house. Then I was going upstairs to get another delegate to chew off the big guy's penis. I *had* to kill them all.

---

* "Death organs" was Joe's neologism for the vital organs.

322

"Mike was the leader. He made me leave the basement. He picked up my coat in the doorway to the stairs, carried it with one hand, guided me with the other hand. He was like a seeing-eye dog to a blind man, a hero in Leonia who saved his daddy's life. The police were on their way. They would have shot at us to kill.

"As we left the basement, Maria Fasching was standing in her own blood. She was turning from right to left and looked like she was dancing."

Joe and Mike ran through the small New Jersey town of Leonia. Cars came close to hitting them, and they ran on.

Because Maria Fasching was standing when Joe last saw her, he felt that he had failed to kill in Leonia and that his world massacre wasn't advancing. He wanted to get rid of the gun, which was fully loaded, and especially of the hunting knife. He had hallucinated that his penis was on a hunting knife and didn't want that knife around. The knife also symbolized what he thought was his failure to kill in Leonia.

Mike warned Joe that throwing things away would give the police clues that might lead to arrest. For this reason Mike had left in the Romaine house a suitcase he had filled with loot. But within a single block Joe threw away the rings, bracelets, and watches that he had in his pockets, as well as the gun and the hunting knife. As the gun and the hunting knife fell into some bushes, he felt momentarily free.

His thoughts since childhood had been drenched in blood. Now he was tormented by the blood on his shirt, the few drops on his shoes, and his hands, sticky with blood. He kept seeing Maria Fasching drenched with blood swaying from side to side. He saw the hunting knife in his hand stabbing the "death organs." Yet he thought he had not succeeded in killing her.

Joe and Mike came to a park at the bottom of a hill, ran into the park and onto a baseball diamond. At the baseball diamond there was a puddle of water.

"I took off my coat and jacket, then my tie and shirt," Joe told me. "I kneeled down beside the puddle and put the bottom of my shirt into it. The bloodstains didn't come off. I took the shirt out and washed my bloody hands. Mike was looking around, waiting for me. His face was red. He was panting and short of breath. Very near us a big dog was barking.

"I got up from the puddle of water, wiped my hands on the shirt, kept the shirt in my hand, and ran with Mike. We stopped at a basketball field. A boy about Mike's age was bouncing a basketball. We passed him, ran a few feet, stopped. I gave my coat and jacket to Mike. With the shirt I wiped a few drops of blood off my shoes. Mike helped me on with my jacket and coat. I went on carrying the wet and bloody shirt. I felt better with the shirt off. Mike and I kept moving all the time. Mike held one of my hands and in the other hand I carried the shirt. I didn't want that shirt, just as I hadn't wanted the hunting knife.

"We came to a green toolshed right off a road, a couple of feet from the driveway. We stood there for a minute, then I flung the shirt and the tie into the shed.

" 'Don't do that!' Mike warned. 'You'll get us caught.'

"He started to pull the shirt up, but I stopped him by grabbing his hand. We went on running. Mike wanted to go back and get the shirt, but I wouldn't let him. I knew a laundry label with the name Kallinger was in the collar of that shirt, but I left the shirt, Flora, and I don't know why I did that.

"We heard police sirens as we were running up a hill. Back on the street, we ran into bushes whenever a police car came. We ran back to the street after the police car had passed. At one point we stepped out from some high hedges and waved at a red-and-tan bus. It was not a bus stop and the bus passed us. I began wondering whether people would notice that under my heavy black double-breasted overcoat there was no shirt or tie.

"Just after the bus passed, a police wagon came toward us. Seeing it, Mike took me into All Styles Barber Shop. When the barber asked if he could help us, I told him that I was supposed to meet someone there. After I looked around, I said I didn't see the person I was looking for and this was probably the wrong place. A man who was getting his hair cut gave me a funny look. Mike and I walked out.

"We got a bus for New York. I sat there like a dumb-dumb—nothing was in the head. At a terminal in New York I went to the men's room and Mike into a store to buy me a shirt. He had the shirt—it was black—when I came out and I went back and put the shirt on.

"Mike and I left the terminal, got pizza at a stand on a corner outside, walked to Penn Station, took a train to Philadelphia's Thirtieth Street Station and the el from there to Huntington Street. We walked to our house.

"Betty noticed that my shirt was different from the one I wore when I left home before four A.M. that morning. I didn't try to explain. Mike went to the Lighthouse for sports. I lay down on my sofa-bed.

"At one moment I saw the woman in the basement (I still didn't know her name was Maria Fasching) dancing from side to side—but alive. The next moment I saw her dead.

"I thought of the hamsters: Winko, Jellyroll, Popsicle, and Humpty-Dumpty. Even though I had wanted them to live, I was responsible for their deaths. That was long before the double and Charlie, delegates from God the Destroyer, had ordered me to wipe out mankind. I planned to carry out the order. But I had killed only *one* person, the woman in the basement, and I wasn't even sure that she *was* dead. I couldn't get her dancing movements out of my mind: I could see her dancing forever and ever, blood pouring out of her wounds, her bloody mouth screaming my name.

"I fell into a light doze and dreamed that I was sitting in a graveyard, on the edge of a grave, with a skull in my left hand. I was looking at its grinning face and talking to it, talking to Death, my bride.

"When I awoke, I knew my godly mission had just begun. The weight of the responsibility was heavy on me, for in killing three billion people I would become God—but also the greatest murderer of all time."*

The covering on the windows in the basement of the Romaine house allowed just enough daylight for Sergeant Robert MacDougall of the Leonia Police Department to see. He listened for sounds:

---

* On January 8, 1975 Joe had not yet remembered the murders of his son Joey and of José Collazo. When he told me about José on June 27, 1977 and about Joey on July 4, 1977, he said that the memories had just returned.

Nobody seemed to be here. But then his attention was riveted to the vinyl floor. A woman lay on her back, her head toward the staircase, her feet toward the south wall. Alongside the woman was a blue woolen jacket. Bloated with cakes of old blood solidifying and with blood still coming from the mouth and nose, the woman's face was hideously distorted. Sergeant MacDougall squatted close to the face, then reached for the wrist. Pulse: negative. "I had five years as a soldier," he told me, "but I never expected to see anyone butchered like that."

Hearing a muffled moan from the boiler room, Sergeant Mac-Dougall went in there. He cut the tape from Frank Jeffrey Welby's face and freed his hands. Welby said he had heard terrible screams from the basement area.

"Is she alive or dead?" Welby asked. "Did they kill her?"

MacDougall said she was dead, but that she was so messed up he didn't know who it was.

"Maria Fasching," Welby said.

Sergeant MacDougall had been the partner on the Leonia Police force of Al Fasching, Maria's father. MacDougall had known Maria from the time of her birth. "A real sweet, beautiful kid," he said. "When she was little, I used to see her on the swings in Wood Park next to headquarters. Well liked. She had no enemies."

Sergeant MacDougall went upstairs to the living room to report to Police Chief Manfred Ayers. Lieutenant Paul Dittmar, who had come down to the basement soon after MacDougall, had already told the chief that Maria had been murdered. Chief Ayers assigned Detective Mashinski to stay with the body. Lieutenant Dittmar had known Maria since her birth; Detective Mashinski had been with her at school parties.

Retta Romaine, who didn't know that Maria was dead and thought she was still a prisoner in the basement, had called the Fasching family. (Retta was one of the three women lightly bound in the living room.)

Al Fasching rushed into the room where the officers were conferring.

"I want to see my daughter," he cried.

"Not the way she is," Sergeant MacDougall replied gently as he put his hand on Mr. Fasching's shoulder. "Later, Al."

Al Fasching pushed past MacDougall, saying, "It's my daughter!"

The police had to restrain Mr. Fasching. At no time that day or night did they allow their friend and former colleague to see his daughter.

Chief Ayers assigned Sergeant MacDougall to secure the outside perimeter of the Romaine house. This was a routine police action, but it seemed especially important in this instance because the police thought the armed men were still in the house and passersby and curiosity seekers, seeing the police cars, had begun to gather. The sense of calamity had spread throughout the small town. The omens were seen in the police cars that came to join the police force from the surrounding communities and in the reports that the Leonia police had sent to headquarters. Besides, Retta Romaine, one of the two women bound in the living room, had, after being released by Sergeant MacDougall, telephoned the families of Jeffrey Welby and Maria Fasching, to report that Jeffrey and Maria were bound in the basement.

The trail to Joe and Mike began with Eva Rumi, a neighbor of Sergeant MacDougall's. When he went home to get refills for his fountain pens, his wife was talking with Mrs. Rumi on the telephone. Mrs. Rumi had called to say that while she had been walking her dog in Sylvan Park that afternoon, something had happened that she had to share with the police. She had called both police headquarters and Sergeant MacDougall. A few minutes later the sergeant picked her up in a patrol car. They drove to Sylvan Park.

While driving, Mrs. Rumi recalled that when she and her dog were halfway around the park's baseball field for a second time, she saw a man and a boy running hand in hand down a hill. Never before had she seen people run that fast. Then she saw the man bend over; it seemed as if he was washing his hands or planting something. His back was turned to her and she couldn't be sure. Her dog started barking at the man and the boy. She saw the man take off his coat and what looked like a shirt. Again she wasn't sure.

As she was on her way out of the park, she was walking with her dog along a macadam driveway up a hill leading to the street. The dog suddenly became very wild. He ran toward the south side of the driveway. She turned left to follow him and found him near some

327

shrubbery. She called to him. As he came toward her, he was dragging a man's shirt.

The dog rolled on his back with the shirt. He smelled it, cried, and smelled it again. Mrs. Rumi put a leash on him to take him home. He pulled back and cried. She managed to take the shirt away from him. The shirt was white with a gray print background. And it was stained with blood! Her dog had been in the shrubbery when Mrs. Rumi found him with the shirt. She threw the shirt back into the shrubbery. By the time she got home, the shirt was no longer in her thoughts.

When later Mrs. Rumi learned that something was wrong in Leonia, she thought again of the bloodstained shirt. For the first time she wondered whether there was any connection between the shirt and the man she had seen in the baseball field.

When Mrs. Rumi and Sergeant MacDougall reached the south side of the macadam driveway, the bloodstained shirt was in the shrubbery where she had left it. She also pointed out where she had seen the man and the boy running down the hill. She took the sergeant to the puddle of water at the baseball diamond point, where she had seen the man bend over and either plant something or wash his hands.

Sergeant MacDougall got a signed statement from Mrs. Rumi and informed Chief Ayers about what had transpired. Adjacent to the shirt the sergeant had found a wide blue-gray tie. He had also seen footprints in the mud. The footprints were in the baseball diamond and also near the shirt and tie.

Police and press would describe the murderer of Maria Fasching as a "sex slayer." Yet, according to the autopsy and a laboratory report, neither vaginal rape nor fellatio had preceded the murder.

Dr. Thomas J. Lynch of the Bergen County Medical Examiner's Office did the autopsy on January 9, 1975. He testified at the trial as he had already stated in his report: "There was no evidence of rape. There was no evidence of any attempt that we could see of any kind of sexual invasion."

A laboratory report requested by Investigator E. Denning of the Bergen County Prosecutor's office, dated March 11, 1975, stated: "No seminal stains were detected on the mouth swabs, the vaginal swabs, the rectal swab, the pantyhose or on the white underpants."

Joe told me that he stabbed Maria Fasching because she had refused to obey his order to chew off Jeffrey Welby's penis. It was not true that he killed her because she had refused to have sex with him, as was generally believed. Maria Fasching was the first person Joe had ordered to "chew" or "eat" another person's sexual organs in his abortive campaign to destroy mankind. If she had obeyed him, he would not have killed her as soon as he did, nor would she have met her death in the same way. She would have died, however, along with the other victims in the Romaine house: All the people in the world, according to Joe's delusion, were to fall to the thrusts of Joe's knife.

Maria Fasching also fell victim to a grotesque distortion that sprang up in Joe's mind. I shall never forget my horror and dismay when he told me:

"Flora, Maria Fasching commanded her own death. She said, 'Kill me. I don't care to live,' with firm conviction. I get the strangest feeling about this. She had problems—some deep disturbance. Her life was not a complete one, Flora. She didn't want to live. If you look into it, you will find that I am right."

Shocked, I replied, "Joe, don't you realize that she was probably saying that she preferred death to having to chew off a penis?"

"No, no," Joe insisted. "She didn't want to live. She ordered her own death. If she had said anything else, pleaded, it wouldn't have happened that way. It wouldn't have happened *then*. As it was, her command turned on the switch, and I started stabbing a few feet into the basement."

Joe paused, and then said, "She disobeyed me, and completely upset my plan for killing everybody in that house. If she'd done what I told her, then she would have been killed the way I was going to kill the others. They all had to die."

At the trial, Larry McClure, the prosecutor, remarked, "Whatever he [Joseph Kallinger] was demanding of her [Maria Fasching] cost her her life."

What Joe Kallinger had demanded of Maria Fasching was so horrible, so delusional and insane, so completely beyond the annals of usual crimes as to be alien to the speculations of lawyers, the press, and the public.

BOOK FIVE

Out of the World Forever

20 "You are an evil man"

On Friday, January 17, 1975, nine days after he had killed Maria Fasching, Joe closed his store at seven o'clock as usual. After dinner Betty, Jimmy, and eighteen-month-old Bonnie went into the living room of 102 East Sterner Street, the home of Anna Kallinger. Critically ill after a stroke and with a gangrenous condition in her leg, Anna was in the nursing-home wing of Episcopal Hospital. That afternoon Joe had visited her and had given permission for the amputation of her gangrenous leg.

Bonnie played on the living-room floor. Betty and Jimmy watched *The Rockford Files* on television. In the adjoining room, Joe and Mike sat at the dining-room table, examining coins. Joe had been a coin collector for many years; he read coin books and often sifted pennies, nickels, and dimes he got from customers in the course of business. He and Mike had stolen coins since their partnership had begun in the winter of 1973–1974.

There was a knock at the front door, then a second knock. Betty turned down the sound from the television set and yelled, "Who is it?"

"Police officers. Open up!"

Joe and Mike charged away from the dining-room table and bounded up the stairs. They ran through the wooden door that was common to the two contiguous houses, Anna's at 102 East Sterner Street and Joe's at 100 East Sterner Street, also known as 2723 North Front Street.

Her hand on the knob of the front door, Betty asked whether the police had a warrant. Before she could open the door, the police broke it down.

Law-enforcement officers from the FBI and three states, Pennsylvania, New Jersey, and Maryland, burst into the living room. There were six officers from the homicide unit of the Philadelphia Police Department, five Pennsylvania state troopers, two officers from Dumont, New Jersey, and one from Baltimore, Maryland. There were two investigators from the Bergen County, New Jersey, Prosecutor's Office, one of whom had traced the ownership of the blood-stained shirt Joe had left in Sylvan Park. There were also two detectives from Dumont, and one detective from Baltimore.

"Where's your husband?" an officer asked.

"My husband?" Betty replied. "What do you want Joe for? He didn't do anything." At first Betty had suspected that the police had come because of something the kids might have done.

The officers were moving through the house. Three of them ran up the stairs. An officer who stayed with Betty said, "Your husband is wanted for rape, robbery, and murder."

"Oh, my God!" Betty gasped.

Joe had told Betty that he and Mike were robbing houses. When they went out in the morning, sometimes even before dawn, she got up and made breakfast for them. Joe also told me that if he and Mike lost each other during the day, each would call Betty to say where he was so that she could report this to the other. But Betty couldn't believe that Joe could murder. It was also difficult for her to comprehend that Joe had raped, for he had been impotent with her for many months. She had been largely outlawed from the cruel kingdom of his psychosis and did not know that Death, Joe's bride, had become her successor.

Betty went back to the television set, which she watched hypnotically for a few minutes. Then she jumped up and screamed obscenities at the policemen:

"You fucking sonsabitches, you have no right to do this!"

She returned to the set, watched the show briefly, then jumped up again to scream more obscenities. The police ignored her.

Meanwhile, back in the living room of his own house, Joe picked

334

up the telephone and started to dial Arthur Gutkin. Michael stood beside Joe. Above them footsteps thundered along the hall on the second floor. Then a cop with a shotgun pointing at them was racing down the stairs. From behind him came a familiar voice, tense and gravelly:

"That's the man!" said Lieutenant James O'Neill, the tough cop who had vowed in the Roundhouse not quite four months ago that he would get Joe Kallinger.

"Don't move!" yelled the cop with the shotgun.

O'Neill grabbed the phone before Joe could finish dialing and threw it on the floor. The cop with the shotgun took a position beside the stair banister. His legs and thighs spread, his arms high, one hand on the stock grip, the other cradling the barrel, he menaced Joe and Mike with the weapon.

"Show me your warrant," Joe said to O'Neill.

A third officer, who had come down the stairs behind O'Neill, grabbed Michael by his shirt and dragged him upstairs. O'Neill put his lean, firm hands on Joe's shoulders and ordered, "Walk!"

Pushing Joe up the stairs, O'Neill growled, "Kallinger, you killed your kid, Joseph, Jr. I *knew* you were going to kill again. You killed that nurse in Leonia! God! If we'd only gotten you before, she'd be alive today."

O'Neill pushed Joe along the hall and through the doorway that connected the two houses, then down the stairs into the living room of Anna Kallinger's house.

O'Neill walked to the other side of the room to speak with another officer. Not daring to move, Joe watched the police ransacking closets and drawers. He heard some state troopers say that they were going next door to search the other house—Joe's house—and the shoe repair store. Joe thought of the jewels in the dust pipe of his shoe repair finisher, the precious stones saved from the watches and rings he had thrown into the Delaware River.

Lieutenant O'Neill came back.

"Look at this," he said as he handed the arrest warrant to Joe.

They arrested me in the wrong house, Joe thought as he handed the warrant back to O'Neill. A false arrest. We'll get the cops on this.

At 11:00 P.M., FBI agents and Philadelphia detectives led Joe out of the house that had been his prison in childhood and that, before his incarceration at Holmesburg, he had turned into a prison for his wife, his children, and himself.

Both Joe and Mike, who had been led out separately, were arrested on fugitive warrants and charged with four counts of kidnapping, four counts of robbery, and one count of burglary in connection with their alleged attack on four women in Susquehanna Township, a suburb of Harrisburg, Pennsylvania. Both Joe and Mike surrendered without resistance and were taken into custody.

Joe was brought to the Roundhouse manacled and under tight security. Assembled there were the top law-enforcement brass from Susquehanna Township and Harrisburg in Dauphin County, Pennsylvania, and also from Dumont and Leonia in Bergen County, New Jersey, Lindenwold in Camden County, New Jersey, and the City of Baltimore, Maryland.

The bloodstained shirt and tie that Joe had left in Sylvan Park had led to the arrest. As Joseph C. Woodcock, the Bergen County district attorney, told the press, "If we did not have this hard piece of evidence, we would still be looking."

The garments were turned over to the New Jersey Crime Laboratory, then to state police laundry-mark experts, and were traced both to Berg Brothers, the Philadelphia store where the custom-made shirt had been purchased, and to Philadelphia's Bright Sun Cleaners, which had cleaned the shirt and inserted into it the name of the customer.

With only a New Jersey charge against Joe and Mike, it would have been difficult to hold them in Pennsylvania. However, one of the fingerprints found at the scene of a December 3, 1974, robbery in Susquehanna Township, Pennsylvania, matched the fingerprints on file for Joseph Kallinger. It was for this reason that he—and Mike—were arrested on a Pennsylvania charge.

Arrested on the Susquehanna Township charges, Joe and Mike were taken to the Dauphin County Jail in Harrisburg, Pennsylvania. They were driven handcuffed in an unmarked police car. About halfway to Harrisburg Mike was taken out of the car and Joe watched his "strength and courage" disappear into the darkness.

When Joe arrived at the jail, it was just before dawn, January 18, 1975. He had known when he had left Holmesburg a year and five months earlier that while there something "deep" had taken place within him. At that time he didn't know "how far it would go." It had gone so far that Kallinger was now a man who had been hunted by three states and for whom charges followed charges in quick succession.

On January 20, 1975—two days after arriving at the Dauphin County Jail—Joe was charged in New Jersey with two armed robberies (Dumont and Leonia) and the murder of Maria Fasching.

On January 27, 1975, a preliminary hearing was held on the Susquehanna County charges. A judge ruled that there was enough evidence for a grand jury to consider indicting Kallinger. This ruling was based on the testimony of three of the four Susquehanna Township victims, who had identified Kallinger as their assailant. That day there were also lineups at which both Joseph and Michael were viewed by eighteen witnesses from the states in which the crimes of which they were suspected had occurred.

On January 28, 1975, Joe was indicted by a Camden County grand jury on charges of robbery and rape in Lindenwold. Among the seventeen counts in the two indictments were charges of conspiracy, burglary, armed robbery, rape, assault, possession of a gun and knife, contributing to the delinquency of a minor, debauching the morals of a minor, and threatening to kill.

On January 28, 1975, Baltimore police charged Joe with robbery.

It had gone so far, this something "deep" that had taken place during Joe's first incarceration, that he had committed three murders. Of the three the Fasching murder was the only one with which he had been charged and the only one he remembered. At least he remembered the stabbing. Because Maria Fasching had been alive when he left the basement, he still resisted believing that she was dead. In his delusional state, his sense of persecution in full throttle, and his need for retaliation churning within him, he believed that the murder charge—and indeed all the other charges—had been slapped on him because the Philadelphia police were persecuting him for the two civil suits he had filed against them in October 1974.

He couldn't understand the Camden allegation of rape, because he knew he hadn't raped in Lindenwold. Why Baltimore had charged him only with robbery and Dumont with armed robbery he didn't understand. In both places there had been fellatio. But his greatest confusion turned on what had happened in connection with the Susquehanna Township case. Three of the four women he had watched the double kill had testified against him at the preliminary hearing and had identified him at the lineup. As far as Joe was concerned, the double had killed these women. Joe's hallucination had been so strong that to him the double's murder of the women and the husband could not be doubted.

At Dauphin, Joe hid his psychosis and torment behind a mask of hypercompetency. He instructed his lawyers, Malcolm W. Berkowitz and Arthur L. Gutkin, to state publicly that their client had categorically denied committing any of the crimes of which he was charged and that the charges grew out of the Philadelphia Police Department's harassment of Joseph Kallinger.

At Dauphin County Jail, Joe was regarded as a model prisoner and was "in population," which is the standard prison and jail term for the quarters where prisoners who cause no trouble are housed. Nevertheless, there were a few unobserved lapses from normality.

On the day of the preliminary hearing and the lineups, Joe discovered that the Susquehanna Township women were alive. At the hearing Mrs. Bogin testified that he had cut her in the left breast with a knife. There had been blood, but the wound was not serious enough to require stitches. After the wound had been cleaned it had been covered with a Band-Aid.

That night, alone in his cell, Joe heard his old laugh ascending from the depths of his belly and then roaring around him. It had not occurred since the day he had sent Joey to the trailers.

Though Charlie was absent, the double was not. The double's voice told Joe not to murder but to wait patiently for an eventual return to the mission God the Destroyer had commanded. Joe was well behaved because he felt sanguine that he and Mike would return home to resume world massacre. He had resisted facing his killing of Maria Fasching, even though, as part of world massacre, killing was right.

While at the Dauphin County Jail he also had to face the death of his adoptive mother. The day he had been arrested, he knew that her end was close, but now that it had come, he was saddened and shocked. He was then in a religious period and forgiveness came

338

naturally. He wished that he could have attended her funeral. As it was, before he was told about her death, she had been buried in Whitemarsh Cemetery where her husband and Joey lay.

Joe had been told that Mike was in the juvenile section of the jail, and he had two glimpses of him at a distance in the hallway. "Not very long seeings" was Joe's way of describing the glimpses.

After a few days at Dauphin, however, Michael was sent to the Lancaster Detention Home, and on March 6, 1975, the day that Judge William W. Lipsitt adjudicated him a delinquent, he was sent to the Youth Development Center at Cornwells Heights. Twenty-one days later he was transferred to the Youth Development Center at Warrendale, an institution for the rehabilitation of delinquent adolescents. Judge Lipsitt thought Michael was "salvageable."

A psychologist who tested Michael reported that he was rebellious, hostile, and always on the defensive; that he could be reached only through long-range analysis and extensive psychotherapy, but that as long as he had his own way he was not a threat. Another psychologist predicted that he would act out his hostility and aggression through fighting and deviant behavior, but that before doing so he would try to manipulate events and people. Still another psychologist strongly recommended that he be removed from his home environment.

At Warrendale, where Michael remained for a year and a half, he showed, according to an official document, "a remarkable history of sustained progress."

In September 1976, while still under the custody of Pennsylvania, Michael went to live with foster parents. The foster mother, a relative of Betty Kallinger's, had been concerned with the entire Kallinger family and especially with Michael.

While Michael was at Warrendale and even after he was in foster care, New Jersey challenged Pennsylvania's right to have custody of him. After a long battle between the two states, the Supreme Court of Pennsylvania handed down an opinion that the extradition of Michael Kallinger to New Jersey was mandatory. New Jersey had charged him with delinquency in connection with the violation of three criminal statutes: two armed robberies and the murder of Maria Fasching.

At a closed hearing on January 26, 1979, before Judge Arthur Minushkin of the Bergen County, New Jersey, Juvenile and Domestic Court, Michael pleaded guilty to two counts of armed robbery (Leonia and Dumont). He pleaded guilty in exchange for dismissal of the murder charge. Although he was suspected of a sexual attack in Dumont, no action was taken.

Prosecutor Roger W. Breslin recommended dropping the murder charge, since Michael did not actually participate in the murder. The prosecutor also proposed suspending sentence for the robberies, "since the youth is rehabilitated and living with foster parents in Pennsylvania." He also said, "To further institutionalize him would undo all the good that's been done for him."

Michael was put on probation under Pennsylvania jurisdiction until December 25, 1982, his twenty-first birthday. Two conditions of his probation were that he finish high school and that he not write anything about the case. He was legally returned to his foster parents.

Joe went through two trials on the Susquehanna Township charges: four counts of robbery, four counts of false imprisonment, and one count of burglary. The first trial, which began on June 19, 1975, ended in a mistrial because a sheriff's matron supervising the sequestered jurors talked to some of them about the case. She said that Kallinger was guilty of these charges because he also had New Jersey charges pending and everybody knew that he had killed his son, Joseph, Jr. A second trial began on September 8, 1975.

At both trials the defense lawyers—Malcolm W. Berkowitz and Arthur L. Gutkin—maintained that the Commonwealth of Pennsylvania had failed to prove Kallinger guilty of the charges beyond a reasonable doubt; that Kallinger was not accountable for his actions recently because of the cumulative effect of inhaling toxic chemicals; and that at the time the crime was committed, Kallinger did not know the difference between right and wrong and therefore could not be held responsible for the crime even if he had committed it.

Elizabeth (Betty) Kallinger testified that her husband frequently heard voices and saw things in front of him that were not there, and she quoted him as saying that he was receiving instructions directly from God about what to do.

Frederick Rieders, a chemist who formerly was chief toxicologist

340

for the Philadelphia Medical Examiner's Office, testified that fumes from toluene, one of the chemicals Kallinger used, could cause intoxification, brain damage, and deranged behavior.

University of Pennsylvania psychiatrist Dr. Robert Sadoff testified that several diagnoses of Kallinger showed evidence of schizophrenia and paranoia, but that he appeared to be a borderline case. "Under periods of emotional stress, in addition to the effects of the glue," Dr. Sadoff said, "there have been times when he tipped over into psychosis, as evidenced by the hallucinations his wife described." The psychiatrist added that sophisticated psychological testing was necessary to determine whether Kallinger could tell right from wrong. Dr. John Hume, the prosecution's psychiatrist, who not only examined Joe but studied him during the trial, testified that he was *not* psychotic.

The only testimony that was given at the second trial and not at the first came from Joe himself. He testified that he talked directly to God, that he was one thousand years old, and that he was once a butterfly.

The jury, after deliberating less than an hour, found Joe guilty of all nine counts of burglary, robbery, and false imprisonment with which he was charged. In arriving at this judgment, they were, of course, pronouncing Joe sane.

At the end of the trial Joe was transferred from the Dauphin County Jail to prison: the State Correctional Institution at Huntingdon (SCIH). At Huntingdon, which is in the southern Allegheny Mountains of central Pennsylvania, he was an uncommitted—that is, an unsentenced—prisoner from October 7, 1975, until December 16, 1975, when he was returned to the Dauphin County Jail for his sentencing.

Judge John C. Dowling of the Dauphin County Court of Common Pleas, who had presided over both trials and declared the mistrial, now had the responsibility for sentencing Joe. During the trials, the judge had been judicial and made no personal comment about the defendant. But at the sentencing Judge Dowling expressed his own feelings, saying, "You are an evil man, Mr. Kallinger, utterly vile and depraved."

He sentenced Joe to a minimum of thirty and a maximum of eighty years in prison.

Joe had expected two to four or five to ten years. "The life sank out of me," he told me on March 28, 1982. "I knew I was never getting out."

Joe had not stood trial for murder. He had been tried for burglary, robbery, and false imprisonment. Yet his minimum sentence of thirty years was longer than is generally imposed for murder. On average, a life sentence for murder means parole after fourteen years.

Over lunch at the Bar Club in Harrisburg on May 27, 1977, Judge Dowling told me, "I could have given him a very minimal sentence. I could have put him on probation. I could have told him to go home and not do it again. Of course, the community wouldn't have tolerated it. But theoretically I could have done it. The key thing that violated my sense of decency was the involvement of his son."

Judge Dowling leaned across the lunch table and said, "I looked at his age and decided on thirty to eighty years. *I wanted to make sure he would never be on the street again.*"

When Joe was returned to SCIH on December 22, 1975, he was Prisoner K-2719, a committed—that is, a sentenced—prisoner. He was still on B Block, what prisoners call "the hole." He was not permitted to go to the library, but he could read the library books he asked the guards to bring him. He read about law with the same intensity he had lavished on medical tomes in connection with Bonnie's illness. By understanding the law, he thought, he would find the means to set himself free.

Soon after his arrest he had entered a religious period. He took a correspondence course and became a minister of the Universal Life Church. During both trials he had a standard Bible with him and read it during the court procedures. "Religion was now an obsession," Joe told me on March 29, 1982, "like bowling and horseracing had been in their day. It is ridiculous how these obsessions came and went, how intense they were while they lasted, and I'm embarrassed to look back on them." (In talking of religion as an obsession Joe was not referring to his visions of God and the "divine commands" he received.)

Looking back, Joe was also embarrassed that at the second trial he testified that he was one thousand years old and that he was once a butterfly. He had said this during a sodium amytal session administered by Dr. Robert Sadoff, the defense psychiatrist. The defense lawyers asked Joe to repeat the assertion in court, for the amytal interview could not be used as evidence. On the conscious level Joe as a child wanted to make his home with the butterflies. Perhaps at that time he wanted to do so because as a child he subconsciously thought he himself *was* a butterfly, for that was what the sodium amytal—known as truth serum—revealed. As an adult Joe was embarrassed at the trial when the district attorney, LeRoy Zimmerman, cited various species of butterflies and asked Joe which of them he had been.

"You're laughing at me," Joe said to the district attorney.

In the world and at the Dauphin County Jail Joe had been meticulous about his appearance. At SCIH, both before and after his return, he seldom shaved, didn't care about his grooming, stuffed up his toilet and let it overflow, and threw food from his trays around his cell and through the bars into the runway.

He panicked about his health and complained that there was blood in his urine. Prison doctors maintained that what he called blood was plum juice he himself had poured. He insisted, and still insists, that the blood was real, the plum juice the prison's cover-up.

Joe sometimes broke into the Kristorah chant. Overhearing him, a guard recorded on an observation sheet: "Kallinger mumbling Greek."

The double didn't appear. Charlie did. Some nights Joe went to sleep on the floor because Charlie just wouldn't get off Joe's cot.

One afternoon Joe had a bad headache because Charlie was floating around the cell. Joe complained about Charlie to a guard. Charlie would go away, the guard said, if Joe shook the blanket. Joe did what the guard told him, but Charlie stayed in the cell, bobbing in the air a few feet above Joe's cot and looking at Joe with a malicious twinkle in his eyes. Then his long hair slowly closed over the featureless face. Joe told the guard that Charlie was still there, so the guard separated them by taking Joe down the hall and putting him into a worse cell.

Joe went to sleep on the cot in the new cell and dreamed about the Devil. His dreams at this time either were about the Devil or, as he believed, came from the Devil. It was a different image of the Devil from the one Joe remembered from his childhood and from the one who, in the early days of his second marriage, commanded Joe to set fires.

"Eyes rolled up in the Devil's head," Joe told me, "eyes became white. I was under the control of the Devil and went into a world that was evil. I saw the Devil in the forms of evil things. For the first time I thought that Charlie came from the devil-world itself. His eyes rolled up and looked like the Devil's eyes."

Charlie kept coming back. "He told me," Joe recalled, "to flood toilets, to throw feces on the walls. He ordered me to throw food around the cell and into the runway outside. I did it. I was flipping. I did it when Charlie told me. I did it by myself. I often didn't know whether I was doing these things by myself or because Charlie was ordering me to do them. I kept telling the guard, 'Charlie did it.' The guards laughed at me. Dr. Wawrose, the prison psychiatrist, didn't believe Charlie was real. 'You've never said, "There's Charlie," ' Dr. Wawrose protested. What was I supposed to do, Flora? Say, 'Now, Charlie, you wait till Dr. Wawrose gets here.' In his way, Dr. Wawrose was also laughing at me."

Joe knew he had to get rid of Charlie. "Those eyes on me all the time," Joe recalled, "that loudspeaker voice ordering me around. He told me once he was afraid of water. So I filled thirty cups of water and put them outside my cell. I did this over and over again. Bars couldn't keep Charlie out. Water was the only thing that could keep him away."

Joe was now more afraid of Charlie than he had been in the past. "With lots of time to see him and think about him in prison," Joe reminisced, "I realized he was the symbol of death with his head just hanging there, bobbing up and down, no body, nothing under that faceless face, just air, the symbol of death, *my* death."

As Joe stood in the middle of his cell, he felt his blood rushing from his head to his feet. From his head to his toes he had a wet, cold feeling. He was certain that he was face to face with death.

He fell to the floor and screamed. His heart stopped, he thought. His heart started to beat again. He knew that he had passed through the valley of darkness and that behind the mountains he had seen on both sides of him was heaven.

On the middle finger of his right hand there was a heavy gold ring with a red stone. At first he thought that the ring, like Charlie, was the symbol of death. Later the ring symbolized life. It heralded a future in which he was affluent and dressed in fine clothes. His suburban dream had not vanished.

Joe was convinced that he had died, had had an experience out of his body, and had come back to life. Getting up from the floor, he remembered that this was January 17, 1976, the first anniversary of his arrest. He remembered the spirits of January and wondered what they were. He also asked himself what there was about January that always led to turning points in his life. His first arrest was in January 1972. His second and, with thirty to eighty years ahead of him, his final arrest was in January 1975. Now, on the anniversary of his second arrest, he thought he had died and had come back to life.

On February 26, 1976, Joe was transported from SCIH to the Bergen County Jail in Hackensack, New Jersey, to await trial for the Fasching murder. At SCIH Joe had never been in prison population. He had even been in the glass cage, the worst cell in the prison. SCIH warned the Bergen County Jail that he was a difficult and disruptive prisoner. As he left SCIH, the guards yelled after him: "And take Charlie with you."

21 Not Free to Die

On July 19, 1976, Joe had been at the Bergen County Jail in Hackensack, New Jersey for almost five months. He was awaiting his murder trial.

They had been bad months. He had refused to cooperate with his lawyer, Paul J. Giblin. Even with his defense psychiatrists, Dr. Irwin N. Perr and Dr. Jonas R. Rappeport, he was essentially uncommunicative. At times his behavior was so unruly that he had to be strapped to his cot for his own protection and that of the guards.

Lying naked on the floor of the Green Room,* a one-man isolation cell for disruptive and suicidal prisoners, Joe had cried "Mama" and had played with paper airplanes. He made the airplanes from a writing tablet he had bought at the commissary before he was isolated. A guard leaned over, pulled the airplanes away from Joe, and punched him in the kidneys.

Joe was back in the Green Room on July 19. A guard ordered him to get dressed for his interview with a writer. Dressing, Joe fantasized that the writer, Flora Schreiber, was a CIA agent coming to probe his mind for his innermost secrets. What better way, he

---

* In this isolation cell, according to complaints received by the State Office of Inmate Advocacy and released by it in April 1977, prisoners were beaten and subjected in other ways to cruel and unusual punishment. The complaints were unverified; there were no witnesses except the prisoners themselves. However, on the recommendation of the Inmate Advocacy Office, the Green Room was abolished.

346

thought, for a spy to get to him than to say she was writing a book about him?

The Bergen County Jail has five tiers flanked on two sides by a high dome-shaped rotunda. Seated at a metal table in an alcove on the second tier, I saw a guard in a brown uniform and a prisoner in a regulation suit of grayish green come toward me.

The prisoner had a full head of jet-black hair. His black beard with touches of gray was neatly trimmed. He was frail and thin. About five feet nine inches tall, he seemed shorter, for he cowered within himself as he shuffled along, with a slight stoop, beside the guard. His face, sallow and waxy, bore the imprint of incarceration.

The guard left to wait outside the alcove. Anthony Pistilli of the Giblin office, who was with me, turned to the prisoner and said, "Mr. Kallinger, this is Professor Schreiber."

"How do you do, Mrs. Schreiber?" (Actually it should have been "Professor or Miss Schreiber.")

"How do you do, Mr. Kallinger?"

Kallinger sat down opposite me at the table. The corners of his lips slid back slightly. He was trying to smile. In five months he would be forty, but he looked younger than his age—except for the eyes. Even though he could see, the staring brown eyes were like those of a blind man. They seemed dead. He was awaiting a trial for murder, and even though he was under tight security and without weapons I had the irrational fear that he might kill me.

Even though Joe and I started out by being afraid of each other, the interview and the one that followed two days later went well. My fear of the man changed to pity for the child, for the eyes that had seemed dead were now filled with sadness and pain. It seemed to be the pain of a lost child. Joe's fear of me had also disappeared. In replying to Giblin's request for some tapes Joe had in bank vaults, Joe wrote: "I have no remembrance what's on any of the tapes I made so I'm not able to cooperate. In fact, until now I forgot all about the boxes. Remembering is thankful to that nice lady, Mrs. Schreiber."

But it looked for a time as if Joe and I would not meet again: The Sheriff's Office said that I would need a court order for further interviews. The court refused to grant the order, and Giblin appealed the decision to the Appellate Division of the Superior Court. He argued that I was necessary "to the full preparation of the defense" because I had not only "gleaned pertinent information concerning the defendant's past, but also succeeded in gaining his confidence and trust."

We won the appeal; the Appellate Division gave me access to Kallinger. Larry McClure, the chief prosecutor of the pending murder trial, however, appealed the decision to the Supreme Court of New Jersey. The Supreme Court sustained the Appellate Court's decision, and on August 25, 1976, I resumed my interviews with Joe. I also saw him on August 26, 27, 30, and 31 and September 1 and 2.

Now in a normal cell, which overlooked the parking lot, Joe looked out of his window every night to watch my car arrive. One night he designated to me a spot in the parking lot where he wanted Betty to linger with three-year-old Bonnie. This took place as planned. He wanted to see Bonnie, but he also wanted Bonnie to see him. "What do they tell Bonnie about me?" he asked. "They should explain that I didn't choose to go away." He was afraid that Bonnie thought he had abandoned her.

I had gained Joe's trust, but on the night of September 2 we both knew that this might be my last visit. I was going to appear before a panel of three judges the next morning in Brielle, New Jersey, because McClure had asked the Appellate Division to cite me for criminal contempt. He claimed that in speaking to reporters on the day I resumed interviewing Kallinger, I had willfully defied a court order not to publish in writing or orally until after the trial.

The panel of judges, headed by Robert A. Matthews, disagreed. Judge Matthews said that the coverage following my conversations in the press room had not been extensive; that in Brielle he had heard nothing about them. He said that the court would not cite me for criminal contempt and that I could continue interviewing Joseph Kallinger.

A few days before the murder trial began I was with Joe when suddenly his arms moved back and forth across the table. His eyes were dazed. I tried to talk to him. He didn't seem to hear me. For about ten minutes his arms continued to go back and forth on the table. His eyes were open but unseeing.

He came to himself and asked, "Where were we?" I went on with questions as if there had been no interruption.

The next night he came toward me with an unsteady gait; he didn't greet me by name but only with a facial grimace. He sat down opposite me. I tried to talk to him. The only reply was a chirping sound accompanied by an intensified version of the movement of the arms I had seen the night before. Then he seemed to be chanting. I thought I heard something like "Kristorah."

He slipped from his chair to the floor. His hands continued to writhe. So did his body. The movements were graceful, like those of a dance. The chirping and the chanting continued. I leaned over him, asked if I could help him. No reply. I tried to get him off the floor, but couldn't. Wanting to have him put to bed, I called a guard. As he pulled the prisoner up from the floor, he said, "C'mon, Joe. Show time's over."

I felt that Joe's behavior was a manifestation of some profound inner disturbance. When I learned more about his past, I realized the behavior was an intensification of the snakelike movements his adoptive father had noticed when Joe was fifteen, and that had also occurred intermittently at moments of tension in his first and second marriages.

At the murder trial, Joe's body writhed, his arms and hands waved. He danced. He moaned and groaned, made sucking and blowing sounds. He foamed at the mouth, fell off chairs, and stuck his tongue out at the judge. He chirped like a bird and intoned unintelligible sounds, among them "Kristorah."

The erratic behavior began during jury selection, and Judge Thomas F. Dalton dismissed the prospective jurors so that they would not be prejudiced against the defendant. The judge ejected Kallinger from the courtroom, saying that he could come back when he was ready to behave himself. As the dismissed prospective jurors filed out, one looked at Kallinger with a glazed stare and told her companion, "Thank God we can leave. Let me get out of here."

When Kallinger came back thirteen days later, a jury had been selected and was at work. The jury, consisting of ten men and six women, including four alternates and representing a cross section of Bergen County, made up of wealthy suburbs and blue-collar towns, now saw the defendant for the first time. His head continued to bob and jerk as he sat at the defense table, but he was quieter than he had been during a legal argument that preceded the entrance of the jury.

The jurors included secretaries, service employees, skilled crafts workers, business executives, and a housewife. The panel, which was to be sequestered during the trial, was chosen after more than 150 prospective jurors had been interviewed in the course of five and a half days. Most disqualified panelists said they were too prejudiced against Kallinger, because of pretrial publicity, to serve fairly. One said, "If he wants to go for insanity for rape or robbery, that's fine, but I don't think for murder!"

The anti-Kallinger feelings were so strong that special security measures were taken. Persons entering the courtroom were screened by the type of metal detector used at airports to reveal the presence of guns, bombs, or other metallic weapons.

In this atmosphere, for three weeks, forty-two witnesses testified. Among the witnesses for the defense were Betty, Stephen, and Mary Jo. Also testifying to Kallinger's insanity was Richard Kimmel, Joe's employer after he left Mahoney's shop and before he took over the Kallinger shoe repair store.

Kimmel said that Kallinger was "one of the best shoemakers" in Philadelphia, but also described his flareups of erratic behavior that made some people refer to him as "Crazy Joe."

Betty, Stephen, and Mary Jo described Joe's basement torture chamber. In telling how her father had burned her with a hot spatula Mary Jo in effect recanted her earlier recantation of the 1972 child-abuse charges. The family's testimony horrified spectators (and probably the jury) but didn't convince them that Kallinger was insane.

During the trial at one point he had a jagged piece of eyeglass lens in his hand. He was about to cut his wrist, but a defense lawyer and sheriff's deputies wrestled the piece of glass from him. Kallinger's second suicide attempt in three days was averted. Earlier he had tried in his cell to cut his wrists on a pants zipper.

To spectators the suicide attempts seemed as phony as the movements and gyrations, and as far from indicating insanity as the family's testimony.

Five prosecution witnesses identified Kallinger as the man who broke into the house where the murder occurred on January 8, 1975.

To spectators, this testimony convicted Kallinger beyond a shadow of doubt.

In his opening statement at the trial, Giblin said Kallinger was "totally crazy" and that psychiatrists would testify that he did not know right from wrong on January 8, 1975.

McClure, in his opening statement, said that the state would put on the stand psychiatrists "who have watched [Kallinger's] machinations and will testify that they are feigned to make his condition seem more serious than it is. He wants to be found insane." The prosecutor also said that the evidence would show "clearly and unequivocally that Joseph Kallinger killed Maria Fasching and that his actions were the calculated actions of a sane person." McClure said, "Any person who could do this is abnormal to a certain degree," but he added that testimony would show that the defendant knew the "nature and quality of his acts" and therefore was legally sane at the time of the killing.

The psychiatrists for the defense, Dr. Irwin N. Perr and Dr. Jonas R. Rappeport, testified that Kallinger was psychotic. Dr. Perr classified him as a "borderline schizophrenic with violent and sexual energies intermixed." Dr. Rappeport said that Kallinger was suffering from paranoid schizophrenia.

The prosecution psychiatrists, Dr. Norman C. Jablon, Dr. Frederick Wawrose, Dr. John Hume, and Dr. Joseph F. Zigarelli, argued that Kallinger was not psychotic but had a personality disorder and was an antisocial personality—a psychopath or a sociopath.

It was what Dr. Jablon had said at Holmesburg in 1972, and the diagnosis, with various interpretations, had remained. Of the four prosecution psychiatrists, Dr. Zigarelli was the only one who hadn't had contact with the defendant before this trial. Dr. Wawrose knew Kallinger at Huntingdon, Dr. Hume at the Harrisburg trial and at the Dauphin County Jail.

What Dr. Jablon said in 1972, he said again after examining Kallinger at the Bergen County Jail in 1976. He added that now the personality disorder included not only inadequate personality, his chief finding in 1972, but also indications of sexual deviancy and paranoid, obsessive compulsive, and schizoid features.

Kallinger was depressed, Dr. Jablon said, but "it's not unusual to

351

find depression in people who are in jail." In spite of Kallinger's depression, the doctor pointed out, "in his current life situation he looks forward to his talks with the woman who is writing a book about him."

Kallinger was malingering,* Dr. Jablon also said. During the examination the prisoner had made animal noises and had given the doctor a Bronx cheer.

Dr. Wawrose told about Charlie and the cups of water with which Kallinger had tried to keep Charlie out of his cell. But the doctor said that Charlie was an imaginary companion and not a hallucination and that at Huntingdon Kallinger showed no evidence of "any organized delusional system."

At first, Dr. Wawrose testified, he had thought that the defendant was suffering from a Ganser syndrome.† Later he decided that the defendant was malingering. This seemed evident when he chanted in some jargon that sounded like Greek or Latin. "I did not feel," the doctor testified, "that it represented a legitimate behavior that would be associated with a mental illness."

Only when Kallinger told Dr. Wawrose that the Lord was going to come for Kallinger, and that he might get some type of sign from the Lord, did the doctor think that perhaps this was a delusion. He dismissed the possibility of delusion, however, because he felt that "Mr. Kallinger was embellishing his symptoms, was, you might say, trying to fool us into thinking that he was psychotic."

Dr. Wawrose testified that at Huntingdon Kallinger was suffering from an emotional disturbance, but not from a major mental illness. He said that at SCIH he had thought of sending Kallinger to Norristown State Hospital, a mental hospital, not because Kallinger was psychotic, but because after a stay there he could become a better-adjusted prisoner at SCIH. He also testified that after examining the defendant in connection with the present trial, he found that "Mr. Kallinger was not psychotic, that he knew the difference between right and wrong in a very concrete and literal sense. I felt that Mr.

---

* "Malingering" is a conscious simulation of illness used to avoid an unpleasant situation or for personal gain.

† "Ganser syndrome" is a diagnosis that is commonly used to characterize the behavior of prisoners who seek to mislead others with regard to their mental symptoms.

Kallinger had emotional problems, but that he was not mentally ill in a legal sense."

Dr. Hume testified that Kallinger "was generally cooperative and did not seem in any way to be in a world of his own or withdrawn. I saw no evidence of any abnormal or peculiar behavior on the part of Mr. Kallinger." Dr. Hume had given Kallinger neurological tests in Harrisburg and from those tests concluded that he was malingering. When Dr. Hume examined Kallinger for the present trial, he noted that he "could reach goals, and people who have schizophrenia are not able to reach goals. Their thoughts go off completely on tangents that are unrelated to the matter at hand. He was able to respond to questions relevantly."

Dr. Zigarelli testified that the defendant knew the difference between right and wrong when he allegedly held seven persons hostage and murdered a woman in Leonia. "In my opinion," Dr. Zigarelli said, "he knew the nature and quality of his acts."

Kallinger's movements, Dr. Zigarelli said, showed he was feigning the symptoms of choreoathetosis (also known as Huntington's chorea). The doctor also testified that Kallinger during the examination seemed mildly depressed and "his affect, though appropriate, was somewhat flattened."

Dr. Zigarelli made the diagnoses of "a personality pattern disorder with evidence of schizoid and mildly paranoid features," but said the defendant was definitely *not* schizophrenic. The doctor also told the jury that Kallinger knew he had done something wrong because he allegedly fled the scene of the crime and discarded a bloody shirt which authorities later traced to him. "When you do something wrong, you try to run away," Dr. Zigarelli said.

Dr. Perr and Dr. Rappeport, the defense psychiatrists, countered that Kallinger was insane and did not know right from wrong at the time of the murder. Dr. Rappeport said that he was suffering from the results of paranoid schizophrenia of the chronic and severe type and that his behavior at the time of the murder had been controlled by his illness.

Dr. Perr, who had spent seventeen hours with the defendant and had him tested at Rutgers, testified that his mental condition had been getting worse for several years.

"He had an awareness that these acts were illegal and likely to get him into trouble," Dr. Perr said. "But," he added, "to know right from wrong can be defined to mean the defendant was able to make rational judgments.

"He could not really appreciate his own behavior, though he had an awareness of some aspects of it."

Dr. Perr referred to the Hoffmann–von Schlichten–Levitt diagnosis and prediction of 1972. "That prediction came true," Dr. Perr testified.

The psychiatrist also said that the defendant was suffering from "a psychosis in which there is a veneer of rationality."

Cross-examining Dr. Perr, Larry McClure asked if the defendant had not shown rationality in bringing a gun, a knife, and tape to bind people, and to take other "necessary steps for a successful robbery."

"No," Dr. Perr replied. "He used stupid, poor judgment. He wasn't successful. It was inevitable he would be caught, and he was caught."

"He successfully got away the day of the crime," McClure pointed out.

"He left some calling cards," Dr. Perr replied.

"What calling card?" McClure asked.

"A shirt with his name on it," Dr. Perr said.

But why should the jury have believed Perr and Rappeport when it could believe the bigger team of Zigarelli, Hume, Jablon, and Wawrose?

A tragic and brutal murder: a girl of twenty-two was killed by a madman's knife. The jury's sympathy was naturally with her and not with the killer. Even if he was sick, the jury wasn't interested. The jury of five women and seven men took six votes—one on each of the five charges, murder, robbery, armed robbery, possession of a dangerous weapon, and contributing to the delinquency of a minor, and one vote on the insanity question. The jury reached a unanimous first-ballot decision on each charge after deliberating only one hour and forty minutes.

As the jurors left the motel where they had been sequestered during the trial, some of them told the press that they didn't believe Kallinger was insane when he went on his crime spree. One juror reported that insanity testimony by defense psychiatrists had no impact "on everybody I talked to. We just went by what the witnesses said." He said that testimony that Kallinger was insane in 1972 was rejected "because we didn't care what he was like in 1972. We just went by what he did in 1975." The juror also said that the tearful testimony by the occupants of the house where the murder took place was "vivid and convincing and their account of the crime influenced the jury most."

Another juror said, "I think Kallinger's crazy, but he's not insane. It [i.e., his behavior] made me laugh. It was just an act." To this juror Kallinger's behavior in court and not the psychiatric testimony was the decisive influence.

A juror Paul Giblin met after the trial told him that she believed Perr and Rappeport, but she was afraid that if she found Kallinger not guilty by reason of insanity, he would be back on the street after spending a little time in a mental hospital.

Joe didn't belong on the street, because his delusions and hallucinations made him dangerous by inciting him to kill. But keeping him off the street did not magically remove the delusions and hallucinations. These could be controlled only in the highly structured environment of a mental hospital, where, along with other therapies, Joe would have been given psychotropic drugs. By sending him to prison, where he would not receive treatment, this jury and judge, like the jury and judge in Harrisburg, put at grave risk both Joe's life and the lives of the other inmates, for without the drugs and therapies, Joe's hallucinations and delusions, erupting within the prison walls, would incite him, as we shall see, to kill again.

At the time of the trial I didn't know the facts about Joe's childhood and his development that I learned later and have presented in this book. These facts were known to Drs. Arieti and Robbins at the time they examined Joe and made their diagnoses of paranoid schizophrenia. But these facts were completely unknown at the time of this trial (and at Joe's other two trials). Dr. Perr and Dr. Rappeport did know about Joe's orthopedic experiments, which clearly indicated to them a delusional system and psychosis.

At the Bergen County trial, nobody knew what Kallinger had asked of Maria Fasching and certainly not that what he asked grew out of the pivotal trauma on which his psychosis turned.

355

Nobody knew about the double or the "frames" Joe saw, or that Charlie, who had been described in open court as an imaginary companion, not a hallucination, was in the basement spurring Kallinger on to murder.

Nobody knew of Joe's world-massacre plan or of the genesis of his psychosis from child abuse, and in spite of the Perr and Rappeport testimony, hardly anybody believed that Kallinger was psychotic.

Kallinger's movements and gyrations were regarded at the trial as a performance of craziness to win an insanity defense. But the movements, I now know, and even sensed when I first saw them in the jail, were not invented for the occasion. They had first appeared when Joe was fifteen years old.

Kallinger's state of mind and purposes on the day of the murder were unknown at the trial. The general belief was that he was in the Leonia house just to steal and that the murder, tragic as it was, was incidental to the felony of robbery. The belief was that the murder occurred because Kallinger had tried to rape Maria Fasching or to have fellatio with her and she had refused to submit. The autopsy report showed no evidence of rape or fellatio, but nobody paid any attention to it.

An insanity plea is generally regarded as a "cop-out." The jury did not perceive or care to perceive that in this case insanity was not a mere plea, but was real. Joe's psychosis existed before he committed a single crime, and his crimes sprang directly from the psychosis, perhaps nowhere more clearly than in what he asked of Maria Fasching in the basement. Only a terribly sick man would make that request: that she chew off a man's penis. But Kallinger was regarded as not sick, but bad, just as he had been when the senior Kallingers put the lock on their bedroom door and Anna filed the incorrigibility petition.

Judge Dalton, in charging the jury, had instructed them that "some criminal acts spring from wickedness and others from sickness." In entering its verdict on October 12, 1976, the jury had, of course, said that Joseph Kallinger was not sick, but wicked. It was an echo of Judge Dowling's "You are an evil man."

On October 15, 1976, Judge Dalton sentenced Joe to a mandatory life sentence at New Jersey State Prison. The sentence was to be consecutive to the thirty to eighty years Judge Dowling had imposed in Pennsylvania.*

"I expected it," Joe told me. "But I knew nothing worse could happen than had already happened in Harrisburg. I also knew that because of the time I got in Harrisburg, I would never actually serve this New Jersey sentence."

Yet the man who had conceived the plan for world massacre couldn't bear the stigma of being a convicted murderer. He took flight by becoming preoccupied with the gravity of the illness he thought he had. After hearing Dr. Zigarelli, who was a neurologist as well as a psychiatrist, say he was feigning the symptoms of choreoathetosis, Joe was convinced he had it.

It was in this state of mind that after his sentencing in Hackensack, Joe left for a county jail in Camden, New Jersey, to await his trial on the Lindenwold crimes.

* Parole on the life sentence for murder was possible after *fourteen* years and a few months. In the Harrisburg sentence, which was not for murder, parole was possible only after *thirty* years.

22 Counselor in Handcuffs

On the day of his sentencing in Hackensack, Joe was brought to the Camden County Jail. His record of prison and jail misconduct having preceded him, he was transferred after a few hours to the jail's Lakeland Annex in Blackwood, New Jersey, where he was put into a cell for disruptive prisoners.

He was locked up in what prisoners call "the hole." Isolated behind a steel door, he had none of his belongings with him and he was not allowed to leave the cell. In his first letter to me from Lakeland Annex he wrote neologistically: "I wasn't in their jail long enough to do any Bad Behavior. They shipped me over here on their own singling-out feelings. I never did anything to deserve that treatment."

Even though he wanted to die, he was afraid that the other prisoners might kill him. He thought that the strange twisting and turning of his body might turn them against him.

On March 15, 1977, he tried to kill himself by setting fire to his cell. He was committed to the Vroom Building of the State Psychiatric Hospital in Trenton, New Jersey. There he stayed from March 15 to April 5.

At Vroom Joe made another suicide attempt: He tried to choke himself with the plastic cover of his mattress. After that, his bedding was removed and he was kept naked in his cell, where he could be seen by patients and hospital personnel.

He sued Vroom for this and other abuses. The case was settled out of court on December 20, 1979, by the attorney general of New Jersey and Joe's lawyer in this matter, Assistant Federal Public Defender David A. Ruhnke. The state awarded Joe $1,000.

An out-of-court settlement was necessary because Joe, in 1979, had been declared incompetent to stand trial. He had been declared competent in Harrisburg, Hackensack, and Camden. But in 1979, he had been a patient at the Farview State Hospital, Waymart, Pennsylvania, since May 18, 1978, and Farview psychiatrists had declared him incompetent to stand trial.

From Vroom Joe wrote me many letters. They were on long rolls of toilet paper; he couldn't get anything else to write on. One letter deals with a delusional experiment Joe performed in his cell. "That morning," he wrote, "my wrists were on a wild excursion." His fingers were red and raw; he had eaten the skin away. The movements of the wrists abated, but the pain in his fingers was intense. From the tips of the fingers oozed a yellowish fluid.

Joe lay on the floor and stared at the wall. He watched with fascination a cockroach moving down the wall and then crawling along the floor toward him. "We seemed to be communicating," Joe wrote.

He lifted the roach onto a small piece of toilet paper. "The paper was so small," he wrote, "it covered the tiny body like a blanket."

He held the roach in his hands, turning it over and over again, and finally squashed it. He let the fluids from the roach pour onto the red raw skin of his fingers. The fluid dripped from his fingertips. Over his skin a yellowish caking began to form. The pain in his fingers lessened and they seemed to be healing.

"All this," he wrote, "was proof that the roach's mystic powers were at work. That power was working to draw all the evil and heal. This mystic power works in the same way as fluid from a woman's vergina heals skin lesions on arms and legs, removing the spiritual evil power, deadening them to the body cemecals. Cockroaches and juse can heal the evil spirits that work under the outer layer of the skin."

On April 12, 1977, a week after Joe had returned to Camden, he poured a glass of milk over a new prisoner. He was punished by not being allowed to telephone me. He kept asking and asking and met

359

with repeated refusals. He threw a lighted package of matches into the trash that had accumulated in the far corner of his cell.

Cell One on E Block went up in flames. The cell block was evacuated. Jail telephone wires had been burned. The telephones were out of order. Kallinger was sent back to Vroom.

"It was like a child's temper tantrum," Joe later remarked to me of the fire. "I had no care. I wanted to burn up the whole world."

After two days at Vroom, Joe was shipped back to Camden. The paddy wagon stopped at the main Camden County Jail. Another prisoner got out. Joe was told that he was going back to the Lakeland Annex in Blackwood. During the ride he tore off his bright-orange jumpsuit, the regulation garb for Camden County Jail prisoners. He wrapped the suit around his neck. A guard foiled the suicide attempt.

At the Lakeland Annex on this April 14, 1977, Joe was hand-cuffed to a bar of his cell. Warden Carroll, formerly of the main jail and one of the jail officials against whom Joe had filed a suit, ordered the handcuffs removed. Three hours later Joe was back in Cell One, E Block.

The cell was a shambles because of the fire. The sink and toilet weren't working. Joe was angry at the conditions under which he had to live and dissociated himself from the fact that he himself had caused the conditions. He was even angrier that he was denied his telephone privileges. Yet on the individual discretion of the guards, he was permitted to call me. The running gag in the jail was: "If you don't let Kallinger call Flora Schreiber, he'll burn the place down."

On April 17, 1977, Joe wrote me the letter quoted in the Prologue and which entreated:

"Please come to help me here at the Camden County Jail. I need help to find my self and I only feel comfortable when talking to you face to face as we did for so long in Bergen County Jail. I trust you, and I always felt better after our talks.

"If we can clear my thoughts that I can tell between visions and life lived, then it's important for not only me but very important for me to tell the court here.

"The trust is important to me. And I must know the truth or life is not worth living and I only trust you."

360

On April 20, 1977, Eugene Salerno, deputy warden and commanding officer of the Camden County Jail, sent Joe to the Salem County Jail in Salem, New Jersey. The transfer was to be temporary. At Salem Joe's automatic movements were so severe that the jail doctor made a diagnosis of St. Vitus's dance (chorea).

Joe was feeling better when he returned to Camden on May 31, 1977. Twelve days later he had a pretrial hearing that he himself had requested. His delusions submerged. He was rational, coherent, and purposeful when he explained to Judge I. V. Di Martino that he wanted to dismiss counsel and be his own lawyer. His defense, he said, would be based on his automatic movements.

The judge remarked that in effect the defense would be that Kallinger "was incapable because of his mental condition to have formulated the necessary *intent* to commit these crimes" (the Lindenwold crimes). Actually it was Kallinger's "mental condition," the delusion of world massacre, that had *created* the intent. This was unknown.

Joe assured the judge that he could get doctors as expert witnesses. He also said he was capable of examining and cross-examining the doctors. The trial prosecutor, Arnold Golden, said that Kallinger was not fit to serve as his own lawyer and cited his "antics" at his murder trial in Bergen County as a reason. This behavior, Joe replied, was why "the defense I'm seeking must be granted." He argued, moreover, that the doctors he would get to testify at the trial would explain that the so-called "antics" were caused by a neurological problem.

Judge Di Martino said that he was "not completely interested" in what Kallinger had done elsewhere, and that he had the right of self-representation. Joe left the hearing as his own lawyer and now even the prosecutor would write to him as Joseph Kallinger, Esquire.

To find expert witnesses on Huntington's chorea, Joe wrote to one hundred doctors in various parts of the world. He also wrote to various organizations concerned with the illness. But his diligence as a lawyer was hampered by his being a prisoner. He didn't have access to law books. Because of his fires, he didn't even have access to his own legal papers, which had been removed from his cell. And except for instructions on how to prepare and file a motion, he had no help from Bruce Robboy, whom the judge had appointed as his legal adviser.

In desperation Joe began writing numerous and lengthy letters to the judge. And, losing the control he had maintained since returning from Salem, Joe set his third fire at the Camden County Jail.

On June 23, 1977, a hearing was held to reevaluate Kallinger's fitness to be his own lawyer. The hearing had been prompted not only by the fire, but also by the Bergen County psychiatric reports Judge Di Martino had read since giving Kallinger the right of self-representation. The judge had learned from the prosecution psychiatrists that Kallinger was a sociopath and that his automatic movements were indeed "antics." The sheriff's officer who had guarded Kallinger at the Bergen trial was brought to this Camden hearing to testify about the "antics." From the defense psychiatrists the judge had learned that Kallinger was a paranoid schizophrenic. In the courtroom "paranoid schizophrenic" had the same ring that "atheist" would have from the lips of the Pope.

Another reason for the reevaluation was that Joe had written the Court to subpoena medical records of his natural parents from St. Vincent's and various other documents from Joe's safe deposit boxes. There was a legitimate reason for doing so: Dr. Edward Bird, one of the doctors to whom Joe had written, had asked him to obtain information about his genetic background. But the judge thought that in asking for these subpoenas Kallinger was just trying to delay the trial.

An exchange between Judge Di Martino and Kallinger about Kallinger's letters, as recorded in an official transcript, shows how wide was the gulf between the legalistic, punctilious world of the courtroom and the world of a man desperately trying to rise above being mentally ill and a prisoner:

"Lawyers don't write to the Court every time they have a problem. Mr. Kallinger, many, many of the matters that you refer to in your letters are completely irrelevant, and they're frivolous."

"But," Joe explained, "cruel and unusual punishment is . . ."

"That has nothing to do with the trial of this case," the judge replied.

"When you're chained and beaten," Joe said, "it affects getting things done."

362

"You have asked me as the judge to provide you with statutes, with decisions, with annotations. Do you believe that's the function of the judge, to do your research for you?"

"No," Joe replied. "I didn't know whether the judge could do it or not. I thought it would be up to you to make a decision how it would be done. The jail has no way of doing it."

"I walk in my office every morning," the judge said, "and I find a letter under my door."

"I thought I was being cooperative with the Court."

"I walk in my office in the afternoon and I find another letter."

"Are you saying," Joe asked, "I shouldn't write to you at all?"

"I told you the last time you were here, Mr. Kallinger, that the only thing I wanted to hear from you were proper motions."

The angry father had rebuffed the little boy who asked: "Are you saying I shouldn't write to you at all?"

At the end of the hearing, Joe, no longer his own counselor, returned to the jail with its narrow runways and serious overcrowding. In the jail there was not only the Joe who set fires, but also the Joe who took care of an epileptic prisoner who was housed in the runway outside Joe's cell. Here, too, was the Joe who in his cell fed a pigeon that had flown in. Joe was under twenty-four-hour watch, and one of the guards assigned to watching him taunted him with: "To me this is a wasted post. If you hang or smother yourself and die, just think of the money the freeholders will save." But there was also the guard who told me, "Kallinger doesn't belong in jail. He should be in a hospital."

To others Joe was a man convicted of murder and to be feared. He himself often said as I left him, "Walk as far away from the cells along the runway as you can. They have all kinds in here. You don't know what they can do to you." He was still separating himself from other prisoners, as he had done in Holmesburg long ago.

The two-week Lindenwold trial, with Robboy, not Kallinger, as defense attorney, began on July 11, 1977. I moved into the Cherry Hill Inn, Cherry Hill, New Jersey, close to Camden, for the duration of the trial. During the day I sat through the court proceedings. When the court was adjourned, I returned to Cherry Hill for a swim and dinner. Then I went back to the Camden County Jail to spend three to five hours with Joe. We had been meeting since, on the day he was appointed his own lawyer, he obtained a court order for me to visit him in the jail. We were now meeting in the empty infirmary mentioned in previous chapters. The torment of the present was the backdrop against which Joe disinterred the dire revelations of the past.

Joe was not on trial for murder, but even though the charges (breaking and entering, robbery while armed, assault with intent to commit rape while armed, etc.) were different, the Lindenwold trial was virtually a repeat performance of the one in Bergen County. For both the defense and the prosecution had exactly the same psychiatrists as in the earlier trial: Drs. Perr and Rappeport for the defense, Drs. Zigarelli, Jablon, Wawrose, and Hume for the prosecution.

Joe had asked to be examined for Huntington's chorea, but the judge had ordered the case to trial without further postponements, with the result that the doctors who examined Joe for this illness did not testify. Dr. Howard Hurtig, a University of Pennsylvania neurologist, examined him on July 15, 1977, while the trial was in progress. Dr. Edward Bird of Addenbrokes Hospital, Cambridge, England, a specialist in Huntington's chorea, did his examination on August 9, 1977, after the trial was over. Both doctors examined Joe as a private patient and wrote their reports to me. They reported that he did *not* have Huntington's chorea, but they took the movements seriously and did not regard them as mere "antics."

Dr. Hurtig postulated, as I reported at the trial on July 21, 1977, that the automatic movements stemmed from psychotic mental processes, from some profound disturbance, capable of "producing strange motor activity at an unconscious level." The doctor said that a psychiatrist with skills in hypnosis could get at the psychogenesis of the specific movements.

On July 22, 1977, the jury found Joe guilty in the Carty house of breaking and entering or entering without breaking, with intent to steal; breaking and entering, or entering without breaking, with intent to steal while armed; robbery, robbery while armed; assault with intent to commit rape; assault with intent to commit rape while armed; and the threat to kill the victim of all these charges. Joe was also found guilty in the Miller house of breaking and entering with intent to steal and of larceny.

364

This was the third jury to reject Joe's insanity plea and by implication to find him sane. Sentencing was scheduled for August 11. Joe remained in the Camden County Jail. Through the kindness of Judge Di Martino and Deputy Warden Salerno, my interviews with Joe continued.

He spent a day at the Adult Diagnostic and Treatment Center at Avenel, New Jersey. He was sent there that August 4, 1977, for the purpose of ascertaining whether he fell under the purview of the New Jersey Sex Offenders Act. If he did, he would be sent to a hospital for treatment as a sex offender. If he didn't, he would be sent to prison. Yet the question was academic. He already had two sentences that would keep him in prison for the rest of his life.

At Avenel, Dr. Charles P. Gnassi and Dr. Basil Campean diagnosed Joe, on the basis of both the examination and his history, as suffering from "a schizophrenic process starting at an early age." The psychiatrists also stated in their report that "the content of his delusions and obsessive thinking is largely a fusion of aggression and sexuality."

"There was considerable care taken," the doctors explained, "in determining that Mr. Kallinger was not malingering by presenting himself in a pathological way. It can be said with some assurance that the dynamics discussed are a true representation of his personality functioning. The evidence for this statement lies not in the content of his psychosis, which can be easily falsified, but in the sequence in which his pathology revealed itself on the unstructured Rorschach test. It required persistent prodding by an examiner for a reluctant Mr. Kallinger to expose his more aberrant thinking."

The doctors concluded: "Considering the history of schizophrenia and the current examination, it would appear that this individual's behavior [attempted rape in Lindenwold] resulted from a thought disorder rather than a compulsive type of psychosexual pathology. It is the opinion of these examiners at the present time that this individual does not fall under the purview of the New Jersey Sex Offenders Act."

The Avenel doctors were on target. Without knowing the biographical facts or the psychodynamics, they recognized the fusion of sexuality and aggression that had characterized Joe's behavior since adolescence. Without specific knowledge of what happened in Lindenwold, they also recognized that Joe had attempted rape not because

of psychosexual pathology but because of hallucinations and delusions.

Sentencing took place on August 11, 1977.

"I think everyone agrees," said Bruce Robboy, who had been
reinstated as defense counsel, "that Mr. Kallinger is a sick man and
in need of treatment. I would ask that the Court take this into con-
sideration when determining the type of sentence. I would also ask,
on behalf of Mr. Kallinger, that any sentence that this Court hands
out be run concurrently with the sentences that Mr. Kallinger is
presently serving because of the length and nature of the other sentences. And, also, because of the fact that these incidents occurred
within a quite short period of time, and Mr. Kallinger has no prior
criminal record of any substance prior to this so-called 'crime spree'
in late '74 and early '75."

Joe had said nothing during his sentencing in Harrisburg and
Hackensack. This time he read a statement that he and I had prepared in the Camden County Jail. The statement represented the
conviction I had arrived at by this time: I was certain that had Joe
been hospitalized in 1972, as Drs. Hoffmann and von Schlichten had
recommended, the crimes committed in 1974 and the first month of
1975 would not have taken place.

It is impossible to say how effective the hospital treatment would
have been, but just by virtue of Joe's not being on the street, he
could not have committed these crimes. Judge Bradley, in sending
Joe home, followed the recommendation of Dr. Jablon, who, con-
trary to Drs. Hoffmann and von Schlichten in their first and second
examinations, did not diagnose Joe as psychotic.

Judge Bradley put Joe on psychiatric probation, but the therapist
Joe saw said he didn't need therapy. It was a tragic misjudgment on
the part of many people. Joe was still on probation but without
therapy and Judge Bradley was still weighing whether to give him a
new child-abuse trial when news of the "crime spree" broke.

"I stand before you convicted by a jury," Joe told Judge Di
Martino. "Yet I still believe that the word *guilty* should be tempered
by the word *sick*.

"I did what I did because I was mentally and emotionally disturbed. I not only did not know the difference between right and wrong, but I actually thought that wrong was right.

"I need therapy. I need it now. I needed it in 1972 when a pair of psychiatrists, Hoffmann and von Schlichten, recommended it to the Court. Instead the Court sent me home.

"If I had received treatment in 1972, I would not be standing before you now, because the events of November 1974, for which I have been on trial here, would not have taken place.

"I still plead sick and the answer to sickness is therapy.

"This therapy, too long delayed, should be given to me now.

"I thank you for listening."

Death, not therapy, was what Arnold Golden said he deserved. "He's probably," the prosecutor told the judge, "a prime example of why we occasionally need the finality of the death penalty. Unfortunately, since we don't have the death penalty, the best that we can do is to put this man away for as long as is humanly possible.

"I think it's the obligation of this Court not to take any chances on prior sentences and not to take any chance of this man ever hitting the street again.

"I would therefore ask the Court to impose the maximum sentences allowable and to make them consecutive to sentences previously given."

The Adult Diagnostic Treatment Center at Avenel had stated that Joe did not fall under the provision of the Sex Offenders Act. Judge Di Martino therefore had to sentence him under the Crimes Act.

"I do not believe that Mr. Kallinger can ever be rehabilitated to a point where he can be a useful citizen. I base this on everything I've read and reports on the testimony of the doctors who have labeled him as an antisocial and inadequate personality. [This statement overlooked the conclusions of the doctors at Avenel, the doctors for the defense, and Dr. Hurtig.]

"The present sentence, I hope, will insure that he will not be re-admitted to our society for such a period of time that our present generation will not have to fear him or his potential criminal activities."

Judge Di Martino sentenced Joe to not less than forty-two nor more than fifty-one years in New Jersey State Prison. These sentences are consecutive to all sentences presently imposed by any other court in Pennsylvania and New Jersey.

On Joe's last night in the Camden County Jail, we talked about his return to the State Correctional Institution at Huntingdon, Pennsylvania, to continue serving the thirty-to-eighty-year sentence Judge Dowling had imposed. We also talked about the revelations he had made to me at Camden.

"As it was coming out," he said, "I sounded like Dracula. But, until just before I told you, it [the murders of Joey and José Collazo] were memories blocked out, something suppressed beyond recollection."

He lapsed into silence, then said, "Three people dead because of me. That little kid [José Collazo] was just flipping a lighter. He was behaving himself. Wasted. Senseless."

Another long silence. Then he murmured, "I wasn't pursuing this kind of life. My pursuit was to be a shoemaker. I was living in two worlds. Even though I thought I was going to become God, there was a fight between me and a demon all the time.

"I think this body was inhabited with a demon, yes. I think the demon is destroying me. The devil himself and all his spirits who are working in this."

He leaned forward and very quietly confided, "But when I snap out, I still want to destroy the world. In jail it takes it out in water incidents, suicides, fires. It's still going on. I can't stop it. But who is *I*?"

He was saying that when he committed his crimes, he was totally at the mercy of a hallucinatory process (although at that time neither he nor anybody else had yet labeled the process as hallucinatory). He was saying that in the face of that process, the "I" he thought of himself as being in "normal" life was nonexistent.

"I'll write you," he said as I walked out of the infirmary for the last time.

The next day, August 12, 1977, Deputy Warden Salerno told me in a telephone conversation that Kallinger had left.

I knew that Joe was on his way to prison. I believed that society had a right to protect itself against what he had done by removing him from it. But I didn't think that prison was where he belonged

368

On the basis of most present-day findings and thinking in the behavioral sciences, I do not subscribe to the traditional moralistic bent of the criminal law which holds all criminals fully responsible for their actions. On the same grounds I do not believe in a "killer" instinct, nor that there are people born with this instinct as they are born with blue eyes. I do not believe that destructive aggression is a deeply seated universal drive. In Joe's case, certainly, it was created not by nature, but by nurture.

23 Prisoner K-2719

In Harrisburg Joe had received a thirty-to-eighty-year sentence to the State Correctional Institution at Huntingdon, Pennsylvania. Since his victims in Dumont, New Jersey, and in Baltimore, Maryland, had decided not to press charges, he would not be going back to a county jail. SCIH was where he would remain.

Joe's cell was in BAU, the Behavioral Adjustment Unit. BAU is on B Block, which prisoners call "the hole." B Block was where Joe had been during his entire first SCIH incarceration. During the drive from Camden he had been appalled that "no one talked to me one word." Here he felt he "didn't have a chance. A card over the cell door had my name on it when I arrived."

The first eighteen days in prison were mostly bad; he had several attacks of automatic movements which he now called "my mind and body problem." In addition, he wrote me, "My head was like a wheel spinning with eveal thoughts one after another as my eyes stayed closed and I tossed from side to side, wanting to kill myself."

On other days, however, he was able to write, "I'm up again and trying. I'm going to be that Poet. Enclosed find poems: *Love, Custom, Style* and *Vitality*."

He looked up from his cot on the afternoon of Friday, August 26, 1977. Standing on the other side of the bars was Dr. Wawrose. Joe remembered him from the Bergen and Camden trials. Testifying for the prosecution, Dr. Wawrose was one of the four psychiatrists who had labeled him as an antisocial personality—and not psychotic. Joe also remembered that Dr. Wawrose in his role of SCIH psychiatrist had been skeptical about Charlie. Charlie likes Huntingdon, Joe thought. It is his roost. Poor Charlie. He is the most misunderstood person in the world.

"Did you ask to see me or did they have your name put on my list?" Dr. Wawrose asked.

"They want you to see me for the purpose of locating me in their population."

Joe spoke of his "mind and body problems." He read aloud Dr. Bird's report and started to read Dr. Hurtig's. (At the Camden County Jail, Dr. Bird and Dr. Hurtig had examined Joe as a private patient.) Dr. Wawrose said he didn't have time for a second report.

"Is it all right," Joe asked, "if I have these reports sent to you?"

"Yes."

"Because of these problems," Joe said, "I don't feel I can handle population without psychiatric help." He was afraid that other prisoners would make fun of his automatic movements. He was also afraid that, having been isolated from other prisoners since having left the Dauphin County Jail in 1975, he might not be able to make the adjustment to living and working with them.

"There's no help," Dr. Wawrose replied. "It's population or B Block. I won't recommend that you stay in B Block. *You* tell them that you want to remain in self-confinement. People do that for years and years. Then you can remain right here."

Joe felt he needed psychiatric help. He was angry because Dr. Wawrose was not going to see him again. He was frightened at having to make the choice between population and B Block. He felt that, as he wrote me, "to stay in self-confinement means to rot. What to do was the question. I decided to try population!"

Events moved swiftly. He appeared before a review board. Dr. Wawrose's report to the board read "process normally." On August 30, 1977, he was transferred to population, which he himself had chosen. This was the first time that he was not on twenty-four-hour watch since he had left the Dauphin County Jail in October 1975. On September 2, 1977, Joe also had a job. Ecstatically he wrote me that night, "Today was my first day on the Job, yes, since that last day on the Job, January 17, 1975. Some two years eight months later I'm in Huntingdon Prison Shoe Repair Shop!"

Joe worked in the shoe repair shop with three other prisoners under the supervision of Mr. Wakefield, an employee of SCIH. Of the five Joe was the only shoemaker by trade. He knew that the others knew that he had had his own shop in Philadelphia. He also knew that this could prove embarrassing. He decided to keep a low profile. Yet that first morning he helped a worker who was struggling with a shoe that had been caught in the stitcher, and, noting that Mr. Wakefield was sanding a pair of sole edges without using the trimmer, told him how to use it. Observing that the shop was in bad shape, Joe thought of ways of turning it into one that "would cater to officers and women personnel in the front office."

The last four months of 1977 and the beginning of 1978 were a good time for Joe. When he started working again in a shoe repair shop, "it was," as he wrote me, "as if the world stood still and no time passed from January 17, 1975 to that day in 1977. All returned instantly. There was no Pause in the great Hands that gently take a shoe on its jurney to rebearth. Each stroke on the machines, each touch with the tools on the last, each operation of the shoe was as skillful as on January 17, 1975, and no time stood between."

Joe basked in the praise of prison officials. They brought him their shoes, and insisted that only he repair them. He began a self-help manual about shoe repair and wrote poems prolifically. He read a poem, "My Jury," at a poetry workshop held at the prison. The poem is a powerful statement of his agony and his alienation; he writes of "cannibals that elatedly feed on my decay."

He often went to the prison library to read, took art lessons by mail, became interested in nutrition and isometrics, and worked out in the prison gym. At the prison he took a typing course, and GED courses in basic English and math for which he received diplomas. After he had completed all his GED courses, he planned to go on to college courses.

His letters to me included many questions about what he was learning, such as: "Is it true, as my English teacher says, that a colon is used for business letters, Dear Joe: and a comma for friendly letters, Dear Flora,"? He asked both John Shapiro, my assistant, and

372

me to send him books about prosody. He also asked for a book "that has distilled meanings about things like occupations, sleep, truth, spirit, hope, eyes, anything that gives more meaning than a dictionary does, that tells something about things used or smelled in life."

Joe wrote us his explications of Poe's "Annabel Lee," became interested in T.S. Eliot's "Burnt Norton" and "The Hollow Men," and amazed his teacher by reading from Joyce's *Finnegans Wake* in his English class.

Joe created what he called his "learning center." He hung cardboard next to the curtain on the front wall of his cell. To the cardboard he taped his homework, his poetry, and flash cards for drill. One of the cards contained "ninety-seven words of simple everyday things I don't know how to spell." On other cards were his addition and multiplication exercises. "Other inmates," he wrote us, "have dirty pictures on their walls. I have a Learning Center!"

On the last day of 1977, Joe wrote letter 108. It read:

"Why I don't even see these walls today. I see this [the prison] as one big learning center—a chance at life to live. I mean really live. To be me, not a carbin copy but an original. I see myself pulled up by the hand of life from the Pit I was in and given a second chance to live, to be me, to start again, for surely where I came from I was dying.

"I wasn't even me there. There was a brain in my body never used, never turned on, brand new. Now it's on and just beginning. Just think of the vast things in the unaverse I can learn about, the character I can mold myself to be.

"In a few hours New Years will start. I certainly have the spirit of the New Year in me. I certainly want the old year not to be forgotten, for much has been learned in it. *Perhaps more so than any other year in my life, for it was the beginning to finding me.*

"The very fact that today I spent time to get a mop bucket, a ringer, broom cleanser and scrub brush. I took my cell apart and worked up a sweat cleaning the old year out so now I am ready for the new year. For great things to happen, new beginnings.

"I spend this evening daydreaming like a school child. Why I am truly in my second childhood. I am dreaming about my GED diploma, College, and thinking all the things I'd like to be.

"Flora, I intend to be a creator of shoes and most of all Poetry, and not a destroyer!"

On January 9, 1978, Joe was promoted to training instructor in the shoe repair shop. He was also appointed a trustee who distributed new shoes to inmates. Instantly he had big plans. He was going to increase the number of men in the shop to ten, then twenty, and expand the work load by having work shipped in from other prison facilities. He realized that new equipment would be necessary, but planned to buy it inexpensively through army (and other) surplus outlets.

He wrote these and other proposals to SCIH Superintendent Lowell D. Hewitt. When I had lunched with the superintendent on June 13, 1977, he had described Joe during his first incarceration as "a certainly below-average-type inmate in behavior bound to be generally uncooperative." But the Kallinger of the second incarceration was a star.

I remembered my conversation with the superintendent and was startled by Joe's letter 119, dated January 9, 1978, which read:

"I made a bold request to Superintendent Hewitt for new rules for the prison. I was saying to the Superintendent, take a look at my training program for the men at Huntingdon. Now that you have put me in the official position, let's give some men something to be proud of, to take home with them into the world. Let's not just have the Shoe Shop on Paper as existing, but let's make it something to be proud of."

The next day four inspectors from the Commonwealth's central corrections office came to the shoe repair shop, praised Joe's work, and left their shoes to be fixed under his supervision. He suspected that, because of his "bold request," he was being tested.

Joe seemed to be a well-adjusted prisoner. Yet he had had occasional facial grimaces and slight movements in the right hand. On some nights the cadences of "Kristorah" sounded in his cell. At times the wheel of destructive thoughts kept turning. As early as September 14, 1977, he had written me in letter 25 that "things in reality have been going well, but there's a big crash coming. I try hard to change my thoughts and make them conform to outer reality. I'm fighting on till I can't fight any longer.

"I can't banish the sick thoughts and I don't get any medication. Nothing since Vroom started giving me stelazine and they continued it at Salem and Camden. God, I try to free myself of the thoughts. I wish I could say all is well. That be a Heaven. But it really appears that I am doomed for my own Hell and shows the same pattern as when I was in the world. Then I had everything going: a nice business, mother's estate coming with me as the sole heir—and I went to Hell then. Now the same thing is happening. There's no end to my destruction."

Only days after Joe had become a training instructor, the double appeared in the shop. An image of a shop worker (but not the worker himself) moved toward the double, opened his fly, and with a lip knife sliced off his penis. The scene was repeated with the double and another phantom worker.

Joe was sure that the two men, his friends until now, were going to slice off *his* penis and let him bleed to death. They were going to do to him, he thought, what at twelve and a half, he had almost done to the little boy whom he lured to the creek. It had been a lip knife then; it was a lip knife now!

Back in his cell, Joe wrote to the superintendent, the deputy superintendent, and Dennis R. Erhard, deputy superintendent for treatment, that two men (Joe named them) in the shoe repair shop were planning to kill him. Hallucination and reality had merged.

Once again "the spirits of January"* were abroad. For on January 16, 1978, after a hearing Joe was removed from the shoe repair shop. He had been in the shop four months and two weeks. He was removed, as he wrote me, "just one day short of being three years to the date of the end of the world." He meant January 17, 1975, the day of his arrest.

Saturday, January 28, was Joe's first day working in the P.M. kitchen, the kitchen that prepares evening meals, where he had been transferred. For half an hour he cut the dark spots out of potatoes. Then he was ordered to mop the floor. The floor was already covered

* "The spirits of January" were not spirits, but Joe's way of saying that in January crucial things had happened to him. He had been arrested for child abuse in January 1972. In January 1975, there followed the arrest that led to his present sentences. At SCIH in January 1976, he had experienced being out of his body.

with water. He looked at the floor and told the supervisor, "I have my slippers on. They have big holes in the bottom. Lemme go back to my cell to change shoes."

"Okay," the supervisor replied, "you won't have to mop today. It'll take too long to get your shoes."

Later that morning Joe was moved to another population cell. While he was carrying a box of legal papers to the new cell, he slipped and hit his head and neck. He was sent to the dispensary for salve and a painkiller and was told that he would see a doctor on Monday. He was also told that he didn't have to return to the kitchen until then.

Joe returned to the kitchen on Tuesday, January 31. He was assigned to mop detail and KP each day from 12:25 P.M. to 6:25 P.M.

"Peeling potatoes and anything else," Joe wrote me, "I'm very upset. I will not do that. I am upset." To the P.M. kitchen supervisor, copies to several officials, he wrote, "As of today (131-78) I can no longer work in the kitchen."

He was sent to B Block—"the hole." A state supervisor who passed on a conducted tour remembered him.

"Kallinger," the supervisor said, "who will fix my shoes now? Hurry back to the shoe shop."

The review board before whom Joe appeared conceded, "It was not a good idea to put Kallinger in the kitchen."

After a week Joe was back in population. He resumed his classes. He sent me two new poems with letter 149. Two lines from the letter read: "It will not be easy for a while to rebuild the lost week. But now I'm running like a kitten."

Joe began working in the SCIH clothing plant on February 10. He was still excited about his classes and his poetry, his letter-writing and his pushups. Yet twelve days after he began working in the clothing plant, the world, as he wrote me, was changing to "eveal" more frequently than at any other time during his second SCIH incarceration. He concluded the letter with words that made me fear that the mythology he had had in the world, while he planned world massacre, had returned. He wrote: "I'm not a prisoner. I'm God. If not, then a delegate of God."

This supernatural role, this grandiosity, did not allay mortal fears. For increasingly Joe feared that his death was at hand—that in this huge hive of cells, passageways, and walls somebody was going to kill him. Under the spell of this delusion he built what he called a button-strangler to protect himself.

He took one layer of mattress-cover material and one layer of prison pants material. Around them, he sewed from one end to the other ten strips of brown cloth. Using this as a core, he sewed onto each end a brown cloth handle. In the handle he fashioned a slot so that he could grip the strangler tightly with his hands as he wrapped it around the neck of anyone who might try to kill him.

Overall the strangler was two feet long. It was one and one-quarter inches wide and one-quarter of an inch thick. Onto both edges of one side he attached with the factory press machine sixteen metal buttons. Each button had a small center shaft that extended one-quarter inch above the surface of the button. He snapped on fifteen double-edged razor blades to fifteen of the sixteen buttons on each edge. Now he had thirty cutting elements and the strangler was a cutting as well as a choking instrument.

Then, on a long sheet of paper, he made a full-scale ink drawing of the strangler. His caption was: "The Button Strangler (designed to choke any size neck by hand)."

He hung the strangler on the bulletin board he called his "learning center." The strangler, side by side with his homework and his poems, was a curious representation of his persecution complex and his sadism. His caption—"The Button Strangler (designed to choke any size neck by hand)"—reflected grimly his public-relations and advertising flair. The instrument itself, the drawing, and the caption were tragic perversions of his strongly imaginative and inventive bent.

As his fears of persecution became stronger, he wore the button-strangler whenever he left his cell. He had it around the small of his back, the buttons facing outward, the handles tucked into the sides of his trousers.

On March 13, 1978 he wrote me: "I'm being B Block I'm in big trouble. Need to be gotten out of here. Murder charges here be filed against me—for here. [signed] Joseph Kallinger." (Entire letter *sic*.)

As in the Bogin house, where he had had the hallucination of his double killing four women and one man, Joe believed that the death of a phantom prisoner he had watched the double kill in his cell early on the morning of March 13 was real. So strongly did Joe believe what he had seen that he thought he had been charged with murder and that he was about to be thrown into "the hole." In reality there had been no murder, and Joe was not charged, nor put into B Block. Calling the prison upon receiving his letter on the morning of March 15, I learned that there was no change in his status.

The next day, March 14, Joe wrote me a second letter. He explained that he had written the March 13 letter right after he had watched the double kill the phantom prisoner. But, Joe went on in his letter, the hallucination had ceased, he had returned to reality, and he was writing to tell me so.

However, by the time I received the second—the March 14— letter, Joe had been put into B Block, and he now *was* "in big trouble."

On the day after he wrote the second letter, on March 15, 1978, at 8:00 A.M., the same morning I called the prison, Joe sat down at his sewing machine in the clothing factory. He threw the switch and began working on his section of a pair of man's undershorts, one of the items of clothing the factory made for the inmates of the Pennsylvania prison system.

By 10:15 A.M. he had finished his section of the material and turned off the sewing machine. The cream-colored cloth felt rough on his hands. It sparkled like snow crystals falling through a beam of light. Everything seemed unreal.

Suddenly Joe couldn't breathe. He felt as if his chest were being crushed. He looked down at his clothing to see what was interfering with his breathing. His prison jacket was unruffled. There was nothing else.

Like a fish out of water, Joe opened his mouth wide. Not only couldn't he breathe, he couldn't swallow. Maybe, he thought, my throat's all stopped up, like plumbing.

He looked at the prisoners working on either side of him, then shot furtive glances at the rows of inmates sitting at their machines in the large room. He wondered which prisoner was going to kill him.

A prisoner near Joe said that he looked sick; another said Joe should see the doctor. They helped him out of his chair; he walked shakily to a half-open window in the rear of the room. Through the window he saw the prison yard and the sky, reminders that forever he was locked into a fortress cut off from the world by high brick walls with towers manned by armed guards. His feeling of suffocation grew.

He turned from the window in terror that someone in the room was getting ready to kill him. He was as determined to live as he had been determined to die in the hospital in Hazleton, the Philadelphia Detention House, the Bergen and Camden County Jails, and at the Vroom Bulding in Trenton.

His back to the window, he thought of the button-strangler under his jacket and of the nine-inch pair of scissors he used in his work and had in his pants pocket. These weapons reassured him.

He saw someone striding toward him *through* the sewing machines. The figure was carrying a button-strangler, a duplicate of Joe's. It was the double. For a moment Joe thought that the double was going to kill him. Then he realized that, as in the days of world massacre and repeatedly in the past few days, the double was ordering him to kill. For the double was slipping the button-strangler over the head of a phantom man.

Joe had an erection. After it he took a short step from the window where he had been standing toward the man at the surger, which was near the window. Joe had chosen Earl Dean Eller, a twenty-three-year-old Maryland man serving a one-to-three-year sentence for burglary, as impersonally as three years and two months earlier he had chosen Maria Fasching.

Joe asked Eller what he was doing. Looking up at Joe, Eller replied that he was sewing pockets.

Eller did not know Kallinger, but he knew of him. He hadn't worked with Kallinger, but had worked around him. Once they had watched television in a group. He looked down again and, thinking Kallinger had walked away, went back to work on a pocket.

Standing right behind Eller, Joe slipped the button-strangler over Eller's head to his neck. Eller put his hands to his neck to remove the strangler. Cut by the razor blades attached to the buttons of the strangler, his hands dripped blood.

Joe held the handles of the button-strangler with his right hand. With the pair of scissors in his left hand, he stabbed Eller again and again in quick succession, first to the neck and then to the back.

When Eller slumped to the floor, Joe bent over him and still held the handles of the button-strangler. Eller tried to crawl away, but couldn't use his hands. He held his hands in the air, got on his knees, and moved a short distance. With a hand dripping blood, he tried to grab the scissors out of Joe's hands. Joe tightened his grip on the scissors and also on the handles of the button-strangler. Then he stabbed Eller in the back. It was the twentieth stab. For the first time, Eller screamed.

Charles T. White, the factory foreman, was up front. He hadn't seen what was happening. But, hearing what he described as a "Hey, don't do that" scream you hear in prison, he turned. He saw Eller and Kallinger scuffling. He ran to them.

Eller was on his knees. His head bent to the left. Both his hands were in the air. Kallinger, bending over Eller, was about to strike the right side of Eller's neck and his right shoulder with the scissors.

"Stop that!" White yelled.

"The yell," Joe told me, "sort of woke me up. The scissors fell out of my hand. I dropped the button-strangler to the floor."

White hit Joe on the chest. He grabbed the front of Joe's jacket and ordered, "Get into the corner!"

Joe walked to a corner. White pushed him against a wall.

"Please get my belt for me," Joe asked White. "It's over there on the floor."

White picked up the "belt," Joe's euphemism for the button-strangler. On the strangler were fresh blood and hair.

White took the button-strangler and the pair of scissors to the office of Deputy Superintendent Kelly as evidence of the assault. Guards took Joe to B Block—"the hole."

Eller was rushed in the Huntingdon firemen's ambulance to the town's J.C. Blair Memorial Hospital. He was treated for stab wounds of the back, the neck, the throat, and both hands. The left hand was severely injured. The hospital reported that he had numerous cuts requiring multiple sutures and that he was in "stable" condition. After one night, he was released from the hospital to the SCIH infirmary, where he recovered.

Police were unable to find any reason for Kallinger's attack on Eller. There was no argument, nothing to provoke the incident, the police declared. The police couldn't have known that the provocation had come not from without but from within.

Joe had given the prison warning of what was happening within himself. He had done so by filing, in late February and early March, seven requests to see the psychiatrist.

The March 1 slip read: "Request to see Doctor for: murdering thoughts to cut apart."

The March 8 slip stated: "Request to see Doctor for: I am being compelled to kill with my 'button-strangler.' I need help medically."

On March 9 Joe filed a slip stating that he had been "refused psychiatric help by total denial to call me to see doctor."

An officer warned, "You're not to put any more doctors' slips in. I am not attesting anymore. I haven't been to the doctor for ten years."

The officer hadn't read the danger signals. Joe was saying that he was in such an acute emotional crisis that he was being *compelled* to kill. The officer acted, however, as if Joe were just a bad boy who, by filing requests for medical help, was contributing to the prison staff's paperwork and to the overloaded schedules of the prison psychiatrist and psychologists. The officer didn't see the difference between his seeing a general practitioner for a checkup and Joe's having to see a psychiatrist or psychologist to avert danger for himself and others. In this instance, as is too frequently the case, mental illness was disregarded because it wasn't accepted as real.

At a preliminary hearing, Huntingdon District Court Judge James H. Kyper ruled that "the Commonwealth has submitted sufficient evidence [in the assault on Eller] for me to hold Mr. Kallinger for the next session of Court."

Joe's double was present more frequently than at any time in the past. With a phantom "button-strangler" the double killed phantom men and women, their faces indistinct. Powerless to execute the double's commands to kill, Joe wanted to be free of him. But only by killing himself, he felt, would he ever be free of the double.

On April 30, 1978, I sat with Joe in the SCIH visitors' room. He refused the cold drinks, potato chips, and candy that on other visits we bought from the prison's vending machines. He explained that this was the first day of his hunger strike.

I tried to dissuade him. He was not to be shaken. To my dismay he asked me for a cigarette. He hadn't smoked since his amnesia in Hazleton in 1959, seventeen years before I met him. He started to chain-smoke now.

Before I left, he handed me a page of yellow paper with instructions to send the message on it as a mailgram.

The mailgram was to Judge Malcolm Murray, U.S. District Court, Williamsport, Pennsylvania. The judge was going to hear the civil-rights suit Joe had filed against SCIH. Among the abuses he had cited were the denial of medical treatment and the deplorable conditions of Joe's rat- and cockroach-infested cell. He had mailed to the judge the tail and three legs of one rat, the tail and four legs of another rat, and the feces of a third. He had also sent the judge thirty-six cockroaches.

The mailgram read:

> This is to inform the Court that as of April 30, 1978 I have begun a hunger strike in order to secure the various rights stated in the body of complaints I sent you.* This includes the need for medical treatment and the 5 Civil #1983 complaints filed with the clerk of the Court, United States District Court, Middle District, Scranton, Pennsylvania.
>
> Very truly yours,
Joseph Kallinger, K-2719
State Correctional Institution
at Huntingdon
Huntingdon, Pa. 16652

Joe had told me, however, that he was going on a hunger strike to get away from the double. He had to get away, and he could do so only by dying—the only weapon he had was starvation.

He had been denied his confidential correspondence with me since he had been brought to B Block after the stabbing of Eller. Yet in the next few days he was able to get through to me a few laconic notes keeping me abreast of the hunger strike:

"—May 2, 1978. Doing badly at end of this day. Two poems enclosed."

---

* The case was settled out of court. SCIH agreed not to do these things to Joseph Kallinger again. At SCIH, before the hunger strike but after the stabbing of Eller, Joe, in my presence, instructed Gutkin to drop all Kallinger suits against the City of Philadelphia and the Philadelphia Police Department.

"—May 4, 1978. I'm of course doing badly. Still going strong on the cause. Another inmate also started as of 5-3-78 noon. I had a hearing May 3, 1978 on two major misconducts. Found guilty on both counts. Every civil right was violated. Action will be taken."

"—May 5, 1978. 10th. day of hunger strike. I am still determined and the newest signs read: *to death do us part.* I'm in a new cell, 427 B Block. Weight 5/6: 186 lb.; 5/7: 181 lb.; 5/8: 178 lb.* Doing badly through 5/7, 5/8, 5/9. Hanging in though. All rise, please be seated!"

I hoped that the prison authorities would step in and keep him from dying. My conviction held firm that even though he had committed the crimes of which he had been found guilty, he did not belong in a prison. He needed the help that SCIH had denied him: the intervention of a psychiatrist and of psychotropic drugs. He had had no such treatment since leaving Camden.

Before the hunger strike and nine days after the assault on Eller, I wrote Superintendent Hewitt that on the basis of my special observation of Joseph Kallinger, I believed that SCIH "should consider the possibilities of his commitment to a mental hospital where he could receive therapy."

On the same day I also sent a letter to the Honorable Fred W. Jacobs, chairman of the Department of Probation and Parole in Harrisburg. After explaining that this was not a probation or parole matter, I wrote:

"I am convinced that Mr. Kallinger requires medical attention and that incarceration without such attention will inevitably result in the violent acting-out [the assault on Eller] that has just occurred.

"Mr. Kallinger functions well for a time only, then to become violent in accordance with his psychosis. At the Camden County Jail he was given daily doses of Stelazine and Cogentin.

"Ideally, of course, Mr. Kallinger should be in a mental hospital. Certainly he does not belong on the street, but neither does he belong in prison without medical attention. He needs, as the enclosed medical reports [Hoffmann–von Schlichten; Bird; Hurtig] indicate, medical help not only for his own good, but also for the sake of prisoners

---

* Joe had been frail at the Bergen County Jail, had gained weight at Camden, and at SCIH had become heavy.

like Earl Dean Eller, who become the victims of the destructive thoughts growing out of his psychosis."

I received replies to these letters, but no action was taken.

The stabbing of Eller, followed by the hunger strike, belatedly brought Joe the psychiatric and psychological attention he had been seeking. Dr. Wawrose saw him on April 14 and 21 and May 5 and May 10, 1978. On May 10, Dr. Don Brian, chief psychologist at SCIH, also saw him. Joe had been filing requests to see Dr. Brian since August 1977, the time of Joe's arrival from Camden.

"I'm sorry," Dr. Brian remarked. "I guess it's like after the fact."

"Locking the barn after the horse got out," Joe replied.

Joe talked of waking up to find things out of proportion. He described h. bloody thoughts of cutting and slicing, and Dr. Brian, obviously moved and horrified, summed up the horror the hallucinations had caused Joe by saying, "You *are* tortured!"

Joe thought that Dr. Wawrose and Dr. Brian had come to see him because the U.S. marshal had served them with his complaints. The real reason was the hunger strike. Because of it Dr. Wawrose had filed a petition under the Mental Health Procedures Act. He asked in the petition for Joe's ninety-day involuntary commitment to a mental hospital.

The hunger strike was still in full force on May 17. This was the day of Joe's mental-health hearing, which was held in the SCIH visitors' room before Morris Terrizzi, the judge of Huntingdon County. Joe was represented by Charles Swigart, Esquire, a public defender.

At the hearing Dr. Brian testified that there was a contradiction between the "aberrant content" of Joe's "thinking patterns" and the cogent "way, manner, style, and order" in which he presented these patterns. For this reason Dr. Brian diagnosed him as "clearly psychopathic." It was the same antisocial personality, sociopath diagnosis made in the past by prosecution psychiatrists, and initially by Dr. Jablon at Holmesburg.

Dr. Wawrose testified at the hearing that Joe was "rather manic depressed" at the present time. He attributed the depression to legal problems that had brought Joe "to the point where he stopped trying to maintain himself and continue to have the will to live."

Joe, the psychiatrist said, was "severely mentally disabled within the meaning of the Mental Health Procedures Act." "He needs treatment in a less restrictive environment," the psychiatrist went on. "He may need medication. He most certainly will need some assistance in trying to get him to eat, which we can't offer him here."

Dr. Wawrose also recommended that Joe be given treatment that would resocialize him and get him to be more active. He should also be given, the psychiatrist said, "anti-depressant medication either voluntary or involuntary." And, if Joe continued his hunger strike, Dr. Wawrose said, "an I.V. might be necessary."

The judge asked whether Joe was dangerous either to himself or to others. Dr. Wawrose replied, "Well, it's hard to say about others. He has attacked other people in the recent past. Whether that was deliberate or the result of some mental illness, it is really not possible for me to say at this point. I believe he is a clear danger to himself since he hasn't been eating."

Dr. Wawrose was now more flexible about Joe than he had been in the Bergen County and Camden County trials. Then the psychiatrist thought Joe definitely responsible for his acts; now he wasn't sure.

The judge asked whether Joe had a history of mental illness. Dr. Wawrose replied, "That matter is debatable, long and involved. [That] Mr. Kallinger has emotional problems is clear. To the extent that he is responsible or not responsible for his actions, I believe is a debatable point."

By the time the eleven-minute hearing was over, Judge Terrizzi, on Dr. Wawrose's recommendation, had committed Joe, for a period not to exceed ninety days, to the Farview State Hospital.

Now, at last, on May 17, 1978, six years after Judge Bradley had failed to issue such an order, there was a court order to send Joe to a mental hospital. Hospitalization, however, as in Vroom in 1977, was recommended for purposes of coping with an emergency. Joe was sent to Farview for a diagnosis and resocialization. But chiefly he was sent there to get him to eat.

24 The Endless Hills

On May 18, 1978, the nineteenth day of the hunger strike, Joe arrived at Pennsylvania's Farview State Hospital for the Criminally Insane. Farview is a maximum-security hospital for men. One-third of its patients are civil cases, the other two-thirds criminal. In the second group are those serving prison sentences and those a judge, at the conclusion of a trial or hearing, has committed directly to Farview.

In his prison garb, Joe walked with a P.S.A. (psychiatric security aide) toward Ward CC2. Here patients stay briefly in locked rooms until, after physical and psychological examinations, they are assigned to wards with dormitories and a few private open rooms.

Joe's locked room had a wooden door and a barred window. Through the window he could see grass and another building. He was impressed because the room was clean.

The P.S.A. told him that there was a dayroom where twice a day for an hour he could watch television and make collect phone calls. When he got to a ward with dormitories, he would be allowed two or three WATS calls a week. The hospital wanted the patients to be in touch with their families and friends.

Joe was weak but still determined to die. He was going to continue his hunger strike; debilitated, he was sure he would not live much longer. It would have made more sense, Joe said to himself as he looked at the sky through his window, for Judge Terrizzi to

386

have shot him in a rocket to the moon. Death's bridegroom, Joe, was eagerly looking forward to embracing his bride.

A half hour after his arrival at Farview, Joe was escorted to a CC2 conference room, where he faced a six-person treatment team. Told that he was going to be given a tray with food, he replied, "I won't eat. *I'm* in control of this situation."

"There are six of us, only one of you," Dr. Ralph E. Davis, a clinical psychologist, replied firmly. "The more determined *you* are to kill yourself, the more determined *we* are to save your life."

"Mr. Kallinger," Dr. Davis went on, "you strike me as an intelligent person. You can do it the easy way by eating. Or it can be done the hard way. We have the means here to force-feed you. Intravenous feeding. Tube feeding. All sorts of things. If you intend to commit suicide, it's a no-win situation. *We'll* win in the end."

Dr. Davis paused, then asked, "What do you want to do, Mr. Kallinger?"

Joe hesitated for a few minutes. Then, realizing that he was *not* in control of this situation, that it was hopeless, he said, "I'll eat."

Dr. Davis felt he had scored a therapeutic triumph. A P.S.A. took Joe to his room and brought him a tray. The main course was chicken, which he loathes, but he ate it. It tasted good. Soon afterward he vomited.

Joe paced back and forth. There are other ways of dying, he said to himself. *They* had won the first battle. But by killing himself, he would win in the end.

He had been at Farview three days when a P.S.A. noted on Joe's chart: "Patient started to pray in some mystic tongue. He stood in the middle of his room, kept waving his hands overhead and kept repeating the same phrases over and over again. He kept this up for forty-five minutes."

The "mystic tongue" was, of course, the "Kristorah" chant.

That night Joe went to bed early. At 3:45 A.M. he got up and paced. About a half hour later the double appeared. With a lip knife he was slicing off the penis of what appeared to be a boy.

Joe had an erection induced by murderous thoughts. He couldn't kill anybody, not even himself, without weapons. Security in this respect was tighter than in prison.

He decided to kill himself by suffocation through smoke. The window was closed. Good! He placed his plastic mattress against the wooden door, then he unwound a roll of toilet paper. He lit two packages of matches, set the toilet paper on fire, and placed the toilet paper under his sheets and blanket.

The sheets, the blanket, and the plastic mattress began to burn. The room filled with smoke. The smell was bad. Joe sat on the floor. He hoped that the inhalation of smoke would kill him.

The door opened, the burning mattress fell to the floor. A P.S.A. dragged Joe into the hallway. Brown blisters broke open on the tips of the little finger of his right hand and on the four fingers of his left hand. These were the only injuries.

At 4:30 A.M. Joe was taken to CCI. This is the maximum-security section of this maximum-security hospital. In CCI he was not allowed out of his locked room and was placed on suicide watch.

The testing that originally would have taken place in CC2 proceeded normally on CCI. And for the first time Joe's mental illness was taken seriously enough for him to receive therapy. His therapist was Thomas Brennan, a psychologist.

Joe was given various clinical tests: WAIS, Figure Drawings, Incomplete Sentence Blank, Rorschach.* The test results confirmed the diagnostic impression of Dr. Eun Sook Yoo, a psychiatrist and at that time the hospital's clinical director. She had told me on June 1, not quite two weeks after Joe had come to Farview, that he was "very sick." On July 31, she told me that the tests showed that "Joseph is primarily paranoid. But so many other kinds of schizophrenia showed up during the tests and the psychiatric examinations that, in diagnosing him, we used the broader classification of schizophrenia, chronic undifferentiated type."

Dr. Davis wrote that "the tests established the presence of a schizophrenic process of long duration. Mr. Kallinger's history shows early emotional deprivation. His illness is always active and breaks through periodically. The nature of his psychosis is destructive, and directed both externally and toward the Self. When this occurs, he is totally out of contact with reality and helpless to exert any con-

---

* Chiefly on the basis of the Rorschach test, doctors at Avenel in 1977 had concluded that Joe was schizophrenic, as recounted in Chapter 22.

trols over reality or himself. Mr. Kallinger is very seriously ill, and in need of intensive treatment."

Dr. Yoo and Dr. Davis discussed Joe's condition with me for several reasons: He had listed me as "next of kin," I had filled out a detailed social-service form the hospital had sent me about him, and the doctors wanted me to work closely with them. They knew that I had studied Joe since July 1976, and they wanted to be able to utilize my research. On June 1, 1978, Robert J. Hammel,* the superintendent of the hospital, had arranged a luncheon at which I met members of the staff who worked with Joe. We exchanged records and observations.

Joe remained in CCI for five weeks and fluctuated between control and the lack of it. Once he cut his mattress into strips to make a rope to hang himself. But before he could make the rope, a P.S.A. discovered feathers and pieces of foam scattered on Joe's floor. Joe was again put on suicide watch. His dosage of Stelazine, a psychotropic drug, was increased. For several days he was not allowed to use a mattress. When, however, he was in "good contact with reality," as his chart stated, he was admitted to CC2. A month later Dr. Yoo and Joe's treatment team decided that he was ready for a regular ward. They decided to send him to BBI, the best ward in the hospital. BBI had two floors. Upstairs there were dormitories and a few private rooms. Downstairs there were three dayrooms and a kitchen.

Joe was terrified. He had not been in contact with groups of men since he had left the SCIH clothing plant after stabbing Eller. He hadn't shared a lavatory since 1972, when he had been in the Philadelphia Detention House. He told the team that he wanted to stay in CC2, where he was safe from doing harm. "We think he's ready for BBI," Dr. Yoo told me. "It's therapeutically important for him to be there, and we have to take the risk."

Two days after Joe was transferred to BBI, Dr. Norman Wenger, the captain of Joe's BBI team, sent him back to CC2. Joe had made the request, and the doctor agreed that he needed a little more time

---

* After Mr. Hammel resigned on March 5, 1980, Joel H. Hersh, Dale E. Newhart, and David W. Jay were, in this order, his successors.

on CC2 before making the adjustment to "continuous interpersonal contacts."

The next day Joe asked to be readmitted to BBI. He was. But he also served notice that since his present ninety-day commitment to Farview was about to be up, he wanted to return to SCIH. He was recommitted to Farview for another ninety days and remained in BBI. But intermittently he asked to be returned to prison. He had discovered that if one wants to commit suicide it is easier to do so in prison than at Farview.

Joe mingled little with the forty men on the ward. He lay on his bench in the dayroom, paced, smoked, and talked to me over the telephone. When he was taken off Stelazine and put on Prolixin, another psychotropic drug, he protested that they were "both in the same class of medication" and he could do just as well on Stelazine. He refused Thorazine and Elavil because they made him sick. He took Haldol even though, as he put it, "it messes me up and takes away my whole personality. I feel like a walking zombie."

Another patient noticed Joe's "shuffling gait while standing still," and Dr. Davis, who was now Joe's therapist, observed his "dazed, slow, robot-like manner." Sometimes, as Dr. Davis also noted, Joe "beat his face, shoulders and back with his hand and invariably the slow choreoform gestures ended with a big slap. It looked as if he were punishing himself."

The movements now, as Dr. Hurtig had suggested in Camden, seemed directly related to specific incidents in Joe's life, and I wondered whether he was reenacting the beatings he had received as a child.* I also speculated that Joe behaved in a robotlike manner because the senior Kallingers had adopted him not because he was a child, but for a fixed purpose: turning him into a future shoemaker.

When Dr. Davis and I talked about this, he said, "Joe was treated as a nonperson. This was the origin of his schizophrenia. He was treated as an object and a performer who had to perform according to the wishes of his adoptive parents to receive from them even the basic necessities of life. This treatment and the institutional care he had received before coming to the Kallingers denied him a sense of self. As an adult, he had to fight for a sense of identity."

* Joe didn't talk to me about these abuses until after I had confronted him with what neighbors had told me. This happened in his early days at Farview.

Looking for identity, Joe as a child and adolescent had had many dreams and fantasies about his real mother, whom he did not remember ever having seen. He had even gone in search of her, although he knew that if he found her he couldn't possibly have recognized her because he didn't know what she looked like. He had become a brutal killer who received hallucinatory and Olympian messages from God, but he was also an acutely sensitive little boy for whom his mother through the years had remained a vitally important absent presence.

I tried to find her. From the records of the senior Kallingers I had her name: Judith Renner. A private detective I engaged turned up nothing. But by sleuthing in court, hospital, real estate, and other records, Arthur Gutkin located the half sister Joe didn't know he had. Her name was Mrs. Muriel Gotshalk and she lived in a Philadelphia suburb very like the suburbs Joe and Michael had invaded.

Just after Thanksgiving 1978, Gutkin and I knocked on Mrs. Gotshalk's door. She wasn't home. We returned on December 5. A dog barked. We waited. A woman opened the door halfway. She peered at us nervously. She was petite. The hair streaming over her shoulders was black, the color of Joe's hair.

"Who are you?" she asked. "What do you want?"

"I'm a lawyer," Gutkin replied. He handed her his card.

"What business do you have with me?" She was tense.

"Family business," he replied. "We want to talk to your mother." (We didn't actually know whether Judith Renner was alive.)

"What member of the family does it concern?" she asked.

I had been standing to the side of the door. I came closer and said, "Your brother."

I couldn't be sure that she was Joe's sister. If she was, I had no idea whether she knew she had a brother. But when she heard the word "brother," her manner changed.

"Come in," she said.

We went into a well-appointed living room. Gutkin sat down in an easy chair near the door. I took a straight-backed chair on the other side of the room.

Still standing, the woman turned to me.

"What's *your* name?" she asked.

"Flora," Gutkin replied.

"Flora Schreiber," she said. "You wrote *Sybil* and you're writing a book about my brother. I knew you would come. I just wondered how long it would take. I'll call my mother."

"Mom," Muriel said after dialing the living-room telephone, "come right over. It's important." Her voice was tense, anxious, as she added, "I'll tell you when I see you."

Within fifteen minutes we heard a car park. Muriel opened the front door. Judith Renner,* now sixty-three, looking perplexed and worried, moved slowly up the long walkway toward her daughter. Stepping into the living room, Judith shivered, pulled her black velvet coat close to her body, and stared fearfully at Gutkin and me.

"Come upstairs, Mom," Muriel said softly. "Come upstairs."

"My feet won't move, my feet won't move," Judith kept repeating.

Mother and daughter climbed to the head of the stairs. Gutkin and I could hear them whispering. When they came back, Judith told me, "I'll talk to you, but not here. I don't want anybody to hear *this*."

"It's *berschert*," Judith said when we were seated beside each other in her charming apartment. "You came here and it was *berschert*." She had used a Yiddish (also German) word for "fated."

I had Joe's and Betty's family album with me and showed Judith a photograph of Joe at the age of nine. Anna Kallinger was standing beside him.

"So stiff, so unfeeling," Judith remarked of Joe's adoptive mother in the photograph.

I told Judith about a few of the abuses to which Joe as a child had been subjected—the "bird" incident, the bare knees on coarse sandpaper, the "I'll give you zoo" and the "I'll send you back."

"I didn't know," Judith said. "I didn't know. They [the Catholic Children's Bureau] told me it was a good home. I didn't know. I thought the Kallingers could do more for Joe than I could. They had more money. They told me they had a fund for sending him to college. I promised I wouldn't interfere."

Judith asked about Betty, her daughter-in-law, and about the

---

* She was Judith Renner Weiss, a widow. For ten years, she and her husband had run a retail business and she was now retired.

grandchildren. I showed Judith and Muriel, who had joined us by now, their photographs.

"We knew about Joe's trouble," Muriel said. "We followed his story from the time of the child-abuse trial. When he was in Bergen County, we were going to go to him. But we didn't."

Judith looked at Muriel with foreboding and asked, "What are we going to tell Dave?" Dave is Muriel's husband.

"The truth," Muriel said in a hoarse whisper.

"What will he think of me?" Judith asked.

"He has to know!" said Muriel.

"He's a good man, Dave is," Judith replied. "Yes, we'll tell him."

I told them that Joe was at Farview, where he had been diagnosed as a schizophrenic. I said I had studied him carefully since July 1976 and was convinced that his crimes were the result of his illness. He was, I also said, a charming and intelligent person.

I asked whether Judith wanted to see Joe. She showed strain, but after a moment said yes. Then she suggested that we go on December 11, his birthday. We agreed, however, to visit Joe on December 16, 1978, Judith's birthday. At the age of forty-two Joe would meet his mother for the first time.

Joe was both eager and perplexed by the approaching visit. He scribbled questions for his mother and read them to me over the telephone. They were:

> Why have you left me?
> Did you think of me through the years?
> What would you have wanted for me?
> Did you miss me?
> Why did you see me so seldom while I was at St. Vincent's?
> Why were you so anxious for me to become adopted?
> Is my father your husband?
> Who wanted most to put me away, you or he?
> Were you sorry after you did it?

We walked to the section of the Farview visitor's room where Joe was waiting. He was wearing slacks and a pink shirt. He was standing near a low round table, his head bent forward, his eyes gazing at the surface of the table. He was trembling slightly.

Judith had arranged for a little ritual, which we followed. She wanted Muriel to introduce her to Joe.

"Joe," I said as planned, "I'd like you to meet your sister."

They hugged each other and kissed. Muriel nodded to Judith. Judith came closer. Muriel said, "Joe, meet our mother!"

Joe and Judith embraced and kissed. Tears filled their eyes. Joe remembered that as a child he had thought, "Everyone has people, right? The butterflies are *my* people."

Arthur Gutkin and I had drawn back. But then the moment was over. We all sat down, Joe and Judith on a love seat, the rest of us on chairs.

Nobody talked of separation. Joe didn't put to his mother the questions he had prepared. The conversation was social. When he did finally ask about his father, Judith froze. He told her that the doctors (he was thinking in particular of Dr. Bird in Camden) wanted to know about his genetic background. I added that they were also concerned whether there had been any mental illness or crime.

Judith replied that in her family and in Joe's father's family, there were doctors, lawyers, and other professionals. I said that among professionals there could be mental illness and crime. She replied that there had been neither.

After four hours Joe walked with us to the door of the visitors' room. He could go no farther. Judith and Muriel kissed him good-bye. He had a pained smile as we left him.

"I expected him to be resentful. But he was extremely polite," Judith said with relief. "I can say one thing for the Kallingers: They reared a very well-mannered man."

We walked along the hallway to the front door. We looked back and saw Joe waving to us.

"He looks like a little boy," Judith said as we kept walking.

"That's what he is," I replied, "a deserted little boy."

Judith and Muriel had been excited about seeing Joe, but they were so afraid of the consequences of the visit that in signing the Farview visitors' book they had used assumed names.

This fear of the consequences was expressed in a telephone conversation I had with Muriel's husband, an engineer. "I thought I married an only child," Dave Gotshalk told me, "and then I heard about this person she calls brother. I've been drinking martinis ever since. We'd have to leave Pennsylvania if anybody knew we were related to Kallinger. And I'm scared about heredity. Do my wife, children, and mother-in-law carry a criminal gene or maybe a gene for insanity?"

However, Dr. Silvano Arieti, a leading, if not actually *the* leading, authority on schizophrenia, did not think that Joe carried a criminal gene or a gene for insanity. He thought that Joe's illness had been induced not by heredity but by what had been done to him as a child.

On February 22, 1980, I brought Dr. Arieti to examine Joe as a private patient. I was present throughout the three-and-a-half-hour examination in a Farview conference room. Dr. Davis was with us most of the time.

Dr. Arieti diagnosed Joe as a paranoid schizophrenic. Among the symptoms the psychiatrist cited in addition to the hallucinations and delusions were neologisms, strange stereotyped or rhythmic movements, and a private language and chant. Hallucinations and delusions, according to the doctor, "compelled the patient to fantasize and sometimes perform the most brutal sadistic acts."

"In my opinion," Dr. Arieti wrote, "the patient must be considered not only psychotic, but also legally insane according to the M'Naghten law and the Durham law* because, although he knew the nature and quality of the crimes he committed, he did not know that they were wrong; in fact, they were commands from God, and presumably good. He was not able to appreciate the wrongfulness of his conduct or to make his conduct conform to the requirements of the law. Because the fantasies and the hallucinations persist, Mr. Kallinger must be considered still an extremely dangerous individual. Were he to find a partner in some way similar to his son [Dr. Arieti did

* According to the M'Naghten law the accused is not responsible for the crime if he was "laboring under such a defect of reason, from disease of the mind, as not to know the nature and quality of the act he was doing; or if he did know, that he did not know he was doing what was wrong." The Durham law states that an accused is not criminally responsible if his unlawful act was the product of mental disease or mental defect. The test proceeds on the assumption that when the criminal act of the accused is the product of his mental illness, the suggested conclusion is that the accused should be hospitalized for treatment and possible rehabilitation.

not know that the son's name was Michael], he would be extremely likely to repeat these crimes."

Dr. Arieti said that Joe's schizophrenic symptoms had led directly to his crimes and that "a specific childhood incident, which we were able to retrace,* became the origin of both the low self-esteem that is conducive to schizophrenia and of the nature of the sadistic acts."

"The patient," Dr. Arieti continued, "was filled with hostility, rage, and vindictiveness because of what his adoptive parents alleged had been done to his sexual organ [the "bird"]."

Joe, according to Dr. Arieti, wanted to exterminate mankind because this was a mechanism of defense to which the hostility had led. Dr. Arieti thought that it was appropriate for the actualization of the plan to have begun with the murder of two children. Joe himself had been a child when he was symbolically castrated. Sadistic pleasure, Dr. Arieti maintained, restituted to Joe the power for sexual excitement that he thought he had lost.

Dr. Arieti said he believed that Joe belonged in a hospital and not in prison; that it was a great tragedy that he had been led into this dangerous schizophrenia by what had been done to him in childhood.

Dr. Arieti was certain that Joe was schizophrenic not because of a genetic defect but because of the Kallingers' abuses.

"Even if Mr. Kallinger had a predisposition to schizophrenia," Dr. Arieti told me, "he would have been a mild schizophrenic if not for the abuses. His mother's abandonment did not make him schizophrenic. But it did make him more vulnerable to the Kallingers' abuses."

Dr. Arieti recommended that Joe be taken off Haldol and prescribed Navane for him. The hospital followed the recommendation.

On March 8, 1981, at Farview, Dr. Arieti, in my presence, examined Joe for a second time. All the findings of the first examination were confirmed. This time Dr. Arieti also ascribed Joe's persistent delusion of the double to what is called at times autoscopic syndrome, at other times Lukianowicz syndrome.

Between the first and second examinations the doctor had read some of Joe's poems. He shrugged and said when we left the hos-

* See S. Arieti and F. Schreiber, "Multiple Murders of a Schizophrenic Patient: A Psychodynamic Interpretation," *Journal of the American Academy of Psychoanalysis*, Vol. 9, No. 4 (1981), pp. 501–524.

pital, "It's a pity. A great pity. He could have been a fine poet." Poetry, we agreed, was just *one* of Joe's potentialities that had not been realized.

The shift to Navane brought back some of Joe's old alertness. In BBI he had also begun to improve in other ways. A loner all his life, he had developed relationships with the other patients. With Jerry Fox he established a real friendship which continued with a flow of letters and cards even after Jerry left Farview.

Joe had been a Catholic until the collapse of his first marriage. He had become a Protestant during his second marriage. And now, after discovering that his mother was Jewish, he had enough energy to take the initiative in becoming a Jew. He also had the drive to begin a book entitled *Ten Murderers*, which will be based on interviews with men he knows at Farview, with psychological commentary by Dr. Davis. Joe also has taken pleasure in string art.

He has developed control. During a hallucinatory episode, he asked to be taken to CCI to keep him from killing somebody. Normal thoughts returned within a few days and he was safely back on BBI. He is on PRN—code letters signifying that a patient can request extra medication when he feels he needs it. Whenever he has a hallucination, he asks for PRN, which deflects him from acting out the hallucination.

One night Bobby Lobman, another patient, tried to kill himself. He did so by eating cheese that in combination with Parnate, his medication, is fatal. In an effort to save Bobby, Joe telephoned me. In a businesslike voice he told me what had happened. He asked me to call Dr. Davis. I did. Dr. Davis called the night supervisor, and Bobby was rushed to Scranton State Hospital. Joe, who had wanted to destroy mankind, had saved a life!

Nevertheless Joe still wanted to go back to prison to kill himself. As on his first day at Farview, he was determined "to win in the end." And in spite of Joe's progress, Charlie, who had been absent since Joe's early days at the Bergen County Jail, appeared at Farview on the night of May 20, 1980. He floated in the darkness at the foot of Joe's dormitory bed. For the first time Joe connected Charlie with Joey.

Joe remembered that at SCIH during his first incarceration Charlie had said that he was fourteen years old. Joey had been fourteen and five months on the day Joe and Michael killed him, drowning him in the stagnant pool of water beneath the surface of Philadelphia's Ninth and Market streets. In the last moment Joe had seen his son alive, Joey, chained to the ladder floating in the water, had turned his head through the rungs and cried, "Daddy, help me!"

Watching Charlie floating above the foot of his bed that May night in Farview, Joe remembered that the only part of Joey that had been visible in the water had been his head, and that when Joey had looked at his father for the last time, his wet hair lay partly over his face. For an instant Joe had seen the whites of Joey's eyes, the pleading brown irises having risen behind the bones of Joey's skull; and then his son's face had turned back to the water and to death.

Like Joey in the stagnant pool, Charlie had hair over his face, and Joe could see, when the hair parted, the whites of Charlie's eyes. Lying in his bed in Farview, hearing only the night sounds of the breathing and turning of other patients, Joe suddenly realized that Charlie was Joey transformed through the murder into a devil: Joey renamed, his body and the features of his face destroyed by death.

Charlie, rolling his eyes in his head in the BBI dormitory, also reminded Joe of the way Joey used to roll *his* eyes. Joe looked at the faceless face and thought: Could it be that way because the coroner wouldn't let me see the decomposed body of my son?

Charlie was Joey transformed into a devil that controlled Joe. Since childhood Joe had seen, as he put it, "the forms of things that were evil." Joe, not wanting anybody to think he was talking to himself, was afraid to tell Charlie to go away. Sick and guilt-ridden, Joe turned over, went back to sleep, and had bad dreams. When he woke up he saw that Charlie was still there. It was 2:00 A.M.

"Kill yourself," Charlie ordered with his controlling megaphone voice.

Joe believed that Charlie was real and that other people could see and hear him, even though Charlie had told Joe a long time ago in the shoe repair shop that he was invisible to everybody but Joe and that nobody but Joe could hear him. Looking around to see whether Charlie's voice had awakened anybody, Joe decided that he had to get rid of Charlie—*permanently*.

Two days before, Joe had had suicidal thoughts. But now that Charlie had ordered Joe to kill himself, Joe wanted to live. He hated Charlie and knew that Charlie hated him. On the floor next to Joe's bed was an extra sheet. Joe reached for the sheet, ignited a package of matches, put the flame to the sheet, and threw the sheet at Charlie. Joe was infuriated when the sheet hit the floor and Charlie, evidently unharmed, just floated away. A P.S.A. saw the flames, rushed to the scene, and put them out. He did not make any connection between the fire and Joe Kallinger.

Joe expected Charlie to come back, for to Joe, Charlie was real and could be killed. On April 29, 1982, Joe told me, "Maybe Charlie doesn't come back because he's afraid next time I'll *really* kill him."

On December 11, 1981, Joe's forty-fourth birthday, a private room became available. He got it. Alone there he heard on the local radio "Seasons in the Sun," which he called "Joey's song." He was deeply depressed by the song. He was in the room only ten days when, under the influence of the double, he made a grandiose suicide attempt. He secured permission to rest in what was known as the Quiet Room. He was going to barricade the steel door of the room with a bed. Then he planned to break the glass partition in the door with a pool-table cue ball. Through the opening in the door he could be fed. For he planned to stay for days before he killed himself.

"Everybody will stay outside, coaxing me not to do it," he told me on the telephone. "The press must be informed. I want to go out in style."

He also said that after he had killed himself he would lie beside Joey in Whitemarsh Cemetery, "ironic as that seems." Joe also talked wildly and in typical schizophrenic fashion about how in heaven Joey had his own private nurse: Maria Fasching, because "they have something in common. They were killed by the same man."

In BBI Joe removed the cue ball from the pool table. A P.S.A. took the ball away from him. He then removed locks from his lockers and trunk.

The locks would take the place of the cue ball. Supper was called. He went to supper with the group. When he came back, he was going to stage the suicide attempt in the Quiet Room. But by now the double was also inciting the murder of a patient or a staff member.

Joe's face was distorted. He walked with strange, jerky movements. Anthony Falvo, the evening "charge," knew something was wrong. While Joe was at supper, he sent a P.S.A. to search Joe's room. The P.S.A. found the locks. He took them away.

Joe was taken to CCI. His regular dosage of Navane was increased. Within a few days he was better. He was returned to BBI, but lost his room. On April 3, 1981, he was again assigned to a private room. His behavior had been good.

At Christmas 1981, following the Quiet Room incident, Joe and Michael, for the first time since their arrest, were in touch with each other. They talked by telephone and exchanged Christmas cards. They have had other telephone conversations. Michael has promised that he will come to Farview to visit his father.

Besides Joe and Michael, no member of the Kallinger family knows about the murder of José Collazo. They all know about the murder of Joey. Betty once remarked to me, "Joey made you climb the wall. But to kill him?" I explained that Joe killed not out of wickedness, but sickness. "Joe is a human being," I said. Betty replied, "So was my son." She has since come to understand that Joe is mentally ill. On that basis she forgives him. As she put it, "That judge should've sent Joe to a hospital in 1972. If he had, my son would be alive. And that nurse. I cried for days when I heard about her."

Judith and Muriel do not know that Joe killed Joey. But they do know that Joe is mentally ill. Judith, as if to erase the past, treats Joe as if he were a baby. She blows kisses to him and calls him "doll" during their weekly WATS-line telephone conversations. When she visits him at Farview twice a year, she sits close to him, strokes and pets him, and pleads with him to lose weight.

Joe had been in the BBI for three and a half years and had had a room of his own for five months when on March 16, 1982, that facility was closed because of a long-term renovation and reconstruction program. Just before Joe left BBI, he told me over the telephone, "We won't see the groundhog anymore." He had taken great pleasure in watching the groundhog through a window.

There were also other losses in being in P Ward, where Joe was now housed. The ward was overcrowded and had no private rooms, and in its rigid rules it created some of the atmosphere of a prison. However, Joe made a remarkably good adjustment.

On June 25, 1982, Joe was transferred to S-1, a thirty-bed ward with eighteen beds used as an infirmary and twelve beds used for permanent residents. Joe has one of the twelve beds.

Farview is the first institution to treat Joe for a psychosis and the Farview psychiatrists the first to find him incompetent to stand trial. Because of this repeated finding, the charges against him for the assault on Eller were dropped in August 1979 and Joe's mental illness was at last recognized by a *court*!

The severity of that illness was recognized by Dr. J. E. Olivier. Examining Joe on July 23, 1982, four years and two months after he had come to Farview, Dr. Olivier found him still "floridly psychotic." It was Dr. Olivier's conclusion that "were he to be transferred back to prison where weapons are freely available, he would become extremely dangerous, even when maintained on psychotropic medication. I expect he will need to remain in this facility for the rest of his life."

At Farview Dr. Davis* directed Joe's therapy toward helping him to understand and ultimately to control his hallucinations. To control the hallucinations is also to control the desire to kill. For Dr. Davis believes that I am the only person Joe wouldn't kill while having a hallucination. This is so, Dr. Davis says, because I am the only one he trusts.

The trust had become so strong that Joe made me a mother figure and allowed me to enter into his most private thoughts. At times when he expressed great remorse I reminded him that the abuse of him as a child was the origin of his psychosis and through it of his crimes. I said I had been raised according to the best principles of child care by loving and enlightened parents and that if I had been subjected to the abuses he experienced as a child, there but for the Grace of God I, too, might have gone.

I hope that Joe, who at the time of going to S-1 had been at Farview four years and five weeks, will not leave Farview in the fore-

---

* After Dr. Davis left Farview, Dr. Marcella Shields became Joe's therapist. When Dr. Shields left, she was replaced by Dr. Ronald Refice.

seeable future. That he should remain there was stated by Dr. Arieti and again on December 11, 1981—Joe's forty-fifth birthday—by Dr. Lewis L. Robbins.

For four hours on December 11, 1981, Dr. Robbins, a psychiatrist with impressive credentials,* examined Joe as a private patient in a Farview conference room. I was present throughout and Dr. Shields some of the time.

In his report about Joe Dr. Robbins wrote: "I can only concur with Dr. Arieti's finding and that of the Farview doctors that Mr. Joseph Kallinger chronically suffers from paranoid schizophrenia and that his criminal behavior is a manifestation of his illness."

Dr. Robbins also stated: "In retrospect it seems evident that had his illness been recognized earlier and treatment instituted when he was arrested for child abuse before he committed any crimes and had he subsequently been committed to a hospital rather than considered sane and hence imprisoned, the course of events might have been less pathological."

Dr. Robbins also made clear in his report that in prison "there is much greater hazard [than at Farview] that he would and could act upon one of his hallucinatory impulses" and that "Farview State Hospital has provided Mr. Kallinger the security he feels he needs."

While Joe was waiting in BBI for Dr. Robbins and me to arrive, he wrote me the following letter. The letter reflects marked improvement in Joe's use of language. The syntax is his own. I have corrected his misspellings, but there were fewer of them than in his earlier letters.

This is my heart speaking to me as I pace this floor at Farview while I wait for your visit on my forty-fifth birthday. Here the hours are long and dreary, although days and weeks and months pass quickly. Each one of these hours is filled with love for you. I think of many things and feel many emotions toward you no words can tell.

You found the little boy in me. You found little Joe and made him feel wanted. I am removed from the world. You gave a portion of that world back to me. You took a convicted murderer and made him your friend.

* Dr. Robbins for many years held top positions in the famous Menninger Sanitarium and Menninger Foundation. After that he was medical director of Hillside Hospital, New York.

402

I often wonder how it would have been if *you* raised me. If you had, I do not think I would have needed psychiatric help. But if I needed it, I would have gotten it at the *first* sign of mental illness.

You would have been my life conscience as you are today while we speak two and a half hours each day on the phone. It is the loving and understanding person that you are that makes it easy to tell you of my most inner thoughts and feelings. You know instantly when I'm depressed and when I need understanding. I feel free to tell you when I masturbate, when I have images, when the double appears or Charlie. You are someone I can trust with the deepest, darkest, most dreadful thoughts.

If you had been my mother, Flora, all that happened to my victims and me would not have been. I know it. I know it.

Long ago I asked you to find the trigger that made me what I am. Well, you found it. The force that changed me into a killer was an illness. That is now clear to me. But the double and Charlie are real. They exist in my life now and forevermore. They drove me. Does that mean I will always be driven? That Navane in a Lily cup of orange juice is the only thing that can stop me? That, Flora, and talking to you. You may not know it, but you control me, hold back my hand from letting my hallucinations rule me.

An illness? Yes. But three people are dead because of me. They were all young and innocent. I wish each day I could bring them back. I am glad that I spared the rest of my victims. With what I had in mind, they are lucky to be alive. And mankind? I thought I would become God by dooming it, all of it, eliminating it. But I know I'm not going to be God. I no longer want everyone to die. But whenever I say "I don't want medication," and they don't make me take it, world massacre comes back.

At Huntingdon it was the opposite of world massacre. It was different from what happened to me in the world. Maybe at Huntingdon I thought everyone wanted to kill me out of revenge for the three people I killed. I wanted to kill to protect myself from being killed. I had absolutely no medication there to control me.

Dr. Wawrose sent me to Farview because of the hunger strike. But Farview paid more attention to my assault on Eller. If it were only the hunger strike, they would have sent me back at the end of the first ninety days. Send me back? Does that sound familiar, Flora? My adoptive parents were often telling me they would send me back.

I knew they were strict. But not until late in our conversations, when I was already at Farview, did I realize how deep the Kallingers' destruction of me had been.

I fantasized about you as my mother. You did bring my real mother to me. This brought me great joy—a joy at finding my roots. But there's still frustration. She doesn't tell me about my father.

She turns off when I ask questions about the past. She keeps it a secret from me. She keeps me a secret from all her friends, won't let me write her at her address (I have to write her c/o Muriel). She's afraid the mailman will recognize the return address, or a neighbor might get the letter by mistake. To her I'm someone who belongs in a dark closet and no one has the key but her.

Back to the world. If Michael hadn't been with me, my sentences would have been lighter. But if he hadn't been with me, there wouldn't have been any crimes. I'm not saying he proposed the plan. He was my strength and my courage. Without him I couldn't have acted out my hallucinations with a plan of action.

I love Michael very much. I am looking forward to seeing him here. Mary Jo's visits are glorious. She loves her daddy and her daddy loves her. My Sunday calls to her are a high point of my week. She brings her children to see Grandpa and I have a relationship with them. Seeing Bonnie, oh so rarely, but seeing her, brings me great joy. Jimmy. I'm so proud of him with a good job in New York. I feel he's going to make it big. But he still has time to visit me, and talk to me several times a week. Betty? She's a good girl, loyal to me when I made it hard for her to be loyal. I wish I had given her a different life.

I hope I'm not dreaming about what your book about me can do for humankind. Maybe people will learn from it what mental illness can do to a human being. If I had gotten help on time, I wouldn't be this way. I *wouldn't*! People out there are ashamed of mental illness. And they're afraid of it or they make fun of it. They refuse to believe it even when all the signs of mental illness are right under their noses. Or they think it's criminal, even if the sick person never did a wrong thing in his life. Or they just walk away from him and say he's *bad*. But the mentally ill should get a better deal from the society and the right treatment. Mental illness can happen to *anybody*. We are all brothers and sisters, all made of the same stuff. So what can happen to one person can happen to *all*! Like you told me, Flora, "There but for the Grace of God go I." Maybe Mr. Jones and Mrs. Smith are falling into the demon world of madness, where it is always thick and foggy night. If *this* world under the sun were different, we'd all go running to help them. But no! We don't. We stand aside to watch them suffer. And we make them suffer more with our stupid attitudes. It's a real puzzle: If a person breaks a leg or comes down with a disease, he gets treated. So why not mental illness? If my illness had been caught early, I wouldn't be in these endless hills. That's what the people around here call the Moosic Mountain.

I'd like to be a great poet. I'm taking the bits and pieces of what I remember from my dreams and turning them into poetry. All my dreams end in chaos, but I'm trying in my poetry to give the chaos form.

I want to express feelings through images—especially the feelings of what it's like to be mentally ill. I'd write for myself and for all the other crazy people in the world: for the ones wandering in pain on the streets, for the ones whose families treat them like second-class citizens, for the ones who couldn't make it in life.

They've just called to say you and Dr. Robbins are waiting for me. I have to go.

Your son,
Joe

Appendix I
Poems by Joseph Kallinger

A NEW DAY

In the darkness of night
I rise to begin my day.
Memories flow in the silence
Of yesterdays and tomorrows
Which are fading flowers,
Lilacs and royal roses,
Sprays of regret
For the might have been
And the never will be.

The Agèd Eagle said:
All time is eternally present,
All time is unredeemable. So
the past is fixed and I am
Unredeemable.

On the ward I pace, in the
Cool silence feel the hot flush of
Memory: Footfalls echo in my memory
Down the hall I paced at home.
A shoemaker, I wanted all men to be
Fleetfooted,
For fleet of foot, their minds would be
Fleetfooted too.

Dawn breaks with sounds of trays and carts
Sizzling bacon for the unredeemables.
Between sips of coffee
I talk on the phone with
Angel Flora, saintly woman
Of my soul, I hear your
Voice and I feel the
Paradise of your presence
Around me, saving me, and
Listening to you I am
Redeemed not in time
But out of time, hearing you
A joy of endless moments
Out of time unredeemable,
Redeemed out of time
In the golden of your voice
Speaking of endless moments.

Farview
October 11, 1982

LIFE AFTER DEATH

There is no Hell, but only a Heaven
After death. Hallelujah!
In Heaven there are no rewards:
Everyone is treated equally
(Some, of course, more equally than others)
(Even in Paradise there can be raw deals)
I come from Heaven
Heaven is where I'll go
When I die and from
Heaven I'll return to
This earth as
Another spirit
In a new born baby.
Hallelujah!
Other people have different
Thoughts about Heaven, Hell, and
Reincarnation.
How do I know
I'm right about

What I think?
It is not a matter of logic,
Or even of religious conviction.
It is thought that
Courses through me,
Flowing through my blood
Beating with my heart.
It is a thought that
has brought consolation in
Dark hours, in twisted times
And has remained firm
Through my forty-five years.
To Heaven I believed I would go
After my Divinely inspired
Mission had been accomplished,
And as God I ascended my Throne.

Farview
October 10, 1982

MY DOUBLE

through a window of the ward
shines a sunray
my double and the woman,
death's dancers,
glide
through the motes of dust
sparkling on the shoulders
of his dark coat, on the blood
flowing from her belly.

from window to wall
they glide through the sunray
slowly
in time to the unheard music
of the knife in my double's hand
going in and out of the woman's
belly
her screams silent counterpoint to the
silent voice of the knife,
devilish music for an unredeemable.

my double looks like me
I look like him
but we are not each other
he is my fear and my master:

in the unheard music I hear
his command to kill, to pluck out
eyes, cut breasts, slice bellies,
testicles and penises, rip
vaginas.

he is the delegate of God
bringing the day of wrath
bringing the day of doom
to mankind
through me
(delegate of a delegate)
when I shall become the God of Glory.

Farview
September 11, 1982

CHARLIE

he's after me, riding air currents
like an angry balloon

floating, his long hair is parted in front
curled back at the sides. his mean brown eyes
stare at me, pin me to the wall
where i wriggle.

(i cannot free myself from charlie)

he has no body and below his eyes his faceless face is
just a tight tissue of skin wrapped around jawbones
rounding in a fleshy chin.

(i cannot free myself from charlie)

bodiless rider, he rides thunderbolts in Hell
with the Devil sings doom songs

through his mouthless face
then comes to me with bloody instructions

(his favorite word is *kill*)

but charlie is real, like you and me
someday i'm going to waste him
someday i'm going to kill him
someday i'm going to puncture him
with a knife
he'll shrivel like an airless balloon.

but maybe charlie's going to kill me first
at night i lie with one eye open

(i cannot free myself from charlie)

Farview
September 10, 1982

THE UNICORN IN THE GARDEN

When I was a little boy,
My adoptive parents,
Anna and Stephen,
Killed the unicorn in my garden.
The nightingale died, too, and
The lilacs and roses perished.
I wanted to be an actor,
Playing with the unicorn in my garden,
But they said: "You will be a
Shoemaker, like your father,
Dummkopf! If you don't,
You will be a bum!"
So I grew up in my adoptive father's shop,
Hearing the cutting of leather,
Smelling the odor of glue,
My music the whirring of machines,
Idiot's delight.
Exiled from the street,
Isolated from other children,
I lived among shoes and knives and hammers.

Unknown, unwanted, unloved,
I learned to shape soles, replace heels, drive nails.
My own soul was hidden from me by the shop's
Dead world.
A robot to their will,
I died with the unicorn in my garden.

Farview
September 3, 1982

DOWNHILL

When I was in the world
I had seven children,
A wife, and a business of
My own.
We were a comfortable family
Until—
One cannot pinpoint the moment
That I lost my mind;
It was not a day, a week, or
Even a year.
Life flames rising, the surges
Came, the invocations, the
Orders from the Devil, then
From God!
My determination grew
To destroy mankind and so fulfill
God's will, reach my apotheosis
And become God Himself!
The route was strewn with corpses,
Multitudes imagined, a few real.
The first reality was one of my own
Sons; after that I began to go steadily
Downhill, and no longer were we a comfortable
Family, or a family that was whole.

Farview
August 31, 1982

THE SHADOW STAND

I am a man whose whole shadow
is only as big as his head:
it lies at my feet and
acts as a stand to hold me up.

Farview
August 28, 1979

THE EVIL WHISPERINGS

The chilling voice from nowhere
came whispering out of the air;
as I listen, then open the door
and
I rushed into the parlor,
'cause anything was better than to stand
in the dim hallway and hear
the evil whisperings,
for I was in intense fear
and silence;
even the music held its breath

Farview
August 20, 1978

SECRET LIFE

I discovered
a secret
of life
in a single line
of poetry.
that was a week ago.
today, I celebrate
a new week yet
have forgotten
what the secret was.
Oh, as life goes on,
I shall discover it
again in other lines

of poetry
that is, assuming
there is a secret.

Farview
July 20, 1978

LAST REIGN—RAIN

When I was king,
I made my rain
—but now my rain
is made by those
who carry keys
to walls and doors
of brick and steel
—and memories.

Farview
July 12, 1978

MY MIND AND YOU

My mind is chainless,
only you can bind it.
through my open window
pass odors of freedom.
the guard paces up
and down the corridor
outside my cell.
My body is in chains.
Brightness fills the air
this fall day.
for my mind is chainless
which only you can bind.

Farview
June 8, 1978

A NEW BREATH

When a child is born
it's a new breath
in an old world,
heart beat of young and old:
but it will never die,
for each new day is glory
when a child is born.

Farview
June 5, 1978

HARD WIND

The wind blew hard as I made my way
along the trail. My hat blew off
and blew across the grass until
it caught on a turtle who swore he was
caught by a human, then all swallowed
up in one gulp as he groped around
in the dark surrounded by the smell
of a human. A child saw the hat
and after picking it up saw
the turtle, and said, shaking his finger:
you naughty boy, you ate him all up.

Huntingdon
March 3, 1978

PAST AND FUTURE

Christmas, the time of year
that has the impact
of a childhood story
and the dreams of the future
all rolled into the present
that we give our loved ones.

Huntingdon
March 3, 1978

414

PRISONER IN COURT

unable to speak
there was nothing;
all the symptoms
of madness were going on
as described by judge
and the newspapers,
who were there
and there was I
in my flowing movements
like a doll swimming
in a sea
of spleen and hatred
(back in my cell the guards
had beaten me, as always)
all watched and taunted and laughed
'cause my head was tilted down
my eyes weren't working right
and I could not speak
I could not speak

Huntingdon
March 3, 1978

MY FINAL WAKING BELL

As I rise this morning
I roll out of bed
to the noise of the food cart
being rolled on to the
head of the block,
the banging sound of the large
stainless steel lids
being taken off the trays,
being laid on top with a bang:
These sounds open my eyes
and as I look around
the guards march by
with three trays of food
for the men back in the main hole
of this prison,

415

and then I hear the clanging sounds
of each spoon being counted, each
being dropped against the stainless
steel tray: my final waking bell.

Huntingdon
February 22, 1978

MY HOME

My home is my
castle and I pray
nothing evil will
ever come cross my door.

Camden
August 7, 1977

ODD MAN

odd man at the trial
odd man all the while.
what journalist's eye
could write my fearful fright?

Camden
February 6, 1977

Appendix 2
Notes from the Author

This book goes to press almost eight years after Joseph Kallinger's arrest in January, 1975 ended a terrifying spree of torture and murder. My first research was in Leonia where the one known murder occurred; and I continued my research in Philadelphia and in other cities and by reading thousands of documents and every word in print on the subject. I didn't meet Joe until July of 1976 and then the research moved on two levels. One was the inner world of Joe Kallinger; the other, the outside world.

I developed warm, personal relationships with Joe's wife and children, his natural mother and sister. The wife and some of the children spent weekends at my apartment and together we visited Joe at Huntingdon and Farview. I talked with his judges and his jailers, his defense lawyers and district attorneys and with other institutional personnel. Judge Bradley refused to be interviewed.

I established close contact with some of the victims. Joan Carty and her husband visited me in my John Jay office and my apartment. Helen Bogin invited me to lunch and I ate at the table where Joe's sinister double had served his fiendish banquet. Over coffee and carrot cake in Mrs. Bogin's home, I later visited with Annapearl Frankston and Ethel Fisher Cohen, two of the ladies who didn't play bridge at the Bogins' the day Joe and Michael were there.

I did not meet Joe's first wife. I talked with her by phone, but James McLain of my staff did meet her face to face. She is a quite different person today from what she was during her marriage to Joe. Then she was very young, "mixed up," as she put it, and her behavior was the product of her immaturity and confusion. Today she is a comfortable, middle class housewife who does not exhibit the slovenly traits she did as a teenager. Joe's daughter Annie is also a comfortable middle class housewife.

I interviewed neighbors of Joe and his first wife. They provided some of the data I've used in the chapter about the first marriage. I also interviewed neighbors who had known Joe as a child. They regarded the senior Kallingers as highly respected people in the community. They liked Stephen, but considered Anna old-fashioned, pushy and eccentric. Several neighbors pointed to the fact that little Joe was not allowed out to play with other children and one of the neighbors told me about the time that Anna hit Joe over the head with a hammer because he asked to go to the zoo. The neighbor, who was in the store during the zoo incident, regularly played bingo with Anna. She gave me my first clue to the kind of life Joe lived in the Kallinger household. As she was walking with Anna to a bingo game, she saw little Joe inside the Kallinger house. He was looking sadly through a window and tapping on the pane. She waved back but Anna didn't. When the neighbor asked Anna why Joe wasn't allowed to play, Anna replied, "He is not here to play. He is here to work. We gave him a home and he must pay us back. We adopted him to be a shoemaker, and he's going to inherit the business and take care of us in our old age. He has to learn the business. He can't waste time playing."

The Kallingers had no relatives in the United States. Henry Kallinger, who brought Stephen to this country, had died. But Anna had a brother and nephew in Canada. They told me that Anna and Stephen were hard-working and life-denying.

My knowledge of the abuse of Joe as a child first came from outside sources and not from him. I had known him more than three years before, in response to my questions based on what these outside sources had told me, he reluctantly and slowly revealed the abuses he had suffered. Slowly I learned that I was dealing with the etiology of a psychosis that drove Joe to perform sadistic acts and to murder.

My research method was inductive. I picked up clues from people. I got the notes of testimony of the four Kallinger trials and also social service reports and police records—indeed, every printed word about Joe and his family. I fed Joe questions based on these data, and cross-interviewed the people involved in a scene.

After I had learned of Joe's tormented childhood of sexual abuse—psychological in the "bird" scene and physical in the tank—I began to see the connection between his crimes and his childhood. I saw that, because of these experiences, he had become psychotic before he committed a single crime. I also saw that the crimes sprang directly from the psychosis: from the delusional system and the hallucinations the psychosis had spawned. I brought in doctors to examine Joe as a private patient because I wanted a diagnosis free of the defense, the prosecution, and the courts. My doctors included Dr. Hurtig and Dr. Bird at Camden, Drs. Arieti and Robbins at Farview.

My intense study of Joe Kallinger, involving daily contact for over six years, has raised urgent questions about American justice. He is clearly psychotic, yet three juries, in denying his insanity plea, implicitly found him sane. He was sent to prison where, driven by hallucinations, he attempted to murder another inmate. In prison, where he was not regarded as psychotic, he received no psychotropic drugs. Yet to prison he can be returned at any time because it was to prison, and not to a mental hospital, that he was committed.

This calls into question concepts with regard to the removal of an offender from society. We must learn to distinguish between crimes committed by sociopaths that lead to prison sentences and crimes by psychotics that reveal mental illness. The mentally ill belong not in prison, but in mental hospitals: when their illness is denied in court, they are sent on a path that intensifies the illness and its consequent criminality. Sentencing will become civilized when *why* a crime is committed is understood. Only then will real insanity be distinguished from a mere insanity defense.

Michael Kallinger repeatedly refused to be interviewed, and I have been unable to get his versions of the murders of José Collazo and Joseph Kallinger, Jr. In my letters to Michael requesting an interview, I wrote, "Your voice must be heard in these pages. It is important from your own point of view to speak to me. I want to give you the opportunity to set the record straight with regard to your part in the story."

Joseph Kallinger, Michael's father, wrote to Michael, urging him to see me, and Michael's brother James Kallinger tried to arrange a meeting between Michael and me at their cousin's house. Michael never answered his father's letter, and the meeting at the cousin's never took place.

Michael's foster parents, who assured me that eventually I would interview Michael, joined me in a visit to the law offices of Arthur F. Abelman to discuss the terms of the projected interview. Mr. Abelman asked the foster parents to have their lawyer call him to discuss the terms, and they agreed to do so. I reminded Michael's foster mother many times of the agreement, but Mr. Abelman never received the phone call from their lawyer.

My attempts to interview Michael were finally defeated by a letter I received from Malcolm Waldron, Jr., Esquire. The letter, dated June 7, 1978, read:

"Please be advised that I represent Michael Kallinger to whom you have addressed a letter dated May 25, 1978. Michael Kallinger will not under any circumstances be interviewed by you in the foreseeable future."

A few weeks later Mr. Waldron told John Shapiro, my assistant, who had telephoned him on an unrelated matter, that I didn't have "the chance of a snowball in hell to see Michael Kallinger." According to Mr. Shapiro, the lawyer added, "I don't know what Mr. Kallinger and Mrs. (sic) Schreiber are trying to do to Michael, but it doesn't matter because there *is* no Michael Kallinger—*Michael Kallinger doesn't exist anymore.*" Michael had changed his name.

On May 31, 1977 Michael's foster parents had given me what they claimed was Michael's version of some of the events surrounding the death of Joseph Kallinger, Jr. The first conversation about Joey's death was between Michael and his foster father while they were

420

sitting in a snowmobile. Later, Michael talked with both foster parents about Joey's death.

According to the foster parents, Michael's story admits that he was with his father, Joseph Kallinger, at Ninth and Market Streets in Philadelphia on July 28, 1974, the day the murder was committed. That day, Michael said, Joseph Kallinger suggested to Joey that they go to Ninth and Market Streets to take pictures of the site as a memento because a construction company was going to build on it. Michael told his foster parents that his father had also asked *him* to come along and that his father had said that he would bring wooden planks and chains to the construction site. Near a shaft or deep hole somewhere on the site, Joseph Kallinger ordered his son Joey to lie down on the plank so that his father could take a photograph of Joey lying on the plank and covered with chains. After Joey had lain down and his father had loosely draped the chains over him, Joseph Kallinger said to Michael, "Shove Joey into the hole." Michael told his foster parents that he refused to do it. His father threatened to shove *him* into the hole, but Michael refused to push the plank over the edge. His father then took off the chains and pushed the plank with Joey on it down the shaft into the water. According to Michael, Joey cried out, "Daddy, what are you doing? Mommy!"

We thus have from Michael some of the same elements reported by his father, Joseph Kallinger: the place, the chains, the hole, the drowning and Joey's cry for help, although the cry that Michael quoted to his foster parents is somewhat different from the cry that Joe quoted to me. That Michael was present at his brother's murder is a fact, and it is also a fact, according to Michael, that he didn't participate in Joey's murder.

After Michael had talked to his foster parents about Joey's death, his foster mother telephoned the office of the Philadelphia district attorney and made an appointment for Michael to go there. That was in March of 1977. Michael failed a lie detector test. When the examiner asked Michael whether he was just being vengeful, Michael answered that he was not being vengeful and that everything he had said was true. The district attorney's office took no action.

During our May 31, 1977 conversation, Michael's foster parents also gave me Michael's version of the attempt to kill Joey by gasoline. Michael said that three weeks before the murder of Joey, Joe Kallinger rented a U-Haul truck, filled it with gasoline and shoved Joey into it. Michael stated to his foster parents that Joe told him to lock the truck, but he didn't, thus making it possible for Joey to get out.

According to Joseph Kallinger, the gasoline incident took place in a C.T.I. container that was mounted on a flatbed trailer in the Niehaus parking lot. The fire department records, which I have, and Jack Griffin, a Niehaus employee quoted by Edward P. Aleszczyk, a retired fire marshal whom I retained to do investigative work for me, point to the presence of Joseph Kallinger, Jr. at the scene of a trailer fire that occurred on the Niehaus parking lot at 6:38 A.M., July 25, 1974, three days before the death of Joey.

Jack Griffin told Mr. Aleszczyk that he remembered a trailer fire due to unusual circumstances on the day in question. Mr. Griffin stated further that a young boy, the Kallinger boy who was later found dead, had come into Sam's Luncheonette, which was adjacent to the trailers, and had alerted them to the fire. Griffin went on to say that he saw the boy there but not the father. Griffin had been a customer of the Kallingers' Shoe Repair for a number of years and knew both by sight.

The Report of Fire Alarm states that at 6:38 A.M., July 25, 1974, Engine Companies #25 and #31 were sent to the trailer "to extinguish fire in the interior of the trailer, then to remove three unspilled bottles of gasoline and take up equipment. The above duties took fourteen minutes."

The foster parents, however, did not mention the projected attempt to kill Joey in Hazleton nor the murder of José Collazo. Michael's brother James Kallinger told me that Michael had told him that there was a *third* murder, one more besides the murders of Joey and Maria Fasching. That was *all* Michael said, so that all we know is that Michael was aware that a third murder (presumably that of José Collazo) had been committed. This might imply that Michael was present, and it represents neither an admission nor a denial of his involvement.

As a result of Michael Kallinger's refusal to be interviewed by me, the chapters ("The Last Song" and "The Test of Strength") dealing respectively with the murders of Joseph Kallinger, Jr. and José Collazo represent the only picture possible based on accessible sources.

* * *

The blackmail by Judith Renner (Chapter 2) was reported to Joe when he was still a child by the senior Kallingers. Judith herself has denied it.

Psychiatrists have asked me about Joe's drug history. The answer is that there is none. He was not on drugs at any time, and it was only during his first marriage that he drank more than an occasional VO. His "trips" were induced only by the inner forces of his psychosis.

General Index

Adult Diagnostic Treatment Center (Avenel, N.J.), 365, 367, 388
Apellate Division of The Superior Court, New Jersey, 347–48
Arieti, Silvano, 95, 145, 178, 250, 355, 395–96, 402
Arrests, 171, 196, 201, 271, 335–36, 342, 345, 375
Ayers, Manfred, 326, 327

Balger, Harold, 200–1
Baltimore, Md., 306–8, 311, 320, 336–37, 370
Berg Brothers, 336
Bergen County, N.J.
  jail, 18, 158, 250, 345–47, 393, 397
  juvenile and domestic court, 340
Berkowitz, Malcolm W., 198, 254, 338, 340
Bird, Edward, 362–64, 371, 383, 394
Blair, J. C., Memorial Hospital (Huntingdon, Pa.), 380
Bogin, Helen, 294–300, 302, 304, 306, 312, 320, 322, 338, 372, 377
Bradley, Edward J., 182–86, 190, 196, 204, 366, 385
Bradley, Michael, 183
Brennan, Thomas, 388
Breslin, Roger W., 340
Brian, Don, 384
Bright Sun Cleaners, 336
Bryant, James, 185

Camden, N.J., city of, 269, 363, 370
Camden County (N.J.) Jail, 18, 58, 147, 188, 203–4, 207–8, 215, 222, 232, 249, 266, 268, 277, 311, 357–58, 361, 362, 365, 368, 371, 383, 390, 394
Campean, Basil, 365
Caristo, Christine Baker, 255

Carty, Joan, 281, 283–90, 296, 298, 301, 364
Catholic Children's Bureau, 32–34, 37–39, 110, 392
Center city, 219, 270
Charges, 184, 196, 200, 268, 336–41, 364, 401
Civil suits, 254, 256–72, 337, 359–60, 382–83
Cohen, Ethel Fisher, 298, 299, 300, 301, 302
Collazo, José, 211–18, 235, 246, 287, 325, 368, 396, 400
Comer, Harry, 128, 138, 146, 180, 182, 183, 184, 215
Cooper Hospital, 269
Court order for 90-day commitment, 384–85
Crimes Act, 367
Criminal contempt, 348
Criminal intent, defined, 361
Custody, 203–4

Dalton, Thomas, 349, 356
Daly, Joseph, 24, 26, 27, 28, 29, 36, 37, 48, 58, 59, 64, 71, 77, 78, 79, 84, 88, 90, 109, 122, 211, 236
Dauphin County (N.J.) Court of Common Pleas, 341
Dauphin County (N.J.) Jail, 336, 338–39, 341–43, 351, 371
Davis, Ralph E., 387–90, 395, 397, 401
Demolition site, Ninth and Market Streets, 239–48, 282
Diamond Square Park, 74
Di Martino, I. V., 361–62, 365–67
Dittmar, Paul, 326
Divorce (civil), 109
Donovan, Robert, J., 201
Douglas School, 195, 198, 204
Dowling, John C., 341–42, 356–57

Downington Camp, 74, 77, 93
Dumont, N.J., 307–8, 311, 320,
  336–37, 340, 370
Durham Law, 395
Dwyer, Carol, 195, 198, 204

Eastern State School and Hospital,
  201–4
Eller, Earl Dean, 379–82, 384, 389,
  401, 403
Episcopal Hospital, 202, 333
Erhard, Dennis R., 375
Extradition, 339

Facison, William, 248
Falkenstein, Robert H., 201
Falvo, Anthony, 400
Fareira, John, 198
Farview State Hospital, 385, 387–90,
  395, 397–404
Fasching, Maria, 310, 313–15, 319,
  321–23, 325–27, 333, 337–39,
  345, 351, 353–56, 368, 377, 379,
  399
Fillinger, H. E., 248
Frankford Hospital, 265
Frankston, Annapearl, 299, 300, 302
Funk, Ed, 249

Gallun, Charles, 180, 181
Gibbons, Thomas J., 251
Giblin, Paul J., 346–47, 351, 355
Glancey, Joseph, 185
Glass, Deborah, 183, 185
Gleeson, Gerald A., 38, 39, 128
Gnassi, Charles P., 365
Golden, Arnold, 361, 367
Gotshalk, Muriel Scurti, 32–33,
  391–95, 400, 404
Grand Canyon, 219–24, 234–38
Gutkin, Arthur L., 196, 198, 255, 258,
  260, 271, 335, 338, 340, 382,
  391–92, 394

Hackensack Court (Bergen County
  Superior Court), 158
Hackensack Hospital, 310
Hammel, Robert J., 389
Harrisburg, Pa., 297–99, 336, 342,
  353, 355, 357, 370
Hazleton, Pa., 224–25, 230, 233, 251,
  296
Hazleton State Hospital, 121–22, 187
Hersh, Joel H., 389
Hewitt, Lowell D., 374, 375, 383

Hoffman, Francis H., 174–78, 182,
  186–87, 354, 366, 383
Hoffmaster, Kenneth F., 198–99
Holmesburg Maximum Security
  Forensic Unit, 178–80, 182, 188,
  194, 198, 204–5, 209, 220, 251,
  336–37, 363, 384
Horn and Hardart, 257
Hume, John, 341, 351–53, 354, 364
Huntingdon District Court, 381
Huntington's chorea, 353, 357
Hurtig, Howard, 364, 371, 383, 390

Ibler, Hans, 107
Iezzi, William, 95
Incompetency to stand trial, 401
Incorrigibility petitions, 94, 200–1
Independence Mall, 270–71
Insanity (legal), 341, 354–56, 365,
  395

Jablon, Norman C., 180, 181, 183,
  187, 351–52, 354, 364, 384
Jacobs, Fred W., 383
Jaske, Pamela, 307
Jay, David W., 389
John Jay College of Criminal Justice,
  18
Jones Junior High School, 89
Juniata Park, 266, 268

Kallinger, Anna (adoptive mother),
  23–29, 31, 34–36, 42–43, 70, 81,
  92, 94, 103, 105, 135, 183, 192,
  240, 252–53, 266, 333, 335, 338,
  356, 375, 390, 392, 396, 403
Kallinger, Anna (daughter), 101, 105,
  106, 108, 109, 114, 132, 192
Kallinger, Bonnie Sue (daughter),
  204, 260, 267–68, 278, 284,
  289–92, 333, 342, 348, 404
Kallinger, Elizabeth (second wife),
  111–14, 119–20, 122, 124–26,
  147, 156, 158, 163–64, 169, 176,
  186, 189–92, 200, 209, 220, 238,
  246–48, 252–53, 261–62, 267–68,
  271, 290, 307, 325, 333–34, 340,
  348, 350, 397, 400, 404
Kallinger, Henry, 35
Kallinger, Hilda Bishop (first wife),
  85–90, 94, 97–109, 114, 209, 397
Kallinger, James (son), 132, 163–64,
  190, 219–20, 222–28, 252, 260,
  268–71, 317, 333, 404
Kallinger, Joseph, Jr. (son), 132,
  140–41, 146–47, 153–54, 162–66,

168–69, 171–72, 183–86, 190–91,
193–99, 200–5, 219–29, 231–35,
237–44, 246–47, 249, 251–54,
256–57, 259–60, 268, 279, 282,
287, 296, 317, 325, 338, 368,
396–97, 400
Kallinger, Mary Jo (daughter), 126,
132, 134, 140–41, 146–47,
156–60, 162–69, 171–72, 174,
176, 182–84, 186, 190–92,
193–94, 195, 198, 209, 220, 252,
266, 268, 283, 291, 317, 350, 404
Kallinger, Michael (son), 17, 132,
146, 153, 163–64, 171, 183–85,
190–91, 193, 195, 198, 205–16,
219–22, 224–48, 251–52, 260,
262–63, 265–66, 268–71, 277–90,
292–96, 298, 302–7, 309, 311–15,
320, 323, 333–37, 339–40, 391,
396, 398, 400, 404
Kallinger, Stephen (adoptive father),
23–29, 31, 35–40, 42–44, 70, 81,
103, 131, 191–92, 244, 252, 305,
339, 349, 356, 390, 392, 394, 403
Kallinger, Stephen (son), 105, 106,
108, 109, 114, 132, 147, 148, 174,
192, 238, 252, 317, 350
Kensington, 36, 137, 195, 246–47,
251, 308, 325
Kensington Assembly of God, 198,
252
Kiddie City store, 265–66
Kimmel, Richard, 35, 128
King, Lew, 202
Kyper, James H., 381

Lancaster Detention House, 339
Law Department of the City of
Philadelphia, 255
Leonia, N.J., 17, 308–10, 323–26, 336,
340
  police, 324, 325, 326, 327, 334
  Sylvan Park, 323–24, 327, 334, 336
Levitt, Albert, 176, 183, 187
Lighthouse, The, 74, 292, 306, 325
Lindenwold, N.J., 277, 281–84, 289,
292, 296, 303, 307, 311, 318, 320,
337, 361, 365
Lipsitt, William W., 339

MacDougall, Robert, 325–27
Mahoney, James, 126, 128, 151
Mann Recreation Center, 210
Marinacci, Anthony A., 252, 253
Mashinski, Detective, 326

Matthews, Robert A., 348
McClure, Larry, 348, 351, 354
McGovern, James A., 249
Medaglia, Anthony, 200
Mental Health Procedures Act, 384–85
Miller, Mr. and Mrs. Wallace Peter,
277, 301
Minushkin, Arthur, 340
M'Naghten Law, 395
Munio, Pasquale, 185
Murray, Malcolm, 382

Neshaminy, 226, 231
Newhart, Dale E., 389
Niehaus parking lot, 230–31, 237
Norristown, 106, 352
Northeast High School, 93–94
Northern Liberties Hospital, 32, 40,
89

OK Restaurant, 238–39, 251
Olivier, J. E., 401
O'Neill, C. J., Funeral Home, 252
O'Neill, James F., 255–57, 259, 261,
263–65, 294, 335
O'Neill, Joseph, 255

Patelli, Tony, 32, 34, 41, 87, 394
Perr, Irwin N., 122, 346, 351, 353,
355–56, 364
Philadelphia *Bulletin*, 202–3, 251
Philadelphia City Hall, 180
Philadelphia Coroner's Office, 248–49
Philadelphia Court of Common Pleas,
94, 173–74, 186, 201, 204, 265,
393
Philadelphia Department of Public
Welfare, 265
Philadelphia Detention House, 171,
389
Philadelphia Fire Department, 233–34
Philadelphia General Hospital, 201
Philadelphia *Inquirer*, 64
Philadelphia morgue, 249, 251–52, 259
Philadelphia Municipal Court, 38, 40,
185
Philadelphia Office of the Medical
Examiner, 248–49, 341
Philadelphia Parents' Organization,
198
Philadelphia Police Department, 266,
382
  Administration Building (The
  Roundhouse), 250–51, 254–56,
  258, 260–61, 265–68, 335–36

Homicide Division, 249, 256–58
Juvenile Aide Division, Morals
    Squad, 200–1, 203, 247
6th District, 248, 271
24th-25th District, 171, 247, 255,
    266, 269, 280
Philadelphia School District 5, 198
Philadelphia State Hospital, 182
Philadelphia's Youth Study Center,
    201
Pistilli, Anthony, 347
Police brutalization, 264, 267–68, 272
Price, Deborah, 265, 266

Rappeport, Jonas R., 346, 351, 353,
    354, 355, 356, 364
Recantation, 196, 200, 204–5, 254–55,
    350
Refice, Ronald, 401
Renner, Judith, 31–34, 37–41, 72, 87,
    391, 392, 393, 394, 395, 398,
    400, 403–4
Rieders, Frederick, 340
Robbins, Lewis L., 178, 355, 402, 405
Robboy, Bruce, 362, 363, 366
Romaine, Mr. and Mrs. Dewitt,
    310–11, 314, 323, 327, 356
Romaine, Randi, 310
Romaine, Retta, 310, 326, 327
Rosenstein, Daniel, 249
Rudolph, Mary, 307, 308
Ruhnke, David A., 359
Rumi, Eva, 327

Sadoff, Robert, 108, 341–43
Saint Boniface, 46, 50, 53, 61–62, 64,
    135
Saint Christopher's Hospital for
    Children, 204, 265, 266
Saint Mary's Hospital, 23–24, 31, 34,
    48, 51, 105, 109, 110, 120, 187
Saint Vincent's, 23–24, 33–34, 36, 37,
    40, 61, 183, 362
Salem (N.J.) County Jail, 361
Salerno, Eugene, 361, 365, 368
Sam's Luncheonette, 234
Schreiber, Flora Rheta, 18, 145, 147,
    176, 203–4, 347–48, 352, 358–60,
    362–64, 371–74, 375–78, 383,
    389, 392–96, 401–5
Scranton State Hospital, 397
Seasons in the Sun, 222, 226, 239,
    242, 267, 399
Sentencing, 18, 186, 196, 340–42,
    348ff., 356–58, 366–68, 370, 404

Sex Offenders Act, 365, 367
Shapiro, John, 371
Shields, Marcella, 401–2
Silver Bridge, 80, 91
Specter, Arlen, 185
Standard Evening High, 101
State Correctional Institution at Hunt-
    ingdon (SCIH), 341–43, 345,
    352, 368, 370, 372, 82–83, 397
State Office of Inmate Advocacy, 346
Storm, William, 251
Suden, Thelma, 298, 300, 302
Supreme Court of New Jersey, 348
Susquehanna Township, 294–95, 299,
    308, 311, 336
Swigart, Charles, 384

Terrizzi, Morris, 384–86
Trials, 183–86, 196, 200, 255, 297–98,
    340–41, 349–56, 361–64, 385
Tumolillo, Joseph G., 40–41

U.S. District Court, Scranton, Pa., 382
U.S. District Court, Williamsport,
    Pa., 382
University of Pennsylvania, 349, 364

Visitation School, 81–88
von Schlichten, Alex, 177, 183, 186,
    187
Vroom Building, State Psychiatric
    Hospital, Trenton, N.J., 358–59,
    375, 385

Wawrose, Frederick, 344, 351–52,
    354, 364, 370–71, 384–85
Welby, Jeffrey, 315, 318, 319, 320,
    322, 326, 327
Wenger, Norman, 389
White, Charles T., 380
White, Thomas A., 173, 180, 185
Williams, Robert, 182
Woerle, E., 248
Woodcock, Joseph C., Esquire, 336

Y.W.C.A., 80–81, 187
Yoo, Eun Sook, 389
Youth Development Center,
    Cornwells Heights, 339
Youth Development Center,
    Warrendale, 339

Zigarelli, Joseph F., 351, 353–54, 357,
    364
Zimmerman, Le Roy, Esquire, 343

Psychological Index

Abandonment, 73, 105–6, 111, 168, 170, 171, 220, 348, 396
Abhorrence for destruction of life, 132, 153
Adoption, 23, 34, 35, 38–39, 40–41, 81, 114, 191
Affinity for discarded objects, 62
Aggression, 71, 79, 80
  first act of terror, 77–78
  wedding use of knife to feelings of, 92, 138, 166, 321, 369, 383
Alienation, 43, 48, 56, 62, 72–73, 75, 84, 98, 190, 371
Ambitions
  actor, 73, 81, 83, 100, 101, 105, 128, 156, 295
  poet, 404
Ambivalence, 56, 73
American Academy of Psychoanalysis, paper presented at, 20
Amnesia, 121, 175, 187, 382
Anti-social personality defined, 181, 182, 187–88, 351, 353, 362, 367, 371, 384
Automatic movement, 90–91, 100, 102–4, 187, 231, 338, 348–49, 356, 358–59, 361–62, 371, 374, 379, 390
Autoscopic syndrome, 396

"Behave yourself," 49, 60, 286, 297–98, 313–15
Behavioral sciences, 369
"Bird," 26, 27, 28, 29, 30, 31, 37, 49, 59, 62, 64, 70, 88, 94, 95, 96, 103, 108, 114, 115, 236, 287, 288, 305, 317, 318, 355, 396; see also Symbolic castration

Child abuse
  physical, 29, 31, 44, 46–47, 49–50, 52–54, 62, 65, 66, 70, 96, 257, 294, 318, 390, 392
  psychological, 19, 20, 24, 29–31, 36, 43–44, 44–49, 50–53, 55, 56, 58–62, 64, 66, 78, 82–83, 87–88, 94–96, 126, 131, 135–36, 158, 196, 199, 204, 220, 388, 390, 392, 403
Child care, 33
Childhood health, 94, 96, 110
Competency to stand trial, 178, 180–81, 359
Compulsions, 123–24, 134–35, 137
Cup runs dry, 229–30, 233–34, 288, 296–97, 306–8, 320
Crimes inseparable from psychosis, 20, 395–96

Defense mechanisms, 72, 308, 396
Delegation, 134, 138, 165, 199, 205, 214, 231–34, 237, 251, 320–22
Delusions, 18, 70, 76, 79, 84–85, 87, 91, 96, 103, 104, 108, 110, 113, 114, 123, 134, 151–53, 155–56, 159, 161–62, 171, 192, 199, 204–5, 207, 209–10, 220, 230, 244, 245, 252, 262, 263, 272, 278–79, 280, 284, 288–92, 294, 298, 301, 307, 316–17, 319–20, 322, 323, 325, 336, 338, 342, 344–47, 352, 357, 359, 364, 369, 376, 396, 398–99, 404; see also Orthopedic experiments and Schizophrenia
Demon, 31, 59, 64, 70, 72, 77, 79–80,

84, 88, 91, 114–16, 118–19, 142,
144, 222, 235–36, 288, 317, 368
Developmental process, 19, 59, 71, 79,
199, 355
Devil, 27–28, 87, 118–19, 127,
144–45, 177, 219–20, 267, 279,
290, 344, 368, 398
Discarded objects, affinity with, 71,
73, 75, 111, 124–25, 133–34,
162, 240
Dreams, 54–55, 59, 62, 110–11, 206,
239, 247, 275–77, 279–80, 282,
288, 303, 312, 318, 325, 343–44,
405

Family dream, 97, 99–100, 102, 108,
111, 113–15, 120, 124, 132,
162–63, 169
Family man, 100, 106, 110–11, 113,
116, 121, 176, 182, 198, 229, 291
Fantasies, 24, 29, 36, 37, 42, 45, 47,
59, 70, 71, 72, 80, 84, 87, 99, 102,
104, 108–9, 159, 163, 168, 232,
282–83, 298, 308, 394; see also
Restitutional fantasies
Farview State Hospital for the
Criminally Insane, 386, 387, 388,
389, 390, 393, 394, 396
Fears, 71, 80, 83, 84, 85, 90, 91, 92,
99, 115, 117, 138, 153, 174, 176,
209, 308, 321
Feelings
as adult, 101, 103, 106, 107, 108,
138, 140, 157, 176, 189, 190, 262,
398, 401, 402
as child, 25, 29, 43, 48, 49, 50, 51,
53, 54, 55, 56, 59, 62, 71, 73, 75,
76, 79, 83, 91, 96, 98, 99, 100,
216, 294
Fire, 118–19, 126–28, 143, 170, 360,
362

Ganser syndrome, 362
Guilt, 72, 398

Hallucinations, 37, 71, 72, 91, 96, 104,
117–18, 127, 131, 132, 133, 138,
140, 141, 142, 144, 145, 152, 154,
157, 159, 161, 162, 163, 165, 168,
169, 175, 180, 205, 206, 207, 209,
211, 214, 215, 218, 219, 220, 221,
222, 224, 225, 226, 227, 228, 229,
230, 231, 234, 235, 236, 237, 239,
247, 248, 262, 277, 283, 286, 287,
288, 294, 295, 296, 297, 298, 300,

301, 302, 305, 312, 313, 315, 317,
319, 338, 340, 342, 355, 360, 368,
375, 379, 384, 400, 401, 402
Charlie, 263, 265–67, 272, 280,
291–93, 303–4, 306–7, 311, 316,
318, 320–22, 325, 343–45, 352,
356, 371, 397–99, 403
compelling power of, 395
The Double, 292–96, 298, 300–5,
307–8, 311–12, 322, 325, 338,
343, 356, 375, 378–79, 381, 382,
387, 399, 400, 403
Hernia operation, 23, 24, 27, 34, 47,
48, 50, 62, 77, 108, 109
Holes, 69–70, 84, 88, 104, 108–9,
116, 127, 140, 142, 145–47, 156,
159–60, 189, 232, 235, 240, 307,
318–19, 322–23, 350
Hunger strike, 370ff., 386–87
Hysteria
with conversion reaction, 122
dissociative, 122

Identity, search for, 55, 59, 62, 91,
390–91, 393–94
Imaginative life, 52, 57, 69, 70, 72–73,
75–76, 79, 84, 92, 144, 205–6,
341, 343
Inner child of the past, 134, 138, 199,
264
Insanity, not a plea but real, 356
Intruder, 206, 294

Killer instinct, 369
Knives, 21, 24–26, 58–59, 62, 69, 70–
71, 72, 77–80, 87, 92, 102, 116,
118, 165–67, 232, 234, 278–80,
282, 285–88, 291, 295, 297–300,
305, 306, 308, 312–14, 318–19,
321–24, 375, 377, 379–81
Kristorah chant, 143–45, 305, 343,
349, 352, 374, 387; see also
Schizophrenia

Learning center, 373
Left hand
hand of power for world massacre,
279
multiple erections by holding knife
in, 116
power of, 69, 75, 76, 77, 283,
287–88, 321
prolongation of sexual fantasies by
holding knife in, 116
stabbing hand, 69, 79–80, 322

Life, respect for, 102, 132, 153
Lukianowicz syndrome, 396

Madness
  consequences of, 173
  denial of old fear of (Hoffman-
    von Schlichten examination), 175
  episodic nature of, 156
  exploration of, 19
  spasms of, 146
  loneliness and, 80
  origins of, 31
Magical thinking, 50–52, 64, 74, 76,
    105, 113, 278, 306
Malingering, 352–53
Masturbation, 57, 70–71, 76, 88, 104,
    109, 116, 146, 218, 232
Mental hospital vs. prison, 383
Mental illness, 91, 92, 94, 95, 96, 103,
    105, 121, 124, 126, 128, 142, 177
  confused with wickedness, 94, 95,
    185, 356, 362, 366, 381, 404
  getting worse for several years
    (Perr), 353
  psychosis full-blown between 1969
    and 1972 (Arieti), 182
Morbidity, 176, 177
Murder, genesis from child abuse, 20

Nature vs. nurture controversy, 96,
    361, 395, 396
Neologisms, 161, 322, 358

Obsessions, 342
Orthopedic experiments, 91, 92, 104,
    123, 125, 132–34, 137, 152, 158,
    160, 167–69, 205, 209, 220, 279,
    355

Persecutors, 160, 161, 162, 164, 165,
    167, 168, 172, 174, 375, 377–78;
    see also Schizophrenia
Personality transformations, 76, 77,
    79, 81, 156, 159
Play, belated, 94, 100, 295
Poems by Joseph Kallinger, 45, 53,
    73, 301–2, 370, 371, 373, 376–77,
    396
Potency, restoration of, 112
Power, restoration of, 305, 308
Premonition, 100, 138
Primal scene, 54, 57, 58
Primitiveness, 177; see also Holes
    and Obsessions
Provocation from within, 381

Psychiatric intervention, lack of, 20,
    93, 123, 186–87, 355, 366, 371,
    375, 381, 383–84, 400, 402–4
Psychological testing, 176, 388
Psychopathology, 177, 187
  of anxiety state, 109
Psychosis, 20
  created crimes, 356
  genesis of, 356
  see also Schizophrenia
Psychotic killer, definition, 19
Psychotropic drugs, 355, 375, 383,
    389, 390, 396, 397, 400, 403
Public relations flair, 377

Rage, 19, 33, 49, 51, 53, 61, 66, 71,
    92, 126, 159, 161, 284, 291, 292,
    396; see also Symbolic castration
    and Tank episode
Rebellion, 49, 57
Regression, 346
Remorse, 368, 401, 403
Restitutional fantasies, 71, 77–79, 90,
    96, 308, 396
Retaliation, 78, 214, 229, 322
  against adoptive parents, 30, 308
  against boys in tank, 77
  against police, 269, 270–71, 275,
    294–95
Rhyming, 16; see also Schizophrenia
Robberies, 206, 295, 300–1, 306,
    313, 335
Rorschach test
  revealed pathology, 365
  in diagnosis of schizophrenia, 388

Sadism, 127, 146, 153, 159, 168, 238,
    306, 322, 377, 395, 396
Saving a life, 397
Schizophrenia, 59, 79, 90, 95, 96, 102,
    110, 120, 128, 133, 136–39, 140,
    142–51, 153, 155–57, 159–65,
    167, 168, 172, 174–78, 180, 186,
    187, 199, 215–17, 235, 246–47,
    250–51, 256, 263–64, 268, 287,
    291, 296, 305, 320–23, 325, 334,
    337–38, 341, 343, 349, 351–53,
    356, 360, 362, 364–66, 368, 383,
    384, 399, 400–1, 403; see also
    Delusions and Hallucinations
Sensitivity, 39
Separation from self, 138, 140
Sexual development, 31, 57–59, 69, 70,
    71, 74, 84, 87, 89–90, 93, 94, 99,
    100, 101, 103–4, 107, 113,

115–16, 127, 132, 153, 157, 159, 175–76, 199–200, 209, 213, 218, 221–22, 232, 282, 284, 287, 288, 289, 290, 296, 297, 305, 307, 311, 313, 316, 318, 319, 320, 322, 334, 338, 365, 379, 396

Sexual organs as trophies, 215, 234, 237, 321–22

Shoemaker, Joseph Kallinger as, 17, 83, 89, 91, 94, 100–1, 120, 132, 182, 190–92, 198, 260, 350, 368, 371, 372, 374, 375

Suburbs, 17, 36, 74, 78, 80, 109, 113, 172, 206–8, 262, 281–90, 294–302, 304, 306–8, 311–12, 320, 336–38, 345

Suicide, 121–22, 128, 172–73, 182, 187, 235, 350, 358, 360, 370, 379, 381, 382, 386–90, 397, 398–400

Sybil, 17, 19, 20, 216, 392

Symbolic castration, 27–29, 31, 48–49, 62, 71, 77, 80, 95, 237, 305, 318, 321, 337, 356

Tank episode, 59, 77

Thief label, 51, 63–64, 66, 77, 169, 301

Thought disorder, 365; *see also* Schizophrenia

Total gods, 171, 184, 191, 193, 198, 204–5, 219–20, 256

Trailer fire, 231–34, 237, 251

Traumas
the "bird," 96
of first marriage, 114
inferiority to "macho men," 117
tank episode, 59, 77

Victim(s)
impersonal choice of, 379
Joseph Kallinger as, 96

Vulnerability, 31, 95, 396

Wanderlust, 29, 162, 199

World massacre, 169, 173, 206, 208, 211, 212, 213, 215, 220, 221, 229, 232, 235, 272, 278, 280, 287, 288, 290, 292, 294, 298–99, 300, 302–8, 312, 314, 316, 318, 320, 322, 323, 325, 338, 356–57, 361, 368, 376, 379, 403

Worthlessness, feelings of, 50–51, 62, 83, 96, 103, 108, 396